# Going Native

**Thomas Weber** is a Reader in the Politics and International Relations programme at Melbourne's La Trobe University. He has been researching and writing on Gandhi's life, thought and legacy for almost thirty years. His Gandhi related publications include: *The Shanti Sena: Philosophy, History and Action*; *Gandhi, Gandhism and the Gandhians*; *Gandhi as Disciple and Mentor*; *On the Salt March: The Historiography of Gandhi's March to Dandi*; *Conflict Resolution and Gandhian Ethics*; and *Hugging the Trees: The Story of the Chipko Movement*.

BY THE SAME AUTHOR

*Gandhi, Gandhism and the Gandhians*

OTHER LOTUS TITLES

| | |
|---|---|
| Ajit Bhattacharjea | *Sheikh Mohammad Abdullah: Tragic Hero of Kashmir* |
| Amarinder Singh | *The Last Sunset: The Rise and Fall of the Lahore Durbar* |
| Anil Dharker | *Icons: Men & Women Who Shaped Today's India* |
| Aitzaz Ahsan | *The Indus Saga: The Making of Pakistan* |
| Alam Srinivas & TR Vivek | *IPL: The Inside Story* |
| Amir Mir | *The True Face of Jehadis: Inside Pakistan's Terror Networks* |
| Ashok Mitra | *The Starkness of It* |
| Dr Humanyun Khan & G. Parthasarthy | *Diplomatic Divide* |
| Gyanendra Pandey & Yunus Samad | *Faultlines of Nationhood* |
| Hamish McDonald | *Ambani & Sons* |
| M.J. Akbar | *Have Pen, Will Travel: Observations of a Globetrotter* |
| M.J. Akbar | *Kashmir: Behind the Vale* |
| M.J. Akbar | *The Shade of Swords* |
| M.J. Akbar | *Byline* |
| M.J. Akbar | *Blood Brothers: A Family Saga* |
| Maj. Gen. Ian Cardozo | *Param Vir: Our Heroes in Battle* |
| Maj. Gen. Ian Cardozo | *The Sinking of INS Khukri: What Happened in 1971* |
| Madhu Trehan | *Tehelka as Metaphor* |
| Mushirul Hasan | *India Partitioned. 2 Vols* |
| Mushirul Hasan | *John Company to the Republic* |
| Mushirul Hasan | *Knowledge, Power and Politics* |
| Nayantara Sahgal (ed.) | *Before Freedom: Nehru's Letters to His Sister* |
| Nilima Lambah | *A Life Across Three Continents* |
| Robert Hutchison | *The Raja of Harsil: The Legend of Frederick 'Pahari' Wilson* |
| Sharmishta Gooptu and Boria Majumdar (eds) | *Revisiting 1857: Myth, Memory, History* |
| Shashi Joshi | *The Last Durbar* |
| Shashi Tharoor & Shaharyar M. Khan | *Shadows across the Playing Field* |
| Shrabani Basu | *Spy Princess: The Life of Noor Inayat Khan* |
| Shyam Bhatia | *Goodbye Shahzadi: A Political Biography* |
| Zubin Mehta | *The Score of My Life* |

FORTHCOMING TITLES

| | |
|---|---|
| Jaiwant Paul | *The Revolt of 1857: Some Heroes and Villians* |
| Masood Hyder | *State Under Pressure* |

# GOING NATIVE

## Gandhi's Relationship with Western Women

Thomas Weber

LOTUS COLLECTION
ROLI BOOKS

Lotus Collection



First published in India in 2011
The Lotus Collection
An imprint of
Roli Books Pvt. Ltd.
M-75, Greater Kailash II Market, New Delhi 110 048
Phones: ++91 (011) 4068 2000
Fax: ++91 (011) 2921 7185
E-mail: info@rolibooks.com
Website: www.rolibooks.com
Also at Bangalore, Chennai, Jaipur
Mumbai & Varanasi

Cover Design: Bonita Vaz-Shimray
Production: Shaji Sahadevan

ISBN: 978-81-7436-820-1

Typeset in Adobe Perpetua Pro by Roli Books Pvt. Ltd.
and printed at Rajkamal Electric Press, Haryana

# Contents

# Acknowledgements

This project started with an inspiration at the Gedong Gandhi Ashram at Candidasa in Bali. Although the Gandhian founder, Ibu Gedong Bagoes Oka, was no longer alive, the institution still preserved the spirit of her strong Gandhian presence. One day, in the ashram library, I came across Mary Barr's collection of the letters that the Mahatma had written to her. From that little book I realised not only Barr's closeness to Gandhi, but also that she had vanished from the Gandhi story as it is most often told. I quickly made a list of the other Western women who should also have been remembered as part of that story, and about whom I should have known much more than I did. To the Gandhi Ashram, and the ashramites, especially I Nyoman Sardra and Agustina Asti who made my stay so enjoyable and productive, my sincere thanks.

I would also like to thank George Paxton and Charles DiSalvo for sharing their insights into the life of Sonja Schlesin; Hoger Terp and Tine Elisabeth Larsen who helped me with the Danish disciples; Sharon MacDonald who gave me more of the background to the life of Mary Chesley; David Hopkins, for assistance with the section on Saralabehn;

and Margit Frank and Laurie Cohen for sharing information and the letters exchanged between the Standenaths and Gandhi that were in archives in Vienna and had not made it into the Indian collections or into Gandhi's *Collected Works*. At the Sabarmati Ashram in Ahmedabad, where I read most of the letters to Gandhi from the women who form the core of this book, I would like to thank Amrutbhai Modhi for looking after me; and the office and library staff, in particular Kinnari Bhatt who almost became my personal research assistant; and Tridip Suhrud who had ensured that the material I needed was waiting for me when I arrived. In Mumbai, as usual, T.K.R. Somaiya of the Bombay Sarvodaya Mandal was my considerate host, and the staff and librarians at the nearby Mani Bhavan are owed thanks, in particular Dr Usha Thakker who discussed Gandhi's relationship with women at length with me. Dr Y.P. Anand and Dr Varsha Das at the National Gandhi Museum Library in Delhi, and the librarians at La Trobe University's Borchart Library helped me with some obscure sources; and at Vedchhi I had the good fortune of spending some time in discussion with Narayan Desai, clarifying some of the larger themes in the book. My able translators were Marja Koskela (from German), Swati Desai (from Gujarati) and Sandhya Mehta and Avni Lavasa (from Hindi). I could not have completed this work without them. Finally, to those who read and commented so constructively on earlier drafts of chapters or the whole manuscript, especially Maureen Bond, Charles DiSalvo, Ruth Fluhr, Leela Gandhi, Meg Gurry, Delene Hutchins, Marja Koskela and Sharon MacDonald – my gratitude to you all.

1

# Introduction

## Gandhi, the Feminine and the West

Gandhi's relationship with women has proved irresistibly fascinating to many. Very often people who know practically nothing about the Mahatma will make a comment on his 'sleeping' with young women in his old age. Much of this comes from prurient interest fostered by sensationalist biographies or books aimed at debunking the 'myth of the Mahatma.'[1] Gandhi often talked about women as the stronger sex (and this has been seen as a form of patronisation by, especially feminist, critics) and how he wanted to be like a mother to his followers. Not surprisingly, the collections of his letters and speeches 'on women' are many. What is surprising is how little scholarly work has been undertaken on his attitudes to, and relationships with, women.

In 1953, Eleanor Morton published a book titled *The Women in Gandhi's Life* (*Women Behind Mahatma Gandhi* in the British edition of the following year). The book provides a chronicle of Gandhi's life using his significant female relationships as the vehicle. The women are, naturally, firstly his mother Putlibai and wife Kasturba; followed by some Western friends and influencers including Annie Besant, Olive Schreiner, Millie Graham Polak and Sonja Schlesin; then noteworthy Indian women such as Anasuya Sarabhai, Vijaya Lakshmi Pandit, Sarojini Naidu, Rajkumari Amrit Kaur, and Sushila Nayar; and other prominent Westerners including Muriel Lester, Mirabehn and Lady Mountbatten. The main problem with the book is that it is not referenced at all and many of the incidents mentioned seem to be based on hearsay. Since then, besides many generally superficial book chapters on Gandhi and women, only Martin Green's book, *Gandhi: Voice of a New Age Revolution*, has taken a serious and scholarly interest in the topic; and, most recently, Girja Kumar's weighty tome, *Brahmacharya, Gandhi & His Women Associates*, has provided the first dedicated, if more journalistic and disorganised consideration of the subject. Sudhir Kakar's book about Gandhi and Mirabehn (*Mira and the Mahatma*), while a novel, is based on reasonably well-researched sources.[2] Given all that Gandhi had to say on women, and given his close relationships with many of them, including many very well-known ones, why, until recently, has there been such a paucity of research and writing on the topic?



The reason, at least partially, seems to be because the Gandhi story is generally closely intertwined with the story of India's independence struggle. And here the main actors were men. As I have discussed elsewhere, this gives us a very limited picture of Gandhi.[3] Narayan Desai, one of the few remaining Gandhians who knew the Mahatma intimately (his father was Mahadev Desai, Gandhi's chief personal secretary, and he grew up in Gandhi's ashrams), was a leading figure in the post-Gandhi Gandhian movement and is a recent Gandhi biographer. He notes that Gandhi gave three great gifts to humanity and that *satyagraha*, Gandhi's nonviolent activism, representing the political Gandhi, is only one of them.[4] This aspect however is the one on which English language books about Gandhi tend to focus. With this focus, Gandhi's co-workers, the ones who take on starring roles in the biographies, are powerful male politicians such as Jawaharlal Nehru and Sardar Vallabhbhai Patel and leading Western male supporters such as the Reverend Charles Freer Andrews and sympathetic British socialists. The political Gandhi, however, is a greatly diminished person and a more complete analysis of the Mahatma would include comprehensive reference to other important co-workers.

Gandhi was not merely interested in freeing India from the British yoke. He also wanted a certain type of free India, and political independence for the country was no guarantee of it. For this reason, he worked tirelessly at what he called the 'constructive program' for village uplift and communal harmony. Gandhi often claimed that the constructive program was more important than the political civil disobedience campaigns that he was leading. Without it, the necessary fundamental changes would not be made, and civil disobedience, if it succeeded in overthrowing a set of oppressors, would merely exchange one group of leaders with another similar group.

Political biographies seem to be more exciting and spectacular than those focussing on the social and moral aspects of Gandhi's life. His women disciples, including the Western ones, tended to be constructive workers and as the constructive *sarvodaya* (uplift of all) activities of Gandhi's life are down-played, these women are largely unknown, despite the fact that many of them wrote books. They have simply disappeared from the record even though they were at least as important to him as his political co-workers. The constructive programmes, in Desai's scheme, is the second of Gandhi's great gifts.

But there is even more to the Mahatma than this, something obvious to Desai, but of which most biographies make far too little. Desai points out that there was a third gift from Gandhi: his eleven vows, a set of rules which established the code of conduct for his ashram inmates and which are key to understanding Gandhi's religious quest. Gandhi firmly believed that life could not be compartmentalised, that actions and the reasons on which they are based, whether they be political, economic, social or spiritual, are interrelated, and that these actions have a direct bearing upon the achievement of personal liberation, the ultimate aim of life. Again, the spiritual Gandhi does not fit too comfortably in primarily political biographies except to set up the Mahatma as the conscience of humanity, or an eccentric old man who had great problems with his sexuality. However, without understanding Gandhi's spiritual quest, we do not understand Gandhi. As he is secularised into a comprehensible and less controversial actor on the political stage, we are left with no easy way of coming to terms with a more whole Gandhi. The problem is that the process is almost inevitable in any biography of a reasonable length and degree of coherence. Where a different aspect of Gandhi's life becomes the focus of a study, that focus seems to be the main motivating force behind the actions of the Mahatma. For example, on reading Kumar's book that examines Gandhi's life through his *bramacharya* experiments, one could almost come away without realising that Gandhi was a political actor. Nehru and Patel are barely mentioned. And this present book may make it appear that all of Gandhi's closest associates and devotees were Western women. How to get the balance right is the dilemma for biographers of characters as complex as Gandhi.

With some notable exceptions, most of Gandhi's women disciples[5] (as opposed to political or constructive co-workers) were ashramites, trying to follow the spiritual discipline of their master. So, again, even though many of them have left autobiographical writings, they too have tended to disappear from the record, and this is particularly true for his Western women disciples. Of course there are exceptions. Mirabehn could not be left out as she was so often physically at Gandhi's side, and because of her previous status, as the daughter of a British admiral, she made good copy. But she was not the only one and indeed not the first Western woman disciple to 'go native'. The others also deserve to be remembered.

The closest of Gandhi's Western women devotees formed a personal rather than a (merely) politically supportive or philosophically like-minded relationship with him. To adequately describe these personal relationships, I have tried to rely on correspondence instead of later biographical or even autobiographical accounts. Letters obviously have a far greater immediacy and are not written for posterity, the way much later autobiographical writings are. Often, however, only the Gandhi side of the correspondence has been preserved. Once Mohandas Gandhi was the revered 'great-souled' Mahatma,[6] his secretarial staff preserved copies of his letters, and those to whom they were addressed tended to keep them and very often allowed them to be reproduced in the one hundred volumes of *The Collected Works of Mahatma Gandhi*. The letters to Gandhi are a little more problematic. Important ones, or ones from certain people or covering certain dates, have been preserved in the archives at the Sabarmati Ashram in Ahmedabad or in the Nehru Memorial Museum Library in New Delhi. However, a great many have also been destroyed. It is very likely that Gandhi received more letters during his lifetime than anyone else. Presumably most were not worthy of preservation, and even many that may have been were replied to and then recycled as note paper. Fortunately, many of the letters had questions to Gandhi and even when they did not, in his responses he very often alluded to the content of the letters he was replying to so the conversation is not necessarily one-sided even when only his letters to friends and devotees are available.

What I have tried to do through these letters and other writings is to look at Gandhi's relations with Western women. Who were they? Why were they attracted to him? And what does this tell us about him? However, before individual women and his relationship with them is explored, some context is necessary.

# Gandhi on Women

From the early-1940s onwards, there have been many collections of Gandhi's writings on women including: *To the Women*,[7] *Women and Social Injustice*,[8] *Women*,[9] *Women's Role in Society*,[10] *The Role of Women*,[11] and more recently *Gandhi on Women*.[12] And it is *de rigueur* for general collections of Gandhi's thoughts to carry sections on women.[13] On looking through these collections, several themes emerge.

Not surprisingly, given the time and place in which he lived and his intellectual capital was built up, Gandhi had an essentialist view of the nature and role of women: they were simply more peaceful and more moral than men. Perhaps surprisingly, this did not mean that he saw them as in any way inferior because of what he perceived as their biology and psychology. In fact he categorised them as different but equal or even praised them as superior. In answering those who held that the sacred Hindu texts deemed women to be the subordinates of men, he declared that 'all that is printed in the name of scriptures need not be taken as the word of God or the inspired word', and that bad interpolations should be removed and sections which 'have no moral value or are contrary to the fundamentals of religion and morality' should also be removed.[14]

Gandhi's writings on women contain many aphorisms, such as: 'Woman is nothing if she is not self-sacrifice and purity personified';[15] 'Woman is the incarnation of *Ahimsa*. *Ahimsa* means infinite love, which again means infinite capacity for suffering. Who but women, the mother of man, shows this capacity in the largest measure?';[16] 'To call women the weaker sex is a libel; it is man's injustice to woman. If by strength is meant brute strength, then indeed is woman less brute than man. If by strength is meant moral power, then woman is immeasurably man's superior';[17] 'To call woman a member of the weaker sex is a libel. In what way is woman the weaker sex, I do not know. If the implication is that she lacks the brute instinct of man, or does not possess it in the same measure as man, the charge may be admitted. But then, woman becomes as she is, the nobler sex. If she is weak in striking, she is strong in suffering. I have described woman as the embodiment of sacrifice and *ahimsa*';[18] 'There is no occasion for women to consider themselves subordinate or inferior to men. Languages proclaim that woman is half of man and by parity of reasoning, man is half of woman. They are not two separate entities, but halves of one. The English language goes further and calls woman the better half of man. Therefore, woman should resort to civil rebellion against all undesirable and unworthy restraints';[19] 'Man has converted her into a domestic drudge and an instrument of his pleasure, instead of regarding her as his helpmate and better half! The result is a semi-paralysis of our society. Woman has rightly been called the mother of the race. We owe it to her and to ourselves to undo the great wrong that we have done her';[20] '... somehow or other, man has dominated woman from ages past, and so woman has developed an inferiority complex. She has believed in the truth of man's interested teaching that she is inferior to him. But the seers among men have recognised her equal status';[21] 'Woman is described as man's better half. As long as she has not the same rights in law as man, as long as the birth of a girl does not receive the same welcome as that of a boy, so long we should know that India is suffering from partial paralysis. Suppression of woman is a denial of Ahimsa';[22] 'I am uncompromising in the matter of woman's rights. In my opinion she should labour under no legal disability not suffered by man. I should treat the daughters and sons on a footing of perfect equality',[23]and 'More often than not a woman's time is taken up, not by the performance of essential domestic duties, but in catering for the egotistic pleasure of her lord and master and for her own vanities. To me, this domestic slavery of woman is a symbol of our barbarism. In my opinion, the slavery of the kitchen is the remnant of barbarism mainly. It is high time that our womankind was freed from this incubus. Domestic work ought not to take the whole of a woman's time.'[24]

If women were different from but equal with men, how could this equality be achieved as a social norm? Gandhi championed women's rights and saw more for them than the usual lack of education and early marriage. In his words, his ideal was that 'A man should remain man and yet should become woman; similarly a woman should remain woman and yet become man. This means that man should cultivate the gentleness and the discrimination of woman; and woman should cast off her timidity and become brave and courageous.'[25] According to Gandhi, one way of achieving equality was for women to cease to be the plaything of men, and his panacea for this was *brahmacharya* (or sexual celibacy[26]), even in marriage. To Western feminists this may sound more than a little problematic, however Hardiman claims that it 'had a particular value for women, for it could provide a means for resisting male domination in a way that was legitimised in their culture.'[27] The Indian feminist writer and activist, Madhu Kishwar points out that in Gandhi's view women were, by and large, the passive objects of male sexuality. Therefore his sexual obsessions and experiments should not be 'dismissed as a mere product of personal eccentricity' but had to be seen as a 'part of his social revolution and vision of a new man-woman relationship.' Especially given that his 'advocacy of sexual restraint was addressed to men', because, for him, male sexuality was 'almost synonymous with aggression towards and humiliation of women.'[28] Woman was more a victim than a temptress, and moreover, 'under the prevalent social circumstances, *brahmacharya* had a very liberating potential for women. In the existing social structures, this was perhaps the only way women could free themselves from household drudgery and the burden of childcare to an extent sufficient for them to become active participants in social change.'[29]

Gandhi had come to see marriage generally as an impediment to the life of service he wanted to lead and the type of life that those he most admired, especially the Western women he held up as models, were leading. It is no accident that most of his close Western women supporters were unmarried and were engaged in lives of valuable service; and no accident that they became associated with him, someone who seemed to be preaching, as a norm, something they were doing as an aberration. When Gandhi was imprisoned in the Yeravda jail in Poona following the Salt March, he wrote a weekly letter back to the inmates, mostly women and children, who remained in the Sabarmati Ashram at Ahmedabad, in which he examined the principles of the observances at the ashram. They were later published as *From Yeravda Mandir*.[30] One of the sections is titled '*Brahmacharya* or Chastity'. There he makes the point that nonviolence is impossible without utter selflessness, because, for him, *ahimsa* (nonviolence) means universal love and this is impeded by marriage:

> If a man gives his love to one woman, or a woman to one man, what is there left for all the world besides? It simply means, "We two first, and the devil take all the rest of them." As a faithful wife must be prepared to sacrifice her all for the sake of the husband, and a faithful husband for the sake of his wife, it is clear that such persons cannot rise to the height of Universal Love, or look upon all mankind as kith and kin. For they have created a boundary wall around their love. The larger their family, the farther we are from Universal Love. Hence one who would obey the law of ahimsa cannot marry, not to speak of gratification outside the marital bond.[31]

Gandhi expressed similar sentiments to Mary Barr, one of his close Western associates: 'Anybody wishing to serve humanity in any special way, will be able to do so more fully as a Brahmachari, for, having no self-possessions, he possesses the world, and having no special service to render to one group (his family), he is free to serve all.'[32] Years earlier, complaining to Hermann Kallenbach, his closest friend and associate from his South Africa days, about his own wife, Gandhi noted: 'My point is that you cannot attach yourself to a particular woman and yet live for humanity. The two do not harmonise.'[33]

To Gandhi, the ideal woman is a sexless being for whom legitimate sex is only there for the purpose of procreation. This is because he sees sex as lust, something which blocks progress towards higher meanings in life. In this, women are the victims of men. Although he never spoke out directly against the institution of marriage, Gandhi, who was married at thirteen and spent much of his adult life campaigning against underage marriages, noted that those who wanted to lead a socially useful life should remain unmarried. However, even within marriage, he advocated unions that eschewed sex, with the partners living together as brother and sister. He believed that only after he had achieved such a state did he manage to forge a truly loving relationship with his own wife. Women in India had very little social space in which to manoeuver outside marriage. He wanted them to serve the poor and downtrodden in his constructive programmes as selfless and devoted social workers, and this could only be done if they had no families. His Western women associates had far more leeway in acting outside of traditional norms, yet, still, most of them were unmarried.

Gandhi advocated the equality of the sexes, however, this did not necessarily mean equality of occupations or power. He still saw a division of labour between the sexes as not only useful but ordained by natural abilities and inclinations. As he said: 'Adam wove and Eve span.'[34] (Nevertheless he made spinning his symbolic sacrificial labour and so broke down one of the social norms which downplayed the dignity of what was seen as essentially 'women's work.') He claimed that men and women were 'equals in life, but their functions differ',[35] and in 'trying to ride the horse that man rides, she brings herself and him down.'[36] Regardless of this, he also noted that no vocation 'is exclusively reserved for one sex only.' While there may be natural inclinations to certain types of work, he pointed out exceptions and noted that 'today in Europe we find women shining as lawyers, doctors and administrators.'[37] In other words, Gandhi the essentialist still allowed for nurture and the environment to play a role in shaping the destiny of women. For him, nature was not everything.

Many of Gandhi's claims about the superiority of women will not stand scrutiny in light of modern psychological analysis or feminist theory, and would not be applauded by critical modern feminists. While Gandhi seemed to characterise a male-female dichotomy in terms of 'active' and 'passive', Kishwar points out that this 'has been an important ideological device for denying women any chance to acquire power and decision-making ability in the family and in society.'[38] While Gandhi sought to oppose the unjust domination of women by men, this position was inherent in the very role, that of 'complement' to man, that Gandhi envisaged for women. It appears that while Gandhi did not want a wife to play an excessively subordinate role to her husband,[39] Kishwar notes that he did not seem to be against them generally playing a subordinate role. While he was able to see that women's belief in their own inferiority was the result of man's '[self-] interested teaching',[40] he failed to see that his views on the division of labour were also part of this same 'self-interested teaching', that 'resulted in the confinement and subordination of woman.'[41] Interestingly, and much to his approval, his closest women disciples, especially his Western ones, played no subordinate role to men, except when some of them became obsessed with him.

In summary, Gandhi gave women a role in Indian society, made them realise their freedom and gave them confidence in themselves. He told them that they were equal to their husbands, empowering them in family and marriage; he not only made it possible for them to be involved in political movements, but he also told them that the national struggle could not succeed without their involvement.[42] It was through him that they became active participants in Indian political life, particularly from the time of the Salt Satyagraha of 1930.[43] As one perceptive observer has noted, Gandhi's advocacy of women as political actors was not contrary to his conception of them as nurturers and care-takers of the home because 'the participation of women in *satyagraha* was seen as an extension of her special mission as the care-taker of humanity.'[44]

Devaki Jain points out that while many of Gandhi's ideas about women may now seem old-fashioned, or even extremist, he was reacting to the 'terrible fact' of their subordination. He seems to have been 'intuitively attuned to them' and saw their potential more clearly than other religious or political leaders. 'He perceived women as equal, but different. In their difference, Gandhi himself identified with women', taking up women's 'ways and issues' such as the campaign against liquor, and the quest for self-reliance in household production.[45]

However, for all Gandhi's attempts to create equality between the sexes and for his continual encouragement for women to become workers in his movements, as Kishwar points out, 'most of the women who came in close contact with him ended up functioning primarily as his devotees.'[46] And while in some instances this pattern was repeated with his Western women associates who remained in India after coming under his influence, they also provided notable exceptions in the case of the Anne Marie Petersen, the Khedi workers, Marjorie Sykes and Catherine Mary Heilemann.

Gandhi, for all his revolutionary approach to gender relations, in the end remained a patriarch. Given his background and social and historical context, he could not undertake an adequate structural analysis of the origins of women's exploitation. At his core, he remained an essentialist who denied 'pure', 'self-suffering' women any sexuality. This very essentialism meant, paradoxically, that his newly awakened powerful woman could only break out of her given roles by denying her biology.[47]

Nevertheless, Hardiman notes that few fellow nationalists or activist women subjected him to any strong criticism for his patriarchal attitudes. His followers, even those who managed to carve out important and independent roles for themselves, still called him Bapu (father) and 'accepted his patriarchal persona without a murmur.'[48] While later Indian feminists have been more forceful in their criticisms, often even they have tended to applaud him for the role he provided for women in the political arena in a conservative and patriarchal society.

# Gandhi as Woman

An intimate friend of Gandhi's at the time of his South African transformation from successful lawyer to political activist and questing New Ager, Millie Graham Polak wrote that

> Most women love men for such attributes as are usually considered masculine. Yet Mahatma Gandhi has been given the love of many women for his womanliness; for all those qualities that are associated with women – great faith, great fortitude, great devotion, great patience, great tenderness and great sympathy. Women could sense that in him they found a fellow traveller, one who had passed ahead along the road they too were travelling, and could give him an affection deep, pure, and untouched by any play of sex-emotion.[49]

Later, she added that he 'was himself rather womanly, having the qualities of loyalty, trust, devotion, faith and purity.'[50] A 'respectable' Gujarati woman who could not be 'accused of blind worship' added that, 'There are some things relating to our lives which we, women, can speak of to, or discuss with, no man. But while speaking to Gandhiji we somehow forgot the fact that he was *man*.'[51]

Gandhi, himself, explained that 'I have always had a passion to serve womankind. Ever since my arrival in India, the women have recognized in me their friend and servant. They have come to look upon me as one of themselves',[52] and he talked to them about his womanliness: 'I know you have not missed the woman in me.'[53] Erik Erikson, in his psychoanalytical study of Gandhi, argues that while Gandhi may have believed in the natural superiority of women in important virtues such as love, kindness and selfless sacrifice, this brought on a competitive attempt for him to become 'more maternal than the most motherly of mothers.'[54]

Talking about women's craze for jewellery and adornments, Gandhi said that:

> If I was born a woman, I would rise in rebellion against any pretension on the part of man that woman is born to be his plaything. I have mentally become a woman in order to steal into her heart. I could not steal into my wife's heart until I decided to treat her differently than I used to do, and so I restored to her all her rights by dispossessing myself of all my so-called rights as her husband.[55]



But there was more to Gandhi's affinity with women than his trustworthy stereotypical feminine nature or the championing of their rights. He was, as hinted at by the above quote, in a sense actively trying to be a woman. In a letter to a friend, he noted: 'The idea is that a man, by becoming passionless, transforms himself into a woman, that is, he includes the woman into himself. The same is true of a passionless woman. If you visualize the state of passionlessness in your mind, you will understand what I say. It is a different story that we do not come across such men and women.'[56] His mission for himself was to become one, and the test of his success was to be ascertained through his most controversial experiments? Gandhi noted that a full *brahmachari* was 'capable of lying naked with naked women, however beautiful they may be, without being in any manner whatsoever sexually excited.'[57]

Gandhi's grandniece, Manubehn Gandhi, was his closest companion in the last year or so of his life. She was the focus of his most intense *brahmacharya* experiments during his peace pilgrimage in violence-torn Noakhali,[58] and was one of the two women on whose shoulders he was leaning when he was assassinated. She was not yet twenty when he died. Gandhi claimed to be Manu's mother: 'Have I not become your mother? I have been father to many but only to you am I a mother.' Manu herself noted that, 'For me ... he was a mother. Generally it is not possible for a man to become a mother to any one because he has not been endowed by God with a mother's loving heart. But Bapu appropriated for himself a share of even this divine gift.'[59] And she called her small book of the relationship *Bapu – My Mother*. Rajkumari Amrit Kaur, another close follower and sometime participant in Gandhi's *brahmacharya* experiments, backed up Manubehn's comments, explaining that 'We found him not a "Bapu" – a wise father, but what is more precious, a mother, before whose all-embracing and understanding love all fear and restraint vanish.'[60]

In keeping with Hindu teaching, Gandhi saw men's spiritual power as being dissipated through sexual emission and that therefore self-realisation required celibacy[61] (something that in perhaps somewhat different permutations seems to be shared by many major religions): 'Even one who has observed *brahmacharya* for some period will notice the increase of mental and physical powers and, having once secured this philosopher's stone, will guard it with care like very life.'[62] One of his close Western women friends, albeit more a respectful co-worker than worshipping acolyte, Muriel Lester remarked in a tone of a 'veiled sneer' that Gandhi was one of a small group of idealists who had sublimated his sex energy in creative action in the cause of nationalist politics.[63]

Gandhi's disgust with sex,[64] stemming from a particularly disturbing childhood experience and his self-confessed sexual obsession in his early married life, made him characterise men as brutes and aggressors. His aim in life was the achievement of self-realisation, and, in the darkness and mayhem that accompanied the gaining of independence by India and Pakistan in his final years, he needed all the spiritual power he could muster in order to be able to make a difference in a subcontinent gone mad. Woman was sexless and infinitely more capable of suffering. She was the embodiment of nonviolence, the quality above all that he wanted to cultivate in himself. Nonviolence was the only path to Truth (with a capital T) and 'As I have often said if there is one true satyagrahi [one practising satyagraha] it would be enough. I am trying to be that true satyagrahi.'[65] Earlier he had said that it is 'an axiomatic truth that even if a single satyagrahi remains, he will win',[66] that 'if a single satyagrahi holds out to the end, victory is absolutely certain',[67] that 'Even one man ready to live a life of non-violence to perfection will be able to subdue the entire world.'[68] He had to neuter himself and demonstrate to himself that he had achieved this state of nonviolence, that he had become a true satyagrahi who would be capable of bringing peace to his country and to himself. That he could not achieve this peace meant that there was something wrong with his nonviolence, that there was 'some serious flaw deep down' within him 'which is responsible for all this.'[69] Perhaps it was 'because I have temporised in the matter of *brahmacharya*.'[70]

Nirmal Kumar Bose, who was Gandhi's chief personal assistant during his Noakhali pilgrimage, was repelled by Gandhi's concern about the private and personal life of those around him. However, he later realised that 'it was a deep, spiritual attitude on his part which was the by-product of his attempt to conquer sex by becoming a woman.'[71] And given the darkness around him, the killing and his growing personal marginalisation by the new power elite, it was necessary for him to rise to new heights of nonviolence to make any difference. And such heights could only be achieved by women.[72]

# Gandhi and Women

As noted above, Gandhi's thoughts on women and womanhood and his message to women have been collected in many volumes. In these books we get a glimpse of Gandhi's desire to nurture his own feminine side and there are some books authored by others, such as Millie Polak's, Mirabehn's, Nilla Cram Cook's, Mary Barr's and Manu Gandhi's, that touch on his motherly relationship with the authors in particular and, at times, women in general. There has also been a substantial number of books on Gandhi's wife Kasturba and his relationship with her (the latest of which is Arun and Sunanda Gandhi's *The Forgotten Woman*). Given this, it is surprising that more studies of Gandhi's association with women, rather than thoughts on them, have not been undertaken. Eleanor Morton's *The Women in Gandhi's Life*, some analytical observances aside, is really little more than a Gandhi biography that mentions many more women than is usual, and Girja Kumar's book on Gandhi's relationship with women in light of his *brahmacharya* experiments draws out very little in the way of conclusions.

Rajkumari Amrit Kaur was one of the most westernised of Gandhi's Indian women disciples. She was born into a princely family that had converted to Christianity, had been educated at Oxford and was a member of Gandhi's ashram from the mid-1930s. She noted that 'no man has evoked such whole-hearted devotion from women.' This she put down to his ability to 'put himself into the shoes of another person ... especially ... the underdog.' She continued, saying that 'A passionate lover of humanity, an implacable foe of injustice ... it is small wonder that Gandhiji early espoused the women's cause.'[73] As someone who lived closely with Gandhi, she was able to observe that in his institutions and work programmes in India 'he has paid equal attention and given equal place to women and girls', while in his ashrams 'there is an air of freedom and self-confidence in the girls and women who have lived with him or been under his care.' She added that this 'is a joy to behold and rarely visible in Indian society elsewhere. Nothing delights him more than the success of women in any sphere of life.'[74]

Rameshwar Nehru adds that Gandhi saw women as better able to bring about his ideal world than men as they made better soldiers in his nonviolent army, and this, in turn, means that 'he has confidence in them, and that is why they are so forcefully drawn towards him.'[75]

Muriel Lester, one of Gandhi's close English supporters and his host in London during the 1931 Second Round Table Conference to discuss India's constitutional future, notes that Gandhi was 'that rare creature whom George Meredith describes in several pages of stately prose as "the friend of women".' She adds that 'A few such men are to be found in every age. Women recognise them at once. These friends are wholly without that sentimentalism which leads men to substitute an exaggerated gesture of respect for the real thing. These friends expect in women what they normally find in any man, courage, straightforwardness, frankness.'[76] After a meeting of the All-India Village Industries Association where the discussion revolved around the gender composition of the board, Mary Barr recorded in her diary that 'Certainly, there is absolutely no sex-superiority in Bapu – a rare gift among men, one which reminds me of Jesus and which makes women instinctively trust and love him.'[77] Amrit Kaur has remarked that, from what he said and wrote, as well as from her intimate association with him, 'no one knew and no one appreciated womankind better than he'.[78]

Gandhi may have enjoyed the company of women and fought for their rights, but not everyone believed that he understood them at all. Although Margaret Sanger, the famed American birth control advocate and champion of women's rights, admittedly only had two days with Gandhi, those two days were entirely concerned with debating the position of women. In his interview with Sanger, Gandhi insisted that he had studied women, knew them and understood them. Sanger had more than mild doubts: 'Gandhi maintained that he knew women and was in sympathetic accord with them. Personally, after listening to him for a while, I did not believe he had the faintest glimmering of the inner workings of a woman's heart or mind.'[79] Still, going by the recorded testimonies of women who had had close contact with him, such appraisals were in the minority.

Looking at the course of Gandhi's life through his association with his closest women companions, some key life-altering instances can be discerned. Having no daughters, Gandhi's relationship with women in his family centred on his mother and his wife. His mother Putlibai was deeply religious, prone to fasting and taking vows.[80] In many ways he seemed to be trying to live up to her example throughout his life:

> My mother's inner life would reflect itself in her austerity. If you notice any purity in me, that is not my father's but my mother's. My mother died at the age of forty, so I have seen her in the prime of life, but I have never seen in her any frivolity, recourse to beauty aids or interest in the pleasures of life or hypocrisy. The one lasting impression that she left on my mind is that of saintliness.[81]

His wife Kasturba was a woman of strong character even though she was not educated, and in early life she probably saw a normal household existence ahead for herself. For better or worse, she married someone who became a Mahatma and in many ways she fought a rearguard action against the overwhelming force of the trajectory of his life. Gandhi claimed that her strong will, stubbornness and silent suffering in the face of his domination, taught him patience and nonviolence:

> I learnt the lesson of non-violence from my wife, when I tried to bend her to my will. Her determined resistance to my will on the one hand, and her quiet submission to the suffering my stupidity involved on the other, ultimately made me ashamed of myself and cured me of my stupidity in thinking that I was born to rule over her, and in the end she became my teacher in non-violence. And what I did in South Africa was but an extension of the rule of satyagraha which she unwillingly practised in her own person.[82]

His wife not only taught him nonviolence, but seemingly she also taught him how to relate to women in a truly loving and equal fashion rather than in a way that is not only complicated but also lessened by sex:

> From that day when I began *brahmacharya*, our freedom began. My wife became a free woman, free from my authority as her lord and master, and I became free from my slavery to my own appetite which she had to satisfy. No other woman had any attraction for me in the same sense that my wife had. I was too loyal to her as husband and too loyal to the vow I had taken before my mother to be slave to any other woman. But the manner in which my *brahmacharya* came to me irresistibly drew me to woman as the mother of man. She became too sacred for sexual love. And so every woman at once became sister or daughter to me. ...
>
> ... But I have never believed that all contact with women was to be shunned for the due observance of *brahmacharya*. That restraint which demands abstention from all contact, no matter how innocent, with the opposite sex is a forced growth, having little or no vital value. Therefore natural contacts for service were never restrained. And I found myself enjoying the confidence of many sisters, European and Indian, in South Africa. And when I invited the Indian sisters in South Africa to join the civil resistance movement, I found myself one of them. I discovered that I was specially fitted to serve womankind.[83]

Regardless of his identification with his South African Indian 'sisters', it has been pointed out that if one reads Gandhi's version of his South African story, apart from family members, there is very little about the Indian women who took part in his campaigns. While the European women who shared his life at Phoenix Settlement are central characters, there is precious little personal record of the Indian women who were at Phoenix and Tolstoy Farm. His writings merely comment on their courage.[84] Most of the Indian women he dealt with were poorly educated, illiterate and, consequently, not his intellectual equals in the way that Sonja Schlesin and Millie Polak were. But in India, he did attract highly educated and highly capable Indian co-workers and disciples. They are no longer totally missing from the record, and certainly in India are far better know than any of his European disciples, with the exception of the ever present Mirabehn. The ones who engendered turning points in his life were Indian.

From late 1919 until the end of 1920, Gandhi was infatuated with Saraladevi Chaudhurani, the aristocratic niece of India's great poet and cultural icon, Rabindranath Tagore. She was everything that his own wife Kasturba was not: cultured, extroverted, intellectual, a politically active nationalist campaigner and publicist, and attractive. She did more to publicise *khadi* (the hand spun, hand-woven cloth that Gandhi wanted to be the livery of the freedom movement), by wearing it than Gandhi himself could ever achieve by his preaching. Gandhi stayed with her for some months in Lahore while her husband was in prison and then toured the country with her in the nationalist cause. In her he found a 'soul-mate' whom he called his 'spiritual wife'.[85] The platonic nature of the relationship was sorely tested and Gandhi almost fell. The way Gandhi talked about her to associates, and letters between them at the height of their closeness, betray something of a teenage-like crush. Gandhi became hyper-critical of his wife who not only seemed to be offering him so little intellectually but seemed to be holding him back in his spiritual and political progress the way he seemed sure that Saraladevi was not.[86] Later in life he admitted how close he came to giving in to his passion,[87] and looked back on this period with some horror realising what he could have lost if he had left his wife for the object of his infatuation.[88] While it is beyond the scope of this book to discuss this particular relationship in any detail, it continued to haunt him throughout his life and it coloured some of Gandhi's relationships with his Western women associates.[89]

Bose, the chronicler of Gandhi's Noakhali *brahmacharya* experiments (he resigned his position as Gandhi's interpreter and assistant over disagreements with the Mahatma on this), noted in his psychological analysis of what Gandhi was doing that perhaps Gandhi's attitude to women could be understood in consideration of his relationship with his mother.[90] Gandhi had struggled with celibacy since 1899,[91] but it was not until he was thirty-seven years old, in 1906, that he finally took a vow of *brahmacharya*. Bose notes that since that time

> ...his relations with members of the other sex was progressively "purified" and he felt that he was becoming a fitter instrument for the practice of the highest virtues of non-violence. We may be permitted to assume that the repression of the sexual instinct was not only a means to a lofty end, but it was also the penance which

> Gandhiji voluntarily imposed upon himself for having proved untrue to his father during the last moments of his life.[92]

And we can only speculate as to the changes the Noakhali *brahmacharya* experiments with Manu could have brought about on the personality and practices of the Mahatma if he had lived longer.

# Gandhi and Western Women

Early in his life, Gandhi had strong regard for the British Empire, believing it to be a fair and civilising influence. Later he lost this faith and professed a horror for at least some elements of Western civilisation. The nineteen-year-old Gandhi went to England to study law in 1888, not only because of professional ambition, but also because if 'I go to England not only shall I become a barrister (of whom I used to think a great deal), but I shall be able to see England, the land of philosophers and poets, the very centre of civilization.'[93] After arriving, initially he was intent on turning himself into a proper English gentleman by way of the expensive lodgings he stayed at, the fashionable clothes he wore and the dancing, French, elocution and violin lessons he took. Soon, however, his financial position forced him to modify his extravagance and the discovery of vegetarian restaurants helped not only to appease his hunger but also put him in the company of an impressive circle of New Agers, Socialists and esoteric Christians. They had a profound impact on the young Mohandas as did the Christian missionaries, who became his first close friends in South Africa.[94] Further, it is revealing to see, for example, how often themes and phrases from the Western texts that Gandhi read crop up in his speeches and writings even decades later. This was evident during the time of his early philosophical explorations in London and South Africa (when he still had time to be building his intellectual capital). Reading Tolstoy's *The Kingdom of God is Within You*, John Ruskin's *Unto this Last*, Henry David Thoreau's *On the Duty of Civil Disobedience*, or Plato's dialogues of Socrates (especially the *Apology* and *Crito*) are genuine eye-openers in this regard; many of Gandhi's favourite sayings or examples, and even whole areas of his philosophy, have been taken almost verbatim from these sources. Gandhi himself claimed that Ruskin's work transformed his life and provided the basis for his economic ideas.[95] His personal secretary and primary biographer, Pyarelal, has gone so far as to endorse the claim that Tolstoy was the 'founder of Gandhism'.[96]

While the formative influences stayed, his respect for Western civilisation took a sharp downturn. As early as 1909, in his seminal political manifesto *Hind Swaraj*, Gandhi was already writing about the evils of modern civilisation. He saw a society which provided an abundance of material goods, but where people had become factory slaves or slaves to materialism, abandoning morality and religion; where rapid railway travel spread plagues and prevented people from having a chance to get to meet and establish kindred feelings with their neighbours on long journeys; where educated lawyers further divided rather than reconciled disputing parties; and where doctors treated symptoms so that causes did not need to be tackled.[97] India required freedom not just from the yoke of British colonialism, but also from the pernicious influence of modern, that is Western, civilisation. This was to be done through his work at social reform via his constructive programme. And here is where he hoped that his Western women associates would play a part. And those who did seemed to be backing his views.

Western women were first mentioned in his life as part of his vow to his mother, before he was given permission to leave for England to read law, as something (along with alcohol and meat) that was not to be touched.[98] Although Gandhi did have a few women friends in London when he was there as a student, with at times comic consequences, his closest early Western women friends there were relatives of South African associates with whom he formed relationships on later visits. During his South African sojourn, Western women had become important supporters, and, in the case of Millie Graham Polak, an extremely close personal friend. In late-October and November 1906, Gandhi was in London as part of an Indian delegation to discuss matters of discrimination in South Africa. At this time he came into close contact with the sisters of Millie's husband, Henry Polak. Polak's parents and sisters received him with such warmth that Gandhi jokingly wrote to Polak that his two sisters, Maud and Sally, were so lovable that if he were 'unmarried, or young or believed in mixed marriage, you know what I would have done!'[99] And, even though he was still a Western, suited, political lobbyist rather than semi-naked, khadi-clad, Hindu holy man, Maud was clearly infatuated with him.[100] She visited him in South Africa and later she worked as Assistant Honorary Secretary to the South Africa British Indian Committee in London. When Gandhi was in London for the Round Table Conference, she (now Mrs Cheesman) came to join his secretariat in the Knightsbridge office.

Gandhi's well-known South African women supporters were feminists, pacifists and socialists. It seems quite logical that they would support a nonviolent campaign by an unfairly treated minority and that Gandhi, in turn, would be drawn to them. At the time he came to know them, he was very interested in the suffragette movement and was experimenting with concepts of equality between the sexes. He was also passionately working through his commitment to nonviolence, and from his London days, when he mixed in socialist circles, he considered himself at least something of a socialist. His South African associates, Emily Hobhouse, Betty Molteno and Olive Schreiner, also admired Gandhi, the principles he professed and the movement he led. There was a mutual respect, and at this stage in his life, Gandhi was still the junior partner in these relationships.

While these British and South African women contacts were friends and supporters, Gandhi also learned much from his observations of the then ongoing feminist struggle in England. The political campaign waged by the suffragettes that he witnessed on his visits to the capital of the empire was to be of deep importance in the formation of his own political methodology.

Just weeks after the launching of the South African Indians' political struggle in late 1906, although at this stage it seems that he had not actually met any of them, Gandhi made close observations of the suffragettes in London and wrote at length about them and their tactics. James Hunt, the premier scholar of this time in Gandhi's life, notes that Gandhi had admiration for the English and their liberated womanhood; and he records that Gandhi received 'significant assistance from a contemporary women's movement at a point when he was formulating his own philosophy of non-violent action',[101] and that this 'yielded valuable results which assisted considerably in the maturing and development of his work.'[102]

In a final act of constitutional lobbying, before commencing the campaign of active resistance in South Africa, Gandhi spent six weeks in London to present his case to the British authorities. During this visit, the women's suffrage movement reached new heights of militancy 'employing tactics and seeking goals strikingly similar to his own.'[103] Three days after his arrival, the Women's Social and Political Union held a demonstration in the House of Commons, resulting in the arrest of eleven of their number. After refusing to pay their fines, the women were sentenced to three months' imprisonment. This was the largest number arrested in the year-long, increasingly militant, campaign. This was not lost on Gandhi who wrote an article for his paper *Indian Opinion* a few days later. He had one of the main protesters announcing that 'I shall never obey any law in the making of which I have had no hand; I will not accept the authority of the court executing those laws; if you send me to gaol, I will go there, but I shall on no account pay a fine. I will not furnish any security either.' He then tied this determination to inevitable success, success that the South African Indians could also achieve with the adoption of similar tactics:

> Today the whole country is laughing at them, and they have only a few people on their side. But undaunted, those women work on steadfast in their cause. They are bound to succeed and gain the franchise, for the simple reason that deeds are better than words. Even those who laughed at them would be left wondering. If even women display such courage, will the Transvaal Indians fail in their duty and be afraid of gaol? Or would they rather consider the gaol a palace and readily go there? When the time comes, India's bonds will snap off themselves.[104]

Following his return to South Africa in December, Gandhi kept up to date with the suffragette campaigns in London and continued to write about them. Following large-scale arrests during marches on Parliament in March 1907, Gandhi wrote that 'We have to follow the example of the women referred to above. They go to gaol, though they are few in number, and thus draw the attention of the world to their cause.'[105] He used the example of the sacrifice of the suffragettes to shame his followers into courageous action: 'While English women do manly deeds, shall we though men, behave like women? … In a few days our mettle will be tested.'[106]

In 1909, the now long-standing civilly disobedient Gandhi was again in London pushing the cause of the South African Indians. During the eighteen weeks he spent there, he finally met members of the women's movement and attended their rallies at a time when the movement was taking a more violent turn with the resisting of arrest, stone throwing, window breaking, hunger strikes in prison and even arson. Gandhi lauded the commitment and actions of the English suffragettes as examples for satyagraha; however, their violence now made them problematic as a model. To get around this, in his earlier writings he did not inform his audience of everything they may have done, omitting references to their destruction of property: 'The systematic way in which they set about their work and their skill deserve the highest commendation', and 'When we consider the suffering and the courage of these women, how can the Indian satyagrahis stand comparison with them?'[107]

Later he voiced his concern at what he saw as the impatience of some of the women, noting that it would prove self-defeating in the long-run:

> Some of these women have grown impatient. It is, of course, an admirable thing that they should go to gaol. No one can have anything to say against their inviting suffering on themselves. … If the British women mean to fight in the spirit of satyagraha, they cannot adopt tactics [such as breaking windows]. There is no room for impatience in satyagraha. Those who want the franchise are in a minority, whereas the majority of women oppose the demand; so the minority has no option but to suffer for a long time. If demoralized by suffering, they take to extreme measures and resort to violence, they will lose whatever sympathy they have and set the people against themselves.[108]

Eventually, he was to realise that the violence was not merely the action of a few who had grown impatient, but that violence had become part of the strategy of the campaigning for some of the leading suffragettes. He noted that as the English respected violence, these tactics may in fact succeed in a limited way but could never bring about any meaningful transformation[109] and may even endanger the whole social fabric.[110]

Although on the question of violence he parted company with them,[111] as Hunt points out, the suffragettes provided Gandhi with an important precedent to cite and a political model to examine. 'It was a living example of the organization of a campaign for rights'.[112] He studied their tactics and methods with interest, first, in 1906 when he needed inspirational examples, he emphasised their courage and faith as a moral model.[113] Later, in 1909 when he was in the midst of his own campaign of civil disobedience, he became more concerned with operational aspects of the suffragettes struggle – fundraising, organisation and publications.[114]

Hunt notes that Gandhi's debt to the suffragettes has never been fully appreciated. He points out that while neither the women activists Gandhi came to know about and observe in London, nor indeed any other Western model, can claim to be the immediate and direct author of what became known as satyagraha, Gandhi often talked about the example of the suffragettes to encourage his South African Indian followers. Moreover, he was doing much more than a year before he discovered Thoreau's essay 'Civil Disobedience',[115] which is often written about as the template for Gandhi's nonviolent political activism.[116]

In later life, Gandhi's Western women devotees may not have been as close to him as his Indian ones, many of whom were directly related to him or his closest co-workers. And no Western disciple was involved in his controversial experiments to assure himself in the last years of his life that he had conquered his lustful passions. At that stage there were no Western women close enough for him to have employed them in this way, and certainly none that could have put him to the test the way young and firm bodied grand nieces could. In a different time, could Esther Færing have fulfilled this role? Or in some more subtle sense, was this the core of his attraction to the 'fallen' woman Nilla Cram Cook? Was he not just a little infatuated with Mirabehn, at least in their earlier years together?

As time went on, Gandhi became less westernised and his Indian women disciples came to dominate his personal life. Nevertheless, his Western women disciples were fundamentally important. They had escaped from the social straight jackets of traditional Europe and he often held them up as models to his Indian women followers. After the publication of Romain Rolland's early biography, *Mahatma Gandhi: The Man Who Became One With the Universal Being* (which inspired the interest of many Western women in him), and before the male authored ones that appeared after the Mahatma's death, his image in the West to a large degree was created by the writer Katherine Mayo and the photographer Margaret Bourke-White. And nobody challenged his ideas on human sexuality the way Margaret Sanger did. Through his relationship with them and the women who 'went native' and threw their lot in completely with Gandhi, we better understand his quest and vision. And even regardless of what we can learn about him through these relationships, most of these Western women associates are so remarkable in their own right that they should not be overlooked by history.

# II

# Western Women Contacts
## Friends, Supporters and Critics

Gandhi's acquaintance with Western women started when he arrived in England to study law in October 1888. On the voyage from Bombay he was too shy to speak with any of the English passengers; however in his first months in London he occasionally stayed in quarters with English and Anglo-English landladies. Some had daughters who must have engaged him in at least brief conversations.[1] Soon he had his own room and was cooking his own meals or eating in the vegetarian restaurants which he had discovered (much to his relief as it meant that he could now eat more than porridge and bread without breaking the vow of not touching meat that he had given his mother before he set sail).

It seems that his first close associate was a woman he had met in his first year during a stay in the seaside resort town of Brighton. An unnamed elderly lady helped the puzzled Mohandas decipher the French menu so that he could determine which dishes were vegan, having realised that his vow, to be in keeping with the spirit in which he had made it, had to include eggs as well. The acquaintance ripened into a friendship that remained throughout his stay in England. He dined with her at her London house regularly on Sundays. He had neglected to tell her that he was married with a wife and child back in India and she had taken to inviting young ladies to the lunches. She attempted to match-make Gandhi with a young woman who was staying with her, and often left the two of them alone together. At first Gandhi was too shy to enjoy the encounters but 'in course of time looked forward to every Sunday and came to like the conversations with the young friend'.[2] Soon he realised that his hostess was trying to get him engaged and that he was getting deeper into a spiral of untruths. He wrote to his elderly friend confessing his marital status, assuring her that he had 'taken no improper liberties' with the young lady, and asked her forgiveness for his deception by omission. Fortunately for him, both the elder and young lady had 'a hearty laugh' over his predicament, and the relationship with his elderly friend continued.[3]

In London, Elizabeth Manning, the Honorary Secretary of the National Indian Association and editor of the *Indian Magazine and Review*, was a friend of young Indians who were in England to study and her house was a meeting place for them. Gandhi seems to have been a regular visitor, although 'When I went to her place I used to sit tongue-tied, never speaking except when spoken to.'[4]

# The First South African Women Friends

After completing his legal education in England, Gandhi returned to India in mid-1891 to practice law. He proved to be a failure in his chosen profession and was relieved when, two years later, an opportunity came to assist in a legal case involving Indian merchants in South Africa. There, Gandhi's first Western friends were the Christian missionaries who befriended him, hoping for his conversion. Gandhi attended their prayer meetings, went to revival conventions, read their literature and apparently did come close to conversion.[5] This circle must have contained the wives of missionaries, but we have only scant records of special relationships with any of the women. In June 1893, on his second day in Pretoria with his new legal firm, he met and befriended an English attorney, Albert Weir Baker. Baker was also the local head of the South African General Mission and a committed lay preacher. The following day Gandhi attended Baker's prayer meeting, and there he was introduced to Miss Harris and Miss Gabb, two 'elderly maiden ladies' who lived together and presented Gandhi with 'a standing invitation to four o'clock tea at their house every Sunday'. He availed himself of the offer and listened to them 'narrate their sweet experiences and talk about the peace they had found.'[6]

A few years later, returning to South Africa from a trip to India, he discovered that he had become a controversial figure with the Europeans who thought that while he was away he had publicly criticised Natal whites, and was now attempting to flood Natal with Indians he had recruited. Gandhi was warned that it would not be safe for him to disembark from the ship until dusk when an escort would be secured for him. When he left the ship, he was soon recognised and surrounded by a crowd. Stones flew, and then fists and kicks. By chance the wife of the Superintendent of Police, Mrs Alexander, who Gandhi knew quite well, came to his aid, sheltering him with her umbrella, and escorting him to the safety of the police station. There were to be other attempts at harming Gandhi later, but in this, the first serious assault he faced, he was saved by a brave woman.[7] The feminist and his later London host, Muriel Lester commented that this 1897 incident perhaps 'typified the new relationship between the sexes',[8] a relationship that was not to be lost on the still youthful Mohandas.

In his own story of these South African years, Gandhi states that many a 'bitter experience has been my lot in life, but I have also had the good fortune to claim a large number of Europeans and Indians of high character as my associates.'[9] His first close Western women contacts were the wives of close male associates and his secretaries, young women who seemed to move quickly from the role of spouses of friends or employees to trusted colleagues in the political struggles Gandhi had taken on, becoming friends in their own right.

Before his family joined him, as a now well settled and relatively wealthy lawyer, Gandhi frequented vegetarian restaurants in Johannesburg. One of the restaurants which he supported financially was owned by Miss Ada Bissicks, who knew Gandhi well enough to invite him to her home. Gandhi either met or built his relationships with some of his closest friends, for example Henry Polak and Hermann Kallenbach, at these restaurants.[10] It was the same with Albert West, a partner in a small printing business, whose female relatives became the first Western women to live on Gandhi's original intentionally created rural community. At Gandhi's request, in 1904, West took charge of *Indian Opinion*, a money-losing paper published in Durban that Gandhi wrote for and financed before finally taking it over completely. He convinced West that the press should be moved to a farm where Indian and European volunteers could labour communally for the same salary and bring out the paper in their spare time. West and Gandhi inspected a property and within a week Gandhi had purchased what became known as Phoenix Settlement. West took up residence to run the paper.[11] Following a visit to his native Lincolnshire, West returned with his new wife (whose 'moral beauty' immediately attracted Gandhi), his mother-in-law and his unmarried sister, Ada. When most of Gandhi's Indian colleagues were imprisoned during his political struggles, the Wests took on much of the burden of running the settlement. Ada (known as Devibehn) rendered services of 'no mean order' to the community by looking after children, teaching English, cooking in the common kitchen, keeping accounts and composing at the press. 'Whatever task came to her, she never hesitated in doing it.'[12]

Western women also made their presence felt at Gandhi's next intentional rural community, Tolstoy Farm, set up with Kallenbach to cater for the needs of the families of those arrested in the Indians' political struggle with the Government. In August 1911, Gandhi invited Elisabeth Knudsen to massage an ailing inmate. She also gave Gandhi pointers in the art of massage[13] and offered to train some young Indian women in the art. She kept in contact with Gandhi, visiting him at his Sabarmati ashram in India in February 1928, and teaching the skills of massage to some of the ashramites.[14]

The English Baptist minister, Joseph Doke, was another of Gandhi's close friends during his middle period in South Africa, and in 1909 became Gandhi's first biographer with his book *M.K.Gandhi: An Indian Patriot in South Africa*.[15] Doke had made the acquaintance of Gandhi in mid-1907 and when, six months later, Gandhi had been assaulted by a fellow Indian for a compromise with the Government, he convalesced at the home of the Dokes, where the daughter, Olive, sang *Lead, Kindly Light* to him.[16] Later she was to teach singing to Gandhi's sons Ramdas and Devdas.[17]

# Women Supporters in South Africa: Emily Hobhouse and Olive Schreiner

The draper Mr Vogl and his wife sympathised with the Indian campaign. Mrs Vogl became the driving force behind the Transvaal Indian Women's Association. She conducted sewing classes for Indian women and from 1910 organised Indian bazaars in Johannesburg where their products, and goods imported from India, could be sold.[18] Even Gandhi made a pair of sandals to be sold at the November 1911 bazaar.[19] That bazaar raised almost £140 that went towards educational work in the community. In appreciation, the association presented Mrs Vogl with a 'beautiful writing-desk'.[20] As a volunteer, she also went to Tolstoy Farm once a fortnight to conduct sewing classes.[21]

Others also supported Gandhi and his struggle, and some of them had the ability to do it at a reasonably high political level. Elisabeth Mari ('Betty') Molteno (1852-1927) was the eldest daughter of Sir John Molteno, the first Prime Minister of Cape Colony, and the sister of James Molteno, the first Speaker of the South African parliament. She met Gandhi while he was in London in 1910. Both she and her friend Emily Hobhouse had been impressed by the Gandhi-led Indian nonviolent struggles against government discrimination. Hobhouse, the English reformer who had done pioneering social work with Boer women, asked her friend Molteno to find out from Gandhi what prejudice the Indian community was suffering at the hands of the Boers. She visited Phoenix Settlement in mid-1912 and called it 'a poem – a dream of liveliness.'[22] She showed keen interest in the Indian way of life and displayed great concern about Kasturba's health.[23] She bought a cottage not far from the settlement and was present, giving support to the satyagrahis, during the crucial stage of the campaign. While Gandhi was in prison in late 1913, she again visited Phoenix and relayed the demeaning stories of imprisonment she had heard from Kasturba to Hobhouse, who in turn took the matter up with General Smuts.[24] During Gandhi's final year in the Colony, the contact between them became close and Molteno served as a conduit for Gandhi to meet important political players: 'What is happening just now is that I am becoming a society man and Miss Molteno is the instrument. She insists on introducing Mrs Gandhi and me to all the families she knows. Yesterday, we went to the great Estate of the Moltenos and met several people. That is the nature of work just now. She is undoubtedly a tactful peacemaker.'[25] And of course, one of the people Elisabeth Molteno introduced Gandhi to was Emily Hobhouse.

Until the death of her widowed invalid father, the Anglican archdeacon of St Ives, in 1895, Emily Hobhouse spent her first thirty-five years in England assisting him and then caring for him.[26] After that, with an inheritance which provided her with a modest but adequate income, she engaged herself in temperance work in America among Cornish miners who had migrated to Minnesota. Back in England before the start of the Second South African (Boer) War she organised an anti-war campaign. When war broke out she became an outspoken critic of her country's belligerent policies, and when she became aware of the high death rate of Boer women and children in British concentration camps, she established a relief fund and went to South Africa on a fact-finding mission in 1900. Her reporting of her findings led to a public outcry in England and humanitarian reforms followed. She was deported from South Africa during a visit the following year, but she returned early in 1903 for seven months, staying with the Smuts family and fellow feminist Olive Schreiner. At the start of 1905 she returned to oversee her new plan: to establish home industries, such as spinning and weaving, for impoverished women and girls in the ex-Boer Orange Free State. As a result of such activities, grateful Boer women gave her the epithet 'Angel of Love'. She spent three years in South Africa between 1905 and 1908, but her poor health forced her home. She was invited back to South Africa in December 1913 to attend the unveiling of a memorial to Boer women in Bloemfontein. During this trip she made the acquaintance of Gandhi. She was concerned that the Boers, who themselves had so recently been the victims of injustice, had joined with British South Africans in perpetrating similar injustices against the Indians out of ignorant prejudice. A champion of the underdog, she now took up the Indian cause.

Hobhouse had the credentials to make a difference. Besides her track record of pressuring her home government to make humanitarian changes, she was a personal friend of General Jan Christiaan Smuts who, from 1910, was the Minister for the Interior, Mines and Defence in the newly formed Union of South Africa, and Louis Botha, the first Premier of the Transvaal and the first Prime Minister of the Union of South Africa.[27] And she used her influence. Gandhi had been arrested in November 1913 as he led a march of over 2,000 protesters in the Transvaal to demonstrate against the breach of the Botha-Smuts pledge which promised to lift the immigration ban and abolish the annual £3 tax on ex-indentured Indian labourers. He was released on 18 December and promptly threatened to recommence the march on 15 January if a resolution of the grievances was not achieved. Gandhi asked Hobhouse for help, and on 27 December she sent a telegram asking Gandhi to postpone the march by fifteen days as a favour to her; pointing out that he should wait until parliament had met and added that there was no point in alienating sympathy through a lack of patience.[28] Gandhi agreed. Two days later she wrote to Smuts explaining that the Indian cause was just and that therefore government force could never prevail against it:

> You see 15 January is the date now proposed for another march. Before then some way should be found giving private assurances to the leaders that satisfaction is coming to them. Their grievance is really moral not material and so, having all the power of the spiritual behind him, he (Gandhi) and you are like Mrs Pankhurst and McKenna and never never never will governmental physical force prevail against a great moral and spiritual upheaval. Wasted time and wasted energy dear Oom Jannie.

> Won't you promise them *recognition* as befits a civilized section of the community with consultation over matters affecting their interests with representatives they should appoint.
>
> I wonder if it would fall out more easily if you had a medium through whom to thresh out an agreement with Gandhi? If you thought me of any use in such a private capacity I am willing, for I *think* Gandhi would trust me and come to see me. Also I *think you* might trust me ... and often in my life I have been able to effect reconciliations and agreements, when it has been awkward for the principals concerned to lower their dignity without a human bridge to help facilitate.[29]

Although Smuts had been trying to crush the Indian movement, he met Gandhi on 13 January, starting a negotiation process that led to the *Indian Relief Act*, which repealed most of the repressive anti-Indian statutes, freeing Gandhi to return to India. It appears that Hobhouse had more than a small part in bringing the antagonists together. Gandhi's close friend, the Reverend Charles Freer Andrews, who was with Gandhi in Pretoria at the time, later wrote that 'There can be no doubt that during the days that followed the influence of Miss Hobhouse with the Boer leaders did much to pave the way to a reconciliation. While we were in Pretoria she wrote again and again both to Mr Gandhi and myself. She thus kept herself in touch with the whole negotiations and took part in them.'[30]

Knowing that her health was poor, Gandhi invited Hobhouse to Phoenix Settlement and promised to nurse her.[31] Finally, in February 1914, Betty Molteno arranged for Gandhi and his wife to meet Emily Hobhouse, who was then a guest at the residence of Prime Minister Botha. Gandhi wrote to Kallenbach that 'Miss Hobhouse has a divine face. Have never seen a diviner face. Gokhale by his features took me by storm. Miss Hobhouse has done likewise, only more so. I feel like gazing at her in awe for hours.'[32] A few days later, following another visit to Hobhouse, where Gandhi met Botha, he wrote to Elisabeth Molteno, calling Hobhouse a 'noble soul', noting that 'To be with her is a spiritual uplifting for me.'[33]

In some way, Hobhouse repaid the compliment by recommending that Smuts should read Gandhi's political tract, *Hind Swaraj*, explaining that,

> I like it *very much* – all about India and the harm English Civilization is doing there. The book has already been prohibited in India – (O

> foolish authorities, will you never learn wisdom?) but he means to devote his life to it in India, and I tell him he is undoubtedly qualifying for deportation from India. It is a book which you would have enjoyed at one period in your life.[34]

Whether Smuts read the book or not, we do not know, however, he came to respect Gandhi because of the way the Indian campaign against government measures was conducted.

During the First World War and after, Emily Hobhouse was engaged in relief work among the poor of war-ravaged central Europe. A secret trip to Germany in the cause of peace during the war had her denounced as a traitor in England. Ill health forced her to retire to London, where she died in mid-1926. Her cremated remains were taken back to South Africa and interred at the foot of the Women and Children's Memorial in Bloemfontein.

On hearing of her death, Gandhi summed up her life and assistance in the South African Indian cause for the readers of his newspaper:

> Newspapers tell us that Miss Emily Hobhouse is no more. She was one of the noblest and bravest of women. She worked without ever thinking of any reward. Hers was service of humanity dedicated to God. She belonged to a noble English family. She loved her country and because she loved it, she could not tolerate any injustice done by it. She realized the atrocity of the Boer War. She thought England was wholly in the wrong. She denounced the war in burning language at a time when England was mad on it. She went to South Africa and her whole soul rose against the barbarity of the concentration camps which Lord Kitchener thought were necessary if the war was to be won. ... Emily Hobhouse, frail as her body was, went again to South Africa at great personal risk to court insults and worse. She was imprisoned and sent back. She bore it all with the courage of a true heroine. She steeled the hearts of Boer women and told them never to lose hope. She told them that though England had gone mad, there were Englishmen and English women whose sympathies were with the Boers and that some day their voice would be heard. And so it was. Sir Henry Campbell-Bannerman swept the board at the general-election of 1906 and made to the wronged Boers such reparation as was possible.

It was after the war and when satyagraha was going on that I had the privilege of being known to Miss Hobhouse. The acquaintance ripened into a life-long friendship. She played no mean part at the settlement of 1914. She was General Botha's guest. Now General Botha had uniformly repelled my advances for an interview. Every time he referred me to the Home Minister. But Miss Hobhouse insisted on General Botha seeing me. And so she arranged for a meeting between the General, his wife and herself and me at the General's residence in Cape Town. Hers was a name to conjure with among the Boers. And she made my way smooth among them by throwing in the whole weight of her influence with the Indian cause. When I came to India and the Rowlatt Act agitation was going on, she wrote saying that I must end my life in prison if not on the gallows and that she did not deplore it. She herself had full strength for such sacrifice. It was an article of faith with her that no cause prospered without the sacrifice of its votaries. Only last year she wrote to me saying that she was in active correspondence with her friend General Hertzog about the Indian cause in South Africa, asked me not to feel bitter against him and told me to tell her what I expected of General Hertzog. Let the women of India treasure the memory of this great English woman. She never married. Her life was pure as crystal. She gave herself to God's service. Physically she was a perfect wreck. She was paralytic. But in that weak and diseased body she had a soul that could defy the might of kings and emperors with their armies. She feared no man because she feared God only.[35]



Gandhi's other high-level supporter and friend in South Africa was Olive Schreiner. Born into a large struggling South African missionary family in 1855, Schreiner grew into a self-educated liberal and feminist.[36] In 1881 she went to Scotland to study nursing but her own health problems forced her to abandon the idea. Instead she completed her first book, gaining public recognition as the author of the first great South African novel, *The Story of an African Farm*, published originally under the pseudonym of Ralph Iron in 1883. The book candidly discussed the experience of marriage and the meaning of freedom for women. She returned to South Africa in 1889, after six years in London literary circles, having been the lover of a youthful Havelock Ellis. In early 1894, she married a farmer eight years her junior and with him took an active interest in the politics of the country. They supported native rights and the Boers in the struggle with the British. Schreiner was also a keen suffragist but as a pacifist she rejected the militant feminism of the London suffragettes. After the South African War, her husband Samuel Cronwright-Schreiner (he had adopted her name on marriage) was elected to the Cape Parliament in 1902. This, and the fact that her younger brother Will was Transvaal Attorney General, gave her access to political circles, and she used them to further the cause of women, the Indian struggle, and peace.

As Gandhi was about to sail for London on 23 July 1909 at the head of a deputation to bring the grievances of the Indians in the Colony to the imperial rulers, 'Mrs Olive Schreiner, a prominent South African lady, and Mrs Lewis [Schreiner's sister] came on board the ship specially to shake hands with us. Both the ladies appeared to have great sympathy for our cause. We saw that the satyagraha movement had won a place in their hearts.'[37] How did this come about?

On board ship on her way back to South Africa from London, Schreiner met the young politician Cecil Rhodes, who was later to serve six years as Prime Minister of the Cape from 1890. He was attracted to her and she at first thought that she 'could almost fall in love' with him,[38] but it was not long before she developed an intense dislike for him. He had revealed his materialism and ruthlessness to her when he remarked that he believed that everyone has their price, and that he preferred men to niggers.[39] Although now world famous, back at home many viewed her with suspicion because of her championing of the rights of Blacks and Indians. When she married in 1894, Transvaal's President Paulus Kruger offered her an annuity of £300. She learned that the money was to come from the funds of the Secret Service Committee and she turned the offer down. Later she came to despise Kruger for his racist attitudes. In the year of her marriage, Gandhi formed the Natal Indian Congress. The Schreiners' Johannesburg household for a time was a meeting place for artists, writers and those of non-mainstream political sensitivities, including Gandhi. Regardless of their position, the Schreiners lived in simplicity and Olive's personal life was an inspiration to Gandhi: 'In her invariably shabby and shapeless gown, and with her thick hair brushed roughly back, she seemed a symbol of the philosophy which Tolstoy preached. Her hands were calloused with daily toil. She cooked and scrubbed and laundered in her modest home.'[40] Gandhi noted that Olive Schreiner's 'love for all mankind was unbounded. Love was written in her eyes. Although she belonged to such a distinguished family and was a learned lady, she was so simple in habits that she cleaned utensils in her house herself.'[41] He added:

> Miss Schreiner was as simple in habits and humble in spirit as she was learned. I had the privilege of being familiar with her. She knew no difference between her Negro servants and herself. Authoress of *Dreams* and many other works as she was, she never hesitated to cook, wash the pots or handle the broom. She held that far from affecting it adversely, such useful physical labour stimulated her literary ability and made for a sense of proportion and discrimination in thought and language. This gifted lady lent to the Indian cause the whole weight of her influence over the Europeans of South Africa.[42]



Unfortunately we do not know very much about the basis of the relationship between the two. Gandhi is rarely mentioned in the biographies of Schreiner and it would appear that he made more of the relationship in his memoirs of the South Africa days than was perhaps warranted. Was Gandhi impressed by her simple way of living when she could have had so much more, by the way she carried on regardless of her debilitating illnesses or by her racial tolerance and championing of the marginalised in an environment where this made someone like her a race traitor?[43] To the degree that Schreiner knew Gandhi as anything more than a passing acquaintance, did she admire him because she knew him and his personal qualities well, or was it more for what he represented in the abstract as a political leader?[44] Eleanor Morton is the only author who makes an attempt to analyse the relationship; however she provides no sources for her conjectures. Morton sees Schreiner (and also Annie Besant) as being important for Gandhi because she is such a contrast to his wife, Kasturba. Schreiner was an intellectual even though she was not formally educated. She had strong global ethical views. She came to simple living because of a conscious choice. Kasturba 'would never be like his friend Olive Schreiner, not even in the everyday life of the home.'[45] Gandhi's wife was forced to accept simplicity and a cosmopolitan life against her will because of the direction of his life. Interestingly, when Gandhi introduced Schreiner to the readers of his account of the Indians' struggle for justice in South Africa, *Satyagraha in South Africa*, he refered to her as the author of *Dreams*, a book that posits a future where there is equality between the sexes in terms of not only work, but also love and freedom (however, one in which 'In the least Heaven sex reigns supreme; in the higher it is not noticed; but in the highest it does not exist.'[46])

Although Gandhi said that he claimed 'the privilege of having been a close friend' of Schreiner,[47] and that she was a person he knew extremely well,[48] after Gandhi had left South Africa for India contact between them faded and there was even something of a formal distancing between them. At the start of the Great War, when he was in London en route to India, Gandhi attempted to recruit an Indian ambulance corps to support the British war effort. Schreiner, who was also in London at the time, took on a strong pacifist position (even breaking with the suffragist movement because of its fervent support for the war). Originally she had hoped to meet Gandhi and Kasturba, but now refused to attend one of his meetings and wrote to him that she 'was struck to the heart with sorrow to see that you ... had offered to serve the English Government in this evil war in any way they might demand of you. Surely you, who would not take up arms even in the cause of your own oppressed people cannot be willing to shed blood in this wicked cause.'[49] Nevertheless, she attended his farewell at the Westminster Palace Hotel on the eve of his departure for India. As a severe asthmatic and angina sufferer, she was often ill. She died in 1920 at the age of sixty-five. Although Gandhi heaped praise on her in *Satyagraha in South Africa*, published nine years after her death, there is no account of any correspondence between them, and minimal reference to her in his writings, between their last meeting and the publication of Gandhi's book.

While Gandhi was in South Africa, he had the strong support of women back in the heart of the Empire. Florence Winterbottom, of the Union of Ethical Societies, was perhaps the main one. When Gandhi led his first deputation to London in October 1906 he made contact with the London Ethical Society and met Winterbottom in order to explain the position of Indians in the colonies.[50] It appears that she was more than sympathetic to what she heard.[51] In December, Louis Ritch, his erstwhile law clerk, now English barrister, delivered a paper on 'The Burden of British Indians in South Africa' at a seemingly well attended meeting of the East India Association, followed by speeches by Gandhi and other delegation members. 'Before the meeting dispersed, a resolution expressing sympathy with the British Indians in South Africa was moved by Miss Winterbottom, the Secretary of the Union of Ethical

Societies, and was passed.'[52] Almost a year later, Gandhi reproduced a supportive letter from Winterbottom in his paper:

> I have just been reading *Indian Opinion* for July 27th and I can forbear no longer sending to you a few words to express sympathy with you, which I have felt over and over again when reading your paper – sympathy with the stress and strain of your struggle, sympathy with the holy nature of your cause, and, above all, sympathy with the spirit in which you are writing, speaking and acting all the time. I want to send you congratulations also in that you have been able to carry on the struggle so strenuously.[53]

She again helped Gandhi, arranging contacts and organising talks during Gandhi's 1909 second deputation to London and contributing funds to the cause of South African Indians. In late 1920, Winterbottom wondered if the Gandhi she knew was becoming a little fanatical and lacking balance in his ideas about nonviolence, which were once seen as a weapon of the weak but which Gandhi now characterised as requiring strength.[54] Further, like many Britons, she was confused and worried by Gandhi's Non-Cooperation movement:

> Do you remember when I first read your "Indian Home Rule" how I was horrified to find that the perusal left me with the impression that it was written by a man charged with bitterness, not to say hatred? And sometimes this impression returns to me on perusing some of your words in "Young India", it returns more or less, at any rate. It is hard to me to link up this impression with my great love and admiration for you as the apostle of love and gentleness. I wonder whether you keep your physical needs supplied enough to keep your spiritual nature serene and happily balanced.[55]

Regardless of this, Florence Winterbottom remained a staunch supporter of the struggle and Gandhi's friend until her death in 1927. On that occasion, Gandhi noted that:

> She was among the rare men and women who find service its own reward, and she belonged to that class amongst the English who seek out and befriend forlorn causes in the teeth of odium, ridicule and

opposition ... she sought us out, she offered me a platform, she studied the question and in a variety of ways helped the cause that at that time had only a few chosen friends in England. She became from that time one of the most constant and painstaking supporters of the cause in South Africa.[56]

# Sonja Schlesin: Secretary/ Co-worker/Critic

The first of attorney-at-law M.K.Gandhi's secretaries was Miss Dick. Although in his Johannesburg legal office Gandhi had up to four young Indian clerks, he needed a typist who had a better command of English than his assistants. As work piled up in the office, Gandhi admits to being 'at my wit's end'. He was happy to engage a European clerk, but was not sure that he could find someone who would not object to serving under a 'coloured man'. Around the middle of 1903,[57] he approached a typewriting agent to find him a stenographer who would be willing to work with him. He sent a young woman, Miss J.S. Dick, who had recently arrived in South Africa from Scotland. She was hired immediately at a salary of £17/10 per month. Some twenty-five years later, in his autobiography Gandhi recalled that

> I was very pleased and straightaway started dictating letters to her. Before very long she became more a daughter or a sister to me than a mere stenotypist. I had scarcely any reason to find fault with her work. She was often entrusted with the management of funds amounting to

thousands of pounds, and she was in charge of account books. She won my complete confidence, but what was perhaps more, she confided to me her innermost thoughts and feelings. She sought my advice in the final choice of her husband, and I had the privilege to give her away in marriage. As soon as Miss Dick became Mrs Macdonald, she had to leave me, but even after her marriage she did not fail to respond, whenever under pressure I made a call upon her.[58]

After Miss Dick, 'who was the very picture of loyalty and purity',[59] left his employment, Gandhi was eventually again in need of a clerical assistant for his legal practice. His close friend Hermann Kallenbach introduced the sixteen year-old Sonja Schlesin to him, probably sometime late in 1906.[60] In Gandhi's recollection, Kallenbach informed him that 'This girl has been entrusted to me by her mother. She is clever and honest, but she is very mischievous and impetuous. Perhaps she is even insolent. You keep her if you can manage her. I do not place her with you for the mere pay.'[61]

Sonja Schlesin quickly became far more than a typist. Unlike Miss Dick, instead of being merely a competent employee and part of the office family, she developed into a co-worker in the Gandhi-led struggle of the South African Indians. At times, in addition to running Gandhi's legal business and taking care of the organisation of publicity for Gandhi's political campaigns, she also played a significant role in the struggle itself[62] and as the honorary secretary of the Transvaal Indian Women's Association.[63] And her talents were not unnoticed. For example, Gopal Krishna Gokhale, Gandhi's political mentor and India's leading nationalist politician at the time, said of Schlesin after his visit to South Africa in 1912 that:

I have rarely come across such purity, single-minded devotion to work and great determination as I have seen in Miss Schlesin. I was simply astonished how she had sacrificed her all for the Indian cause without expecting any reward whatever. And when you add to all this her great ability and energy, these qualities combine to make her a priceless asset to your movement. I need hardly say it and yet I say that you must cherish her.[64]

When Polak was in India, Joseph Doke assumed responsibility for the editorial department of *Indian Opinion* and had the articles he wrote for the paper vetted by her and confided to Gandhi about the importance of

Schlesin's assistance.[65] And Gandhi himself noted how often he accepted corrections and additions she suggested, 'knowing them to be appropriate'.[66] When she was twenty-years old, after receiving her parents' permission, she prepared a speech (read out by Gandhi in Gujarati to an audience of 2,500 Indians shortly before his first imprisonment) reminding the Indian audience of the sacrifices being made by the suffragette women in England and exhorting them to stay the course.[67] Later, Gandhi informed the readership of his book on the South African struggle how hard she had worked for the Indian community, not for a salary but because of her deep sympathy with the cause. He explained that

> Pathans, Patels, ex-indentured men, Indians of all classes and ages surrounded her, sought her advice and followed it. Europeans in South Africa would generally never travel in the same railway compartment as Indians, and in the Transvaal they are even prohibited from doing so. Yet Miss Schlesin would deliberately sit in the third class compartment for Indians like other satyagrahis and even resist the guards who interfered with her. I feared and Miss Schlesin hoped that she might be arrested some day. But although the Transvaal Government were aware of her ability, her mastery over the "strategy" of the movement, and the hold she had acquired over the satyagrahis, they adhered to the policy and the chivalry of not arresting her.[68]



In 1924, Gandhi wrote a professional reference for Schlesin. In the accompanying letter he engaged in some of their light-hearted sparring by telling her that she can accuse him of untruthfulness in not attesting to her slovenliness: 'If you wanted to make it a model of neatness, you have failed badly. The same slovenliness, the same smudging. I can almost see your inky fingers in your letter.'[69] The reference confirmed that

> Miss Sonja Schlesin served me as confidential secretary in South Africa for nearly seven years and during a most important part of my public life. She was entrusted with heavy responsibilities including account-keeping, involving transactions extending to four figures at a time. She came in touch with hundreds of people belonging to different races and nationalities. During my last incarceration in South Africa, she was in sole charge of my affairs. I never once had

> reason to doubt her integrity or ability. Indeed, she did not work for the sake of pay but for the sake of the work itself which she loved. Her services were available to me at all times of the day. Her knowledge of shorthand and literary talents were of great assistance to me. I could not wish for a better secretary. I should like to hear that she was entrusted with a post requiring close attention, strictest honesty and ability.[70]

Who was this extraordinary young woman? Sonja Schlesin was born to Jewish parents in Moscow in mid-1888. Four years later the family settled in South Africa where the father, Isidor, applied for British naturalisation. Kallenbach knew Schlesin and her family because one of her uncles came from his home town in what was then East Prussia. In South Africa she had passed the Intermediate examination of the University of the Cape of Good Hope in 1903, obtaining a first class diploma in shorthand and typing. She was looking for work and, through Kallenbach, became the eventual replacement for Miss Dick. Although Gandhi was willing to pay £20 per month for a good stenotypist, he had no idea about Schlesin's ability and acceded to Kallenbach's suggestion of paying her just £6. She asked for no raise, although eventually Gandhi started paying her £10 'which she accepted with reluctance, and flatly declined to have anything more' because she felt that if she took anything in excess of what she needed 'she would have betrayed the principle' which attracted her to Gandhi.[71]

From photographs of the time, Sonja Schlesin was short but well-built with short dark hair. She dressed conservatively and functionally, often with broad-brimmed hats and neckties, and wore no jewellery. And, as Kallenbach had noted, Schlesin was mischievous. One morning soon after she had joined him, Gandhi came into his office to find her 'sitting on the table, dangling her legs and smoking a cigarette'. He slapped her and threw away the cigarette. She burst into tears and apologized, promising never to do such a thing again, recognising the love in his action.[72] 'But,' Gandhi later noted, 'in a month's time she had achieved the conquest of my heart', adding that,

> She was ready to work at all times whether by day or at night. There was nothing too difficult or impossible for her … she captivated my clients as well as the fellow Satyagrahis by her frankness and readiness to serve. This young girl soon constituted herself the watchman and

warder of the morality not only of my office but of the whole movement. Whenever she was in doubt as to the ethical propriety of any proposed step, she would freely discuss it with me and not rest till she was convinced of it.[73]

She was without racial prejudice, seemingly totally fearless and a strong feminist. At times this translated into tactless candour: 'She would not hesitate even to the point of insulting a man and telling him to his face what she thought of him. Her impetuosity often landed me in difficulties, but her open and guileless temperament removed them as soon as they were created.'[74] How could Gandhi not have liked her? Even twenty years later he was saying that she was one of the few women he had the privilege of coming across who 'had a character as clear as crystal and courage that would shame a warrior.'[75] Soon, according to Gandhi, she was in charge of the accounts and, when the leadership of the movement was in jail, she had control of large funds and even, according to Gandhi, 'led the movement single-handed'. While she was with Gandhi she learnt to speak Gujarati and became a vegetarian.

However, she was also intellectually oriented and not content to remain a secretary. She desired to work for the cause in a greater capacity. Gandhi took her on as an articled clerk on 24 February 1909, even though this was without precedent in South Africa, and probably encouraged her in her endeavour to become a lawyer. In April, Schlesin applied to the Supreme Court of the Trasvaal for an order 'to compel the Law Society to register her articles of clerkship' after the Transvaal Law Society had rejected her application. The court refused the application on the grounds that it went against 'the long practice which has prevailed' and that such a change 'which would mean an enormous difference in the practice of courts in this country' should be made by the legislature rather than the court.[76] Around this time she took on the position of secretary of the Transvaal Indian Women's Association, even though she believed that the position should ideally have been held by an Indian.[77] At the end of the year she became a trustee of the financially troubled Phoenix Settlement, and, although she never lived there, she kept up her interest in the property and the press for decades after Gandhi had returned to India.

Sonja Schlesin did not let opportunities to further herself academically slip by. In January 1911 she passed her Intermediate Arts Examination and in August took up a temporary teaching position in a government school in Mayfair. It is possible that this was a requirement of the teaching certificate she was now working towards. She made it clear that her preference was to work in a 'coloured school'.[78] She was expected back at the start of October.[79] The relationship between the two at this stage is well illustrated by Schlesin's cheekily familiar letters, even though they are addressed to 'Dear Mr Gandhi'. While he was away in Cape Town for political meetings, she reminded him to 'be good and send me a letter daily',[80] and a few days later she thanked him for his letter that she has just received and added: 'I do not think I have ever received such a charmingly written letter from you. Your descriptions are graphic, and make delightful reading. Please now don't fall back into your old slipshod habits.'[81]

In 1913, at the height of the Indian struggle, with the main protagonists in prison, Schlesin took on a leadership role, liaising with those at Phoenix.[82] Later she was to teach at the settlement. One of the young inmates of the community recalled that when someone asked her why she did not have long hair, she replied, 'Why waste time in fixing it? Should only males be allowed to remain free from that? Should all rights be reserved for men?' In a letter to Gandhi (now addressed to 'My Dear Bapu'), the young feminist tells Gandhi about a book she had read that discusses chastity and the notion of women as property.[83] As a teacher she was 'of a jesting nature, amusing, talkative and smart, but when she entered the class for teaching, full calm prevailed.'[84]

After Gandhi left South Africa, they continued their relationship through an intermittent correspondence that was characterised by complaints, jests, misunderstandings and desires to meet again. Early on, Schlesin still saw herself as being intimately connected with Gandhi's close circle. After he had been back in India for a year she wrote to Gandhi disapprovingly about the draft constitution of his new ashram and about what she perceived had become of him. She disliked the idea of vows (which she thought should only be taken after lengthy periods of probation), and picked them apart like a lawyer, pointing out redundancies. She made suggestions about the accommodation, food, methods of resolving complaints and the need to set times aside for visitors so that they did not come at random and disrupt the working of the institution.[85] She was obviously not happy that Gandhi and the group around him were being transformed into something that was alien to her experience of them. In a letter written less than two months later, after wishing Gandhi a merry Christmas, with the caveat that such a phrase may be inappropriate in such a time of strife, echoing the sentiments of Florence Winterbottom, she added:

> ... if, indeed, by this time, merriness has not altogether been renounced by you as a cardinal offence, for I have noticed that the simpler you have become in your life the more sombre and gloomy you have become in [disposition?], though one would have thought that this unburdening of yourself of the complexities of "civilization" would have had a directly opposite effect, would rather have tended to accentuate your natural cheerfulness. This is a problem with regards to yourself to which I still seek a solution.[86]

The feelings of kinship with Gandhi and her Indian friends, whom she had lived with for a decade, were slipping away from her. A few weeks later, Millie Polak wrote to Gandhi, informing him that she sees 'Sonja occasionally, she seems rather lost lately, and one finds it so difficult to draw near her, she goes her own road.'[87]



In mid-1917, at a talk with teachers at the national school in Ahmedabad, Gandhi noted the importance of learning English to the point where a pupil could be able to speak the language with any Englishman without being nervous. He noted his desire to obtain a teacher for the purpose but added that he could 'think of no one at present except Miss Schlesin. If only she would come, we could want nothing better. She is a very capable person.'[88] Two months later, Gandhi wrote to his third son Ramdas (who had remained in South Africa) to 'Tell Miss Schlesin to write to me. I am awaiting her arrival. Tell her also that there are some ten letters from me she has not answered.'[89] In mid-1919, he wrote to Schlesin on her passing her teacher's examinations with distinction: 'You do not want me to congratulate you, I know. I am simply anxious that you should get through your final examination, because I expect you one of these days to take your place in India.'[90]

In 1919, after requesting a loan from Gandhi for her education,[91] Schlesin completed her studies and became a teacher at the high school in Krugersdorp, a small mining town near Johannesburg. She remained there for twenty-three years, spending the rest of her teaching career in this small town, specialising in Latin.[92]

It is clear that it took Gandhi a length of time to feel as at home in India as he had felt in South Africa, and to create an equivalent circle of friends and co-workers around himself. There the workers developed with him, in India he arrived as a Mahatma to whom others attached themselves as assistants. He missed his friends greatly. He made this clear in a very candid letter to Schlesin four years into the final Indian phase of his life:

> Satyagraha is going on merrily. Civil disobedience is expected to commence very soon. How I often wish you were here for more reasons than one! But I must plough the lonely furrow. It often makes me sad when I think of all my helpers of South Africa. I have no Doke here. I have no Kallenbach. Don't know where he is at the present moment. Polak in England. No counterpart of Kachalia or Sorabji. Impossible to get the second edition of Rustomji. Strange as it may appear, I feel lonelier here than in South Africa. This does not mean that I am without co-workers. But between the majority of them and me, there is not that perfect correspondence which used to exist in South Africa. I do not enjoy the same sense of security which you all gave me there. I do not know the people here; nor they, me. This is all gloomy, if I were to brood over it. But I do not. I have not the time for it. I have a few moments of leisure just now. Ramdas' letter reminds me of your existence in South Africa, and I am giving myself the momentary pleasure of sharing my innermost thoughts with you.[93]

There was little communication between the two of them for the next five years. In 1921 Gandhi wrote to Kallenbach asking for news of Schlesin, whom he often thought about, because 'of late I have been feeling anxious about her.'[94] It appears that she did not make contact until 1924 when, after having graduated with First Class B.A. and M.A. degrees from the University of Witwatersrand, she requested the professional reference from Gandhi. In this more formal letter, again addressed to 'Dear Mr Gandhi', Schlesin asked him to read the letter through carefully to the end 'after all it is only once in five years that I am requiring this of you and my writing is, for once, quite legible.' Before she got to the 'business sections' of the letter, she criticised Gandhi for not following through adequately on his work in the Indian struggle, presumably in South Africa. She noted that he earned the respect of the Europeans for the cause, but it did not last; and the fault was his: 'The real task began at the conclusion of the struggle – the task of building up a community of noble, lofty-minded, every way worthy of esteem. That task you shirked.' She added that 'There seems little likelihood of my ever visiting India. For one thing my desire to do so is largely gone.'

The last pages of this eleven page letter concerned her request in 1919 for £24 of her money that Gandhi was holding to go with the loan she had asked for to help her with her education expenses. She notes that it never arrived and she was wondering what had happened to it. Then she castigated Gandhi for the testimonial she had obtained from him when his legal office was closed in 1913. He had asked her to draw it up herself and he had signed it. Now she had realised how 'impractical and even childish and absurd' such a request was. How could a person with the knowledge Gandhi had have signed such a document she asked, and blamed it on his 'usual lack of interest in matters which do not interest you personally'. Now she was providing him with an opportunity to make amends. After the abuse, she asked, 'Will you now please send me a usable testimonial, adequately reflecting my 7½ years' work.' She reminded him that her periods of working for him were from November 1906 to January 1913, and from November 1913 to July 1914. She instructed him, '*Please do not neglect this matter*, and write on good paper with good ink – *legibly*, so far as possible.' She concluded the letter asking him to 'Please write soon and [missing] personally. Don't send the message through other [missing]. I can't be bothered with people and their messages these days.' In a postscript she added that 'I just understand that the great Frenchman Romain Rolland, has taken it into his head to write a book about you. I have ordered it, and, if it is worthwhile and no one else has done so, I may translate sections of it for the Book Reviews column of the local press.'[95] One cannot help wondering what sort of commentary would have accompanied the translation if she had undertaken it.

Two months later Schlesin wrote to thank Gandhi for his reference, but could not refrain from poking fun at it and what he had left out, adding that the 'pious prayer at the end was totally uncalled for'. She informed Gandhi that the letter had completely destroyed her 'philosophic calm' and that she had to reply immediately 'that I may return to that happy state once more'. She continued: 'You ask whether I shall continue to write now that I have commenced, but what is the use of writing to you, even if one has the time for correspondence, if you do not understand what one does write? You have certainly succeeded in making a glorious muck of things and annoying me intensely.'[96] She was livid about his cancelling her debt when all she wanted was a statement of accounts.

In late 1925, Schlesin again wrote to Gandhi noting that she did not have a reply to her last letter of over a year ago and, even though it did not require a response, she could not help wondering if the silence was due to the 'vagaries of the Indian Postal Service, or to your own negligence'. She was still annoyed about her loan and remitted another £40 in repayments, leaving £70 still outstanding. She asked for an acknowledgement and receipt. In this letter she indicated that she had also again warmed a little to the idea of visiting Gandhi: 'Cooks are now advertising trips to India, lasting from December to March, so perhaps I might come along myself one of these days, on one of my vacations.'[97]

In 1927 they again started exchanging regular correspondence ('Miss Schlesin has been of late writing to me regularly, and of course she is as mad and as good as ever'[98]), but the tone soon soured. The publication of Gandhi's *Autobiography* and *Satyagraha in South Africa* caused a great deal of trouble between them. Schlesin complained about Gandhi's 'wretched autobiography', his 'breaches of confidence', 'unholy misrepresentations', 'caddishness', etc.

The outburst of anger started relatively mildly. In May 1928, Schlesin wrote to Gandhi about his breaches of faith, how he was denying a proper education to the children around him, on Catherine Mayo's book *Mother India*, on the possibility of catching up with Gandhi in person and only incidentally criticised the *Autobiography*. The letter was marked '*Personal*' and made a request of the Mahatma:

> Please do not show my letters around, as I understand you are doing; else I shall simply not write to you. Letters and conversations should be regarded as confidential and to publish these without the consent first had and obtained of the writer or speaker is a distinct breach of confidence. I notice again and again in your Autobiography that you mention conversations and incidents which one feels that the people concerned would not have liked mentioned. ... It rather detracts from the good opinion one might have of the author, because *it is not honourable*. Please be more Mahatmalike in this respect.

She continued with instructions to Gandhi to foster the talents of the ashram children instead of wasting their genius by forcing them all onto the one path. She added that if she had a flying machine she would come and rescue those children and see that they received appropriate education. She concluded: 'I see from the papers that you intend going to England this year, but are now deferring your visit to next year. Can't you defer it [to] 1932, when if all goes well, I may possibly visit England too?'[99]

After she had had more time to think about Gandhi's *Autobiography*, her relatively mild criticisms and seeming desire for personal contact erupted into angry denunciations, and demands for immediate corrections in Gandhi's newspaper:

> I must deny your statement of my official Johannesburg position; otherwise I may be hauled over the coals departmentally. The Department not knowing that you are in a mentally unfit state may imagine I have made misrepresentations. ... *on no account* ... publish the allusions to myself in your wretched autobiography in book-form *until* I send you a revised copy. ... I do not require lies and exaggerations to enhance my merit. The whole thing is simply a fabrication of your own fancy – your brain is so tired that you have just the haziest of recollections of things, you jumble up facts and you unconsciously invent. I therefore seriously think you should cease writing until you are in a normal state again. In fact I think you should be interdicted from writing until then. You may place *yourself* in as ridiculous a light as you choose, *but* you have no right to place other people in such a position.

However, she was able to add that, generally, she thoroughly enjoyed Gandhi's account of her own idiosyncracies, and in the letter, which was addressed to 'Dear Mr Gandhi', she did make reference to 'my Bapu'.[100]

Sonja Schlesin was impulsive and her letters certainly showed her feelings. And they did this in more ways than one. When she was angry it seems that she could not control the rapid flow of thoughts upon thoughts, and this comes through on the paper as manic scribble, full of crossings out, margin notes, underlining, interpolations and, often, illegibility. When she is calm, for example when she relates her view on a book she is reading,[101] her writing is orderly and legible. When she wrote to Gandhi concerning the Autobiography, she was very angry.

Two weeks later, Schlesin sent Gandhi a list of her corrections along with an enclosed letter to the editor of *Young India* with a corrected version of her employment status. She added: 'My own candid opinion is that it would be an excellent thing if the whole wretched thing were burnt and you refrained from writing any more auto-biographical nonsense, but, if you will insist on doing so, I have at least the right to insist that no misrepresentations be made about me, I will not be lied about.' She denied at anytime leading the movement single-handed or otherwise, or that she managed thousands (of people or pounds it is not clear in Gandhi's writing) and the paper *Indian Opinion*, asking how this made her look and how it must have made the editors West and Cordes feel.[102]

Kallenbach, who seemed to have some sort of resentment against Schlesin (possibly he saw her as a rival for Gandhi's affections[103]), sympathised with Gandhi over this episode: 'Speaking about your autobiography, I do hope that Miss Schlesin is not hurting you with her eccentric criticism on [sic] a few sentences about her.'[104] In response to the criticism, Gandhi wrote to his other South Africa-based second son, Manilal, and his wife: 'I follow what you say about Miss Schlesin. But then, isn't she half crazy? She has written a sort of wild letter even to me.'[105] The trouble stemmed from Gandhi's depiction of Schlesin in the pre-publication serialisation of his autobiography in his Indian newspaper *Young India*. Of particular concern was his note at the end of the section on her which stated that 'She graduated after the struggle was over, and is now head mistress in a Government Girls' School in the Transvaal.'[106] The correction she insisted upon was carried in Gandhi's paper: 'Miss Schlesin of whom mention has been made in the autobiographical chapters tells me that she is not, as I have stated, principal of a girls' school but that she is a teacher at a High School. The error has given her pain for which I am sorry. I may at once say that she is in no way responsible for the error.'[107] The references to her leading the movement 'single-handed' and that 'She had the management of thousands, a tremendous amount of correspondence, and *Indian Opinion* in her hands, but she never wearied', remained.[108]

Sonja Schlesin also made her assessment, this time more kind, of Gandhi's other book on the South African struggle, *Satyagraha in South Africa*. In a letter, she thanked Manilal Gandhi for sending her a copy of the book (which she could not accept as a present so she sent ten shillings to cover the cost and postage), adding that it is 'much better than the autobiography and it is certainly not nearly so offensive – Bapu was evidently far less tired when he wrote this book.' Still, she did manage to point out some inaccuracies and omissions (for example that Mrs Vogl, who 'worked day and night for the Indian Women's Association', should not have been left out), and recommended that a 'Roll of Honour', listing the names of those who had worked for the cause and had gone to gaol, be appended to the book.[109]

Not long before he set out on the Salt March to Dandi in March 1930, Gandhi was still hoping that Schlesin could come to India to correct the inaccuracies before a second edition was published, but feared that she would not find him at the ashram as he was likely to be in 'one of the king's hotels.'[110] A year and a half later he asked her to send a list of all inaccuracies and omissions so that they could be corrected, but noted in his own defence that 'My book is true, because it is a faithful reproduction of my recollections.'[111]

Regardless of their differences, there was also positive communication, which continued until Gandhi's death. In his old age, Gandhi was still hoping that Schlesin would come to him in India: 'I do not think there is any chance of my coming to S[outh] Africa or going to America. But whether I do or not, of course I expect you one day to drop in here and pass the rest of your days in India.'[112] Schlesin had hoped to meet Gandhi at the San Francisco Conference, to be held between 25 April and 26 June 1945, where the Charter of the United Nations was to be formally adopted, and from there to return to India with him: 'If you are short of secretaries to accompany you to the Peace Conference, call here on your way and I shall come along.'[113] Neither of them made it to the Conference. However, two and a half years later, only three months before his assassination, Gandhi was still hoping she would come to India.[114]

In 1931 Schlesin completed a Diploma of Afrikaans from the University of Witwatersrand and spent the rest of her life as something of an eccentric but inspiring and even brilliant teacher, and as something of a loner, instead of as a political activist. She never married. It appears that she undertook studies in accountancy at the University of Witwatersrand just before she retired from teaching, at age fifty-five in 1943, to become a public servant in the Defence Headquarters in Pretoria. In 1953, the sixty-five-year-old Schlesin attempted to set right the wrong she suffered in 1909 by enrolling to study law at the University of Natal. She had to withdraw from her studies, presumably because of ill-health, in early 1955. She died at the beginning of 1956 and was cremated in Johannesburg.[115]

As Eleanor Morton notes, Sonja Schlesin 'possessed a strange, dramatic quality; she proved to have fire and imagination, but no romantic interests.'

She adds that the relationship with Gandhi was 'wholly impersonal, yet profoundly deep'.[116] They had a teasing and at times competitive, but certainly non-erotic, comradeship. Schlesin was her own woman and Gandhi seems to have admired her outspokenness even when it occasionally caused problems. She was totally committed to the South African Indian cause, obviously thought highly of Gandhi's principles and earned his respect and trust, however to the end she remained 'Miss Schlesin' to him.[117] Although she was certainly far more than an employee, becoming a genuine co-worker, she never became a sister the way Millie Polak did when she and Henry lived in the Gandhi household. This is not to imply that Schlesin had no personal attachment to Gandhi or that she did not feel an acute sense of loss when he left South Africa to return to India. The tone of her letters illustrate the contrary.

Even though Gandhi biographer Geoffrey Ashe considered Sonja Schlesin to be the prototype of all his women helpers,[118] she was in fact unique. Many women were later drawn into Gandhi's orbit because of a strong identification (and at times obsession) with him as a person, rather than with what he stood for politically or spiritually; not so Schlesin. And never again was a woman to play such a leading role in his political campaigns.

# Annie Besant: Gandhi's Last Rival

Gandhi may have had political rivals in his early South African public life[119] and when he returned to India he was not the leading nationalist figure he was to become. However, soon after his arrival, the other great figures of the movement were dead: the 'moderate' Gokhale in April 1915, only a month after Gandhi's return, and the 'extremist' Bal Gangadhar Tilak, in 1920, as Gandhi was starting his first nationwide campaign. After over two decades in South Africa, the third great nationalist, the English-born renowned Theosophist Annie Besant, should have been his staunchest ally, however she was more often his bitterest rival in the political struggle in India. In this sense Besant was his last rival for political preeminence. After the early 1920s, Besant's political star faded and Gandhi was unchallenged as political leader of the freedom movement.

Annie Wood was born in October 1847 in England to a well-off family. Her father had died when she was five and, at the age of twenty, her extremely sheltered life (which included a total ignorance of matters sexual) came to an end when she drifted into marriage with a conservative clergyman, Frank Besant. Although less than certain about a married future, she was unable to call off the engagement for notions of honour that her mother held dear. In rapid succession she had a son and a daughter. It soon became clear that a tradition-bound and loveless marriage was not going to sustain her. As she questioned her faith following the near fatal illness of her daughter Mabel, the quarrels with her husband became increasingly heated and she left him in 1873, taking Mabel with her. The following year she met the crusading atheist and radical politician Charles Bradlaugh, who had a strong interest in Indian affairs. Under his influence she started writing and lecturing for the National Secular Society, of which she became the vice-president in 1874. In 1877 they were prosecuted for immorality after publishing Charles Knowlton's forty-year-old pamphlet on contraception (*The Fruits of Philosophy: or, The Private Compassion of Young Married People*), of which she was the first woman advocate. The conviction was quashed on appeal, but, as a result of the scandal, in 1879 she lost custody of Mabel to her estranged husband. She became a socialist in 1885, and under the influence of George Bernard Shaw joined the Fabian Society and was soon known as the greatest woman public speaker of her time. In 1888 she led a groundbreaking strike of exploited women at East London's Bryant and May's match factory and helped to form their union. As a member of the London School Board between 1887 and 1890, she worked to introduce free public education for all children and the provision of free school meals. Her labour for the poor and oppressed was laudable, however the philosophies of materialism and science in which she had been immersed for years were no longer spiritually fulfilling her.[120]

Annie Besant's life took a dramatic and sudden turn in 1889 when she read the two large tomes of *The Secret Doctrine* and then met the author Madame Blavatsky. By May, she had converted to Blavatsky's brand of spiritualism, known as Theosophy. Following a succession battle among the leadership of the Society on the death of Blavatsky in 1891, she emerged as one of its leading figures. In 1907, Besant became president of the Theosophical Society, an office she held until her death, and employed her brilliant propagandist skills for the cause. Theosophy emphasised human service, a philosophy of spiritual evolutionism drawn from both Western and Eastern esoteric beliefs (including reincarnation and the doctrine of karma), and the role of superhuman masters of wisdom. Its aim was to form a universal human brotherhood through the comparative study of religions, the mysteries of nature and powers latent within humans. Her principal soul-mate in her spiritual quest, Charles Leadbeater, may have been a pedophile; and he certainly had the reputation of being one. That she kept supporting Leadbeater through the several scandals that surrounded him caused a great many defections from the Theosophical Society, and according to her obituary in *The Times* was a main cause of her loss of prestige in later life.

Annie Besant visited India in mid-November 1893 to assist in sorting out the affairs of the Society, which was headquartered there. Initially, her work was to be religious: 'My work in India is entirely directed to the bringing about of a spiritual revival as against the materialistic ideas which are spreading from the Western education to which the youth of India is now submitted.'[121] She extolled the great past of pre-British India in the realms of government, education and industry. Her vision was to 'give back to India her ancient Freedom', to 'rescue India from the materialism which was strangling her true life by the revival of ancient philosophical and scientific religions, and, by the placing of India as an equal partner in a great Indo-British Commonwealth.'[122] At around the time he returned to India from South Africa, Gandhi could have been saying most of the above. Here was the potential for a strong alliance in the struggle for freedom.

In 1895 Besant finally moved to the country, originally making her home at Benares. This was the time that Gandhi left India to make his life in South Africa. She adopted a Hindu persona and engaged in educational and social pursuits as well as popularising Theosophy and India's spiritual mission to the world. In 1898, with the founding of her Central Hindu College in Benares, she concentrated her energies on education in ways that would be taken up by Gandhi in decades to come. For about ten years she dedicated herself to social work, including campaigning for the uplift of women and lower castes, and the protection of impoverished children and animals, then, in 1913, she started a series of lectures with the title 'Wake Up, India' and plunged into political activism. She promoted the cause of Indian patriotism by founding youth organisations (including the world's first Boy Scout organisation for non-whites) and launching and editing the nationalist journals, the weekly *Commonweal* and the Madras daily *New India*, in 1914.

In 1915, with the death of Gokhale, before Gandhi had established himself as a major force on the Indian political scene, Annie Besant emerged into the political spotlight.[123] In September 1916 she formed the Home Rule for India League, and although Britain was at war she kept on with her demand for self-government, making her unpopular with the government. Following the outpouring of Indian public sympathy as a result of her internment, she became enormously popular and was able to have significant influence on the growing nationalist movement. In 1917, at the age of seventy, as a woman and a foreigner, she became the President of the Indian National Congress. She opposed Gandhi's confrontational political activism, fearing that it would lead to violence, but was soon eclipsed by him as a nationalist force. In her spiritualist guise, since 1909 she had been promoting her protégée Krishnamurti as a potential spiritual world leader, until he renounced the position, Theosophy and her in 1929. Her great plans defeated, she died something of a broken person on 20 September 1933 at the Theosophical Society headquarters in Adyar, on the outskirts of Madras.

Gandhi had known of Annie Besant while he was a student in London. Theosophical friends had taken him to Blavatsky Lodge where he met Madame Blavatsky and Besant, who had not long before joined the Theosophical Society. Gandhi 'was following with great interest the controversy of her conversion.' In August 1889, he heard Besant give a talk on 'Why I became a theosophist'. He noted that 'the words she uttered then as she rose to answer the charge of inconsistency have never faded from my memory.' He added that 'the utter sincerity with which, I felt, she spoke these words captivated me and ever since I have followed her career with unabated interest'.[124] He also read Blavatsky's *Key to Theosophy*. Although he declined an invitation to join the Society, these encounters stimulated his desire to find out more about his own religion.[125] The Theosophical Society's rule 'respecting brotherhood' appealed to the young Gandhi, however he had 'no sympathy for its search for occult powers.'[126] He became an associate member of the Society in March 1891, some three months before leaving London.[127] A branch of the Theosophical Society was established in Johannesburg in 1899, and when Gandhi arrived in the city in 1903 he befriended its members. This gave him an avenue to friendship with like-minded whites in the colony.[128]

Gandhi's Johannesburg legal office contained framed pictures of Christ, Tolstoy and Annie Besant.[129] It is obvious that he admired her greatly. Not only was she a woman who was a famous and courageous social activist, but she also sought the truth, regardless of personal cost. When she became a Theosophist, she turned her back on atheism, becoming more sympathetic to the local Indian students because Theosophy validated many of their beliefs. When he arrived in Durban in 1894, Gandhi wrote to Besant to explain that while he was there he 'intended to spread as much as possible information about Theosophy',[130] and in late 1904 he published a translation of her rendition of the *Bhagavad Gita* for circulation among Hindu boys in South Africa.[131] In 1907 he published a translation of an article by Besant under the title 'How to Build a Nation', noting that it was 'serious and thought provoking.'[132] During a trip to India, in February 1902 he briefly called on the ill Besant to pay his respects,[133] and in mid-1909 she had sent Gandhi and 'our Indian brothers' in the struggle for South African Indian rights a message 'of hope, of consolation, of friendship, which may cheer them as they patiently suffer in the hope of better days.'[134]

However, Gandhi also had differences with the more occult parts of Theosophy and soon appeared to be repudiating his earlier enthusiasm. And he had concerns about Annie Besant's naivete. In a letter to a friend, he noted:



> I have held since 1899 the same views that you do about Theosophy. They pressed me hard that year to join the Society but I refused in no uncertain terms, saying that, though the Society's rule respecting brotherhood appealed to me, I had no sympathy for its search for occult powers. I do not think that Mrs Besant is a hypocrite; she is credulous and is duped by Leadbeater. When an Englishman suggested to me to read Leadbeater's *The Life after Death*, I flatly refused to do so as I had grown suspicious of him after reading his other writings. As to his humbug I came to know of it later. All the same, I have drawn from Theosophy the lessons which seemed to me worth drawing. Blavatsky's *Key* had made a good impression on me. Theosophy sent many Hindus inquiring into their own religion. It has performed the same service as Christianity has. Moreover, Theosophists believe in the same basic principles as we do and therefore it is easy enough to come across good persons among them. ... Ritch was a Theosophist. He urged me to become a member. Not only did I not become one, I helped him to be free from that humbug. Polak is a Theosophist, but he stays miles away from the practices and writings of Theosophists. The same is true of Kallenbach. When I was in India, I sent Gokaldas to the College at Benares. Then also I was disappointed. Even after wards, as long as I had not come to see the

light, which I have now, that is, as long as I had not outgrown the fascination for modern education, I used to inquire about institutions like the Benares College and even wished to send the boys there, thinking that something was better than nothing. All that is over now. Cordes, at Phoenix, is a staunch Theosophist. I have not yet been able to get him out of the hold of Theosophy. In himself, he appears to be a sincere man. He has gone to Adyar at present, against all persuasion. Being honest, he will see the fraud that is there and turn his back on it, unless he is taken in. It is worth ascertaining what humbug prevails there safe under the cover of Mrs. Besant's goodness. Her desire to pass off as the "Master" is understandable. One who runs after occult powers cannot but become so intoxicated. It is for these reasons that all our *shastras* have looked upon occult powers and Yogic attainments as unworthy pursuits.[135]



In turn, Annie Besant wrote approvingly of the work Gandhi was doing in South Africa, but developed reservations about his methods. The early mutual admiration, such as it was, was far less straight-forward once they were treading the same political stage. Annie Besant was not a follower or supporter of Gandhi. She was a far better known figure in India than Gandhi, the newly arrived and newly proclaimed Mahatma. Very soon they were political rivals.

Both Gandhi and Besant were concerned with service, self-sacrifice for service, the quest for spiritual evolution, and, by the time they were occupying the same political public space, the political future of India. This, as manifested in their passion for Indian Home Rule and the fostering of Indian nationalism by propounding a great pre-colonial Indian past, seemed, on the surface, to be a recipe for forging a strong and productive alliance. However, very quickly upon Gandhi's return to India, this was proving not to be the case. Their visions for India's future, and the methods for achieving it, meant that they ended up as opponents rather than allies.

From a distance, they supported each other and Besant had praised Gandhi's work in South Africa. Then the relationship became problematic and the troubles started early. In April 1915, only four months after his return, Gandhi visited Annie Besant on two occasions. On one of these, accompanied by his Madras-based publisher, friend and host, G.A.Natesan, Gandhi was taken on a tour of the well-appointed premises at Adyar. Although Besant was 'a pioneer in the matter' of educating 'untouchables', when Gandhi discovered that the school for 'untouchables' consisted of 'an unpretentious shed', 'the contrast between the palatial residence for one set of people and the mean quarters for another was too much to be tolerated' by him. Despite Natesan's protestations that he would insult Besant, who would in turn be annoyed with Natesan, Gandhi changed his programme, and refused to stay the night.[136]

Annie Besant favoured working with the elites for the uplift of India, whereas Gandhi was concerned about the uplift of 'untouchables' and instilling a national spirit in the masses. At this time, Gandhi was still in favour of the British war effort and did not want to embarrass the country in its time of need by undertaking any political agitation. Besant had no such reticence. Later Gandhi was to lose his innocence regarding the goodness of the British Empire, but at this stage Annie Besant was far more radical in her approach to colonial domination.

The strain in their relations was dramatically emphasised on 6 February 1916 at the ceremony following the laying of the foundation stone for the Hindu University at Benares (that had grown out of Besant's Central Hindu College) two days before by the Viceroy Lord Hardinge. The occasion was a grand one. The university was to assist in the revival of a glorious Indian cultural and intellectual heritage. The ceremony was lavish, the speeches were many and the security was tight (forcing the exclusion of many students). After Besant's speech, Gandhi addressed the audience in a way that insulted the Maharajas who were guest dignitaries on the platform. He complained that the speeches were made in English, and about the filth around the temples of the holy town. He pointed out the differences between the wealth of the princes and the miserable condition of the Indian masses. He spoke of anarchy and the possibility of violence. Besant tried to stop him and eventually most of the insulted and outraged dignitaries left the platform. Besant was furious that Gandhi had ruined the occasion but this was really only a crystalized example of their differences of approach.[137]

Nevertheless, even at times of great tension between them, conciliatory moves were made. In June, Besant wrote to Gandhi: 'None of us can wholly understand each other, but we can trust to purity of motive and willingness to sacrifice all. God needs many workers on different lines. Knowing this, I can myself always work with people on any lines on which we agree and leave the disagreements to other lines.'[138] Their public pronouncements regarding each other were also laudatory. For example,

Gandhi stated that, 'The air in the country is thick with cries of swaraj [self-rule]. It is due to Mrs Besant that swaraj is on the lips of hundreds of thousands of men and women. What was unknown to most men and women only two years ago, has, by her consummate tact and her indefatigable efforts, become common property for them.'[139] On 13 March 1918, Gandhi chaired a meeting in Ahmedabad that had been arranged to hear Annie Besant speak on 'national education'. In his introduction, Gandhi announced that

> I cannot do full justice, nor can anyone else for that matter, I am sure, to the task of introducing Mrs Besant. I have known her for thirty years, having followed her activities since my youth, though of course I cannot claim that she has known me so long. "Home Rule" has become a household word all over India, in places big and small; the credit for this goes to this lady. I have often said that there have been, and there may still be, differences between her and me; there are quite a few even today. If I had the Home Rule movement under my charge, I would go to work differently. Having said this, I admit I cannot but look up to her with reverence, honour her, pay tribute to her for her excellent qualities, for she has dedicated her very soul to India. She lives only for India to live thus is her sole aspiration. No matter if she commits hundreds of mistakes, we shall honour her. In my view, Ahmedabad has covered itself with unsurpassed honour by honouring one who has rendered such great services as she has.[140]

When Besant was interned in June 1917, at the urging of some of the leading nationalist figures Gandhi wrote to the Private Secretary of the Viceroy to cancel the internment. He noted that, while he did not like the idea of political propaganda being carried on during the war, the government had committed a 'big blunder' because her propaganda was constitutional, did not subvert the Constitution and was free from violence. Further, the internment had completely backfired because the internment had caused disturbances in places that were perfectly calm beforehand.[141]

Although Besant unveiled a portrait of Gandhi on his birthday in Madras, the differences between the two were by this stage becoming acute. In discussing Annie Besant in early 1919, Gandhi painted her in less than flattering terms, while perhaps burnishing his own image in something of a self-righteous manner: 'Has anyone spat as much venom as she is doing? But is there a trace of hatred for her in me? None at all. Should one condemn or pity her for the perversion of her intellect after growing grey with so many years' splendid service to the country? To condemn her is to kick a falling person.'[142] Less than a month later, Besant wrote to Gandhi accusing him of diverting young followers from the spiritual path, perhaps fearing that she was losing disciples to him: 'You little realise how you have led young men of good impulses, but thoughtless, to break their most solemn [spiritual] pledges by inducing them to take your vows. Truth becomes a farce and honour a betrayal, where former promises are broken to make new ones.'[143] Gandhi responded:

> It saddens me to see in your writings a new Mrs Besant, and not the old Mrs Besant who in utter disregard of man-made laws, whether social or political, stood for Truth against the whole world. It is tragic to think that you should now turn back upon your own teachings and accuse me of "leading young men of good impulses to break their most solemn pledges". I cannot accept the charge, but I would certainly advise everyone to break all the pledges he might have taken if they are contrary to Truth. You deprive a fellow-being of his or her human dignity when you interpose between him and his conscience, an outsider, no matter how high-placed in spirituality he may appear to be. Those of your followers who obey the voice of conscience in preference even to your own instructions are loyal to you as truly as Prahlad was to his father. Surely, your past life is a striking demonstration of the truth of my remark. Is not every reformer an avowed law-breaker?
>
> But I do not want to strive with you. I shall continue to think of the Mrs Besant whom from my youth I had come to regard as a great and living illustration of fearlessness, courage and truth
>
> You have written your note in grief. You do not know what greater grief you have caused and are causing to those who know your services to India and who love you for them.[144]

By this time their positions on respect for the ruling power had been reversed as Gandhi lost his faith in the beneficence of British governance following the massacres at Jallianwallah Bagh in Amritsar on 13 April 1919. Besant wanted India to become an equal partner with Britain in an

Indo-British Commonwealth of Nations (as a move towards a worldwide brotherhood of nations), through constitutional agitation by an elite leadership. Gandhi now wanted complete independence for India, and aimed to achieve it through popular action. In May, Besant wrote to him indicating how worried she was by his methods. She did not approve of his direct action tactics, especially when they involve law-breaking, and she was very hesitant about the mobilisation of the masses. She concluded: 'It is a pity that both you and I have lost our ideal of the other. Time will tell which of us has been the more faithful to India and to freedom.'[145] Time did tell, and it was Gandhi.

When Besant had lost popularity during the 1920 campaign for opposing Gandhi and was shouted down in public meetings, Gandhi sprang to her defence, insisting on her right to speak and demanding that she be treated with respect.[146] Besant also made conciliatory gestures: she started calling Gandhi 'Mahatma', and took up spinning to fit in with Gandhi's discipline for a Congress Party that he now dominated.[147]

When Gandhi launched his non-cooperation campaign in 1920, Besant was not only concerned with the possibility of violence but 'saw it as the very antithesis of her millenarian dream' of true brotherhood; and, even if the method had value, 'humanity was not sufficiently evolved to practice that method with a perfect sense of self-sacrifice and *ahimsa*.'[148] For her, Gandhi's movement was an undisciplined form of mob-rule where there was no free speech, where through wild promises of a glorious future Gandhi had managed to fool at least part of the people. 'And all this midsummer madness has caught the fancy of boys and illiterates, and they shout down the nationalists.' Further, she accused Gandhi of unleashing forces which he could not control: 'He says that he finds that he cannot control the forces he has raised, and is, presumably, rather glad to be relieved from the necessity of trying to do so' because of his imprisonment.[149] When Congress voted to back Gandhi's policy of non-cooperation, Besant publicly disassociated herself from it at the beginning of 1921 in the New Year editorial of her paper *New India*, which she had titled 'The Parting of the Ways'. There she declared her battle against Gandhi, the 'Dictator' whose actions would lead to social collapse. She added that everyone had to choose between those (like her) who wanted to lead India 'along the path of Righteousness, Prosperity and Peace' and those who did 'their best to bring about chaos' through non-cooperation: 'Between these two divisions there can obviously be no peace. They must fight to a finish, for their ideals are incompatible. The struggle is between the forces of construction and destruction, of union and disruption. Each man and woman must choose between them, for India's fate depends upon the choice.'[150]

Besant saw Gandhi as being 'good for other kinds of work' but not that of a politician. For her he may have been a Mahatma and a great saint, but as a politician 'power was not safe with him' because his example 'could betray the ordinary man into disregard of the law.'[151] She added that 'Gandhi believes in suffering, and he is not happy if he achieves his object through normal evolutionary methods. He wants to build character through suffering. That is not my way. He is the martyr type and believes more in suffering than in achievement.'[152] In some sense, Besant was right because Gandhi's methods did lead to violence. However, her vision for a coming world brotherhood being ushered in by an equal Indo-British Commonwealth stemmed from the fact that she was British. In Gandhi's vision, the total dismantling of colonialism did not entail the hindering of a future world brotherhood, but was a necessary precondition of it. And of course Gandhi *was* primarily interested in building character. For him the revolution (and he did want revolutionary, not merely evolutionary, changes[153]) always began with the individual; in fact if the individual character was built sufficiently, that *was* the revolution. There was no need for further political struggle.

In any case, only a few years after the peak of her popularity, the public were no longer interested in listening to Annie Besant. Following the eruption of violence early in Gandhi's campaign, she pointed out that governments had to stop violence and therefore 'before a riot becomes unmanageable brickbats must inevitably be answered by bullets in every civilized country', and the public turned against her. Growing opposition led to her resignation (or to her being 'forced out' as she complained) as President of the Home Rule League in May 1919 and she was succeeded by Gandhi. After the death of Tilak, the other leading nationalist figure, Gandhi emerged as the unchallenged political leader in the country. However, when Gandhi was sentenced to six years' imprisonment and his movement ended in 1922, Besant again came forward with a plan for the leading personalities of the country to frame a new constitution. Nationalist leaders, including the prematurely released Gandhi, failed to endorse her plan and eventually it was to peter out.[154]

Gandhi, who was undertaking a penitential fast because of Hindu-Muslim riots, and so could not attend the festivities, sent a message to be read out at the celebrations for Annie Besant's seventy-eighth birthday in 1924. While he praised her past work, Gandhi implied that her important work was behind her:

> Dr Besant is a world figure. It is no small gain to India that she has adopted Bharat Mata as her mother and dedicated all her matchless gifts to her services. At her time of life, when people should be entitled to complete rest from all toil, she, with amazing energy, is writing, making speeches, moving about, and hatching plans for India's deliverance. Her indomitable courage in the face of all odds, her great organizing power, her literary and oratorical gifts, and many other qualities that I could name are all treasures for us to prize and to utilize. It was painful to me, therefore, to differ from her. It is an equal pleasure to me that we seem to be coming closer. May God give her long life and enable her to witness the establishment of swaraj, for which she and we are all striving, and for the achievement of which she is not to be surpassed by any body in perseverance and ceaseless efforts.[155]



Annie Besant was a great orator, but she spoke in English.[156] She may have dressed as a Hindu and been well versed in Hindu philosophy, but she was English. She was a great inspirer of Indian nationalism but she would always be a *pardeshi* (foreign) rather than a *swadeshi* (of the land) nationalist. She was a constitutional reformer who preferred to work with the educated elites at a time when the national mood had turned to one of mass mobilisation. Further, with her glorification of a great Hindu past, she did not inspire Muslims to join the freedom struggle and may have strengthened the position of upper-caste Hindu conservatives. As the Indian people deserted her for Gandhi, she directed her attention to proclaiming Krishnamurti as the World Teacher. But, towards the end of her life, he too repudiated her plans for him.

Upon hearing of the death of Annie Besant, Gandhi paid the following tribute:

> Whilst the people will thank the Almighty for relieving Dr Besant from lingering illness by sending to her the Angel of Death, thousands

> will, at the same time, mourn the event. So long as India lives, the memory of the magnificent services rendered by Dr Besant will also live. She had endeared herself to India by making it the country of her adoption and dedicating her all to her.[157]

Another of the prominent nationalist figures, the Gandhi lieutenant and poetess ('the nightingale') of India, Sarojini Naidu, in perhaps something of an overstatement, pointed out the contribution Annie Besant had made in priming India for the arrival of the Mahatma:

> If there had been no Dr Besant there would perhaps have been no Mahatma Gandhi. She had sponsored Swadeshi, if not Khadi proper, for long years. She had pleaded with great force for communal peace and harmony. All this programme was taken up by Gandhi later. Under her inspiring lead there was a terrific upsurge of emotion for the freedom of the country from all bonds, but in a way the path had already been paved for him by Dr Besant.[158]

# Muriel Lester and Agatha Harrison: Hosting Gandhi/ Interpreting Gandhi

Muriel Lester was a well-known British Christian pacifist author, eloquent preacher ('whose musical voice enhanced her message'[159]) and social worker. She was born in December 1883 into a wealthy home with the privileges of a good education (which introduced her to vegetarianism), travel and a full cultural life.[160] From her father she acquired a strong religious faith and social conscience and from her mother a love of nature, books, music and travel. Her first experience of poverty was when she glimpsed the slums of London's East End from the window of a first-class railway carriage while the family was on the way to the annual Christmas pantomime. She left school at eighteen and seemed to be on the path to becoming a member of the idle rich, however the religiosity of her family and her independent mind broadened her horizons. As with Gandhi before her, the writings of Tolstoy (particularly *The Kingdom of God is Within You*) led her to pacifism.

In 1902, at age eighteen, Muriel Lester was invited to a party at the Factory Girls' Club which had been established six years earlier by Annie Besant in the Bow district of the East End. What promised to be a pleasant diversion ended up a life-changing experience. She realised that the factory workers, although the same age as her, were not only far more mature and independent than she was, but that for the past five years she had spent at 'delightful boarding school', they had been working for ten or eleven hours a day tending machines. The world was not fair, and she became determined to do something about it. She returned to Bow the next week, and the week after that, and the one after that. Understanding that one never really gets to know a place unless one sleeps in it, she and her like-minded sister Doris left their comfortable home whenever they could to live for periods of time in Bow. In the winter of 1913-14 Muriel went to the Riviera with her family. During the trip, in her words, she 'became more than ever disgusted with myself and with the contrast between the conditions in Bow and on the Riviera. Evil was so deeply entrenched in the world that it was idiotic to fight against it with kid gloves on. I must undergo a more exacting self-discipline, a twenty-four-hour-a-day service.'[161]

Back in Bow, she decided that she and those around her had to do something practical for the poor. She, her sister and some close friends had absorbed the atmosphere of Bow for a number of years, they knew the evils of capitalism, had gone to countless meetings and listened to countless speeches. Muriel Lester knew that the unions and left political parties were doing valuable work; she also knew that they could be dead before these organisations fulfilled their programmes. The question became: what could they do to change the quality of life in their neighbourhood? They founded a men's adult school based around bible study. Muriel Lester dedicated her life to work for social justice. She moved permanently to Bow with Doris and eventually their brother Kingsley, to become a social worker, and to advocate the rights of women (including the need for women clergy) and the special role women could play in the fights against war, imperialism and poverty. The sisters set up boys' clubs, nursery schools and adult schools (Doris was better with children, Muriel with adults). Kingsley died suddenly following operations for a troubling appendix just after England had entered the war with Germany. Kingsley left his money to his sisters who set up Kingsley Rooms to further their work of adult education and wholesome social activities.

In February 1915, with Doris, Muriel founded Kingsley Hall with a donation from their father as a memorial to their younger brother. The disused Strict and Particular Baptist Chapel was purchased and turned into a teetotal pub to provide a congenial evening gathering place for the residents of the crowded slum houses. Most of the clubs and classes that she and Doris had established in the neighbourhood were re-housed at the Hall. Lester explained that the Hall 'was not the outcome of any streak of sentimentalism, of pitying charity. It was an overdue act of justice, recognised as such by all connected with it.'[162] And bravely, given that it was the height of war hysteria, she declared that 'We refused at Kingsley Hall to pronounce a moratorium on the Sermon on the Mount for the duration of the war.'[163] Nevertheless, in 1916, the building was damaged during a German zeppelin air-raid.

In 1919 Muriel Lester had another deepening of her commitment to her life's work. On reading Olive Schreiner's book *Dreams*, she came to the realisation that the possession of luxuries that were still available to her were a source of shame rather than pride. As she started to read Gandhi's works, the sentiment was reinforced and soon her life had become not just one of Christian pacifism, but also of voluntary poverty.

After the war, Lester, who by this time was serving as the socialist alderman in the local borough council, convinced London County Council members to sell to her and Doris several adjoining condemned buildings down the road from the old Kingsley Hall. With the aid of more money from their ninety-year-old father, the sisters constructed London's first purpose-built Children's House, which was opened in 1923 and operated under the directorship of Doris. In mid-1927 construction began on the new Kingsley Hall in Powis Road, Bow. It was ceremonially opened in September 1928, and a second unit in Dagenham, where Ford Motors had established a major car factory which attracted many workers from Bow, was opened the following year. Gandhi stayed at the settlement house in Bow in 1931.

Kingsley Hall in Bow was established by the Lester sisters and 'a group of committed pacifists who formed a disciplined community of prayer, service, and voluntary poverty.' It was dubbed by James Hunt as 'a veritable Christian ashram.'[164] In Muriel Lester's description,

> Kingsley Hall is a center of fellowship in the midst of a large industrial district of East London and is run for the most part by the people of the neighbourhood who work out their own salvation, educationally, socially and spiritually. Ten volunteers give wholetime service and

> receive food, seven shillings a week and a cell on the flat roof as their portion; ignoring barriers of creed, class and nation, they serve in unity, cooking or organising, cleaning or teaching, scrubbing or praying. The strength of Kingsley Hall lies in the practice of the presence of God, as taught by Jesus Christ, and is an effort towards the Kingdom of God on Earth.[165]

How could Gandhi have stayed elsewhere? He would become a guest of Muriel at this special place when he arrived in London to attend the Second Round Table Conference to discuss India's future, following the calling off of the Civil Disobedience campaign that he had launched to secure India's independence.[166]

In 1919, Muriel Lester came upon a bound volume of Gandhi's paper *Young India*. It was a revelation to her: 'I read it from cover to cover, revelling in the discovery that the principles for which a few thousand of us in the West had been standing between 1914 and 1919 were being put forward with power over an Eastern subcontinent.'[167] And when Romain Rolland's biography of Gandhi appeared in English in 1924, Lester realised that nonviolence and Christian pacifism had much to learn from each other. She noted that when 'the book fell into my hands', it 'marked a new epoch for me'.[168] Towards the end of her life, she recalled:

> You can imagine what a pleasure and surprise it was for us to learn that there, in India, was a man who had been carrying out the ideas and principles which we believed in on a vast scale compared with our own small efforts. It gave us enormous encouragement and confidence just to know this, and naturally we wanted to meet him and to discuss our common problems.[169]

Lester first went to India in 1926, following an invitation from poet and writer Rabindranath Tagore's son-in-law Professor Nagendra Nath Ganguli, after he had lectured at Kingsley Hall. With her eighteen-year-old nephew, Daniel Hogg, she arrived at the Sabarmati Ashram on Gandhi's fifty-seventh birthday. Although she quickly developed an intimate relationship with some of Gandhi's close friends, initially she had trouble in establishing a close rapport with the Mahatma himself (unlike Daniel who cleaned latrines with the Mahatma). The friends encouraged her to talk to Gandhi as she talked to them, assuring her that he would be interested. This, however, she found difficult when he was always surrounded 'by so many admirers hanging on his every word', even though Gandhi was quite accessible. For almost a month she worked hard cleaning, scavenging, spinning, and sitting in her room reading, with little contact other than 'polite and pleasant greetings' as they passed each other in the ashram. Finally, a night or two before her visit was to end, her friends ushered her into Gandhi's room. To overcome the embarrassment of silence as she sat there, Gandhi contentedly spinning, Muriel 'suddenly blurted out' that it would be important for Gandhi to come to England. Gandhi responded by noting that his success in nonviolent methods had not reached the stage where he had anything to teach Fellowship of Reconciliation[170] people like her. She interrupted him by explaining that she didn't want him to 'come to England in order to teach us. I want you to come and learn from us'. Gandhi burst out laughing and they became close friends.[171] 'He would love to be surprised in conversation or discussion by a challenging or arresting remark. He would be so pleased, and his face would show this in a happy smile.'[172] Gandhi gave Lester conditions on which he might come to England, but they were such that it would have meant completely changing British policy. The choices of condition were that Lester had to influence the government to grant India independence, or to persuade the Lancashire cotton magnates not to send their goods to India! She asked for an easier condition and, observing that Gandhi was 'going to talk seriously this time',[173] was given the task of rousing public opinion to get the government's liquor and opium policies changed.

She spent the next two months of her India tour looking into this problem, and when she returned to London she was determined to 'go out and spread the knowledge of facts'. She wrote a leaflet on the responsibility of the British for the destiny of the people of India because of their excise revenue policies relating to drugs and alcohol, printed 20,000 copies and, 'accepted every invitation to speak' that came her way:

> I spoke on improvised platforms, soap-boxes, at street corners where Communists poured out torrents of violent abuse on Mr Gandhi because of his principles of non-violence, in the parks where two to three hundred people used to listen with rapt attention, at chapels and churches and lecture societies, at universities and

> temperance meetings, lunches, Rotary Clubs, literary clubs, at international meetings, students' meetings and at branches of the National Council of Women.[174]

After detailing all these activities to Gandhi, she concluded that 'It does rather look as though people are stirred.'[175]

During the thirteen week India trip, she had learnt what Gandhi had done for India. A ranking English Indian Civil Servant informed her that if ten years ago an Indian coolie had crossed his path in a narrow laneway and made his horse swerve, he would have shouted at the man to get out of the way and he 'would have disappeared cowering'. Now, if the same thing had happened, 'the man would stand up straight, look me full in the face, and quietly say, "Why should I?"'[176] And through Lester, the Indians also learned that there was a movement in Britain which accepted the Mahatma's ideals.

It was to be another five years before Gandhi could make it to England. However, when Lester heard that he was coming to the Conference, she wrote to him: 'Now you're coming, don't forget this is the place where you will be happy, Kingsley Hall. You'll find we live extremely simply, you'll find we have cell-bedrooms on the flat roof, little tiny places, you can have one of them and whoever you bring will be treated the same way and you will find that we have our days punctuated by times of prayer just as you have.'[177] He replied that, 'I would rather stay at your settlement than anywhere else, for there I will be living among the same sort of people as those for whom I have spent my life.'[178] In a letter to Charlie Andrews, Gandhi added that at Kingsley Hall he would 'come in touch with the poor of the East End, know something of life in the East End and probably serve the cause better, being in those surroundings', than at more prestigious places with the elite of London's Indian community.[179] In retrospect, Gandhi added that

> It was a good thing that Muriel Lester, the soul of Kingsley Hall settlement, invited me to stay at her settlement and that I was able to accept the invitation. The choice lay between Kingsley Hall and Mr Birla's Arya Bhavan. I had no difficulty in making my choice nor had Mr Birla. But great pressure was put upon me by Indian friends, and that naturally, to stay at Arya Bhavan. Experience showed that Kingsley Hall was an ideal choice.[180]

At Kingsley Hall Gandhi slept in a small room on the top floor, often arriving back after two in the morning, only to be up for prayers at four. After a further short sleep, at five-thirty he would go for an hour's walk before breakfast. Generally he would take these long morning walks with Lester and Mirabehn along the nearby streets and canals where he met the locals, at times venturing into their houses, and joked with the children. When he had the time, Lester included him in evening social activities at the Hall. These activities enabled him to see the slums and come into contact with the poor of London.[181] Many dignitaries (including Charlie Chaplin and Krishnamurti) also came to visit him at the Hall. His stay did much to aid understanding of the Indian cause and to humanise Gandhi in the eyes of the British public. As Lester later noted, as a consequence of the visit, the public were buying books about India and for information 'MPs were presented with copies of other books than "Mother India."'[182]

Of his stay at Kingsley Hall, Gandhi reported that:

> It is situated among the poor of London and is dedicated purely to their service. Several women and some men, under the inspiration of Muriel Lester, have dedicated themselves to such service. Not a corner of the big building is used for any other purpose. There is religious service, there are entertainments, there are lectures, billiards, reading-room, etc., for the use of the poor. The inmates live a life of severe simplicity. There is no superfluous furniture to be found in all that settlement. The inmates occupy tiny rooms called cells. It was no joke to accommodate five of us in that settlement. But love makes room where there is none. Four settlers vacated their cells which were placed at our disposal. Bedding, etc., had to be borrowed. Fortunately, we had all armed ourselves with sufficient blankets and, being used to squat on the floor, most of the articles borrowed could be returned. But, there was no doubt, my presence at the settlement put a severe tax on its times, space and other resources. But the good people would not hear of my leaving it. And to me it was a privilege to receive the loving, silent and unseen services of the members and a perennial joy to come in vital contact with the poor of the East End of London. Needless to say I was able to live exactly as in India, and early morning walks through the streets of East London are a memory that can never be effaced. During these walks I had most intimate talks with those members

who joined me and others whom Muriel allowed. For she was a vigilant guardian of my time whilst I was in the settlement. And she would get easily angry if she heard that my time was being abused by people when she was not by me.[183]

Of Muriel Lester herself, he wrote to the women inmates of his Ahmedabad ashram:

> Muriel Lester who came to stay with us at the Ashram is a daughter of rich parents. Like Mirabehn, she has given away, as a trust to the Ashram founded by her, all her share of the parental wealth. She and her sister Doris have dedicated their all to public service. Doris runs a school for children. She is helped by about ten women teachers who work for a very small pay. Muriel runs the Ashram where I was staying. Day and night the two sisters think only of service. Both have remained unmarried and now they have reached an age when even the thought of marriage would not occur to them. We can see their purity marked on their faces. In Muriel's Ashram no distinction would ever be made between high and low or between whites and non-whites. One may suppose that she could expect some publicity by acting as my hostess. But what shall one say about her having let Tilakam stay at the place? You may ask Tilakam himself how he was looked after there. He went to it as a pauper. I had agreed to pay the expenses on his account. However, Tilakam gave to the Ashram his full services like the others, so that I did not have to pay a single penny on his behalf. Negroes too she admits into her institution, and treats them with the same respect and love. I have many such happy memories of my stay.[184]

Muriel Lester noted that 'before you can say you knew anyone, you need to see them at home, to live with them.' She lived with Gandhi for ten weeks at Kingsley Hall and then travelled the continent with him for a further two. She saw him in a variety of settings, finding him always exactly the same: 'serene, gay, humorous, appreciative, selfless, at one with God and man.' In summing up their time together, she remarked that, 'I welcomed him to Bow as a great man whom I admired. I bade him farewell as a dear, delightful, and wholly reliable friend.'[185]

At the conclusion of the Round Table Conference, Muriel Lester joined Gandhi's entourage that travelled in a leisurely way through France,

Switzerland and Italy on the way to Brindisi, where the India-bound contingent boarded ship. During the trip, the self-appointed protector of the Mahatma managed to put Romain Rolland offside. Following the visit of Gandhi's group, he described her in his diary as 'an intelligent and forceful Englishwoman who works with the poorer classes in London and whose manners are brusque and domineering', noting that while she insisted on escorting Gandhi from her home all the way to Brindisi, it was a service that he believed Gandhi 'would willingly do without'.[186]

Following travels in China and Japan for the International Fellowship of Reconciliation (IFoR) and as a representative of Maude Royden's Peace Army, with her somewhat reluctant niece Dorothy Hogg she joined Gandhi's grueling anti-Untouchability (*Harijan*) tour in early 1934 and visited earthquake-devastated Bihar with him. Dorothy Hogg recounts an amusing anecdote of Gandhi struggling through a large crowd to bring the English friends a tray of tea, announcing that he had their 'poisonous beverage', even though he had advised them against drinking much of it.[187]

In March, Muriel Lester had an interview with the Viceroy Lord Willingdon. A few days later, she reported on her interview to Gandhi, noting that the Viceroy thought that the Mahatma was insincere.[188] During this time, in his paper Gandhi published a talk on Christ that Lester had held with missionaries, noting that 'Many persons have written like Miss Lester before now. The value of her conversation lies in the fact that she endeavours every moment of her life to practise what she professes and preaches in her writing.'[189]

She returned to England with her friend Agatha Harrison, who had also come to visit Gandhi, in mid-June. In January and February 1936, she visited Gandhi in Wardha (where she took part in Mirabehn's scavenging work in nearby Sindi[190]) and Ahmedabad while in India to attend the Conference of the International Council of Women, and was again with him in India, this time with Dorothy Hogg, in 1938/39.[191] During that visit, she spent part of the time as Gandhi's observer of the satyagraha movement against the corrupt ruler in his childhood home town of Rajkot before Gandhi personally intervened.

Lester's last visit to the Mahatma came seven years later, during the chaos of partition in 1946, and here she may have played an important role in the trajectory of Gandhi's life. On hearing about the Noakhali massacres she proceeded there to investigate the situation. In the first week of November, she wrote a report from a relief centre, noting that 'this orgy of arson and violence ... was not a spontaneous uprising of the villagers', and that the 'worst of all was the plight of the women'.[192] She also wrote to Gandhi not to fast to the death as a reaction to the violence but to show a lead to the Muslim boys and children who had 'taken vigorous part in the riots' because 'they need a live experience to save them from their present outlook on life'.[193] Her reports of the situation helped to decide Gandhi on his lonely pilgrimage to bring peace to the riot-torn region, one of the most remarkable times in his long life.

In the 1930s, Lester spent more and more time working with IFoR and turned over the leadership of Kingsley Hall to Doris after returning from her 1934 India trip. From the end of the Second World War until she was in her eighties, Muriel Lester devoted her life to the IFoR cause as its travelling secretary, completing nine around-the-world trips, lecturing and writing and even being imprisoned in that capacity. She also wrote several volumes of autobiographical writings in which Gandhi features large, as well as several volumes dedicated to spreading the Gandhian message. Her relationship with Gandhi was one of a co-worker rather than worshipful acolyte. Even after just leaving Gandhi's presence in 1927, she signed her letters 'yours in fellowship'.[194] She died in 1968.

• • •

Agatha Harrison was another of Gandhi's strong English supporters who had come into contact with him during his 1931 London sojourn with Muriel Lester. Although Gandhi had long believed that the freedom struggle had to be won in India and therefore no special representative was necessary in London, when he was there for the Round Table Conference the reality on the ground forced him to modify his views. His British supporters convinced him that some structure was needed to assist in the dissemination of his and the Congress point of view in England. Gandhi was willing to come up with the funds if a suitable person could be found to do the work. The day before he left London, he called upon Agatha Harrison,[195] who was known for her organisational and investigative capacities, and as a 'woman of immense energy and enthusiasm' and even as 'a bustler, a fixer, a manager',[196] to fill the role. When Harrison asked for advice as to how to undertake the 'staggering task', Gandhi replied; 'God will direct your steps'. Harrison recalled that 'Often I have had to make a decision and not known which way to turn. This time I knew at once what was the thing to do, and found myself saying to him that I would do it'.[197]

Harrison, one of several children, was the daughter of a Methodist minister. When her father died suddenly, her mother had trouble making ends meet. A deal was struck whereby fees would not have to be paid for Agatha's schooling if she undertook part-time work in her school. At sixteen she started earning her living by teaching and helping at Kent College in Folkestone in return for training for the Froebel Certificate for women teachers. On graduation she took a post in a private school running the kindergarten. This was followed by stints as head of welfare departments at Boots Cash Chemists in Nottingham under the social work pioneer Eleanor Kelly, and at a tin box factory in Hull. In these roles she fought for fair wages and decent working conditions for the women workers. She organised cultural outings and picnics, visited sick workers, established branch libraries and sports clubs. She earned the love of her charges and the respect of the bosses. Kelly said that it was in the factory that 'Agatha found her feet', and that she worked miracles: 'All I know is that it was through her we found *our* feet, and we were her miracles. In those days there was a stigma attached to the word factory-girl. She taught us that we counted, that we were of value as citizens. She gave us self-confidence.'[198]

In 1917, although she had no degree, she was recruited to the staff of the London School of Economics because of her practical experience. There, her aim was to make the LSE a centre for training of welfare workers. From the LSE she was seconded to the YWCA to undertake work that would free exploited child labourers in the cotton mills of Shanghai. Several years later, on her return from China, she was invited by the National Christian Council of India to repeat the work she had done in China. However, she thought that it may be beyond her and instead, in early 1925, accepted an offer to work in the United States as the head of the YWCA's Education and Research Division which was then setting up a department for the social sciences and economics. After three years she returned home and took up an association with the Women's International League for Peace and Freedom, spending the first half of 1929 on a speaking tour for the organisation. Her next assignment was as an assistant to the only woman member of the Whitley Royal Commission on Labour in its India investigations. It was felt that her practical experience with factory workers, especially women and children in Britain, China and America, would make her a useful addition to the team. Although she had been attracted to Gandhi from the time she had read Rolland's biography of the Mahatma, her first tour of India was an extensive six-month trip with the Commission from September 1929.

In mid-1931, at the age of about forty, she met and dedicated her life to serving as the secretary of the Church of England missionary Charles Freer Andrews, one of Gandhi's closest friends since the end of the Mahatma's South Africa days. Harrison and Andrews had a long and very close, even loving (many expected them to marry[199]), yet platonic, soul-mate relationship. Andrews and Henry Polak were Gandhi's key English aids and in this way she assumed the role of an important secretarial member of Gandhi's Knightsbridge headquarters and had come to Gandhi's attention. She accepted Gandhi's call and became the secretary and mainstay of the India Conciliation Group, thus, in effect, becoming Gandhi's press consultant. The group included several others, many of them Quakers, who were friends of Gandhi. Among them were Carl Heath (Chairman), Horace Alexander, and Jack Hoyland, as well as Maude Royden and of course Muriel Lester. The Conciliation Group served the position of go-between with regard to British politicians and Congress politicians, both in England and India (where Harrison was of added value to Gandhi because at times she was the only one in his entourage who could use a typewriter and had skill in vetting Gandhi's correspondence 'from the angle of English mentality.'[200])



As the secretary of the Conciliation Group she had no staff and no office (papers were filed in her apartment) but she had a free hand to fulfill the role as she saw fit, noting that,

> in the final analysis I feel the person to whom I am responsible is the man who asked me to do this work. And he has never said to me "do this or that." He works like this, I imagine – picks people and then expects them to do their utmost. Sometimes the work is lonely, but I would not change it for any other. To be "at large," so to speak, working on the mutual understanding of two countries like India and mine, is a humbling experience.[201]

The task was to influence those with a knowledge of Indian affairs or those who were engaged in vigorous journalism to 'educate public opinion and influence the course of events'.[202] She was often in charge of damage control when controversy erupted following Gandhi being mis-quoted or when malicious rumours about his intentions were spread.[203] Although

Gandhi was not overly convinced of the value of the press, Harrison became something of a long distance press secretary. Although she managed to stay in the background, in her role as leader of the group, Harrison had private meetings with viceroys and princes, was on close terms with the leading political figures of both sides and perhaps invented what later became known as 'shuttle diplomacy'. Every week she received a pile of Indian daily papers and anyone needing information about India beat their way to her door. She briefed interested M.P.s and informed the India Office. When in a moment of doubt she cabled Gandhi, who was back in prison in India: 'SHOULD VALUE ANY ADVICE YOU CARE TO GIVE ME AT THIS MOMENT', his reply was simple and indicated the trust in which he held her: 'UNDERSTAND YOUR STRUGGLE. GOD WILL GUIDE YOUR STEP'.[204] As time went on, Harrison's flat became a second home for many Indian students studying in London. She lived frugally, dedicated to her work on behalf of the Mahatma without any thought for the future, on a small stipend from Gandhi. Her friends worried about her financial position and wrote to Gandhi expressing their concern. When she heard about this from Gandhi, she replied that while her friends may have been trying to save her from herself, she fervently echoed the prayer that said, 'Oh, Lord save me from my friends.'[205]

Agatha Harrison had first seen and heard Gandhi in early November, 1929, in Delhi during his meetings with women and the public in Queen's Garden. She became an admirer, returning 'to the Labour Commission with an indelible impression of a remarkable man with whom I wished I could have talked'.[206] Two years later, on the day after Gandhi arrived in London, she went to Kingsley Hall to see him. Although it was his day of silence, she 'came away feeling part of his entourage',[207] and soon she was the backbone of the Conciliation Group. By early 1934 Harrison thought that it was time that she reacquainted herself with India first-hand, and had long discussions with Gandhi in a time of truce in the independence struggle. Her visits were welcomed not just by Gandhi and Indian nationalist leaders, but also by the British authorities because 'it was felt that she would not complicate a difficult situation by playing off one side against the other'.[208] When Gandhi interrupted his Harijan tour in March 1934 to hurry to earthquake ravaged Bihar, Harrison joined him and Muriel Lester in touring the devastated villages, and accompanied him until mid-June on his resumed Harijan tour in South Orissa.[209] This India trip not only brought her into closer contact with Gandhi, but also gave her the ability to speak with great conviction on Gandhi's cause with important British officials.[210]

She was back with Gandhi in India in late 1936 to early 1937 for a six month visit, and again in late 1938, when she spent another seven and a half months in the country. With the looming threat of war, she tried to persuade him to come to Europe and perhaps talk to Hitler or at least give Western pacifists 'the benefit of his deep experience in the practice of non-violence'.[211] Gandhi responded that he had to prove his methods in India first.

She was devastated by the death of Andrews in Calcutta on 5 April 1940. Gandhi wrote to comfort her: 'I do not know what to say or how to console you. Perhaps C.F.A.'s death has hit you the hardest. But you are a brave woman. Let us all forget his death and make him live by working in his spirit at the legacy he has left to us.'[212] At around this time she became a Quaker. From late 1945 until mid-1946, she was again in India helping Marjorie Sykes work on her biography of Andrews and to continue 'the task of behind-the-scenes negotiator and mediator in bringing together the Congress, Muslim League and British Government into constitutional agreement.'[213] In January, after attending the All India Women's Conference in Calcutta, she met Gandhi and the following day accompanied him to Madras aboard the 'Gandhi Special', a train that consisted of nothing but an engine, a guard's van and a third-class carriage.[214]

She continued to work for Indian independence and the Gandhian cause until the end.[215] During the Quit India movement, while England was still fighting for its survival during the Second World War, Gandhi noted that:

> Agatha Harrison sends me cable after cable revealing her deep pain over what I am doing and the Congress is doing. And Agatha Harrison, weak in body though she is, is wearing herself out in removing the cobwebs of misunderstanding. She sees every responsible English statesman who will see her (and let me admit that they all see her) and pleads for India's cause. But she is up against a blind wall. I seem to have lost the credit that I thought I used to enjoy in those circles.[216]

Although most of the letters Harrison exchanged with Gandhi were related to weighty political matters at hand, the relationship was by no means merely a business-like one. She was also deeply interested in his philosophy, partly to be able to better interpret Gandhi to a Western audience, partly because she had a deep spiritual involvement. They discussed matters such as the place of God in the training for nonviolence,[217] and the meaning of beauty. As a replay of Gandhi's debates on beauty with his friend the poet Tagore some twenty years before, in 1946 Harrison asked Gandhi, 'Won't you ask people to grow flowers on a small piece of land? Colour and beauty is necessary to the soul as food is to the body.' She was having a friendly jibe at his suggestion that a millionaire friend should dig up his beautiful flower gardens in order to plant vegetables.[218] Gandhi replied, 'No, I won't. Why can't you see the beauty of colour in vegetables? And then there is beauty in the speckless sky. But no, you want the colours of the rainbow which is a mere optical illusion. We have been taught to believe that what is beautiful need not be useful, and what is useful cannot be beautiful. I want to show that what is useful can also be beautiful.'[219]

While some of his women friends, most notably Maude Royden, lost their pacifism during the war, Agatha Harrison only went as far as hinting that perhaps Gandhi's nonviolence may not have survived being in wartime Britain with bombs dropping around him. Gandhi replied that his faith in nonviolence was growing daily stronger by the day, adding that whether

> it can stand the strain if bombs were dropping near my feet and I was witnessing dear ones being crushed to death, I cannot say. I rehearse such situations, I pray that the faith might not break under such strain. I flatter myself with the belief that I can feel these things from afar. I did shed a silent tear when I read about the damage done to the Houses of Parliament, the Westminster Abbey and St Paul's. Nevertheless this is all speculation. If I fail in the examination, if it ever came to me, I shall have the courage to admit my weakness but I will not deny my faith in non-violence.[220]

Following the Independence of India, Agatha Harrison made two more trips to the subcontinent (January to May 1949 and November 1949 to May 1950) as something of a roving ambassador for the new country. She was planning to visit India again in the latter part of 1954, but death intervened. In his tribute to her, Krishna Menon, India's ambassador to the United Nations, said that 'She had no office or title, and no flags were lowered for her, but all over India people honour her name.'[221] In Horace Alexander's words, Agatha Harrison's 'unceasing, single-minded, and utterly selfless work' continued until India achieved independence in 1947, and 'which, in a slightly different form, still went on until her untimely death in 1954 – due to her determination, at the age of 69, to work as if she were only 39.'[222] An Indian newspaper called her 'C.F. Andrews' gift to Mahatma Gandhi and India.'[223]

# Maude Royden: Gandhi and Peace Armies

During the inter-war period, when she had contact with Gandhi, Agnes Maude Royden was one of the world's best known women pacifists. The youngest daughter of the large family of a wealthy Liverpool shipowner, she was born on 23 November 1876. She studied history at Lady Margaret Hall at Oxford University and, after lecturing in English literature in the University Extension Scheme, became a social worker in a Women's Settlement in the slum area of Liverpool. She went on to become one of Britain's first women preachers and pastors, as well as a prominent champion of women's suffrage.

In her twenties, Royden was greatly influenced by the unorthodox Anglican preacher Reverend George William Hudson Shaw and began working as his lay curate. At age thirty-two she joined the National Union of Women's Suffrage Societies, and for a while edited its journal, *The Common Cause*. In 1914 she decided on a life in the ministry, but as this was not open to women in the Anglican Church, in 1917 she became an assistant minister at the Congregational City Temple in London (although she remained an Anglican). It is reported that 'Her preaching filled the

City Temple to the roof.'[224] During the war she joined the Fellowship of Reconciliation and the Women's International League for Peace and Freedom. Devoting herself to the cause of peace, she took part in a peace mission that toured around the country in a horse-drawn caravan preaching pacifism. After the war she became the secretary of the FoR and later vice-president of the WILPF. In 1920 she started undenominational Fellowship Services at Kensington and later at the Guildhouse which she founded in June 1921, and where she stayed until 1936 using her charismatic personality and power as a preacher to gather a large following. She wrote pamphlets on prayer and women's ordination and women's rights generally, and spoke out on controversial subjects including gender-based sexual double-standards, female sexuality, and birth control. She was made a Companion of Honour in 1930 and was the first British woman to receive an honorary Doctorate of Divinity (from Glasgow University).

Royden had loved Hudson Shaw since he had taught her at Oxford. In between, she maintained a lengthy, loving but platonic relationship with him and his wife. Following the death of the 85-year-old Hudson Shaw's wife, in 1944 Royden married him two months before his own death.[225] She died in London on 30 July 1956 in her eightieth year.[226]

Maude Royden came into close contact with Gandhi over their common interests in poverty alleviation and pacifism. During the Sino-Japanese war, she was instrumental in founding her peace army, which in peace circles is now legendary.

In 1928 she embarked on a world-preaching tour which took in the USA, New Zealand, Australia, Japan, China, Ceylon and India. She had no public meetings scheduled in India; her aim was to meet Gandhi whom she thought was the 'greatest man then living'.[227] Reasonably regularly, since 1925, Gandhi had been spending December at Wardha, the area of his future ashram in the geographical centre of India, with his spiritual heir Vinoba Bhave and his millionaire benefactor Jamnalal Bajaj. It is here that Royden first caught up with him in mid-December, with an introduction from the eminent peace worker Jane Addams.[228] She claimed that the occasion and the atmosphere surrounding Gandhi overawed her and she lost her usual eloquence: 'I would rather the Mahatma had talked to me of God, but my Western shyness overcame me in the presence of so many strangers, and we talked of politics instead.'[229] She had hoped that Gandhi could see some role for Britain to play in the future development of a free India; however, Gandhi disappointed her, noting British arrogance poisons all her gifts. What conversations were held during their other meetings is not recorded; however, given the interest of both of them in pacifism and moral power, it would be fair to assume that they discussed issues surrounding war and its resistance.

Gandhi spoke regularly about nonviolence in times of war. These efforts to explain his philosophy continued during his trips abroad. For example, during a public meeting in Geneva on 10 December 1931, when he was on his way back to India following his attendance at the Second Round Table Conference, Gandhi was brutally clear about his vision of civilian defence. He was asked: 'How could a disarmed neutral country allow other nations to be destroyed? But for our army which was waiting ready at our frontier during the last war we should have been ruined.' These questions were of central concern to those who opposed rearmament and the method contained in the answer was soon to be attempted in practice. Gandhi stated:

> At the risk of being considered a visionary or a fool I must answer this question in the only manner I know. It would be cowardly for a neutral country to allow an army to devastate a neighbouring country. But there are two ways in common between soldiers of war and soldiers of non-violence, and if I had been a citizen of Switzerland and a President of the Federal State, what I would have done would be to refuse passage to the invading army by refusing all supplies. Secondly, by re-enacting a Thermopylae in Switzerland, you would have presented a living wall of men and women and children, and inviting the invaders to walk over your corpses. You may say that such a thing is beyond human experience and endurance. I say that it is not so. … Imagine these men and women standing in front of an army requiring a safe passage to another country, the army would be brutal enough to walk over them you might say. I would then say, you will still have done your duty by allowing yourself to be annihilated. An army that dares to pass over the corpses of innocent men and women would not be able to repeat that experiment. You may, if you wish, refuse to believe in such courage on the part of the masses of men and women, but then you would have to admit that non-violence is made of sterner stuff. It was never conceived as a weapon of the weak, but of the stoutest hearts.[230]

During his London visit, Gandhi likewise addressed several gatherings. He spoke with Quakers and attended their silent 'prayer' meetings and addressed members of the Fellowship of Reconciliation. Gandhi, who had been *Time* magazine's previous 'Man of the Year' and who was greeted by a crowd of 5,000 people on his Folkestone landing, 'had now become such a world figure that he was followed everywhere by reporters and photographers, and reports of his activities appeared in hundreds of publications … everyone wanted to see him and hear him, and he was available to all.'[231]

Given her friendship with Lester and Harrison, it can safely be assumed that at this time Maude Royden attended his meetings and, on 23 September 1931, Gandhi addressed a Guildhouse meeting chaired by Royden where he explained his mission to England and spoke on voluntary poverty. The following day Royden wrote to her good friend H.R.L. (Dick) Sheppard (the well-known Anglican vicar, church reformer and, during the last ten years of his life, pacifist and peace activist) that 'There was a huge crowd. All the police came … and listened to "Voluntary Poverty and Non-Resistance".'[232] In fact, it seems that they enjoyed it immensely when Gandhi noted that even though he believed in voluntary poverty he still had his loincloth, and while he had a body he had to wrap it in something. However, he added with a beaming smile that 'if anyone wants to take it off me, he can have it. I shan't call in the police.' The eighteen police that the government provided to guard him 'burst into a roar of laughter as he turned to look at them, and the whole audience followed suit.'[233] A collection was taken up and donated to Gandhi, who in turn gave it to Royden to use for work with the unemployed.[234]

On 15 October, Gandhi addressed a student meeting held at the International Students' Movement House in Russell Square. In answer to a question about the place of the police and the army in a state founded on his philosophy of nonviolence, Gandhi replied: 'I do not regard it as Utopian to think of a state without an army, but it requires a higher degree of courage and purity.' Gandhi claimed that he could 'ask people to pit non-violence against hordes of an army.'[235]

A few days before the Guildhouse meeting, on 18-19 September, across the world, Japan accused China of blowing up a Manchurian railway line over which it had treaty rights. This 'Mukden Incident' was followed by the Japanese seizure of the city of Mukden and an invasion of Manchuria. The very day before the Guildhouse meeting, China appealed to the

League of Nations against Japanese aggression. Military occupation of the region was completed rapidly and on 18 February 1932, Japan established the puppet state of Manchukno.

In a Guildhouse sermon, shortly after the Japanese invasion, Royden proclaimed: 'I would like now to enrol people who would be ready if war should break out to put their bodies unarmed between the contending forces, in whatever way it be found possible – and there are ways that you do not think of now in which it would be possible.'[236]

Although they did not spend too much time together, there was a degree of mutual admiration between the two. At the time Royden was planning her peace army, Gandhi, back in India and incarcerated in Yeravda Central Gaol in Poona, wrote to his women followers back at his ashram about her virtues:

> DEAR SISTERS,
> I wish to write to you today about a lady. Her name is Maude Royden. She is an old woman. She has remained unmarried. She was the first woman in England to obtain the highest degree in theology. Besides her, there has been only one other woman who has obtained that degree. I am saying this not to show that theology is a very difficult subject, though it certainly is that. My point is that few women have been attracted to it. It does not help one to acquire status or importance in the world. Not only has Maude Royden studied the subject so deeply, but she has also dedicated her life to the service of the poor. Like Miss Muriel, she too makes no distinction between whites and non-whites. Through her own efforts she got a church built, which gives shelter to the poor and in which they hold their meetings. These services have brought the lady great honour. People valued her learning very little, but her services to the poor have made the lady very famous. She is also a powerful speaker, and in her character she is above all reproach. She relies on herself in all her activities and does not regard herself a weak and helpless woman. She has travelled widely and gathered much experience. Perhaps she may even come here to help us in our work. The main question before her will be whether she can be free from her present work.[237]

Royden in turn was to keep Gandhi informed of the developments concerning the 'Peace Army' she tried to establish. Royden explained in a sermon that the idea of interposing unarmed volunteers between combatants had been around 'for many years', and that after the First World War 'we began to look over past records, and found many traces of this idea'. Now Guildhouse members had 'even enrolled a little band of people who have declared themselves willing to put their bodies between the opposing forces if and in what way may be found possible'.[238] Just before Christmas 1931, Royden 'conducted a service of consecration' for 'a small band of people … who had formed a group to study constructive ways of peacemaking' and to 'seek to establish the way of Christ as the basis of civilisation.'[239] This led to the establishment of the 'Peace Army'.

Whether this idea, the first of many peace army experiments,[240] was originally Royden's or the Mahatma's is not ultimately resolvable; however, given that Royden was talking about this soon after the First World War when Gandhi was not long past trying to recruit soldiers,[241] it is likely that Gandhi acquired the idea from her. In any case, the fact that both of them were talking about this groundbreaking idea, at around the same time, says much about the fruitfulness of their relationship.



The idea of the Peace Army received little publicity until the last week of February 1932, when, following renewed Japanese aggression, Maude Royden met with Sheppard and another close friend, Dr Herbert Gray (a Scottish minister and one of the directors of Muriel Lester's Kingsley Hall), and formulated a concrete proposal. The three of them, in Royden's words, 'went into retreat for a few days to ask the guidance of God on our actions with regard to the Sino-Japanese War. We longed for the League of Nations to keep its pledged word to nations attacked, but realized that, if this meant the sending of armed forces, we should fall into the old error of combating war by war'.[242]

The result of this meeting was their famous letter which appeared in the London *Daily Express* on 25 February 1932. The letter urged that 'men and women who believed it to be their duty should volunteer to place themselves between the combatants. … We have written to the League of Nations offering ourselves for service in such a Peace Army.' The Army, to be under Sheppard's leadership, was to act as a human barrier between the combatant parties and thus end the fighting. Royden explained that what they wanted was 'an army of pacifists who should offer themselves to the League of Nations as the 'shock troops' of peace.'[243]

The press generated by the appeal was enormous. Because of the inspirational nature of the call, it gripped the public imagination. However, the Peace Army was never put to the test. Royden, Sheppard and Gray sent their letter to Sir Eric Drummond, the Secretary-General of the League of Nations, with the entreaty that he should not regard the plan as 'fantastic'. Drummond replied that he did not at all consider the idea as fantastic but regretted that it was not in his constitutional power to bring the proposal before the League's Assembly. By way of consolation he, at least tacitly, encouraged them to try to bring the proposal before the Assembly, which was at that time in session, through the formal demand of one of the member states, and released the letter to the representatives of the world's press, ensuring international publicity.

In her correspondences with Gandhi, Royden included copies of her exchanges with Drummond, and sought the Mahatma's blessing for the project which now relegated the India question to the background because of the extreme urgency of the China/Japan situation. Gandhi gave his approval to the action stating: 'I ... felt that you were quite right in concentrating your energy over a situation that threatened to involve bloodshed on a vast scale and that too by the adoption of the method of satyagraha'.[244]

Meanwhile, volunteers enrolled themselves for service in the Peace Army. However, even with the worldwide publicity, the 'army' received barely one thousand recruits. The organisers approached Sir John Simon, Secretary of State for Foreign Affairs and head of the British Delegation to the League, and the leaders of several governments represented at the Assembly with their plan, but with so small a number of volunteers they 'could not expect the League to take us seriously', and they received only 'courteous refusals or silence'.[245]

Royden later lamented that: 'Perhaps we should have sought to go alone. Perhaps three pacifists being killed in a manner so much in the spirit of Mahatma Gandhi might have worked a miracle.'[246] That, however, was not the initial plan and an operation on the scale they envisaged was impossible to undertake on a voluntary basis. Government support was necessary for ships and finance. Without government help, the plan faded. 'While we were writing to Prime Ministers and Foreign Secretaries and awaiting replies,' Royden recalled, 'the opportunity was lost. Fighting spread over a vast front. Our project became impracticable.' And, she added, 'It seems in the highest degree unlikely that it will ever be practicable again'.[247]

Gandhi maintained his contact with Royden after he left England, and she visited him in Delhi on 11 January 1935, when she was in India to attend the All-India Women's Conference. The following year she resigned from the Guildhouse, explaining, 'My reason is that I find the work of the Guildhouse and the work that I do for Peace outside the Guildhouse too much for my strength. … I have to choose; and in the present circumstances of this distracted world I feel that it is the Peace work to which I must give myself.'[248]

On the eve of the Second World War, Royden commented on the strangeness of the fact that the 'best Christian in the world to-day is a Hindu.'[249] She eagerly awaited copies of Gandhi's weekly paper *Harijan*, which to her were 'like a drink of pure water in a hot and thirsty land.' She wondered whether the West's belief in force 'may succeed in undermining the Mahatma's influence with his own countrymen and convince them that force alone can meet force.'[250] However, when Britain became engulfed in the war with Nazi Germany, Royden came to the realisation that Nazism was even worse than war: 'it is more hideously cruel, more blind, more evil – and more important. I am still a pacifist in that I believe … that spiritual power is the right weapon. … The tragedy of pacifism is that it has left the great mass of the unconverted under the impression that the use of spiritual power is simply "doing nothing"'.[251]



She could no longer maintain her pacifism, and Gandhi used her recantation as the basis for sermonising. For his task he quoted an article by her in the December 1941 issue of *The Survey Graphic*. He noted that although she is one of the foremost pacifists of the West, 'Like many she has felt compelled to revise her position and is now most reluctantly but fully ranged on the side of the defenders of the British Isles.' In a 'concluding portion of a touchingly sorrowful article' Royden had written:

> I am a pacifist still in one sense; that is to say, I realize that Christians should be able to meet material force with spiritual power. It is horrifying to reflect that after nineteen hundred years, we are still unable to do it except in individual cases and on a small scale. But to me it seems merely "wishful thinking" to act as though we had a power which in fact we have not and for which we have neither trained nor disciplined ourselves in the past. Such power does not come to those who have not disciplined themselves, at the last moment, in the hour of need. It has not come to us. I would rather, therefore, do what I can in defence of principles which I believe to be both right in themselves and of enormous importance to the

future of the human race, than stand aside and do nothing. It is *doing nothing* that is the worst expedient of all.

When, therefore, my pacifist friends ask me whether I can imagine Jesus Christ dropping a bomb or firing a gun I am entitled to reply: "No, I cannot; but neither can I imagine him standing aside and doing nothing at all."

I am compelled to echo the words of a very dear relative of mine who, loathing war as much as any pacifist that ever breathed, said to me at the beginning of the last war (in which he lost his life): "If you can stop war with spiritual power, do it. If you can't, let me do what I can; and if you are right in thinking that war is so damnable that anyone who takes part in it is damned, then I would rather be damned than let these things go on without doing all I can to stop them, even at the cost of my own life."

Is this not very close to the meaning of our Lord when he said: "He that loseth his life shall save it"?

Gandhi stated that the article demanded a considered reply. He was obviously saddened by Royden's change of heart, noting that

There is no cause whatsoever for despondency, much less for denial of one's faith at the crucial moment. Why should not British pacifists stand aside and remodel their life in its entirety? They might be unable to bring about peace outright, but they would lay a solid foundation for it and give the surest test of their faith. When, in the face of an upheaval such as we are witnessing, there are only a few individuals of immovable faith, they have to live up to their faith even though they may produce no visible effect on the course of events. They should believe that their action will produce tangible results in due course. Their staunchness is bound to attract sceptics. I would also suggest that individuals like Dr Maude Royden are not mere camp-followers. They are leaders. Therefore, they have to live their lives in strict accord with the Sermon on the Mount, and they will find immediately that there is much to give up and much to remodel. …

The advice that Dr Royden's relative gave her and which she quotes approvingly is altogether wrong. If the war is damnable, how can he stop the things that go on by taking part in it, even though it may be on the defensive side and at the cost of his own life? For the defence has to resort to all the damnable things that the enemy does, and that with greater vigour if it has to succeed. Such a giving of life is not only not saving it but a mere waste. I have attended the Doctor's services in her Church where a living belief in the efficacy of prayer is much in vogue. When the impenetrable gloom surrounded her, why did she not find strength and consolation and real action in heart-prayer? It is never too late to mend. She and her fellow-pacifists, many of whom I have the privilege of knowing, should take heart and, like Peter, repent of the momentary loss of faith and return to the old faith in non-violence with renewed vigour. Their return will mean no material loss to the war effort but will mean a great deal to the anti-war effort which is bound to succeed sooner rather than later, if man is to live as man and not become a two-footed brute.[252]



Gandhi, who had supported the British war effort in the previous, far less morally-based, World War, was of course not in London being bombed, and many still see his request to the British to surrender and offer nonviolent resistance to the occupying Germans[253] as something not far short of lunacy. Royden was desperate to act on her pacifist principles but could not see what she could do. She was offered a right of reply by Agatha Harrison, but Royden felt that she had 'no heart to do so, and no right' because she realised that pacifism was a weapon that, unlike Gandhi, she could not use because, as a friend had told her, 'You Pacifists are trying to use a weapon you haven't got.'[254] Towards the end of the war, in an interview with *Collier's Weekly*, Gandhi was asked by the reporter Ralph Coniston whether he wouldn't go to the West 'to teach them the art of peace.' He replied that Dick Sheppard and Maude Royden had written to him at the height of the war 'asking me to point the way'. He said that the answer he gave them then 'would be the same today':

My reply in substance was: Even if one of you can become true in the right sense of the word, that one man will be able to inculcate non-violence among the European folk. I cannot today save Europe, however much I may like to. I know Europe and America. If I go there I shall be like a stranger. Probably I shall be lionized but that is all. I shall not be able to present to them the science of peace in

> language they can understand. But they will understand if I can make good my non-violence in India. I shall then speak through India.[255]

Gandhi was asking Royden and her friends to stay true and work for pacifism in Europe. In the end, through her lack of the weapon he thought she had and she seemed to have lost, it was left to India to lead the way. And in the end, as Royden may have failed him, India, by becoming just another country in regard to its attitude to defence policy, may from his perspective have failed the world. Nevertheless, through the fruitful relationship of Royden and Gandhi, the idea and practice of peace armies continues to progress.

# Ellen Hørup: Gandhi as Beacon

Ellen Hørup was born on the last day of 1871. Her father Viggo was the anti-militarist founder of the Copenhagen daily newspaper *Politiken*. It is probably not surprising that she grew up to be a radical anti-fascist journalist, feminist and pacifist.[256] The income she received from her shares in her father's paper made her economically independent, allowing her to pursue the causes that interested her. There was already a Danish connection with Gandhi through members and ex-members of the Danish Mission Society and she developed an interest in Gandhi in the mid-1920s while she was living in Rome. In January 1929 Hørup and the famous Danish artist Cathinca Olsen visited Gandhi with a letter of introduction from Esther Færing. Anne Marie Petersen thought that a visit to Gandhi would be important to them because Katherine Mayo's salacious book *Mother India* had influenced their view of women in India and because they 'are not believers in God and it may be a real blessing for them to stay in your ashram with you for some time.'[257] They stayed with him for over a week at his Sabarmati Ashram and took their meals communally with the rest of the ashramites.[258] Following the trip, a friend from Copenhagen had reported to Hørup on a talk by Esther Færing about Gandhi and his ashram. In May, Hørup wrote to Gandhi explaining that 'I had the impression from what she said that it is possible to be a member without living there. If it is so, I should like to know the conditions.' Along with the letter she sent Gandhi a picture of Saint Francis preaching to the birds, a copy of her paper with her published article on India and a draft of a second, about to be published article, titled 'Mahatma Gandhi and his ashram'.[259]

Two years later she was back in India for the four months between November 1930 and April 1931 with Norwegian barrister Carl Vett, and the celebrated Norwegian singer and actress Caroline (Bokkan) Lasson. They met Gandhi at a prayer meeting following the death of Motilal Nehru in Allahabad in February 1931. The Mahatma was at the Nehrus' residence, Anand Bhavan, to be with the terminally ill Motilal, the nationalist stalwart, and father of free India's first prime minister Jawaharlal Nehru. Gandhi remembered Hørup's previous visit to Sabarmati well in their discussion, but although she went to many of his prayer meetings they did not have much time together, Hørup noting that she felt that she has no right to take more of his time.[260] During the trip she also visited the missionary school of her fellow, Dane Anne Marie Petersen, at Porto Novo, and while there adopted four boys.

An American lawyer, Edward Holton James, was also present with the Scandinavians at Allahabad. Later he recalled that the two Scandinavian women 'were heroically wearing Gandhi buttons, and later in Bombay and Karachi the Young Women's Christian Association refused to take them in because they were wearing those buttons.'[261] The three of them agreed that James should catch up with Gandhi in Delhi, where the Mahatma was headed to discuss with the Viceroy the ending of the Civil Disobedience campaign that had been launched by his Salt March almost a year before. He was to ask if Gandhi would give them a mandate to form a committee of well-connected and impartial people to investigate alleged excesses in police behaviour during the struggle. Gandhi was in favour of the committee; however, in the course of reaching his struggle-ending agreement with Lord Irwin, the Viceroy pointed out that, even if such excesses existed, he could do nothing about them without damaging police morale. And this was something which he could not afford to do while the threat of a resumption of the campaign was still in the air, a reason which Gandhi accepted.[262]

Later that year, Hørup published a book about this India trip under the title *Gandhis Indien*.[263] About the time the book appeared, while Gandhi was in London for the Round Table Conference, Hørup and Olsen called in on him for an early morning prayer at Kingsley Hall and ended up sleeping in his room.[264]

By this time Hørup was active in her support of Gandhi and India's freedom struggle. In October 1930 she had set up the Danish *Indiens Venner* (Friends of India) society. Two years later, she established the International Committee for India in Geneva, and in 1933 the Committee published a monthly magazine, *Indian Press*, devoted to Gandhi and the Indian liberation struggle.[265] Hørup worked in Geneva between 1933 and 1939 as a foreign correspondent and as an editor of *Politiken* covering news from the League of Nations.[266] She also immersed herself in work as a peace activist and supporter of political refugees. Soon after settling in Geneva, on 7 October 1932, she became involved in the organisation of the first of three international conferences in support of Indian freedom under the auspices of the International Committee, and in the publication of the journal *Indians Venner*, which came out between November 1930 and November 1938.



The second conference was held on 23 March 1933. On the day Hørup decided on the date, she received a letter from Gandhi and could not resist writing to him. In poetic terms she explained what he meant to her:

> I don't know if you ever have been up in the mountains, walking an entire day without meeting a living creature. Up there, the skies and the hills meet in the horizon, and the silence together with the great emptiness brings one closer to eternity. It was in Norway I walked in the mountains, and ever since then, I think of you as my "*varde*". A *varde* is a heap of stones set up as a landmark. The stones are roughly laid upon each other to point you to the right way up in the mountains where there are no roads or path you can follow – not even traces of human feet.
>
> All the "*vardes*" have been built by travellers. They have put stone upon stone to make them high so that they can be seen from afar. It is on the right path that the world's great travel. And to help their fellow human beings, from getting lost, or falling into hidden abysses, they have heaped stone upon stone to show them the way.

> To me, you are such a "*varde*", built by the great of humanity. You are high enough to be seen by the whole world, and I always have my eyes on you. You are the "*varde*" leading me to the right path.
>
> Thus, I don't need to bother you often with letters. But today, when your voice sounded in my ears like the violinist in yours,[267] I had to write.
>
> I try the best I can to follow the path which my "*varde*" gives me, and I thank Fate for making it so high that even I ... [268]

Gandhi replied that 'The knowledge that I am a guiding *varde* to some friends humbles me and makes me more and more conscious of the tremendous burden that I carry on my shoulders. I have to watch myself and incessantly pray to the God of Truth that I may not prove a false guide to anybody.'[269]

The Women's International League for Peace and Freedom's Danish chapter published a magazine called *Fred og Frihed* (Peace and Freedom). In its July-August edition of 1937, the report of the minutes of the organisation noted that they supported Gandhi's candidature for the Nobel Peace Prize. In the magazine's previous issue, Hørup had penned an article titled 'Gandhi and the Nobel Peace Prize' where she noted that the Norwegian chapter of Indiens Venner (established and headed by Lasson) had nominated Gandhi for the Peace Prize.[270] She wrote to two leading and internationally known Gandhi promoters, the French writer and pacifist Romain Rolland and the English minister Charles Freer Andrews, for their support for the nomination. Lasson is reported to have announced that the society would not give in 'until Gandhi received the Prize'.[271]

Hørup understood how busy Gandhi was and did not press herself upon him in person when they were together, and this attitude also ensured that there was only a sparse correspondence between them. As time wore on she drifted from Gandhi, putting more of her energy into the plight of women and peasants in India. In an address to the Danish Friends of India Society, on 23 November 1936, on her relationship with Gandhi, she noted that,

> His ideas, my admiration for him, the longing to meet the man who gave me what I have been seeking all my life – something which together is called devotion, reverence and love – was what led me twice to India. I wanted to see Gandhi, and I wanted to see the 350 million meek Hindus who follow him. While in India, I sought out

only him and his followers. … I identified India with Gandhi. And Gandhi meant, to me, the apostle who would bring, not to only India but to the entire world, the gospel of the future – the abolishing of violence from mankind.

And he still does.

But as the years have passed and after I have been to London attending the Round Table Conference, India now means more than Gandhi to me.

And I have become wiser from reading and from meeting many people from Gandhi's country, and I have learned that there are different movements in India just as there are in any country. And I have drifted from Gandhi in many ways. I follow him on his journey among the peasants and in the cities among the workers. I read what he says about the women, and what he says to them when they ask for advice. Gandhi admires them highly. He has called them out from their isolation, freed them from the purdahs. But Gandhi still has the mind of a man, and besides that, the mind of a Hindu.[272]



Interestingly, here is an admirer and strong supporter of Gandhi slowly distancing herself from him because his feminist credentials no longer seem adequate to her. She may have seen Gandhi as a moral *varde* after meeting him, and she was certainly no apologist for the oft-cited British civilising influence on a barbaric country (in fact her life shows her as being an extremely fervent supporter of Indian independence) but she was not cured of what Anne Marie Petersen saw as Katherine Mayo's influence on her view of women in India. She also criticised Gandhi's anti-untouchability programme, noting that 'the untouchable is a by-product of the caste system, and Gandhi fights for the untouchable but wishes to keep the caste system.'[273] Terp observes that she was one of the few of Gandhi's Scandinavian friends who dared to voice criticism of him.[274] The Gandhi supporter had become an India supporter. Following India's independence, Ellen Hørup became a board member of the Danish-India Friendship Union, founded in 1948.

Gravely ill, she died in 1953 at the age of eighty-one while dictating her last article – a protest against the Korean War.

# Conclusion: Agreements and Disagreements

Ada West and Sonja Schlesin would quite likely not be known outside a very narrow circle if it had not been for their connection to Gandhi. This is certainly not true for the others discussed in this chapter. Emily Hobhouse, Olive Schreiner, Annie Besant, Muriel Lester, Agatha Harrison, Maude Royden and Ellen Hørup were notable international actors in their right. While it is the particular aspect examined here, it should be remembered that their relationships with the Mahatma are only part of their stories, and in most cases not even the largest part.

Not only did Gandhi attract those engaged in social work and feminists (women who were generally well ahead of their time, and often well ahead of him, in proclaiming the rights of women – note how some of them were advocating ordination for women almost a century ago), but not surprisingly, most were also staunch pacifists, often more consistent in their positions than he was. Olive Schreiner and Annie Besant were appalled at his overt support for the British war effort during World War I. However, as his pacifism firmed and he preached nonviolence from afar, some like Maude Royden and Agatha Harrison were to question the, by then, seemingly total pacifism that he was teaching from India as bombs were raining down on them in London.

It is interesting to note how often Gandhi's Western women friends made contact through Gandhi and formed friendships with each other. Maude Royden, Muriel Lester and Agatha Harrison were friends and they knew the Polaks. Often Gandhi's letters to one would include greetings for another, and often Gandhi's Western friends met when an India-based one of the circle visited Europe, or more often when a Europe-based one visited India. This may be quite understandable because of their mutual regard for Gandhi, but it is also of no surprise given the often very similar backgrounds of the women: generally upper class, well educated, from religious backgrounds, unmarried, and with well-developed social consciences.

In the early days, before mahatmaship, and even before Gandhi became a leading political figure in South Africa, Sonja Schlesin was something of a daughter figure and Millie Graham Polak a sister. His later women supporters were influential women in their own right and thus were useful to Gandhi's cause at reasonably high political levels. Except for Royden who was married only very briefly, Besant, who married and then divorced relatively early in life, and Schreiner, they remained unmarried, their energies were directed towards the causes that dominated their lives: local injustice, anti-colonialism, pacifism and feminism. Most worked for the poor, not by way of upper-class charity, but by throwing their lot in with those they worked with, living simple lives that were not the usual expectation of those born to their class. Perhaps to some degree at least Eleanor Morton was right when she commented on the way Gandhi must have perceived Schreiner. Gandhi admired strong-willed women, those that had minds of their own, even when they did not always agree with him. And of course he admired dedication to causes, the larger picture, rather than dedication merely to him as a person. This was something that was to become more of an issue with those who went to see him in India and stayed, needing his physical presence for lengthy periods as disciples and part of his ashram family. There was also another group of women who, while not necessarily dedicated to either him personally or specifically to his cause, helped to define him to a Western audience.

# III

# Western Women Interpreters

## Constructing an Image

Early in his emerging political career, Gandhi was not averse to positive publicity. Some relatively recent works show that, in South Africa, a politically ambitious Gandhi actively pushed his way to leadership positions[1] in a manner that is not reflected in either his *Autobiography* or *Satyagraha in South Africa*; that the first biography of his life, the one by his friend the Reverend Joseph Doke, seems to have been more or less dictated by Gandhi to the writer, and it was Gandhi himself who arranged for its publication.[2] As time went on, the attention he received could become a source of frustration and not all the attention resulted in positive interpretations of the Mahatma.

During his post-South Africa India days, Gandhi was interviewed countless times, probably several times a day on average. It seems that almost everyone who had the opportunity wanted his *darshan* (being in the presence of a holy person, from which the viewer gains merit) and, especially in the case of those from overseas, to exchange words with him. Many of these encounters were brief and inconsequential, not even registering in the notes of Gandhi's secretaries. Often, however, even these brief encounters made it into the pages of books written by those who had been in the Mahatma's presence. These books helped to shape his image in the West and several of the most influential ones were written by Western women.

# Interviewers and Gandhi's Image in the West

Patricia Kendall was one of this multitude of interviewer writers. Gandhi apparently spoke briefly to her in one of the busiest times of his life (although her descriptions of the event seem in part to echo the descriptions in Mayo's book of a few years before a little too closely for comfort, and the recorded spoken words of Gandhi are conveniently similar to his written ones). She used the interview to aid her construction of Gandhi as a dangerous reactionary in her sensationalist book on the horrors of India.

Katherine Mayo had also written about the horrors of India; however she had attempted to use Gandhi to back her case that British rule was needed as a civilising agent. Mayo's book *Mother India* was a sensation, and for years to come set the tone for the understanding of the misery that was India. The book was more about India than Gandhi, with the Mahatma appearing as something of an out of touch reactionary, but one who generally cared about and pointed out the social problems and inequalities of the country.

Margaret Sanger, the champion of birth control as a means of liberating women, also had a lengthy and important interview with Gandhi. She was no mere *darshan* seeker; she was trying to get Gandhi's support for her cause. The interview took on the tone of a vigorous and frank debate on the meaning of human sexuality. She was not in awe of Gandhi and kept pushing him to clarify his position, to maintain consistency. The interview helps us to better understand Gandhi and some of what seem to be his stranger quirks, and history and modern psychology would have to judge that in this case it was Sanger who was taking the more realistic and healthy position.

The photojournalist Margaret Bourke-White gave the world a very different image of Gandhi and India. Gandhi had become something of an established international saint and British rule was fading into the past as she was reporting. Her India certainly had serious problems, but was also full of hope and promise. Her Gandhi may have been a little confusing in his attitude to modern technology in a country that needed all the help it could get, but he came across as a genuine spiritual beacon. The major interview she had with Gandhi, probably the last of his life, produced a classic and oft-quoted passage of Gandhiania. The aging Mahatma attempted to show that even in a terrible age overshadowed by the atomic bomb, nonviolence of the pure at heart can, and surely will, triumph. Her photographs of Gandhi in his last years have helped to construct the image many in the West still hold of Gandhi: the great man in a loincloth at his spinning wheel radiating a simple goodness.

# Katherine Mayo: The Drain Inspector

Born in Ridgeway, Pennsylvania in 1867, Katherine Mayo was educated in private schools and as a twenty-two year old went with her gold-seeking, mining engineer father to Dutch Guiana (Surinam) for eight years.[3] She had her first article published in 1894 and, following the time in Guiana, she returned to New York to pursue a life of research and writing. She characterised her journalistic career as a 'contribution of good citizenship' by 'a volunteer spokesman for the voiceless underdog'.[4] She worked on law and order and police issues in New York in 1917; however, she is best remembered for her books on little-known social evils such as those concerning the US administration of the Philippines (*Isles of Fear*, 1925), and especially an indictment of Indian customs such as child marriage in her landmark book, *Mother India*. Her book on the Philippines was against the early granting of independence to the country because of the sexual exploitation of women that would then be uncontrolled. Her critique was greatly appreciated by the American authorities.[5] This was a precedent for what would follow in India.

Where her seemingly long-held concern with the oppression and sexual exploitation of women, with racial discrimination, and with issues of law and order originally stemmed from is not quite clear. Perhaps things the never-married Mayo saw in the male-dominated mining towns of South America had left a deep and unfavourable impression on her, and she was not impressed by her observations of indentured Indian labourers in the colonies.[6] In any case, it seems that she held a firm belief in the beneficial role of Anglo-US imperialism that would 'keep at bay the demands of various "natives" and their liberal sympathisers for the devolution of greater political responsibility into the hands of the indigenous peoples themselves'.[7]

Gandhi knew that Americans had mixed feelings about India as a land of spirituality or a land of dirt and social evils. He wanted them to study the situation in India carefully so that they would be supportive of the independence movement.[8] Because he was not forewarned of her deep-held prejudices, Mayo seems almost to have come in answer to this call.[9] She spent three months over the winter of 1925-26 in India researching her book. In answer to a letter from her, on 4 March 1926, Gandhi replied to Katherine Mayo that '17th March will be a suitable day for me to receive you at 4 p.m.' at the ashram at Sabarmati.[10]

Mayo insisted that she was going to India to write an impartial study of the country for Americans; after all 'what does the average American actually know about India? That Mr Gandhi lives there; also tigers. ... It was dissatisfaction with this status that sent me to India, to see what a volunteer unsubsidised, uncommitted, and unattached, could observe of common things in daily human life'.[11] Gandhi was happy to oblige, and was obviously pleased with the interview, addressing letters to her as 'Dear Friend', as he corrected drafts and sent additional information.[12] In the interview, Gandhi spelled out his message to America as simply the hum of his spinning wheel, and what it means for the hungry millions in the country, and how the roots of that poverty lie in colonialism. He also strongly criticised untouchability.[13]

A year after the interview, Katherine Mayo's book, *Mother India*, appeared. In it, Mayo championed the British presence in India not only for political or economic stability but also, and particularly, because of what she saw as Hindu social customs resulting in the sexual abuses that stemmed from the practice of child marriage. In short, India was not ready for independence because of a basic deficiency in, particularly, Hindu culture. The book opens with a graphic account of animal sacrifice at the temple of Kali in Calcutta. From there it covers filth, disease (of such an extent, Mayo claimed, that if it became known civilised nations would demand protection from India through the League of Nations), sex, disadvantage and illiteracy, mostly as it affected girls and women, heartless caste practices, the mistreatment of cows, untouchability, Hindu-Muslim enmity, and, of course, woven through the narrative, Gandhi.

The book was published in May 1927 in the US and two months later in Britain. It was a sensation from the moment it appeared. In America the book went through twenty-seven editions by 1958, selling a total of almost 400,000 copies by the mid-1950s, becoming the most popular book on India in the first half of the last century.[14] In its first six months, the British publication went through eight impressions. One critic called it 'the great standard pornographic book on India'.[15]

Many, including most Indians, were convinced that the purpose of the book was not only to slander India and bolster support for British imperialism, but also to discredit Gandhi. Mayo was undeniably an Anglophile and it appears that most of her primary informants were British. The book certainly pleased the British, being not only a vindication of their presence, but also a vehicle to shift discussions of India from the issues of nationalism to those of social problems, the exact opposite direction Gandhi had hoped that American friends would move their thinking about the country. *Mother India* argued that the backwardness of the country was not the result of economic or political causes (for which the British could be held at least partially responsible), but resulted from religious and cultural ones embedded in the very nature of Hinduism.

Gandhi's feisty South African colleague, Sonja Schlesin had mixed feelings about the book and about Gandhi's reaction to it. In her assessment of *Mother India*, Schlesin believed that while Mayo's intentions may have been good, that is to prompt reform, she managed to come to the wrong conclusions, which 'are absurd' and 'not justified by the contents'. She added that the conclusion should have been the preface, because in it she gives a picture of only part of India. Schlesin also noted that it was Mayo's manner, rather than her facts, which were wrong. Although critical of the book, she was not totally in favour of Gandhi's response to it, noting that as a 'passive resister' she had to question his labeling of the author as a 'drain inspector' because it was less than constructive.[16]

The book naturally spawned many rejoinders, some wanting to out-Mayo Mayo by pointing to social problems in the West, others attempting to take a more dispassionate look at the country and its problems, or lauding India as a spiritual lighthouse in contrast to the materialistic West. None of them had anywhere near the impact of the book they sought to debunk.

Some claim that the role of the references to Gandhi in *Mother India* was to demonstrate that the Mahatma was a sham, and, worse, by taking him out of context making him a party to Mayo's attacks on India.[17] There certainly is a tension here – Gandhi was clearly against most of the practices she herself railed against (child marriage, prohibition on widow remarriage, the seclusion of women, untouchability etc.) and she used him liberally as a source. Therefore, he could not dismiss the book out of hand. Neither could he ignore it. Some time after going through the text, although 'I really get little time to read any literature', he wrote to her that, 'I am sorry to have to inform you that the book did not leave on my mind at all a nice impression', and arranged for a copy of his review to be sent to her.[18]

Gandhi's review was titled 'Drain Inspector's Report'. In it he noted four instances where Mayo had told untruths about him. They present a somewhat strange line of attack in that they cover trifling matters: whether he always or sometimes had two secretaries, about the reasons for Gandhi's request for Western surgery to remove his appendix, about the popularity of the visit of the Prince of Wales to India in 1921, and questions about his message to America in his interview with Mayo. Even though the passages Gandhi disputes do not appear to be of first rate importance, it is not entirely clear that she was completely wrong in her interpretations.[19] And most of the customs she abhorred, he, likewise, had long battled against. The real problems with the book lay elsewhere. It impugned Hinduism which Gandhi celebrated while trying to eradicate its blemishes. It championed British colonialism which Gandhi was attempting to dismantle. Whatever truths there may have been in the book, it had slandered his people. His review was angry, but it was also ambiguous. It leaves the impression that it was a difficult document for him to write. In it he notes:

> The book is cleverly and powerfully written. The carefully chosen quotations give it the appearance of a truthful book.[20] But the

impression it leaves on my mind is, that it is the report of a drain inspector sent out with the one purpose of opening and examining the drains of the country to be reported upon, or to give a graphic description of the stench exuded by the opened drains. If Miss Mayo had confessed that she had gone to India merely to open out and examine the drains of India, there would perhaps be little to complain about her compilation. But she says in effect with a certain amount of triumph, "The drains are India". … Her case is to perpetuate white domination in India on the plea of India's unfitness to rule herself. … Whilst I consider the book to be unfit to be placed before Americans and Englishmen (for it can do no good to them), it is a book that every Indian can read with some degree of profit. We may repudiate the charge as it has been named by her, but we may not repudiate the substance underlying the many allegations she has made. It is a good thing to see ourselves as others see us. We need not even examine the motive with which the book is written. A cautious reformer may make some use of it. … But let us not resent being made aware of the dark side of the picture wherever it exists. Overdrawn her pictures of our in-sanitation, child marriages, etc., undoubtedly are. But let them serve as a spur to much greater effort than we have hitherto put forth in order to rid society of all cause of reproach.[21]



And for Gandhi they did serve as such a spur – throughout his celebrated Salt March to Dandi to defy the British salt laws as a start to the Civil Disobedience movement of 1930, and later campaigns, the focus was not merely on an India free from the British, but a certain sort of India – one that was free from the blemishes pointed out in *Mother India*. Gandhi did not or could not dispute the reality of much of what she wrote and the amount of energy he spent on commenting on the book, even years later, shows an almost obsessive relationship with Katherine Mayo and *Mother India*.[22]

During the Civil Disobedience campaign, the American press could not resist the analogy between Gandhi's solemn manufacture of illicit salt and the famous Boston Tea Party.[23] Editorials, even in influential American papers, forecast that as Britain lost America through tea, she was about to lose India through salt. The tables were now turning. The British were worried by American press coverage and angered by American simplification of a complex issue (as not that long before Indians had been by Mayo) – and with good reason: the tempting analogies and the positive publicity following an adherence to nonviolence in the face of brutal British repression had given the nationalists the moral high ground *Mother India* had earlier accorded the British. According to Negley Farson, a US journalist who had witnessed British acts of brutality, they had 'rubbed out Mother India as easily as you clean a child's slate'.[24]

Mayo was undeniably an Anglophile and an Indophobe. She lacked tact or sympathy, was prone to generalisations, and may have been sex obsessed.[25] However, although there is strong evidence that her book was produced with the connivance of British authorities and that her express motive was to aid the British cause in India,[26] she managed to convince Gandhi's English clergyman friend C.F. Andrews[27] that she was sincere in penning her exposé and had not been employed to write the book for political purposes.[28] After a meeting with Mayo, Andrews came to the conclusion that she had undertaken her work 'independently without a conscious political motive' and without payment,[29] however, given her personality, what she wrote about India was 'bound to be a misinterpretation'.[30] Regardless of his friend's charitable conclusions, Gandhi certainly was not convinced that *Mother India* was merely a part of a life-long crusade for improving the status of women on Mayo's part. He commented that, 'I am not shaken in my opinion that the book bears in it patent evidence of a political bias. It contains falsehoods which the authoress must have known to be such. She has since written things which too are probably false. In the face of such patent facts, evidence to the contrary must be held to be irrelevant.'[31]

Katherine Mayo never repented for what she had written, as Gandhi hoped that she would. In fact, she published further volumes on the theme in later years (*Slaves of the Gods*, 1929; and *Volume Two*, 1931) that were so obviously propaganda pieces that even the British authorities felt the need to distance themselves from them.[32]

# Patricia Kendall: Out-Mayoing Mayo

The publicity blurb on Patricia Kendall's book, *Come With Me to India!*, spells out her agenda. It claims that the book is

> an authoritative elucidation of the racial, geographical, and religious history of seething India, as well as all that has happened, and is happening, under British rule. Unlike *Mother India*, this book is not confined to a few phases on Indian life.
>
> It comprises a startling re-examination of India's past and present and charges Mahatma Gandhi with opportunism and with fostering Hindu mysticism, which, the author shows, has by infanticide, child marriage, suttee, phallic worship, and caste made India degenerate.
>
> *Come with Me to India!* will definitely contribute to an understanding of what is going on in India to-day. Its essential thesis has had little consideration in this country: that the Nationalist movement in India is not the stir of a people united by some common danger or intolerable burden or all-consuming ideal – but is the revolt of

Hindu and Moslem against enlightened modern influences which threaten the extinction of a reactionary civilization.[33]

While Mayo merely dedicated her book to the people of India (and an unnamed labourer who saved her life[34]), Kendall dedicated her tome, which was sub-titled 'A Quest for Truth Among Peoples and Problems,' 'To India' because 'the Truth Can Make Her Free.' The English edition was titled *India and the British: A Quest for Truth*. The book is a journey around India woven through with a brutal history that serves to illustrate Kendall's understanding of what she sees as the superstition, degeneracy and general worthlessness of Hinduism, the bloodthirstiness of Islam, and the illiteracy of both. The leaders of the nationalist movement are characterised as self-seeking reactionaries or communists. As a consequence, 'Mohandas Gandhi and Jawaharlal Nehru cast an ominous shadow on the future progress of India.'[35] There is nothing equivocal here, the civilising mission of the British and Christian missionaries are the only hope for a depraved country. Gandhi is painted as a manipulating two-faced reactionary who wants to destroy the railways and preserve child marriages, who admonishes women who resist attacks because this goes against nonviolence, while asking others to resist the British in their attempts to confiscate illegally gained salt until 'blood is spilt'.[36]



Sometime in the first half of March 1930, Kendall had a brief interview with Gandhi. This, just before Gandhi set off on his celebrated Salt March to the seaside village of Dandi to break the salt laws and thus defy British control of India, was one of the most hectic times of his life. The Kendall visit does not seem to have made any impression on him, and neither she nor her book feature in his writings.

Her description of Gandhi says much about her attitude – she described him as having the 'eyes of a strategist; the nose of a dictator; the mouth of a monologist.'[37] The interview, which is strangely not recorded by the two Hindu secretaries 'taking down every word that falls from his lips',[38] does not have the feel of Gandhi's words;[39] and, unlike Mayo, Kendall is not concerned with using those words to back her case of illustrating problems in India; Gandhi is simply a manifestation of those problems.

In Kendall's description of the interview, Gandhi announces that 'It is always delightful to talk to Americans,' before denouncing the child marriage restricting Sarda Bill (soon to come into force as the *Child Marriage Act*) and attempting to turn the conversation to the 'law of love' and the spinning wheel. Kendall does not let him off the hook and pushes the issue further. Gandhi conveniently responds in the 'precise words' that can be found in his writings, linking the Bill with sexual attacks on women in a very convoluted way. He announces that the Indians who recommended and supported the 'satanic Government's act' have 'not yet seen the light'. In contrast to the picture presented in *Come with Me to India!*, Gandhi certainly was against child-marriages and was broadly sympathetic with the Sarda Bill.[40]

Following her recounting of the interview, she presents a potted biography of Gandhi: he is an ingrate who does not mention the Inns of Court or London University in his autobiography's chapter 'Life in London'(although his book was about experiments in truth rather than a mere autobiographical litany), or offer 'a single suggestion of gratitude' for the honours of having lived in London and having received a British legal education. In India he develops into a manipulator with more spiritual prestige than any Messiah of any creed was able to exercise in his lifetime, and one who 'publicised himself as the saviour of the masses'.[41]

The section of the book dealing with Gandhi and recent Indian history loses much of its racy sensationalism. By way of countering nationalist arguments and bolstering the British position, Kendall reproduces out-of-context quotations from Gandhi, lengthy British reports of various disturbances and the types of medical enquiry reports that Mayo relied upon before her, as well as long extracts from anti-Gandhi writers.

Like Mayo, Kendall is another Anglophone American woman who sees the necessity of British rule to prevent India being invaded, prevent India tearing herself apart, or damaging the global economy through a seizure of banking, shipping and railways. For her, the granting of freedom to a country 'whose long history is one of autocratic régimes, where material conditions and mental habits are peculiarly unique, and whose peoples are inarticulate and illiterate' can only end in chaos.[42]

Unlike Mayo's *Mother India*, *Come with Me to India!* prompted no debate about whether the author was a proto-feminist who deeply cared about social issues or whether she was merely a British sycophant. Her journalism is unoriginal and contains little in the way of social crusading. As a writer, Patricia Kendall either has limited analytical skills, resulting in intellectual tunnel-vision, or is engaged on a disingenuous propaganda agenda, or both. For example, while discussing Gandhi's South African experiences, in a reference to problems faced by the 'black and brown', she blithely states that 'our own negroes' were discriminated against in America before the Civil War![43] And, while Gandhi's 'doctrines' appall her, Kendall sees the alternative as possibly worse: 'should Jawaharlal Nehru succeed him, as seems probable, the Communists would no doubt send forces to India as they did into China where they were "keeping the pot of revolution seething".'[44]

Kendall and *Come with Me to India!* seem to have aroused little by way of interest in the Indian or the Western press or consciousness the way that Mayo and *Mother India* did.[45] When Kendall's book was published in 1931, the Civil Disobedience campaign was the dominant news in India and the dominant news about India in the world press, and it was such ground-shaking news that it made apologist-for-the-British, sensationalist writings lose relevancy. Kendall was offering nothing new, and her timing was bad.

# Margaret Sanger: Examining Gandhi's Love and Lust

Margaret Sanger, the founder of the American birth control movement, and one of its international leaders, was born Margaret Higgins in 1879, the sixth of eleven children of a devout Irish Catholic mother who endured eighteen pregnancies in twenty-two years. She wanted to become a doctor but, because of the prohibitive cost of medical school, went on to study nursing instead. She married the socialist artist William Sanger in 1902 and worked with immigrants in the poorer sections of New York City. The tuberculosis-suffering Sanger had three children by 1910, but decided that she did not want to slip into the usual domesticity that was often the lot of wives and mothers. During nurse training, she came to realise the degree to which many women lived in fear of constant childbearing, and, as an obstetrical nurse in New York City, she discovered the relationship between poverty and uncontrolled fertility, and unwanted pregnancies and high death rates from botched illegal abortions. This led her to become a crusading feminist for women's rights, championing contraception to avoid unplanned pregnancies.

From 1911, she edited the *Birth Control Review* and began writing articles for Socialist newspapers and pamphlets on her passion. It was not long before her articles ran afoul of the strict obscenity laws of the day. In 1912, she became involved in socialist political agitation and in the following year she gave up nursing to devote herself full-time to the cause of birth control. In 1914 she founded her own paper, *The Woman Rebel*, but had to flee the country for London to avoid being charged with printing obscene material. Realising that the legal tide was moving in her favour, she returned to the United States in 1916 to face trial; however the charges against her were dropped. Sanger quickly opened the first, and hugely popular, American birth control clinic in Brooklyn. It was declared illegal and closed after only nine days. As a result, in 1917 she served thirty days in prison for maintaining a 'public nuisance'. Paradoxically, her harassment by legal and church authorities helped to popularise the birth control movement. Sanger founded the American Birth Control League (which eventually became the Planned Parenthood Federation of America) in 1921, and she organised the first World Population Conference in Geneva in 1927. She was divorced in 1920 and two years later married James Henry Noah Slee, a wealthy businessman.[46] She engaged in many legal battles against restrictive laws and in 1936, as a result of her bringing a test case, the U.S. Second Circuit Court ruled that doctors could finally prescribe birth control measures not only to prevent disease, but also for the more general well-being of their patients. In later years she was involved in backing the research that gave rise to the oral contraceptive pill. After several heart attacks, the severely ill Sanger died in 1966. Her life mission had been achieved the year before when the U.S. Supreme Court ruled that the use of contraception was a constitutional right.

In 1924 a birth control league was established in Bombay and the secretary wrote to Gandhi, seemingly to ask for his blessings as it would help the Indian population problem. Gandhi responded: 'I am totally opposed to artificial means of controlling the birth-rate, and it is not possible for me to congratulate you or your co-workers on having brought into being a League whose activities, if successful, can only do great moral injury to the people. I wish I could convince you and your co-workers to disband the League and devote your energy to a better purpose.'[47] Margaret Sanger entered the ensuing debate writing to Gandhi in protest. Gandhi replied that he was open to further education on the subject[48] and Sanger started planning a visit to India.

Something had always come in her way, and perhaps partly she was reluctant to go 'because Katherine Mayo's book had left me with such an aching pain I felt powerless to help life [sic] the inertia she described.'[49] However, over the winter of 1935-36, Sanger finally made it and toured India for almost ten weeks. She came following an invitation to speak at the All-India Women's Conference, which the previous year had passed a resolution favouring birth control and now wanted to draw up a practical programme of action. How could she refuse? Here was one of the poorest and most populous countries in the world, a country obviously in need of birth control, a country with a national saint who championed the rights of women, and one whose women were asking her for help. One of India's most famous sons, the Nobel Prize-winning author, and friend of Gandhi, Rabindranath Tagore had written to Sanger a decade before that her movement was 'a great movement'. He noted that, 'In a hunger-stricken country like India it is a cruel crime thoughtlessly to bring more children to existence than could be taken care of, causing endless suffering to them and imposing a degrading upon the whole family. ... I feel grateful for the cause you have made your own and for which you have suffered.'[50]

It seems that India was ready for her; by the time she completed her stay, she had travelled 10,000 miles, presided over more than forty public meetings and had established some fifty birth control information centres. And she was more than ready to take her crusade to the subcontinent and to its perceived moral leader. She had asked the Reverend John Haynes Holmes of New York, Gandhi's leading American supporter, to write to the Mahatma on her behalf requesting an interview. Gandhi's reply reached her on the ship before she disembarked at Bombay: 'Do by all means come whenever you can, and you shall stay with me, if you would not mind what must appear to you to be our extreme simplicity; we have no masters and no servants here.'[51]

Although originally expected to arrive on 26 November 1935, it was not until a week later that, after a bullock cart ride from Wardha railway station, Sanger arrived at Gandhi's headquarters on 2 December, a Monday, Gandhi's day of silence: 'Gandhi was cross-legged on the floor of a room ... He rose to greet me as I entered with an armful of books and flowers and magazines and gloves that I had not realized were there until we tried to take each other by both hands. He beamed and I laughed.'[52]

In her recollection, Gandhi seemed to have a 'luminous aura' around him, and once this had been seen his 'ugliness faded and you glimpsed the something in the essence of his being which people have followed and which has made them call him the Mahatma.' Knowing how influential Gandhi was, she was sure that his 'endorsement of birth control would be of tremendous value if I could convince him how necessary it was for Indian women.' Sanger decided to set herself 'to the task'.[53] The next day, after having accompanied Gandhi on his accustomed early morning walk, she was granted an interview at eleven and it continued till three o'clock.

A transcript of the interview was taken by Gandhi's secretary, Mahadev Desai. It was published in Gandhi's newspaper in an article by Desai. Sanger's assistant, Anna Jane Philips, also took a shorthand record of the interview. Needless to say, the two versions differ somewhat, but more in the order of discussion than the content.[54] Desai's narrative is mainly concerned with what the Mahatma said in a very frank and personal interview, into which he 'poured his whole being'. The Philips account places more emphasis on Sanger's contribution to the conversation.[55]



Margaret Sanger's diary notes that the arguments in the formal interview 'were along the same lines as in the morning', and she felt that 'his personal experience at the time of his father's death was so shocking and self-blamed that he can never accept sex as anything good, clean or wholesome.'[56] During the formal interview, she informed Gandhi that his influence was such that even 'the opposition at home often quotes you in opposing our legislative campaign for birth control', and admitted that her acceptance of the speaking engagement at the conference 'is really only a pretense to come and see you. The real reason I came is to see if we could not agree upon a fundamental principle and some practical means of helping the women of the world.'[57] Gandhi replied that he could not recommend the remedy of birth control to a woman who wanted his approval: 'I should simply say to her: My remedy is of no use to you. You must go to others for advice.' He was forced to admit that 'some great people in the world', including his friends Tagore and India's 'nightingale' the poetess Sarojini Naidu, agreed with her eloquently advocated cause, rather than with his views on the subject.

After Sanger had 'cited some hard cases', Gandhi agreed that they were problematic, and agreed that women should be emancipated and masters of their own destiny, but he did not agree with her solutions. He counselled celibacy:

> I have felt that during the years still left to me if I can drive home to women's minds the truth that they are free, we will have no birth-control problem in India. If they will only learn to say "no" to their husbands when they approach them carnally! I do not suppose all husbands are brutes and if women only know how to resist them, all will be well. I have been able to teach women who have come in contact with me how to resist their husbands. The real problem is that many do not want to resist them.

Not unexpectedly, Sanger raised the phantasmagoria of 'irritations, disputes, and thwarted longings that Gandhiji's advice would bring into the home', citing cases of 'great nervous and mental breakdowns as a result of the practice of self-control.' Gandhi countered that this would only be the case with 'imbeciles', not with 'healthy-minded people'. When Sanger insisted that his advice was not practical, that it would 'mean a revolution in the home' and lead to divorce because 'the average marriage contract assumes that intercourse and the married relationship shall be harmonious', Gandhi tried to draw a distinction between love and lust:

> When both want to satisfy animal passion without having to suffer the consequences of their act it is not love, it is lust. But if love is pure, it will transcend animal passion and will regulate itself. We have not had enough education of the passions. When a husband says, "Let us not have children, but let us have relations", what is that but animal passion? If they do not want to have more children they should simply refuse to unite. Love becomes lust the moment you make it a means for the satisfaction of animal needs.

Sanger did not accept the analogy, explaining that 'sex expression is a spiritual need' and that the quality of the expression is 'more important than the result'. She tried to get Gandhi to admit that he was against 'sex lust' rather than 'sex love'; however when she asked him whether he thought 'it possible for two people who are in love, who are happy together, to regulate their sex act only once in two years, so that relationship would only take place when they wanted a child?', Gandhi answered that 'I had the honour of doing that very thing'. Sanger saw it as 'illogical to contend that sex union for the purpose of having children would be love and union for the satisfaction of the sexual appetite was lust, for the same act was involved in both.' Gandhi explained that he knew that all sexual unions partook of the nature of lust from his own personal experience because

> as long as I looked upon my wife carnally, we had no real understanding. Our love did not reach a high plane. There was affection between us always, but we came closer and closer the more we or rather I became restrained. ... The moment I bade good-bye to a life of carnal pleasure our whole relationship became spiritual. Lust died and love reigned instead.

Sanger responded by asking if that meant that 'the sexual union take place only three or four times in an entire lifetime?' In response to the woman who, like Olive Schreiner thirty years before her, had been a lover of Havelock Ellis, the pioneer of sexology and author of the seven volume *Studies in the Psychology of Sex*, Gandhi responded:

> Why should people not be taught that it is immoral to have more than three or four children and that after they have had that number they should sleep separately? If they are taught this it would harden into custom. And if social reformers cannot impress this idea upon the people, why not a law? If husband and wife have four children, they would have had sufficient animal enjoyment. Their love may then be lifted to a higher plane. Their bodies have met. After they have had the children they wanted, their love transforms itself into a spiritual relationship.

Not long before his discussion with Margaret Sanger, Gandhi received a letter from a councillor of the Municipal Corporation of Bombay asking him to support the opening of a birth control clinic by the Corporation and issuing posters advising people to take advantage of it. Gandhi replied that,

> One may propagate a thing that is spiritually elevating. How can one propagate something that has a lowering tendency? ... Everybody would welcome sex-gratification without having to have children. Therefore the means of ensuring this are spreading like intoxicants. If there is any cause for regret, it is only that what is morally bad is being regarded as morally desirable.[58]

Soon after Sanger's visit, he wrote to the councillor again:

> I had long discussions with Mrs Sanger. The more I listened to her arguments the more I became confirmed in my view. If a gourmand falls ill, what else would a vaid [doctor] advise him to do but to fast? But people will continue to take digestive pills and yet continue to suffer. Understand that it is the same with regard to birth-control. My advice to you is that, in your own case, you may do what you like but should take no interest in the propaganda move. If, however, you have come to definite views on the subject and are convinced of the universal necessity of birth-control, I would have nothing to say.[59]

This sounds almost like acquiescence on Gandhi's part. In her autobiography Sanger notes that even though Gandhi appeared to be going along with her in their discussions, as soon as she stopped he continued 'as though he had not heard you', putting up a 'stone-wall of religion or emotion or experience' which she could not 'dynamite him over'.[60] However, he had heard her, and tried hard to counter her arguments, and perhaps Sanger had slightly more impact on him than she imagined or he admitted to. At the end of the session of interviews, Gandhi conceded that he thought highly of Sanger's purpose, otherwise he 'would not have given time to this subject'.

Towards the end of the late morning interview, she had begged him to 'advise something practical, something that can be applied to solve the problem of too frequent childbearing for the mothers of India?' She claimed that those who were present at the interview 'declared that the Mahatma made concessions he had never made before' and that he remarked to her that 'This has not been a wasted effort. We have certainly come nearer together.'[61] Indeed they had. Only a year before he had totally rejected such arguments when they were put to him by Edith Howe-Martyn and at that time he was very critical of birth control advocates: 'Man easily capitulates when sin is presented in the garb of virtue, and that is what Marie Stopes [English author of *Contraception: Its Theory, History and Practice* and various other works on sex and marriage, and founder of Britain's first birth control clinic] and others are doing.'[62] As a conclusion to the section of his article that contains the interview with Margaret Sanger, Desai wrote:

> And yet as Mrs Sanger was so dreadfully in earnest Gandhiji did mention a remedy which could conceivably appeal to him. That method was the avoidance of sexual union during unsafe periods confining it to the "safe" period of about ten days during the month. That had at least an element of self-control which had to exercised [sic] during the unsafe period. Whether this appealed to Mrs Sanger or not I do not know. But therein spoke Gandhiji the truth-seeker. Mrs Sanger has not referred to it anywhere in her interviews or her *Illustrated Weekly* article.[63] Perhaps if birth-controllers were to be satisfied with this simple method, the birth-control clinics and propagandists would find their trade gone ...[64]

What had induced this change? Later a close friend and member of his secretariate, Rajkumari Amrit Kaur, was to recall how the talks with Sanger 'grew tense and strangely exciting, as if long-buried trains of thought were emerging'.[65] Gandhi biographer Green claims that the encounter left Gandhi exhausted, resulting in his hospitalisation and a breakdown in his health that 'was very painful to him because it involved an episode of involuntary sexual excitement'.[66] Green appears to be making a causal link between Gandhi's seminal discharge and the resurfacing of buried emotions, particularly those that had led to the platonic yet sexually-charged love affair (or spiritual marriage) with Saraladevi Chaudhurani that had fleetingly threatened his own marriage in 1920.[67] This is not an outrageous interpretation. In the interviews, Sanger had put to Gandhi that, 'If we have a choice in our mates [as he did not] there is a natural sex attraction between two people. You then have a different experience and in the experience an expression of love which makes you a finer human being ... and contributes to a finer understanding and a greater spiritual harmony.' Gandhi's response was illuminating:

> I had a woman with whom I almost fell. It is so personal that I did not put it in my autobiography. We have considered if there can be this spiritual companionship. The marriage relationship is a matter of contract. Your parents arrange it in your childhood and you have nothing to do with it. I came in contact with an illiterate woman. Then I met a woman with a broad, cultural education. Could we not develop a close contact, I said to myself? This was a plausible argument, and I nearly slipped. But I was saved. I don't know how. For a time it

> seemed I had lost my anchor. I was saved by youngsters who warned me. I saw that if I was doomed, they also were doomed. I decided I was not right in my argument.

And Sanger, quite logically, questioned whether this was 'a rationalisation or a personal feeling'. Perhaps the intensity of the argument did stir up unresolved issues for Gandhi.

In an article on birth control that appeared in his paper only a few months later, Gandhi reiterated that he would agree to at least consider the rhythm method of birth control, even though he did it reluctantly:

> A co-worker who is a careful reader of my writings was disturbed to read that I was likely to approve of the "safe period" method of birth-control. I endeavoured to make it clear to the friend that the safe period method did not repel me as did the use of contraceptives and that it was open largely only to married couples.
>
> ... birth-controls by contraceptives and the like is a profound error. I write thus with a full sense of my responsibility. I have great regard for Mrs Margaret Sanger and her followers. She impressed me much by her great zeal for her cause. I know that she has great sympathy for the women who suffer because they have to bear the burden of carrying and rearing unwanted children. I know also that this method of birth-control has the support of many Protestant divines, scientists, learned men and doctors, many of whom I have the honour of knowing personally and for whom I entertain high regard. ... But I should be false to my God who is Truth and nothing but Truth, if I concealed my belief from the reader or these great advocates of the method. Indeed, if I hid my belief, I should never discover my error if my present belief is one. Moreover, its declaration is due to those many men and women who accept my guidance and advice in many moral problems including this one concerning birth-control.[68]

Later in the year, Gandhi wrote to Margaret Sanger, addressing her as 'Dear Sister'. He thanked her for her thoughtfulness in sending him an assortment of dried fruit, commented on the 'natural superiority' of the sex to which she belonged, and noted that he had gone through her reproduction of the interview in the journal *Asia* and 'My hurried reading left on me the impression that it was a faithful reproduction'.[69]

Although she had no luck in convincing Gandhi of her position, her lecture tour of India led to the opening of several birth control clinics in the country. When, in 1959, Prime Minister Nehru declared that a large sum of money would go to family planning in India, Margaret Sanger was standing at his side.

To many, Sanger, who was nominated for the Nobel Peace Prize several times in the mid-1950s, was a feminist saint. To others she was the incarnation of evil, the destroyer of family life and the promoter of the murder of the unborn. Throughout her career she aligned herself with various groups that she saw as having the potential to benefit her struggle for freely available contraception. Occasionally her choices, for example when she felt that the women's movement had let her down[70] and she turned to the eugenicists, would end up haunting her reputation in later years. Still, through her sincerity and the objective logic of her arguments, she did manage to dynamite Gandhi over some of his deepest held psychological blocks to human intimacy in the way that no one had previously been able to do.

# Margaret Bourke-White: The Icon Maker

Margaret Bourke-White was not just one of the best-known women photographers of the twentieth century, but simply one of the best-known of all photographers ever. She was born in 1904.[71] Her father was a keen amateur photographer. She studied herpetology at various universities, graduating from Cornell, where she took a photography class in 1927. After completing her university studies, she set up a darkroom in Cleveland, developing pictures in her bathtub to save money on equipment. She specialised in industrial and architectural photography and soon the hobby-photographer became a professional freelancer supporting herself through magazine and corporate assignments and advertising. She quickly gained a reputation for the beauty and originality of her work. In 1929 she became the chief photographer for the newly created *Fortune* magazine, which aimed to document business and industry through photographs. In 1930 she moved to New York, and the following year she photographed the Soviet Union for the magazine. In 1936 she became one of the first staff photographers for *Life* magazine and one of her pictures, of the Fort Peck Dam in Montana, was featured on the cover of its first issue. Her later work, as exemplified by her book *You Have Seen Their Faces* (with husband Erskine Caldwell), on the living conditions of impoverished tenant farmers in the US South, displayed a passionate commitment to social causes.

As a fearless photo-journalist, she pioneered the concept of the photo-essay and travelled the globe on remarkable photojournalist missions, chalking up many 'firsts': she was the first Western photographer allowed into the Soviet Union, she was the first a woman war correspondent covering the Second World War and was the first woman photographer attached to the US armed forces (in the process being on a torpedoed and sunk ship, and documenting the battles of the US infantry in Italy and North Africa). She was the only foreign photographer in Moscow when the Germans attacked the city, she crossed the Rhine with General Patton's First Army, she was the first woman to fly on a combat bombing mission, and was present with the US. troops when they liberated Buchenwald concentration camp in 1945, becoming one of the first to document the death camps. After the War she went to India to photograph and write about the coming of independence. Many of her photographs have taken on the status of icons, and some of the best known portraits of the elderly Mahatma were taken by her.



Bourke-White started her autobiography by recalling that her mother had always told her that she had been 'invited into the world'. She was not the result of an accident, but had been wanted and planned, 'the welcome result of a known and definite act of love between man and wife'. She noted that Gandhi felt the same way, but, unlike her mother who believed 'in warmth and ardor between married partners', would have expected celibacy between the invitations.[72] Bourke-White was no prude and she had many lovers during her life. Unlike Mayo and Kendall, she had no problem with what they saw as degrading Hindu sexuality and practices. There is nothing salacious in her India writings. She came to India for the first time when the wheels of the granting of independence were in motion – the time for championing British imperialism was over. In fact her view of India was extremely positive. She seemed determined to put *Mother India* and *Come with Me to India!* into perspective:

> The sight of some women still wearing veils is of far less significance than the knowledge that many more women are breaking out of their ancient bondage, leaving seclusion to take an active part in the

life of these nations [India and Pakistan]. Of course, I was distressed by feudal landholding systems, the despotism of princes, and the vestiges of caste discrimination, but I was unexpectedly and even more deeply stirred by the heroic efforts being made to correct these inhumanities. To my Indian and Pakistan friends I may seem to have devoted too much space to some of these long-standing iniquities. But I feel that the Western reader needs this background to understand the scope and vitality of the progress being made.[73]

It had long been decided at *Life* that India 'needed a thorough and interpretative coverage'[74] but it had to wait until Bourke-White had the time to stay for a long enough period to do it justice. This was impossible while she was covering the War. She finally arrived in early March 1946, staying for most of the year, photographing and gathering material for a book before returning to the US to write.

One of her first tasks in India was to photograph Gandhi, who was staying in an 'untouchable' colony in Poona at the time. She recounts an amusing story. Even though she had a strict deadline to meet, she was not allowed into his presence until she had endured a spinning lesson. Pyarelal, Gandhi's secretary, had put to her that the camera can only capture outward appearances, but knowing how to spin would help in truly understanding the Mahatma. With humour, she recounted how she was not allowed to talk to or disturb Gandhi during her photography session and how she was only allowed three flash bulbs, the first two of which did not work.[75] The resulting iconic picture has been reproduced countless times since then and ironically has been used as an advertising tool to sell computers.

She travelled in a third-class train carriage with Gandhi and Nehru to Simla and photographed the Mahatma many times afterwards. Gandhi, 'who loved a little joke', quickly found a fond nickname for her: 'Whenever I appeared on the scene with camera and flashbulbs, he would say, "There's the Torturer again".'[76]

While she was writing the book, Ed Stanley, a skilled journalist and editor friend who was assisting her, pointed out that she had relied too heavily on left-wing sources and 'told her bluntly that she did not know enough to write the serious book she had in mind.'[77] She returned to India in 1947 to complete work on the manuscript and to document the great exchange of populations that was taking place between the newly independent neighbours for *Life*. Her work completed, as she was about to return to America to finish her manuscript, in January 1948 Gandhi announced that he would fast to the death if peace did not replace the communal rioting that was sweeping the now two independent countries. She postponed her departure and was present at Gandhi's headquarters in Birla House when the Mahatma commenced his fast. She was also present when he finally broke it, five days later, peace having returned to Delhi.

It was only then that she came to fully appreciate the 'greatness of Gandhi'. Before then she had some concerns about what she saw as Gandhi's inconsistencies: talking with the aid of a microphone while denouncing modern machinery in a country that she thought would have greatly benefited from more tractors, scientific agriculture and modern industry, including more textile mills; staying with millionaires; having a lot of money and effort spent on his comfort when he stayed or travelled with the downtrodden etc. They had coloured her perception of him. But now, 'in the last act of the drama, when he stood out so bravely against the religious fanaticism and prejudice ... I began to glimpse his true greatness.'[78]

On 28 January[79] 1948, Bourke-White presented Gandhi with two photographs she had taken of him for him to autograph. He immediately responded that it would cost her five rupees for each as donations for his Harijan fund. She explained to Gandhi that she was writing a book about India and wanted to talk formally with him before she left the country. Gandhi responded by noting that he had been interviewed by an American woman for a book before. Bourke-White was well aware of Katherine Mayo, noting that,

> Her ghost had persecuted me everywhere. Her *Mother India*, stuffed with half-truths and second-hand information, had aroused such resentment that its reputation dogged me even in remote villages where no one could read. The fact that I was automatically associated with the memory of my countrywoman Katherine Mayo was the only disadvantage I suffered in India through being a woman.[80]

Gandhi asked her if she could be counted on to report his words accurately, rather than misquote them as Mayo had done. She gave her assurances and an interview was arranged for the following day. Although she had photographed Gandhi many times and had exchanged snippets of conversation with him, this was to be the first time that she 'had a chance to sit down and talk with him quietly'.[81]

During the interview, after she had introduced herself as 'the torturer', Gandhi informed her that because of the terrible happenings in the world he had given up his desire to live to be one hundred and twenty-five years-old as is befitting Hindu sages, and helped her to understand his seemingly puzzling attitude to machinery and his wealthy friends in the midst of the poverty of India. He pointed out that tractors replaced labour, that state-controlled nationalised industries would produce 'a nation of slaves', that trusteeship – the holding of their wealth by the rich in trust for the poor – and the growth of handicraft industries could help alleviate poverty and make the country happier. But even more importantly, she realised that

> Gandhi had no ambition to reshape the structure of society. He wanted to reshape the individual human heart. He cared very deeply about calling out the best in every man. If that man was poor it was better for him to remain so, for wealth was riddled with temptation and abundance could lead to indolence and sin. If that man was so rich that he held the destinies of other men in his hands, it was equally important to move his heart. But the inner change of heart, whether in manufacturer or maharajah, must always be by conversation, never by compulsion.[82]

The topic she wanted most to discuss with Gandhi was his thoughts on nuclear weapons which had been first used in anger not that long before. Bourke-White recalls that,

> As we began to speak of these things, I became aware of a change in my attitude toward Gandhi. No longer was this merely an odd little man in a loincloth, with his quaint ideas about bullock-cart culture and his vague social palliatives – certain of which I rejected. I felt in the presence of a new and greater Gandhi. My deepening appreciation of Gandhi began when I saw the power and courage with which he led the way in the midst of chaos. ... Gandhi went on to stress the importance of choosing righteous paths, whether for a nation or for a single man; for bad means could never bring about good ends. He spoke thoughtfully, haltingly, always with the most profound sincerity. ... Since that momentous day, many people have asked me

> whether one knew in Gandhi's presence that this was an extraordinary man. The answer is yes. One knew. And never have I felt it more strongly than on this day, when the inconsistences that had troubled me dropped away, and Gandhi began to probe that dreadful problem which has overwhelmed all.[83]

She asked him how he would meet the atomic bomb with nonviolence. Gandhi answered that he would 'meet it by prayerful action'. When asked what form that action should take, he responded that 'I will not go underground. I will not go into shelters. I will go out and face the pilot so he will see I have not the face of evil against him.' Then, probably guessing what was going on in Bourke-White's mind, he added that,

> I know the pilot will not see our faces from his great height, but that longing in our hearts that *he* should not come to harm would reach up to him, and his eyes would be opened. Of those thousands who were done to death in Hiroshima, if they had died with that prayerful action – died openly with that prayer in their hearts – then the war would not have ended as disgracefully as it has. It is a question now whether the victors are really victors or victims ... of our lust ... and omission. ... The world is not at peace. ... It is still more dreadful than before.[84]



Bourke-White's biographer, Vicki Goldberg, notes that what impressed her the most 'was that, directly confronting the terror at the heart of the modern world, he still believed in the power of the human heart and the ultimate triumph of good.'[85]

As she got up to leave, the interview concluded, Bourke-White put her hands together for the Hindu *namaskar* salute. Gandhi, however, took her hand and shook it in the Western fashion. She wished him goodbye and good luck. The following day he was killed on the way to his evening prayers by a Hindu fanatic who thought that Gandhi was too concerned with the welfare of Muslims.

When news of the assassination reached her, Bourke-White hurried back to Birla House with her camera. Although she was allowed into the room where he was lying in state, her equipment was not. She was not allowed this last photograph of the Mahatma, but did manage to capture the crowds and the cremation of Gandhi the next day.[86]

Soon after, she returned home to complete the book. Her biographer described *Halfway to Freedom* (*Interview with India* in the English edition) as her most politically aware book, one that provided a 'balanced and intelligent, if not scholarly, assessment of a complex situation.'[87] Like her predecessors, Bourke-White discussed the position of women and the princes, the issues of caste, poverty and the labouring classes, and the future of Kashmir and the princely states. Unlike them, her main respondents were Indians and she had access to the likes of Patel, Nehru and Jinnah. The times were different – when she first got to photograph Gandhi, the British were leaving, and when she interviewed him, they had gone. Even if she had wanted to, it was too late to laude the civilising influence of the colonial masters. Her portrayal of India shows a confusing and, at times, confused country. However, her narrative is never condescending. Her Gandhi can be argued with on some policy matters; he can be seen as possibly living in the past, perhaps somewhat deluded by the vision of a long-lost golden age. However, he grows as her narrative progresses and her understanding of him increases. The final two chapters of her India book deal with the last days of Gandhi and something of the saint emerges. It must be remembered that her India book came out more than a year after the Mahatma's death, and her autobiography fifteen years after. Perhaps her positive portrayal of Gandhi is not only because his words and manner convinced her when they finally had time together. Looking back, the interview must have taken on special meaning; after all it proved to be one of Gandhi's last messages to the world, and as Goldberg noted, 'Margaret spoke of Gandhi afterward with reverence and some awe.'[88] Of course Gandhi could not comment on her writing, critics and supporters were now irrelevant. In the years since his death, Gandhi's stature had grown immeasurably. His enemies and detractors had largely vanished. He was now more iconic than any of her pictures, he was the new apostle of peace, and he had touched a deep chord within Margaret Bourke-White. Her books reflect an exciting emerging India and a saintly, even Christlike, Gandhi. The reporter had become a populariser, and, in Western consciousness, her Gandhi had supplanted the disingenuous and vain character portrayed by Mayo.

After the India assignment, Bourke-White covered the Korean War and photographed South Africa's gold mines. She was struck down with Parkinson's disease in the early-1950s. She died from complications of the disease in 1971.

# Conclusion: The Constructed Image

The four American women who came to interview Gandhi did not come as friends and supporters, and certainly not as disciples. But neither did they come as the mere curious or *darshan* seekers. They had different agendas. If one was going to write seriously about India between the anti-British Non Cooperation Movement of 1920 and independence, they simply could not ignore Gandhi. And to give added authority to anything that was written, an interview with the Mahatma was certainly advantageous. Mayo may have been genuinely concerned with the welfare of Indian women, and speaking with Gandhi, who had long championed their cause, was an obvious way of enhancing her argument. Where she and Kendall wanted to champion British imperialism as a civilising agent, an interview with Gandhi which made him look superstitious or reactionary was also useful. And presumably a first hand account of the Mahatma would have helped sales of any book that contained it. Where the books were by outsiders, and where they became popular, as Mayo's *Mother India* did, they also helped construct the image of Gandhi that the world came to adopt,[89] even if only temporarily.

Margaret Sanger was on an even more focussed crusade than the others when she talked to Gandhi. She wanted nothing less than to elicit Gandhi's help in her attempts to popularise birth control. Although the lengthy interview with Gandhi gave her no satisfaction, neither did it turn her against Gandhi (or Gandhi against her). While she maintained great respect for him, because she was not trying to damage the saintly persona of the Mahatma, as Kendall and possibly Mayo had set out to do, it was her 'modern' arguments that Gandhi could not engage with that made him seem out of touch with contemporary knowledge of human psychology. In his insistence on celibacy, he seemed much more unreasonable than when he perhaps naively explained that nonviolence would change the heart of the pilot of an atomic bomber. Sanger, unintentionally to be sure, gave us the Gandhi many Westerners are ambivalent about because of his attitudes to sexuality. Many have explored these issues with prurient interest and even glee if they have little time for Gandhi as Mahatma. In this sense, paradoxically, the broadly sympathetic Sanger may have done more in the long run to problematise Gandhi than the unsympathetic Mayo and hostile Kendall.

Margaret Bourke-White photographed and interviewed Gandhi as part of her job. She did not approach her work with a preconceived negative picture of him, determined to do a hatchet job, as at least Kendall had. She was unimpressed by his ideas on machinery and modernisation, but she warmed to him as a person and highly evolved spiritual entity. However, she was also a good journalist, and work came first; the efforts she went to in order to get the 'scoop' of pictures of Gandhi's assassinated body, even if it alienated the Gandhi disciples she had grown to consider friends, seemed to be a price worth paying. Nevertheless, the pictures which she did take, and the words she subsequently wrote, helped to define the Mahatma for Western audiences.

# IV

# Western Women Disciples
## Going Native

As we have seen, many Western women had a strong religious faith or socialist principles that drove them to work for peace and with the poor and downtrodden. Some like Annie Besant were in India before Gandhi's fame spread, but to several of them, usually in England, it came as a revelation that Gandhi was doing similar work to them in far away India, and that the Empire whose citizens they were, was not necessarily a force for the good when viewed from the perspective of the subjects. They became interested in Gandhi's philosophy and campaigns, paid visits to him in India and added his cause of Indian independence to theirs, or continued with their charitable and political work with Gandhi as a distant colleague or adviser. Often the deep respect was mutual and friendships, although rarely face-to-face, lifelong. However, there was another group of Western women who travelled to India to do their social work or meet this saintly Gandhi they were starting to hear about, who stayed for lengthy periods, even for life, and during their stay 'went native'.

'Going native' was a pejorative term for those of the colonising race, or Europeans in general, who took to living a little too closely with, or like, the 'uncivilised' 'primitive', 'inferior', or even 'degenerate' colonised population. It speaks about a fear of being contaminated by, or, worse, being absorbed into, native life and customs. From the colonialist standpoint, those who 'went native' had lapsed from superior European behaviour and been led into a situation of moral degeneracy. The key indicators that someone had 'gone native' were more than merely identifying with, or showing sympathy to, the oppressed population. They entailed outwardly visible manifestations such as dressing in native garb, eating native foods and engaging in native ceremonies.

Margaret MacMillan, in her book *Women of the Raj*, notes that while some senior memsahibs were 'permitted some eccentricities', most were confined to the conventional roles assigned to them by race, and that the freedom some had carved out for themselves became ever harder to enjoy as the Raj 'reached its full pomp and dignity' in the later nineteenth and twentieth centuries. There were, however, women who went against social conventions. They 'faced the full disapproval of their peers who did not hesitate to speak their minds: "going *jungli*", they said, or worse, "going native", or worse still "letting down the race and the Raj and the British Empire."'[1]

Gandhi's most important Western woman disciple, Madeleine Slade, known as Mirabehn, perhaps best expressed the extreme version of this when she wrote to Gandhi that

> Every day of my life I become more and more deeply in love with the Hindu nature … I just feel as if it were the highest development of humanity which we have in this world, with its inborn gentleness forgiveness and tolerance – its simpleness and natural feeling for God. … I get the feeling that to pass into the Hindu nature is the natural, perhaps *the* road to salvation. Anyway, as long as one remains to any extent outside it, one feels onself to be to that extent a barbarian. I know that barbarism in myself, which I have still hanging on me from Europe, is the cause of most of my difficulties. … sooner or later I will overcome it. If I cannot altogether overcome it in this life, then I ask nothing better than to be born a Hindu in the next birth … [2]

Of course from her standpoint (as her letter clearly indicates), and from that of others who 'went native', they were taking on a morally and even culturally superior, not inferior, role.

Most did not take their identification quite this far, but they were still willing to bend or ignore the unwritten rules to some degree, regardless of the consequences. And this was easiest to do for women who came to India to work rather than join husbands who were part of the ruling establishment. The largest single group of women who had come to India to work were missionaries, health workers and teachers. Although they had to be careful not to embarrass their missions or employing institutions while they remained working members, they were often stationed in smaller, more out-of-the-way locations, and in closer contact with the native population in the schools and hospitals they worked in than were those whose only contact was with domestic servants. Their original motivations for coming to the subcontinent was likely a sense of adventure or because of a call to do good, and this later motive may have been to spread the word of God or to engage in some sort of feminist social or political activity that would improve the position of Indian women. And for a few even the desire to work towards the end of what they saw as an oppressive Raj. MacMillan points out that some missionaries went so far as to 'live in an Indian style, and even to wear Indian dress'.[3]



## INTRODUCING THE 'NATIVES'

Millie Graham Polak was unconcerned with what her fellow Europeans thought and lived with Gandhi on his communal settlement at Phoenix in South Africa (as did Ada West). She lived with Indians, but not in Indian style, because at that time neither did Gandhi. She was as much native as Gandhi was. She was the first Western woman to throw her lot in with Gandhi, but did it as more of a challenging equal than a disciple as those who followed her would end up being.

Some of the unconventional women who entered Gandhi's orbit in India were 'restless souls' who 'sought in India something they did not find in their own civilization. They did not mind the cold shoulders of British society because they had no intention of being accepted into it; indeed they were rejecting everything it stood for'.[4] MacMillan's prime example is Madeleine Slade. Mary Barr, Catherine Mary Heilemann and Marjorie Sykes are other examples. And from the non-English side, Esther Færing, Anne Marie Petersen, Margarete Spiegel, and several others, are equally good representatives.

Sudhir Kakar, a noted Indian psychoanalyst and interpreter of Gandhi and his relationship with women, has written perceptively that

> In his middle and later years, a number of young women, attracted by Gandhi's public image as the Mahatma, his cause, or his fame, sought his proximity and eventually shared his *ashram* life. These women, who in many cases left their well-appointed middle- and upper-class homes to take upon themselves the rigors of an ascetic lifestyle, were all else but conventional. Some of them were not only "highstrung" but can fairly be described as suffering from emotional crises of considerable magnitude. Like their counterparts today who seek out well-known gurus, these women too were looking for the therapist in Gandhi as much as the Mahatma or the leader embodying Indian national aspirations.[5]

And this applied equally to his Western and Indian women devotees. Again, from the Western side, Slade is the primary example. Possibly this description could also apply to Færing and probably does to Francisca Standenath, and it certainly applies to Nilla Cram Cook, Margarete Spiegel, Helene Haussding and Antoinette Mirbel. Of course not all those who came to Gandhi were highstrung or suffering emotional crises. Some of them 'went native' to work in the way their faith told them that they should, with Gandhi providing aid and guidance for their mission rather than filling the position of much-needed therapist. Petersen, Barr and her co-workers at Khedi, and Sykes and Heilemann are the best examples. In short, the reasons that these Western women – disciples does not seem too strong a word – 'went native' were different. What they had in common was Mahatma Gandhi, who had the ability to attract these very different types of followers.

# Too Equal to be a Disciple: Millie Graham Polak

By the time Gandhi commenced satyagraha in 1906, he had built a successful legal career and was living a middle-class life. From 1903 he resided in a well-to-do suburb of Johannesburg, and between 1906 and 1908 in a house shared with Henry and Millie Graham Polak when they were not living on the communal property at Phoenix. The Phoenix Settlement had been set up following the internal turmoil and soul-searching that was moving Gandhi in the direction of a more simplified life of public service, a process that was facilitated by his relationship with Henry and tested by his relationship with Millie.

## MILLIE COMES TO SOUTH AFRICA

At the time when Gandhi was re-evaluating his life, Henry Polak became his most enthusiastic fellow experimenter. Soon, his wife Millie Graham Polak was at the centre of a household that had become a hotbed of alternative health, dietary and educational practices, and she herself quickly developed into more than the partner of a colleague and more than a mere supporter of Gandhi's cause.

The twenty-two-year-old Henry Polak met the thirty-five-year-old Gandhi in Johannesburg in March 1904. As a newspaperman he wanted to talk to Gandhi about the position of Indians in the country and when he discovered that Gandhi was a fellow Tolstoyan vegetarian this desire was strengthened. A few days later the opportunity came when Ada Bissicks told Polak that Gandhi would be attending an 'At Home' at her house the following evening and invited him to come as well. They met, and the meeting changed the current of both their lives.[1]

Polak offered Gandhi his own services, free of charge, as a writer for Gandhi's paper *Indian Opinion* and they were soon soul-mates rather than mere close friends. A little more than a dozen years after their meeting, Gandhi related the event to his secretary and explained how he managed to 'capture' Polak:

> I judged Polak within five hours. He read my letter published in a newspaper and wrote me a letter. He then came to see me and I at once saw what he was, and since then he became my man. He married and started his practice as a pleader only after he joined me. He told me before marriage that he must earn a little for his children. I told him plainly, "You are mine and the responsibility to provide for you and your children is mine, not yours. I am getting you married, as I see no objection to your marrying." His marriage was celebrated at my residence.[2]

While his family was in India, Gandhi was living in a modest room behind his chambers. When Gandhi took larger premises in Troyville in anticipation of the return of his family, Polak took over the Rissik Street room and this 'helped to bring me into closer contact with him'.[3] After hearing the news of the financial plight of *Indian Opinion* from Albert West, Gandhi was worried that it would be forced to close 'with the consequent loss of public service which this would entail'.[4] To set things straight, in September 1904, he had to undertake a hurried trip to Durban, from where the paper was being published. For the journey, Polak lent Gandhi a book that he had just finished reading. That book was Ruskin's *Unto This Last*.[5]

In Durban, Gandhi told West of the impact the book had had on him 'and proposed that *Indian Opinion* should be removed to a farm, on which everyone should labour, drawing the same living wage of three pounds, and attending to the press work in spare time'.[6] The agrarian commune would see Indians and Europeans living together in Gandhi's first intentional community in a simple and healthy environment, and in mutual support, learning from each other.

Polak quickly volunteered to join the community, gave a month's notice at his own newspaper, leaving a potentially secure career, and was soon sharing quarters and running *Indian Opinion* with Albert West at Phoenix. According to Gandhi, Polak took to life at Phoenix 'like a duck takes to water'; however Gandhi needed a legal assistant and he asked Polak to become his clerk and to qualify as an attorney so that they could more quickly finish their work and 'more quickly realise their ideals' of communal life.[7]

Polak was engaged to Millie Graham Downs, whom he had met at the London Ethical Society, before he ventured to South Africa. We know little about Millie except that she was Scottish and a Christian who had no concerns about marrying a Jew, and that she shared a concern about ethical issues with her fiancé. It appears that not long after his meeting with Gandhi, Polak had been invited to shift in to Gandhi's Troyville residence and the two friends rapidly 'began to live like blood brothers'.[8] When Gandhi's family arrived from India to join him towards the close of 1905, Polak wrote to Millie in England that Gandhi (who had not yet fully settled on celibacy as an ideal) wanted her there also, and that they should be married. Millie was not in good health at this time and Henry Polak's father wrote to Gandhi 'begging him to use his influence to postpone the marriage indefinitely,' as he did not consider that she was 'physically strong enough for the strenuous life of the Colonies'. Gandhi replied to Polak Senior that if Millie's health was not robust in London, it was 'all the more reason for her to hasten her departure from it,' so that she could live a simple life 'amidst loving care' in a 'beautiful climate' where 'she could gain the physical strength she evidently needed'.[9] Gandhi also wrote to her, assuring her of a warm welcome in his home: 'I have not the slightest doubt that we shall get on well together, and that you will be a most valuable acquisition to the family'.[10]

She accepted the idea and in a few months was in Johannesburg where she and Henry were married at the very end of 1905 without even the necessity of 'a special dress' or religious rites – their 'common religion' being 'the religion of ethics'. Having a 'coloured' person as best man, and Polak's habit of referring to himself and friends as 'we Indians' meant that the ceremony at the registry office had to be delayed 'pending inquires' to ensure that it was not a mixed marriage. Gandhi had to intervene and obtain a note from the Chief Magistrate to clear up the 'amusing incident'.[11] Millie recalled that her first impressions of Gandhi related to his eyes, 'the kindest eyes in the world, that seemed to light up from within when he spoke. His eyes were always his most remarkable feature and were in reality the lamps of his soul.'[12]

Millie shifted into a joint family household that was a mix of European and Indian styles, customs and people and one in which Gandhi had 'introduced as much simplicity as was possible in a barrister's house'.[13] As there was a houseboy and cook, there was no housework to do, and, although not a trained teacher, Millie took on the work of educating the Gandhi children and also teaching Kasturba Gandhi a few words of English. From her account, Gandhi came to rely on her advice on the furnishing of the household.[14] He became involved with the caring of the two infant Polak children, looking after them in times of illness and assisting in the weaning process, something he had missed doing for his own. Millie in some sense provided Gandhi with a family home for the first time in his adult life, and his only taste of something resembling a nuclear family.

At 6.30 every morning the male members took to the task of grinding wheat for the home-baked bread, both as a practical necessity and as a form of exercise which was supplemented by skipping (at which Gandhi was adept).[15] The Johannesburg house, in a 'fairly good middle-class neighbourhood, on the outskirts of town', was a free standing, two storied, eight-roomed modern villa surrounded by a garden and facing the open space of the hilly countryside. In the hot weather the residents often slept on the upstairs veranda.[16] From here they went to Phoenix with its unlined huts of corrugated iron and rough wooden supports, where the bathrooms were lean-tos with holes in the roof under suspended watering cans, operated by lengths of cord, to serve as showers.[17] Millie was a fellow traveller with a strong enough bond to enjoy a good-natured laugh at Gandhi's expense.[18] A good example is her 'gloriously exaggerated description' of life at Phoenix to Henry's sisters in 1909 when both she and Gandhi were in London. According to Gandhi she gave a 'harrowing picture' without 'a single relieving feature' of Phoenix Settlement with 'beetles everywhere, spiders, ants in the milk, no baths, water bad, people half-naked, filth too, lift a plate and you will find an insect underneath, snakes hanging from the tree'. Gandhi told the sisters to 'accept it as an accurate description'. Without undue criticism, Millie was later able to note that the ideas they had hatched when discussing the simple life and reading about it in the study, ideas that sounded so right and reasonable, 'were often found impracticable when applied to the hard facts of life'.[19]

In June 1906 the suburban household was abandoned and all the members went to Phoenix. Millie did not greatly like the life there and after about a month and a half, because of her isolated life and 'a native rebellion',[20] she left the settlement for Durban before the Polaks returned to Johannesburg in August with Gandhi. He needed to be nearer to his political activities and so ended up living with the Polaks rather than his own immediate family. When they were together, Millie formed a strong bond with Kasturba, who, as a concerned mother, at times felt that her husband's experiments in simplifying his life meant that their children were missing out on a reasonable education and decent clothes. When Millie left Phoenix, she worried that even the little education she was giving the boys would cease. Because she could stand up to and argue with Gandhi, she had often been the go-between, interceding with Gandhi on Kasturba's behalf to get the things she wanted for the children.[21]

Gandhi was an admirer of the English Women's Suffrage movement, and during one of his imprisonments (probably in late 1908 or early 1909) Henry asked Millie why she didn't start some organisation for Indian women in Johannesburg. On 23 March, a hall was found and forty women attended a meeting called by Millie. She explained the details of the political struggle their menfolk were engaged in, and informed them of the women's struggle for political freedom in England. From this point the group met fortnightly and grew into the Transvaal Indian Women's Association. When Gandhi was released from jail and heard about the new movement he was delighted and praised Millie's efforts.[22] When Millie went back to England half a year later, the administration of the Association was continued by Mrs Vogl and Sonja Schlesin.

## MILLIE THE CHALLENGING 'SISTER'

Letters, especially those between Gandhi and Millie, throw some light on their interactions. Gandhi's first letter to her in London welcoming her to South Africa, Millie was later to recall, 'set the tone to the whole of my relationship with him, establishing him in my life as a loving and understanding elder brother and showed the human tenderness of the man.'[23]

Millie's book of the relationship, written a quarter of a century later, presents a picture of a lovable and earnest young Gandhi who was at times so bound up in the idea of absolute principles that he had trouble seeing shades of grey. Millie had no such problem and a large part of the account is a retelling of the debates, debates in which she more than held her own, between the two: 'I cannot think of any human problem that at some time or other I did not attempt to thrash out with Mr Gandhi. Most often, the discussions arose spontaneously and were the outcomes of something he said that would seem to challenge my mind or something deep-seated in me'.[24] And the discussions did seem to deal with all sorts of matters: human nature and psychology, the disciplining of children, diets, the need for comforts or art, whether lying could be justified if it resulted in saving lives, and even the issues around sexuality. For example, on the role of women in marriage, especially Hindu marriage, Millie objected that women were restricted to family duties while men could go off, Buddha-like, renouncing the family to seek enlightenment. Gandhi countered with an argument that women did not have to do this because they were already on some higher plane. Debating the relative merits of the treatment of women in the West and the East, Gandhi pointed out that women were worshipped in his part of the world. Millie responded that in theory it may be the case, but in practice she always found eastern women being dependent on men without any individual life (of the kind she obviously enjoyed). Gandhi's counter was that in small things she may serve man, while in the 'great things' she is man's equal or superior. Needless to say the arguments did not impress Millie.[25] She was equally unimpressed, and told him so, of Gandhi's strengthening belief, or more precisely stronger resolve to put his belief into action, concerning the relative value of celibacy and parenthood.[26]

Millie concluded, 'I sometimes think that Mr Gandhi enjoyed such discussions, not because of their intrinsic merits, but because of the different points of view he would hear stated, and also because he often liked to hear me express myself vigorously, even if he did not altogether approve of my comment.'[27] She also discovered that although Gandhi could argue strongly for philosophical positions, he could also put them aside in the light of practical reality. At a time when Gandhi was arguing strongly against having children, one of the members of Phoenix gave birth. He originally seemed to have nothing to do with or say on the matter, but after the birth, when they visited the mother and child, 'his eyes were alight with affectionate interest'. Millie was at first puzzled but then realised that 'even Mr Gandhi distinguished between abstract truth and human love, and mother-love was always of great beauty and joy to him.' She concluded that 'he often endowed a mother with many attributes she did not necessarily possess.'[28]

Although she often disagreed with Gandhi, and did so fearlessly, it did not dent their relationship. From Millie's account, Gandhi seemed to enjoy their verbal sparring, using her as a sounding-board as he refined his philosophy. During one of his trips to London, where he had gone to lobby for the cause of South African Indians, Millie was also visiting home and he spent considerable time with her. Only a day or so after leaving to sail back to South Africa, he noted that regardless of their differences,

> there is still a subtle sameness running through our thought which makes you most lovable to me. ... Meanwhile both of us are mad after Truth. So we are apart from your being Henry's wife, sister and brother. ... I ... want a sister's full trust and confidence. Will you please express to me all your wants! I am more anxious now that I am away from you. It was a relief to me to meet you twice a week. Now, O God, when shall we who have so much in common meet again! And yet why complain? We are nearer, than the passengers who are sitting in the same room as I am.[29]



It is through her writing and later oral history recordings that we are given an insight into life in the Johannesburg household. Here we get a picture of Gandhi as a man, rather than 'saint or prophet or statesman'.[30] For example, in 1960, an elderly Millie recalled:

> We had many discussions on a variety of topics, and on some matters I would quite disagree with him, because I could not help noticing what seemed to me the glaring inconsistencies in some of his views if carried to their logical conclusion. He, however, would never waver in his belief, and would only smile or shrug his shoulders if I argued that such-and-such a situation might become unjust or absurd.[31]

The closeness of their relationship is hinted at in some of their early letters. He addressed her in his letters as 'My Dear Millie', and ended them 'With love', signing them as 'Brother', and the letters themselves were quite personal in content, touching on the deepest of feelings:

> I see you address me Brother in inverted commas and underlined thrice. We may well call ourselves brother and sister. Our conduct certainly justifies it. But will you give me a sister's confidence? If you say "yes", I shall try to be "brother" to you. ... You could hardly be so sweet as you are if you never needed a friend's help and consolation. Though a brother could never replace a husband, I tried during my stay in London to replace Henry so far as I could. It was no more a wrench to you to separate from me than it was to me to separate from you. We certainly came nearer each other in London than ever before. It was natural.[32]

And:

> You are dearer to me than my widowed sister Gokuldas' mother, whom as you know I worship, though in thoughts a gulf divides us. You are dearer because there is so much in common between us and because I have entered so much into your and Henry's lives – I hope for our common good and the good of humanity. ... Will you not, for my sake, shake yourself free from that little morbidity of your nature? It ill becomes a character like yours. I want a perfect sister and am anxious for Henry that he should have a perfect wife. It is because it is in you to be perfect that I venture to draw attention to what in my opinion is lacking in you.[33]

These letters sound like rehearsals for the types of letters Gandhi would write to Mirabehn almost two decades later. In what we know about their relationship, Millie was the first Western woman to have thrown her lot in with Gandhi more or less totally, even though at this stage Gandhi himself had not yet completely discarded his Western persona. Millie 'went' semi- 'native' with the not yet completely 'native' Gandhi.

In mid-1909, when Henry went to India to plead the South African Indian cause, Millie returned to England. Gandhi arrived a few weeks later as part of the South African Indian delegation. They met often and their discussion and debates continued until Gandhi returned to South

Africa in mid-November. Eventually, Henry came to London and, together with Millie, returned to India for almost a year in 1911. It was after an absence of almost three years before the Polaks were back in South Africa. By this time Herman Kallenbach had taken the Polaks' place as Gandhi's soul-mate, and they were living at Gandhi's next intentional rural community, Tolstoy Farm. At about this time, it appears that Millie wrote to Gandhi asking him about the use of 'Bapu' as his moniker. Gandhi replied, 'Bapu has become the conventional name and that may remain without the signification attached to it. We are and must remain brother and sister, always confiding, always trusting, always loving and helping, but neither entirely leaning on the other.'[34]

Gandhi and Henry Polak had an agreement that when the South African campaign came to an end, the Polaks should return to England so that their children could be 'brought up in an atmosphere free from racial and colour prejudice'.[35] But now Gandhi felt 'the call to return to India' and knew that one of them had to stay in South Africa to 'see the Agreement through'. He asked if Henry would stay 'to serve the Indian community in his place' as he had often done during Gandhi's imprisonments and trips to England. They referred the matter to Millie, 'who told him that, in all the circumstances, though it was a terrible disappointment, she felt that I must free him for his great mission. Who can say what might have been the course of political events in India, had the decision been otherwise and he had been obliged to remain in South Africa?'[36] As Millie watched Gandhi's boat leave, she felt 'an intolerable sense of blankness' come into her life.[37]

Gandhi left South Africa for India via London in July 1914. The Polaks and their two young children stayed on to ensure the implementation of the agreement to remove the poll-tax on indentured Indian labourers and accept the legality of non-Christian marriages with the South African Government following the conclusion of the campaign. In 1916 Henry went to India to help end the practice of indentured Indians being sent to South Africa.[38] Millie followed a short time later for what she thought would be a stay of a few months. They caught up with Gandhi in Ahmedabad and Millie wondered how the time apart might have affected their relationship:

> I knew that during these three years he had travelled a long way in thought, but somehow I felt he had become more Indian and less

universal, and that I should personally find him different from the "brother" I had known in South Africa. But this was not so. To me he was the same; kind, gentle, and sympathetic to all the little things of my life, as well as the bigger problems.[39]

She did, however, notice that 'his natural asceticism had become more pronounced.'

Because of the war, the India trip turned into two years, during which time Millie debated Gandhi's attitude to the conflict. Henry became ill and returned home to England. Millie ended up being stranded with her children when the passenger services between the countries were suspended. She and the children stayed in the Nilgiri hills in the south of India in a great deal of hardship,[40] ostracised by the Europeans because of their relationship with Gandhi, until the service was resumed at the end of the war. Millie left for London from Bombay where she met Gandhi again after almost two years.

Although South Africa was behind them, Gandhi saw his relationship with Millie continuing in a direct way. While she was in the south of India, Gandhi wrote to her about the women working with him distributing medical relief in the villages of Champaran in Bihar (where Gandhi was engaged in the struggle of peasants against their exploitation by British indigo planters), adding that 'I know that you would love this kind of work.' He noted, however, that it was not yet time for her to take up such work, but when her children had grown up and she and Henry 'have had a few years of peaceful life together', she might feel the call 'to work among the villagers here'.[41] While Gandhi may have still seen a role for Millie in his life and work at some later stage, Millie felt the parting keenly and worried about her friend's health. In 1918 she wrote to him: 'I am glad, very glad that you are getting better. I should feel it irreparably, if anything happened to take your strength or health from you. Yes, I know death must come to us, and though it means but a crossing to another land for the one who goes, it leaves desolation to the human near to left. And anyway, you have to stay here for years yet.' She signed the letter, 'With sisterly love, Yours, Millie.'[42]

In the early years of their relationship both Henry and Millie Polak helped shape Gandhi, the prototype Mahatma. Millie was probably the first woman who was close to being his equal and she set a pattern of strong-willed Western women becoming part of Gandhi's close circle.

Even after the Polaks settled back in England, they maintained an active interest in Indian affairs and in particular the issue of Indians overseas. Despite disagreements with Gandhi over some of his campaigns (for example during the Non-Cooperation campaign, Mille wrote to Gandhi that 'Our minds may not see the same road to travel, but our hearts remain unchanged in their allegiance to the ideals that we have loved together'[43]), they kept up a friendly correspondence until the end of Gandhi's life, and to the end, regardless of his fame, Gandhi still signed all his letters to them as 'Bhai' (brother).

# The First Disciples: The Danes Esther Færing and Anne Marie Petersen

Mirabehn may have been Gandhi's best known Western Woman disciple but she was by no means the first. Millie Graham Polak, while not quite a disciple, did 'go native' in South Africa for a while, living at the first of Gandhi's South African ashrams with her husband Henry, Gandhi's first soul-mate. However, the prototype Mirabehn was Esther Færing almost a decade before Madeleine Slade arrived at Gandhi's Sabarmati Ashram. Danish missionaries had been working in South India since the 1860s and the Danes, Esther Færing and Anne Marie Petersen were already in India as missionaries when they came under the sway of Mahatma Gandhi, who was not yet an internationally recognised figure attracting Western visitors, supporters or disciples. Færing, in particular, threw her lot in with the Mahatma. She identified with India and Gandhi to the point of lamenting that she had not been born Indian, to the point of desiring naturalisation as a subject of British India, of seeing Gandhi as her father, of marrying an Indian, and attempting to bring her daughters up as Indians. In short, she identified as an Indian, at least for some time, at least as strongly as Mirabehn did. She was the original Western ashramite 'native'. Petersen too came under

Gandhi's spell, but it seems that through her strong and unusually inclusive non-racist Christian faith and belief in an education system that resembled Gandhi's, as well as her natural comfort with Indians, she was probably destined to 'go native', even without her relationship with Gandhi.

## ESTHER FÆRING: MY DEAR CHILD

Esther Færing was born on 22 June1889, educated as a religion teacher and then as a missionary. In 1912 she was hired by the Danish Missionary Society and in November 1915 went to south India as a staff member of the Society.[1] She met the thirty-seven year-old Danish missionary Anne Marie Petersen when they shared an apartment in Madras where Petersen was working at the Society's school for girls. In late 1916 Petersen toured India, visiting innovative educational institutions in order to be better acquainted with the educational system in the country as a prelude to the Society's conference in Madras in late January 1917 and as a step towards establishing a mission high school for girls. She decided that Færing should accompany her to prepare her for missionary work. They visited several educational institutions in India, including Tagore's Shantiniketan, and spent three days, from 6 January 1917, at Gandhi's first Indian ashram, following his return from South Africa. It was then located in a large bungalow at Kochrab across the Sabarmati River from Ahmedabad.[2] Later, Færing was to recall that, 'Anne Marie Petersen selected me to join her in visiting the schools around India, although I was the youngest. It was then we met Gandhi. My discontent and uneasiness about being a part of an organised society originates from this meeting. He utterly fascinated me and his ideal was mine too from my very youth'.[3]

From the first day at the ashram, unlike Petersen, Esther fitted right in. Petersen later recalled:

> We sat on the floor in the kitchen eating together. Clean and neat it was in all its simplicity. But it was hard for me, as it is hard for many of the visiting Hindus, to eat it. It was made in its own way, without seasoning and spices. But my fellow? She could. She got the most strange ability to submit herself everywhere, especially among Indians. And she were treated as one of their own – even though she had just come to the country. Early 5 pm [sic] all arose, also the little missionaeremissi, while the old laid tired and turned on the hard bed, cold and hungry. No, asceticism suited her not.[4]

Soon after, the correspondence between Færing and Gandhi started. In the following three years he wrote more letters to her than he did to his own grown children. At first Gandhi wrote to Færing as 'Dear Esther', within four months they were addressed to 'My Dear Esther'. Gandhi's first letter to her was a reply to Færing's letter of thanks immediately after the Danish missionaries' stay at the ashram, assuring her that they were members 'of the family', not guests.[5] He is reported as having written later that 'Of course Esther has been more than a begotten daughter, for she is it by choice and right of love'.[6] Only four months after her visit to Kochrab, Færing, who had started wearing khadi, become a vegetarian and try to live by the ashram rules, seems to have begun questioning her duty to the Mission and expressing her desire to live at the ashram. Gandhi responded:

> I am sure that your duty is to fulfill your undertaking with the Mission with all your heart. You can come to the *ashram* only when they relieve you and when you feel in the clearest possible terms that you will come to render the service of humanity in greater fullness. When that time comes, the *ashram* will receive you as one of its own. Meanwhile you are free to go [to] the *ashram* and stay there as long as you like.[7]

In March, Esther wrote to Gandhi's secretary, Mahadev Desai, that Gandhi had become the 'manifestation of the love of God', and so he came into her life as the living ideal of that for which she had been seeking for years.[8] Two months later, on her twenty-eighth birthday, she wrote to Gandhi about the many gifts God had bestowed on her in the previous year: 'but most of all I thank Him, because He sent me to the ashram'.[9] Gandhi gave her permission to address him as 'Bapu'[10] and their association quickly developed into one of several of Gandhi's 'father/daughter' relationships, and by early 1918 Gandhi started addressing his letters to her as 'My Dear Child'. This became the standard address from mid-1919.

At the start of their association, the letters between Gandhi and Færing were exchanged every few days. Besides the usual ashram news, they covered deep philosophical issues, such as killing, self-defence and fear,[11] the difference between desire and the love of God,[12] and the nature of perfection[13] and vows.[14] However, not long after their first meeting obstacles appeared in the path of the growing relationship.

With Britain at war, missionary societies not headquartered in Britain were closely watched, as were foreigners who had contact with Gandhi. Those suspected of supporting or aiding the nationalist movement were particularly targeted and the actions of individuals could reflect on the organisations with which they were associated. Færing's relationship with Gandhi became a 'real embarrassment' to the Danish Mission. The political loyalty of missionaries was under scrutiny and non-British or American mission societies needed to obtain special permission from the government to work, or continue to work, in India. Foreign missionaries were required to sign a statement requiring them to pledge obedience to the government, to refrain from participating in political matters, and if engaged in educational work to undertake that their influence 'shall be exerted to promote loyalty to the Government in the minds of my pupils, and to make them good citizens of the British Empire.'[15]

Færing's relationship with an enemy of the Empire could easily have jeopardised the existence of Danish missionary work in the country. She was pressured to end the relationship, but her letters of frustration did not stop, and Gandhi counselled patience and loyal submission to the Society.[16] A senior member of the Society and chairman of the Missionary Conference, Johan Bittmann gave permission for Esther to visit Gandhi when she was free and Gandhi asked her to pass on his gratitude for Bittmann's leniency.[17] However, Bittmann and his wife Helene were the only ones supporting Esther in this (Petersen being back in Denmark at the time) and her proposed visit to the ashram for Christmas was prevented by the Society. Again Gandhi advised patience:

> It is your clear duty just now to obey those to whom you have given the right to control your movements. You can oppose them only when they clearly hinder your spiritual progress. They receive the benefit of any doubt. You could certainly reason with them that just at this time of the year you will have perfect weather in Ahmedabad, loving attention and no worry. The very change of surroundings is likely to do you good. If you still fail, you have to accept their opposition with resignation.[18]

Half a year later, things had not improved and she wrote to Gandhi that she was considering resigning from the Society because of the restrictions on her contact with him. Gandhi replied: 'I am quite sure that you must quietly go through your contract even though you may be prohibited from coming to the Ashram or writing to me. You will gain greater strength of will and purpose by the enforced discipline and restraint.'[19]

The separation was diminished slightly by Færing sending Gandhi two somewhat ill-fitting vests that she had made for him and that he wore daily, promising to wear them out.[20] Towards the end of 1918, Gandhi's close missionary friend Charles Freer Andrews arranged for Færing to teach English for a while at poet Rabindranath Tagore's nationalist university *Shantiniketan* in Bengal.[21] And in May she asked Gandhi's permission to take the vow of *swadeshi* (the use of locally made goods) even though in her uncertainty as to its meaning it could have implied giving up gifts from her homeland, and informed him that she was ready to apply for naturalisation.[22] Gandhi yet again urged her to fulfill her agreement of work with the DMS.[23]

However, a situation was fast developing which could derail all her Gandhi- and India-centred plans. In mid-1919 there was some suggestion that Færing may be deported from India as her friendship with Gandhi had begun to attract the attention of the government and police. At the end of April she asked Gandhi for permission to publish an article that called him a saint and true follower of Christ even though she thought it may mean her banishment from India.[24] A week later she added that she would rather spend several years in prison than leave the country.[25] Another six weeks later she reported being questioned by police and expressed fear that she would be deported, and that, she felt, would be unbearable.[26]

Bittmann had to take action. He told her to choose between her missionary work and her interest in 'Indian politics'. He reminded her that she was a missionary and, as a Dane, a guest of the British. She offered to resign from the Mission, but realised that this may jeopardise her privilege of remaining in the country. Bittmann advised her 'to keep perfectly quiet and leave off all correspondence with all who in any way are connected with any political work.'[27] This was unacceptable to her and she expressed her desire to go to Gandhi at Sabarmati.[28] In late September, she voiced her impatience at not having received formal permission and asked Gandhi to allow her to go to Bombay and intercede with the governor.[29] Gandhi advised Færing that if the authorities imposed conditions on her which would allow her to stay, she should accept them 'in so far as they are not humiliating'[30] and promised to write to the government on her behalf.

Esther Færing spelled out her position in a letter to Gandhi's ex-ashramite colleague V.A. Sundaram, who forwarded the letter to the Mahatma:

> Monday I received a letter from our chairman, kind and sympathetic he, containing 400 Rs to pay my debt; given to me as a gift from the mission; they do not want to make life more difficult for me, than it already is, they want to remove this stone from my path; moreover there will be no conference or discussion concerning me, as they all feel, they cannot ask me to come back, however much they regret and feel sorry because I have leave the D.M.S.
>
> I am on leave until we have the answer from Denmark and therefore not allowed to take up any other work, before the home board's answer will be here. They want me to go back to Denmark but I cannot do so. I belong to India today more than ever before ...[31]

On 22 August, Gandhi wrote to the personal secretary of Lord Willingdon, the then Governor of Bombay Presidency (the administrative region where Ahmedabad was located), 'on a somewhat personal matter of urgency':

> Probably the name of Miss Esther Færing, of Danish extraction and, up to recently, if not still, working as Superintendent of a Girls' School belonging to the mission in Tirucoilur, has been brought to His Excellency's notice. It was probably two years ago that she, along with another Danish lady, visited my Ashram at Ahmedabad. Both the ladies took a special fancy for the Ashram and its ideals. Miss Faering has since then met me three or four times and she has visited the Ashram, I believe, once after her first visit. She has been a fairly regular correspondent and I believe she is attached to me like a child to its father, simply because, in her opinion, I represent in action the ideals she would fain enforce in her own life and is ever trying to. She loves India as her own motherland and I know it would be a terrible wrench to her if she is ever banished from India, as she dreads she might [sic]. Latterly, it seems she has been a suspect, very much shadowed. It was her intention some time ago to leave the Danish mission, if she could. I think I succeeded in weaning her from the desire. I told her that it was her duty to fulfill her contract with

> the mission, so long as she was permitted to do so. I have just heard that she is no longer in the mission. If this is true and if she is permitted, I would be pleased to take her into the Ashram where she would be associated with me in my non-political work. I believe her to be as truthful and straight a person as is to be found anywhere. She ever lives in the fear of God and does her best to live a Christian life. As her desire is to pass her life mostly in the midst of the people of India, I advised her to become naturalized. I know she took steps in the direction and I revised for her the petition for naturalization. But I do not know whether she has sent it. I can only hope that His Excellency will meet her and form the same opinion about her that I have. If any undertaking is required about her, it can be easily given. If an assurance is necessary, I wish to assure His Excellency that I have not the slightest desire to avail myself of her services in the political field. As probably Lord Willingdon is aware, the largest part of my work is social and moral or religious. My most intimate associates take hardly any part in my political work. The inmates of the Ashram are engaged in agricultural, industrial and educational work, and if Miss Faering comes to the Ashram, she will take part in these activities, and if need be, I will undertake, in no other.

On the same day he wrote to Andrews:

> I have most disquieting news about Miss Faering from Sundaram. I asked him specially to go and see her. He has been there and he tells me she is no longer in the Danish mission and that she is in distress lest she might have to leave India. It would be almost death to her if she is forced to do so. Here is a copy of my letter to Lord Willingdon. I feel most keenly about her. Will you not immediately go to Madras and do what you can to prevent her banishment?

Gandhi followed up Andrews' visit with a telegram to the Governor of Madras Presidency (the administrative region where the DMS was located) requesting him to permit Færing to join him at the ashram.

During a stay in the Nilgiri Hills in mid-1919, Færing had met a young (seven years her junior) Keralan medical student E.K. (Kuhni) Menon and in February of the following year she publically announce their engagement to be married. This caused outrage in the Society and the Hindu community. Gandhi sent her almost daily uplifting verses to help during the height of the storm of criticism in March 1920.[32] A few months before the stricter regulation of missionary societies came into force, Esther resigned from the Danish Missionary Society, saving it from having to answer for her actions. In early August 1919, she wrote her letter of resignation to the Board of Directors:

> As a result of my view and criticism of the Mission, and the missionaries in general, and myself in particular; and furthermore, due to my pronounced sympathy for M.K.Gandhi and his work, I have been subject to much well deserved criticism from several missionaries; and since I, by various imprudent pronouncements have brought the DMS as a whole under suspicion, would hereby like to resign from the DMS. Besides, I have given rise to a great deal of criticism by becoming engaged to a Hindu in June 1919, and unfortunately this has caused indignation too. Therefore, this step in connection with the above mentioned has led me to completely lose all right of being in the service of the DMS.[33]



Bittmann forwarded her resignation letter to Denmark, noting that although he had no choice, it was a difficult thing to do: 'Had it not been for the engagement, I probably would not have agreed to sending it home; but since she has not broken it off, I suppose, this is the only way and she must resign.'[34]

Færing's mission salary was suspended in August and Gandhi asked her to let him know of her 'pecuniary wants' and invited her to come 'at once' to the ashram if she was free.[35] The board of the DMS sent a telegram to Bittmann requesting that Færing return home for negotiation. She refused. It was settled that she would resign from her work at the boarding school in Siloam, where she was stationed, on 2 September, the date when Petersen, who had recently returned from Denmark, could take on her tasks.[36] Between then and when permission to travel to Ahmedabad was granted, Færing stayed with Emilie Bjerrum, another Danish missionary in the south, 'suffering in mind because she is without work and because she is longing to go to *ashram* where she will be able to live and work for her beloved India.'[37] On 6 October the Madras Presidency Governor's Private Secretary finally replied to Gandhi that Esther Færing had permission to join him, if she made the standard application. Finally, on 22 October, she returned to the ashram as an inmate rather than a visitor, just before Gandhi left for Delhi on route to the politically troubled Punjab.

She quickly settled into ashram life, learning Hindustani, looking after and occasionally being alienated by Kasturba who seemed to resent this first outsider being in her kitchen,[38] instructing the ashram children, learning spinning, and desiring to write articles for Gandhi's paper *Young India* (something Gandhi warned her against so as not to 'disturb the Government'[39]). Gandhi saw her presence in the ashram as 'uplifting' and thought of her as 'a good natured girl with all the loftiest aspirations that anyone can be capable of.'[40] However, the prayer meetings were uncomfortable for her as a Christian and Gandhi advised her not to attend if she was not at ease and to pray in her quarters instead.[41] In late January she found lodgings with Gandhi's close Muslim ashramite friend Imam Saheb Abdul Qadir Bawazir as a way to escape tension with Kasturba.

She stayed for nearly three months, however, much of the time Gandhi was not present. They corresponded almost daily, Esther trying to be a good daughter and a conscientious Christian. Gandhi in turn, like a good father, worried about her independence and trusting nature and how easily she could be led astray after she absented herself from the ashram to spend some time at a wedding party of a friend who Gandhi thought could 'befriend her for unworthy purposes'.[42] Some saw far more in the relationship. Stanley Wolpert for example, in his biography of Gandhi, has an obsessed fifty-year-old Mahatma experiencing 'an intensely personal passion for [the] young, golden-haired, blue-eyed Danish beauty'.[43] While Gandhi termed his almost daily correspondence to her 'love letters', this has probably more to do with his state of mind at a time of re-aroused passion in his life, centering around Saraladevi Chaudhurani, with whom he was staying in Lahore, rather than because of romantic feelings for his first European total disciple.

Esther Færing was lonely at the ashram without Gandhi and she spent Christmas with Petersen in Madras. Soon after her return to Ahmedabad her delicate health and personal issues, such as illnesses of family members, forced her to consider returning to Denmark. Gandhi, now touring with Saraladevi, obviously did not want to see Esther go, however, the passion for her, fatherly or otherwise, was no match for the pull of his 'spiritual wife'. Esther left the ashram not long before Gandhi's return in late February and again travelled to south India from where she publicly announced her engagement to Kuhni Menon. Gandhi informed her that he had resigned himself to the marriage and told her to 'do exactly as God guides you. Only always be sure it is the voice of God.' He added that if she was willing to give herself to Menon it constituted proof that 'he is no ordinary young man'.[44] In May she had a few days with Gandhi at Sinhgadh near Poona before she sailed for Denmark on the 19th aboard the *Berlin*. This was the final meeting for some years as the textile labourers' strike in Ahmedabad prevented Gandhi from returning to Sinhgadh as planned. The Mahatma met and approved of the fiancé in August, invited them to live in the ashram, and suggested that they marry but, because it would be difficult to decide on the religion of any children, 'not see each other carnally'.[45]

Years later, Esther Færing recalled that,

> In 1920 I went to Denmark under pressure from the DMS, my father and my sister – and got my dismissal, branded as a heretic, and perhaps as something even worse. When the Grundtvigians [the church movement that championed progressive education and to which Petersen belonged] at the request of Anne Marie, let me speak in the Youth Societies, I was called a renegade. In 1920,[46] I was engaged by my former committee to depart to India in order to help Anne Marie – regardless of my marriage to a Hindu.[47]



Menon, who had stayed behind, joined Færing in Denmark where they married at the beginning of July 1921. Church members saw this as an opportunity to increase their number with Esther becoming 'a tool to drag him into the congregation of Christ.'[48] In Denmark, Esther gave talks on Gandhi and his mission.

The Menons returned to India in December 1921 to help Petersen in her south Indian girls' school, *Seva Mandir*, at Porto Novo (Parangipettai), south of Madras. Although the government had refused to grant Esther permission to return to India, they entered the country without it. Petersen remarked in a letter to a friend that 'Menon says, the British has absolutely no right to deny his wife access to his own country and to be with her husband. But what injustices are they not doing of the time being?'[49] On 5 February 1922, Gandhi wrote to Esther agreeing that her attitude of entering without permission was the right one, adding, 'Let the Government do what they choose.' However he did not publish the news of her return so as not to bring her to the notice of the authorities. Although permission for Esther to enter India was never granted, no issue was made of this and over the years she came and went as she pleased.

Despite Gandhi's suggestions of celibacy (which Gandhi thought had appealed to Menon at the time of their meeting), in 1923 the Menons' first child, Nani (Narayan), was born. In January 1924 Gandhi was released early from his imprisonment following the Non-Cooperation Movement because of ill-health and Esther and Petersen spent a week with him during his recuperation at Sasoon Hospital in Poona. At this time Menon was financed by Petersen's support group, a situation which continued when the family moved to the Kotagiri hill station in the Nilgiri hills as the climate began to affect Esther's health. Menon worked with the poor, but could not earn enough to support the family. Esther wondered if they should take up Gandhi's standing invitation for the family to live at his ashram, but Menon was hesitant and she did not know how to tell Gandhi about her husband's baptism.[50] She did not write to him for over half a year following their time together in Poona.

In October of 1925 Esther proposed writing a biography of Gandhi. He cautioned her against it noting that, 'If you take up the task of writing my biography, you have to pass many months at the Ashram and, may be, even travel to South Africa and visit Champaran and Kheda, probably the Punjab, too. It is a big job if it is done thoroughly. It was in these places I tried to work out non-violence as I understand and know it.'[51] Nevertheless, she pushed ahead and in 1930 the book was published in Danish in Copenhagen under the title *Gandhi: En Karakeristik og Fremstilling* (Gandhi: A Sketch and a Portrayal).

After the birth of their second daughter, Tangai, in 1926, the Menons, with Esther in a 'dilapidated condition',[52] returned to Europe for the 1927 annual meeting of the Porto Novo Mission. With Mission support, Menon then went to Birmingham to obtain British medical qualifications while the malaria-stricken Esther stayed for some years in Denmark with the children, where she presented several programmes on Gandhi on Danish radio. Without her partner and with sick children, Esther was physically and mentally exhausted. She had painful varicose veins, trouble sleeping and lost weight. She had an appendectomy operation in late 1928 but planned to be back in India by the end of 1929. This was not the way things turned out. The wife and children joined Kuhni in Birmingham. He should have finished his studies in 1930, however he only passed his examinations at the third attempt in July 1931. Esther's letters to Gandhi had become infrequent but Gandhi managed to catch up with the family and met the two little girls during his London visit for the Round Table Conference. After his re-imprisonment on his return to India, he sent fifteen letters from Yeravda Prison to the Menons in England.

Petersen was anxious to have the couple back in India at work with her school, however there seemed to be some hesitancy, particularly on Kuhni's part, to return. As a supporter of the independence movement, he was worried about the political situation in the country and Esther and the two girls suffered repeated bouts of malaria; in addition Esther suffered from rheumatism and had to have her teeth removed. The old life of vitality seems to have slipped away for her. She started worrying about what the Indian climate would do to the health of her now relatively robust children. After his graduation, Kuhni took a job working at West Bromwich Hospital for a year. During Gandhi's September 1932 fast in Yeravda prison over the awarding of separate electorates to Harjians, Menon gave up smoking.[53] When the Menons were finally ready to return, their finances would not cover the trip and the patience of the committee and Petersen was wearing thin. The family returned to Denmark in late 1933. The Mission attempted to lend Menon to other mission societies (something Petersen was opposed to) and eventually it was decided to bring them back to India with money raised through a fund.

Finally, in January 1934, the Menons were back, but Kuhni obtained a position in a government hospital in Tanjore, sixty miles south-west of Porto Novo where Esther and the girls were staying. His medical studies had been expensive and he was criticised because this work did not benefit the Mission. Even with his extensive British training, Menon never managed to obtain the type of job he sought and was still not able to adequately support his family. Further, it appears that all was not harmonious in the marriage[54] and, because Esther and the small children could not take the heat of the south Indian plains after eight years in Europe, soon they were living close to 120 miles away from Kuhni in the hill station of Kodaikanal.

Esther's relationship with Gandhi was at its strongest in the earliest years. The letters exchanged between them diminished as Esther entered the more complicated world of being a wife and mother. Her illnesses also took their toll. In the mid-1930s, along with the letters, the Esther Færing/Menon story peters out. Kuhni could not generate enough income to allow him to be free of contributions of the financially strapped *Seva Mandir* and during the war he served as a military doctor before returning to work in hospitals in the south of India. After the war, in the late 1940s the still ill Esther returned to Denmark with her daughters. She paid only a brief visit back to India in 1951 when she arranged for her friend Alice Barnes to edit and oversee the publication of Gandhi's letters to her. All but forgotten, she died in Denmark in the autumn of 1962. Her brief obituary in the *Porto Novo Mission Journal* noted that 'Her life's course was heroic and tragic to an extent that few have experienced'.[55]

## ANNE MARIE PETERSEN: MISSIONARY AND NATIONALIST

In 1869, Peter Andersen became the first Danish missionary to India when he founded the mission at Tirukoilur. By 1900 the Danish Mission Society had an extensive network of missions, schools and hospitals in south India. The DMS grew out of the pious Danish Lutheran Evangelical tradition. There was also another stream of Danish missionary activity: the more liberal Grundtvigian movement[56] which supported the mission of Edvard Løventhal at Vellore.[57]

Anne Marie Petersen, was born in September 1878 and attended the first women's Folk High School in Denmark. In 1900 she graduated as a teacher and taught in schools and pre-schools for several years. In 1907 she heard a talk given by Løventhal during one of his visits home to Denmark. She was inspired, and his comments on the lack of women in the mission spoke to her. On her behalf, her vicar approached the Løventhal mission seeking employment. Although Løventhal was concerned about the suitability of unmarried women working in the mission, she was taken on. To prepare herself for overseas work, Petersen commenced learning English and undertook a year of study at Oxford. She also undertook courses in nursing, obstetrics and child care. Just before Christmas, 1909, the thirty-one-year-old Petersen arrived in India as Løventhal's assistant.

Petersen's first task was to learn to speak Tamil, and her language studies occupied much of her early years in India. To aid her acculturation, she moved out of the Løventhals' house to live alone in a rented property in Vellore. Back in Denmark, a deal was struck between the Løventhal Mission and the DMS for Petersen to work with the DMS on a salary provided by the Løventhal Mission.[58] This arrangement assisted in fostering close cooperation between the two missionary societies. Eventually she ended up working in Madras with the Bittmanns. When the seventy-three-year-old Løventhal left India for the last time in 1914, a question arose as to the future of his mission. The board decided to continue and so Petersen's salary was assured and she took on the task of overseeing two Danish missionary educational programmes.

In late 1916 she undertook a journey around the country gathering information from various educational establishments before the DMS conference was held in Madras. Along with Esther Færing, she visited thirty-two schools around the country, including mission schools, Hindu and British schools, and national schools. The itinerary included a visit to Gandhi's ashram in Ahmedabad and, while perhaps not quite as strongly as her colleague, she too was changed by this experience. Unlike many Western missionaries, Petersen was not steeped in arrogance and racism. She believed in the equality of the races, that Indian churches should be supported, that while missions should convert, they should not attempt to westernise their charges, and that India should be free. Petersen had long wanted to establish her own national Christian women's school and, after her visit to Gandhi, she started planning an institution that took the best from the Danish Folk High School tradition and Gandhi's ashram. At the conference she spoke about her ideas of the foundation of this new school that would conduct its teaching in the vernacular. The conference endorsed the plan, anticipating that 'Miss Petersen, cooperating with Miss Færing if possible, after her return from Denmark, carries out her intention of starting a school for girls within our mission field.'[59] Now that things were in place for realising her dream, she went back to Denmark for a break in mid-1917. This was her first visit home since her arrival eight years before.

During her Danish sojourn, Anne Marie Petersen travelled the country and talked about the situation in India, about the Indian school system, about her vision and how it could be taken on by the Løventhal Mission, while raising funds from the Grundtvigians, and writing several booklets on missionary work in South India, on 'Denmark's World Mission', and on her proposed school. In the book *Our School*, she noted that the teaching would be done in the Indian way with students seated on the floor, dressed, as she herself would be, in Indian clothes: 'Why do I do this? Well, I believe it is beautiful and also, it is perfect for the setting. It is to rid the Christian girls of the foolish idea they have been inclined to fall victim to, that to be a Christian involved showing contempt for everything Indian.'[60] She had a desire to name the project 'The National Indian School Mission', however the business committee of the Løventhal Mission thought that the word 'national' was too dangerous to use as it could upset the British. In the end it was decided to call it 'Løventhal's Mission Continued'.

Anne Marie Petersen hoped to be back in India for the missionary conference in Madras in early 1919, but the disruption caused by the war made it impossible to return until August. Her task in India was to carry on the Løventhal Mission, Edvard Løventhal having died in 1917. The carefully laid plans quickly unravelled. Two weeks earlier her best friend, Esther Færing, had resigned from the DMS, and so could not be her mission co-worker in the new school as they had envisaged. Petersen did not believe that being engaged to a Hindu should preclude Færing from being a missionary, and she shared Esther's nationalist political sympathies. However, she chose to stay with the DMS when they requested her to take over Færing's work at the girl's school in Siloam, and to await the final decision that was to be made about her school at the annual January Missionary Conference. At the conference she requested to be relieved from her work at Siloam as soon as possible 'and made responsible for the beginning of a Christian national girls' school in accordance with her thoughts and ideas.'[61] Although this proposal was passed unanimously, the conference decided that Indian missionaries could not be employed on equal terms with their Danish counterparts. To Petersen this proved 'that the mission societies were still acting as masters and not as servants'[62] and, on 27 April 1920, she followed Færing in resigning from the DMS. She explained to her Danish support group that being away from the DMS might be a blessing in disguise: 'I would rather choose, like Miss Færing, friendship and collaboration with the Indians from a Mr Menon to a Mr Gandhi, even though it might disqualify me of being with a mission society, than I would collaborate with the Europeans.'[63]

On 14 August 1920, she attended a meeting in Vellore where Gandhi was the main speaker.[64] He caused Petersen some embarrassment and helped shape her new direction in life:

> I hoped to be able to hide in one of the fringes of the crowd, but it turned out to be impossible. My peculiar figure caught the eye of one of the leaders, a white woman wearing an Indian dress, and whether I liked it or not, I had to take one of the chairs near the platform. I felt very strange as the only woman and only European in this large crowd of people.

Gandhi recognised her,

> and he – the great – worshiped like a saint by India – put both his hands to his forehead and greeted me. …The leaders standing nearby stared at me with wonder. I was so embarrassed that I did not know where to hide. But Gandhi waved to me: "Come over here Miss Petersen." "No, no!" I said with a deprecating gesture. But the people standing close to me whispered: "Gandhi wants it, Gandhi wants it." So there was no excuse. I had to climb the platform. And there in front of the gazing crowd, he took both my hands in his and said: "I am so happy to see you".[65]

After the meeting she wrote to Gandhi thanking him for his kindness, and noted that the meeting 'more or less decided my future,' because 'I have thrown myself at the feet of India.' She prayed that she would not disgrace God the way 'we Christians have been doing by our behaviour in India.' She added that, 'I feel myself under obligation not only to Christ but to India for His sake at this time of momentous importance for her future.' Gandhi had called for the boycotting of government schools and for the establishment of national ones. This had struck a chord with her. She saw that 'the education the foreign government has given you is not healthy for India and can certainly never make for her real growth.' Her letter concluded:

> Only by indigenous education can India be truly uplifted. Why this appeals so much to me is perhaps because I belong to the part of the Danish people who started their own independent, indigenous national schools. The Danish Free Schools and Folk High Schools … were started against the opposition and persecution of the State. The organizers won and thus have regenerated the nation.[66]

Gandhi reproduced the 'thoughtful' letter in his paper, *Young India*, with an introduction that announced that she 'is about to sever her connection with her Mission for the purpose of giving herself to education that is truly national.'[67] Petersen was now fully immersed in the nationalist project, and Gandhi heartily approved. He wrote to Esther Færing that: 'Anne Marie, that is Miss Petersen, [as she] insists on my calling her, [and] I have fallen in love with each other.'[68] Petersen attended the annual Indian National Congress session held in Nagpur over Christmas 1920. Some months later, she wrote to a friend that the gathering, which was attended by 30,000 delegates, was the 'mightiest I have ever witnessed', and explained why a missionary had to be loyal to the independence movement:

> When we missionaries relate to Gandhi, and participate in this movement to free and reform India in any possible way we are able to as Christians, perhaps we are capable of preparing the way for the Lord. ... On the other hand, by working against the deepest desires and aspirations of the people, and collaborating with the foreign government, keeping these people in slavery and poverty; we make them believe that we are the government's paid agents, and we throw suspicion on ourselves and our ideas, which will render the message we bring impossible.[69]



Petersen commenced travelling in the area to the south of Madras, looking for a site for the school. One night her luggage was stolen at the town of Porto Novo and she decided to stay and teach the people 'the love of God'.[70] Not far from the sea, she purchased land for the school and Kuhni Menon rented a house for her in the town. With money from her support group of Grundtvigians in Denmark, on 17 September 1921 Petersen founded her own National Christian Girls' School at Porto Novo. With a crowd of 10,000 present, Gandhi laid the foundation stone. Her mission in Denmark authorised the change of name of the mission to the Porto Novo Mission. After their return from their visit to Denmark, the newly married Esther and Kuhni Menon joined her. Menon supervised the building of the school.

For three years, until the building was complete, Anne Marie Petersen taught pupils in her rented house. The formal dedication ceremony was held on 20 January 1924. Because he was in prison, Gandhi could not attend. Two weeks later, Petersen and Esther Menon travelled to Poona to share the news with the convalescing but recently freed Mahatma.

The building was an imposing two-storied structure, built in the south-Indian style. It contained two teaching rooms as well as quarters for Petersen, the teachers and the students. She called the school her ashram and named it *Seva Mandir* (Temple of Service). The school coupled working with the hand and the work of the spirit with a more standard academic curriculum. The pupils leart to spin so that they could produce their own clothes, they grew their own food, and studied Indian culture, religions and history. When the school opened it had only thirteen students and was under severe financial difficulties because of cost overruns in the construction.

It goes without saying that Petersen's nationalist sentiments did not endear her to the government. She had signed the required loyalty pledge with caveats. As a result her school received no accreditation or finances for a number of years, she was placed under surveillance, and twice she was denied visas to return to India following visits home to Denmark. In 1922 a new law had been passed which restricted work opportunities in government schools for teachers who had previously worked in nationalist ones. The school struggled financially and in attracting staff until the late 1930s.

Her nationalist leanings did not dilute her Christianity. She clung to the hope that one day India would reject Hinduism in favour of Christianity, and continued to pray that Gandhi would become a convert.[71] The point was that for her the process was to be an organic and culturally acceptable one. Her approach almost ensured that her problems did not end with the British authorities. Even the Grundtvigians were concerned to the point of splitting because some saw her work as being overly political and not sufficiently concerned with gaining Christian converts, and others thought that she had not placed strong enough emphasis on formal Christian baptisms. When in 1922 she was asked to tone down what was seen as her involvement in politics, she answered:

> Now you say: "Do you really take part in politics?" No, I am more and more convinced that we, the missionaries, should refrain from participating in politics. However, in the spiritual struggle, in the fight of the prayers, we must gather all our strength and fight for the victory of freedom and justice, that the suppressed may be freed and the fettered released, because not until then Christ is able to becoming the King of India.[72]

In 1926, during what was to be a restful visit back to Denmark, the underlying tensions came to a head. The religious establishment had their doubts about her and her approach, and she did not help when she spoke out in favour of female ordination. At a meeting of her mission in late

January 1927, it was resolved that the 'Committee of the Porta Novo Mission have agreed on dissolving this committee' because 'it appears that the mission in India run by the missionary Anne Marie Petersen, is more part of the Indian National Movement than it is a Christian piece of mission work.'[73] A new mission committee was quickly established and voted to support Kuhni Menon's medical education in England.

Anne Marie Petersen had great difficulty in getting a visa to return to India. In the end she received one from a subordinate, who did not realise that she had been blacklisted, at the British consulate in Aleppo in Syria. She entered India through Karachi, an unusual entry port where the officials had not been notified to intercept her. Her mission was in economic dire straits. The girls at the ashram were few, the school had no students or teachers with the ill Esther Menon in Europe. The remaining staff were forced onto half salaries and Petersen was consumed with financial worries as money hemorrhaged as a result of Menon's lengthy studies.

Gandhi's new Civil Disobedience campaign, inaugurated by his famous Salt March to Dandi, spawned several local salt marches. This caused some problems for Petersen. She wanted to participate fully in the campaign, but also knew that at any time she could be deported from India. Gandhi and his Madras lieutenant, Chakravarti Rajagopalchari, advised her against being arrested. She decided that rather than 'report for duty', she would hold herself in reserve and 'train the young women, who reported themselves'.[74] Nevertheless, Petersen said a prayer at the start of Rajagopalchari's regional salt march. After the arrest of Gandhi and the rest of the nationalist leaders, Mirabehn toured the country organising resistance. She stayed at Seva Mandir during her trip to the south.

The school stopped buying foreign cloth and other foreign luxuries and, at about this time, Ellen Hørup, who visited Porto Novo, reported on the school: 'Life at the school is conducted in the Indian manner. The language, the attire, the food, everything is Indian. Anne Marie Petersen herself, always wears a saree made from home spun, home woven clothes. We were invited for Christmas. A more beautiful and strange Christmas, I have never experienced.'[75]

During his visit to London for the Round Table Conference, Gandhi urged Menon to return to India. Petersen was almost desperate for the Menons to return. She wrote to a friend, asking whether 'It is so strange that I think Menon ought to come back after his long absence, considering the devastating conditions here, and India's desperate need of its sons?' Later, she added, 'I do not understand why they are not coming.'[76] Tired, physically and in spirit, in March 1933 she wrote to Gandhi how much she needed them and how glad she was that they were finally on the way back. She added hopefully that when Esther and Kuhni did return, with Menons' help she was planning to start 'some work amongst the poor and needy around us'.[77] A week later, Gandhi wrote to Esther Menon on the matter:

> Maria wrote to me the other day and I saw how glad she was that you were at last coming. She is weary with fatigue, both in body and mind. She is almost on the verge of breaking, and I am anxious that, whilst she is still fit, she should run away to Kashmir and give her body and mind a rest for a few months. She needs it desperately.[78]

However, it was not for another three quarters of a year, in early 1934, that the Menons were finally back. As there was no place to set up a medical practice at Porto Novo, Anne Marie Petersen had hoped her friends would settle in the nearby town of Cuddalore, from where Menon could visit *Seva Mandir* on a weekly basis as the school's doctor. Again, she was to be disappointed. Menon had difficulty securing a job, and, when he did, it was far away.

Petersen had a meeting with Gandhi in Bombay when he returned from London at the end of the year in 1931. The following year was hard for her and at the end of 1932 she wanted to go home to Denmark for a spell, but she knew that the British would never let her re-enter the country if she left. The trip was postponed and she went to Kashmir instead for a three month rest stay with her friend Mary Barr. On the way north she visited Gandhi in prison in Poona at the start of April 1933. Gandhi noted that she had lost her vitality and had a 'haggard pensive look' during the visit and attributed her breakdown to having postponed rest for too long. He hoped that the bracing air, and even more the 'relaxation of mind and body', would benefit her health.[79]

Later in the year, she visited the recently freed Gandhi, this time at Wardha, which was to become his base for the next few years. The Civil Disobedience movement was officially suspended by the Indian National Congress in May 1934, and with a less oppressive atmosphere in the country, Petersen finally managed to undertake her trip to Denmark at the beginning of 1935. In late 1937 she was allowed to re-enter India 'through the front door'.

In 1935, the *Government of India Act*, the final British constitution for India was passed. It provided for political autonomy which was inaugurated in April 1937, following elections throughout the country. Congress won most of the provinces, including Madras. Rajagopalchari became chief minister. The autonomous provinces had, amongst other things, responsibility for the education system, and local schools based on Gandhi's educational philosophy were favoured. It seemed that the financial problems of Petersen's *Seva Mandir* might be over. When she returned to India, she found that the school reform programme had 'made her school the object of increased attention from the government and people interested in educational matters since the school already worked in accordance with Gandhi's Wardha Scheme.'[80] In 1939, the authorities assessed the school and concluded that it was:

> established with excellent guidelines. The teaching here is rather different from the normal schools [sic] stereotype teaching. In the free domestic air the teaching is characterized by its naturalness. ...The manager Miss Petersen has transformed a desert to an oasis and brought happiness to many human lives. The musical skills of the children are extremely high ... I cannot find any words to describe my deep admiration for the work done in this, the Home of the Service.[81]

With the outbreak of war, the Congress ministries resigned as a protest at India having been declared as being at war without any say in the matter and the British introduced censorship and martial law. Her local funding ceased as power was again centralised in British hands. Petersen was in poor health and had great difficulty receiving money from Nazi-occupied Denmark and keeping her school functioning. In January 1945, she attended the 'All India National Basic Craft Educational Conference' of teachers in Gandhi's Nai Talim (new education) system at his ashram in Sevagram.[82] There she again met Gandhi, and asked E.W. Aryanayakam, who was the director of the programme, if *Seva Mandir* could be used as a model. While he told her that for 'so many years and before anybody else you have been working for a national school', he noted that there was no hurry in pushing matters further. She replied, 'Yes but for the time being

I have no money.' His response was that money could be found from the Kasturba Gandhi National Memorial Fund, named after Gandhi's wife who had died a year-and-a-half earlier and which supported schools and hospitals working for women and children.[83] Petersen had already applied to the fund and was awaiting a reply.

When the reply came it was disappointing, noting that the Fund 'did not want to support Christian missions'.[84] Petersen was led to believe that only Hindus could apply to the Fund and she wrote to Gandhi to complain about the outcome from a matter of principle even more than one of finances.[85] She obviously felt that she had done enough and expressed her concern over whether Hindus were willing to collaborate with Christians and Muslims. Gandhi assured her that the Fund was non-sectarian[86] and sent her papers to the board of the Fund so that her application could be considered seriously, however, he noted that 'The ideal will be to find your expenses from the surroundings.'[87] The application was again rejected, but with a prospect of funding on the condition that no one at *Seva Mandir* was baptised.[88] Petersen saw this as religious discrimination and withdrew her application. There was a strange irony here: in the mid to late 1920s, the Danish mission committee had criticised her for working more for the Indian national movement than she was carrying out Christian missionary work. Now she was being refused funding because she was running a Christian missionary school rather than being involved with national matters.

In the meantime some money finally came through from Denmark and she used part of it to travel to Bengal at the end of the year to spend some time at Shantiniketan, with a fellow missionary and Gandhi educationalist, the Englishwoman, Marjorie Sykes. Half a year later, she returned to Denmark for the last time. She stayed away from India until the end of 1947. However, her trip home was something of a disappointment. She had not been back for ten years and had a lot to tell to the mission's annual meeting in August 1947, but too few people were interested in what she had to say.

On her return to India, she found that her assistant, Mary Chacko, who was appointed just three weeks before Petersen left, had proved to be an excellent choice. The school was in good condition, there were far more pupils than there had been, and India was free. The new government recognised the value of the school, recommended the establishment of a teacher training institute and started funding *Seva Mandir*. Because the constitution guaranteed freedom of religion, it could continue unhindered as a Christian institution.

A few weeks after her return, Gandhi was assassinated. Petersen remembered the Mahatma who had done so much to influence her life:

> Without Gandhi I would never have become as Indian as I became. What a significance he had on me and on our mission. Also, I came under the influence of this strange man and was allowed to call him Bapu and I felt, that my friendship and love was worth something for him, him whom millions loved, admired and adored. He valued everything that was real and true. ... When he fasted and I was sad fearing for his sake, he wrote and comforted me.[89]

In 1950 she contacted Rajagopalchari, now deputy prime minister, and complained that after having lived in India for forty years as a supporter of the country's independence she was still subject to the *Foreigner's Registration Act*, having to report on her movements outside her area of residence and to annually apply for a residency permit. In December she was finally freed from the control of the *Act*. For the upcoming Christmas party she cooked and made decorations. The Christmas party was a day of feasting and fun for the children. The next morning, however, she could not get up from bed. Menon was summoned and he diagnosed typhoid. She was taken to the Danish Missionary Hospital in Tirukoilur, however on 9 January 1951, she died. The next day she was buried in the garden of her beloved *Seva Mandir*. Gandhi's newspaper, *Harijan*, wrote: 'There was a peculiar spiritual understanding between herself and Gandhi, who used to call her, "My Anni Marie" ... To the last she remained a devoted admirer and follower of Gandhi and she belongs to the blessed group of foreign friends, who served India in complete harmony.'[90]



## THE 'NATIVE' DANES AND GANDHI

Esther, like Mirabehn after her, lived in Gandhi's ashram as a daughter who adopted the wearing of khadi and became a vegetarian. Although she despaired at news of Gandhi's fasts and was elated when they were terminated,[91] she was not obsessive in her relationship with the Mahatma. She was also broad minded. While she may have had a minor struggle with being a Christian in the ashram setting, she never really had to struggle with adapting to India. She realised that her loneliness and absence of friends was most acute when she was among her fellow Danes at the Mission[92] who pitied her 'because I had lost my true mission out of sight and gone astray'.[93] She noted that 'When I came to India, I felt at once at home',[94] and added that she wished that she had been born in India.[95] She readily married a Hindu in the face of church criticism; wanted to bring her children up as Indians 'being proud of India and giving her their best, because they have learnt to feel and think as Indians;[96] and provided her daughters with dolls of different races while she was living in Europe.[97] This did not mean that Færing and Gandhi had no differences of opinion or that they did not carry personal prejudices. Færing was, after all, a devout Christian. While she could not agree with Gandhi that all religions were equally true,[98] she readily allowed Gandhi to instruct her in philosophical issues, and it seems from the letters between them that it was shared ideals rather than an obsessiveness with the person that was most important to her. If anything, an obsessiveness on Gandhi's part for her, his first Western women disciple to actually join his ashram, is evident from his letters. Much of the time Færing was at the Sabarmati Ashram, he was away touring with Saraladevi Chaudhurani, the one woman with whom Gandhi had become truly and disturbingly infatuated. Whether his romantic letters to Færing (like those addressed to Millie Polak a decade before) were in any way a deep psychological defence against his feelings for Choudharani is mere speculation. The initial extreme closeness of their communications aside, this 'native' returned home. Following her departure from India with her family in 1934, the contact with Gandhi was slowly weakened and eventually Esther Færing/Menon's dominant persona became that of mother to her family.

Anne Marie Petersen's relationship with Gandhi was also a loving one; however she respected Gandhi's busy schedule and never forced herself on him ('…is it not selfishness the very craving of one's heart wanting to see you?'[99]), so her letters were relatively infrequent, even though Gandhi asked her not to stop writing to him for fear of taking up his time, as long as she did not always expect a reply.[100] She was at her most touching and most poetic when Gandhi was undergoing one of his lengthy and life-threatening fasts. On one of these occasions she sent him some yarn which she had spun:

> I am trying to do my duty. But this cotton is Devacotton [God's cotton], cannot be used by man and therefore it is for you. It was

> grown in my garden. I plucked it early in the morning when the white soft little cotton children were wet with dew, tears shed from above for our sake. I took the offering, spun it from the seed so that no machine should crush and soil it. I have prayed when I span it and I am now weeping over it for my heart is faint with fear for you and India. Accept this as my love offer.[101]

The next day she had to write again, not to try to get him to give up his fast for the sake of her love, but in the name of the little children who 'were begging you to give up your fast and live for their sake'. After all they were innocent and had done nothing to deserve the curse of his death.[102] And many of her later letters came at similar times and expressed similar sentiments; she wanted him to look after his health because India needed him.[103] We can only speculate on what disappointment she must have felt in the last years of her and Gandhi's life when her beloved nationalist school was not afforded funding by the charitable fund operating in the name of her long-time friend, Gandhi's wife. There is certainly tension in the letters between them at this time.[104] Once she had to fight her own mission over the validity of her views on the ritual of conversion and now she was arguing over the validity of practice with Gandhi.[105] She admired Gandhi, and to a large extent had made herself as much Indian as Danish, but throughout she remained true to her faith, a faith she always hoped the Mahatma could embrace. She had started 'going native' before she had met Gandhi, and probably in some form the process would have continued without the meeting. As it was she became a native Christian who not only longed to join Gandhi's tribe, but hoped that he would join hers.

# The Ultimate Disciple: Mirabehn

Of all Gandhi's Western disciples, male or female, Madeleine Slade, whom he named Mirabehn (or 'sister Mira' after Mirabai, the sixteenth-century mystic Rajasthani poet), was preeminent. There are two main reasons why she simply could not be ignored: her defection 'to the other side', in spite of her status as an elite British woman whose father was an admiral in the Royal Navy; and because for twenty-three years she was so frequently present by Gandhi's side, including during his main overseas trip. But, in some sense at least, she is not typical of Gandhi's Western women disciples. Madeleine *went* to India to be at the feet of Gandhi, the new object of her devotion. Most of the others who 'went native' for any extended length of time also revered the Mahatma, but were engaged in furthering his ideals rather than obsessively wanting to tend him personally. They were in India to do good work and *met* Gandhi along the way. With the exception of Margarete Spiegel, those who did go to India to be at the feet of Gandhi, their 'guru', stayed for a much shorter time than Mirabehn.

In 1953, seven years before Mirabehn's own autobiography,[1] Eleanor Morton wrote a book about Gandhi with a strong emphasis on the women in his circle.[2] Although there is some discussion of Olive Schreiner, Annie Besant, Sonja Schlesin, and Muriel Lester, most of the protagonists are, naturally enough, Indians, and, of the Westerners, the only one who could be classed as 'going native' was Mirabehn. Without the autobiography to refer to, Morton had to rely on Mirabehn's already published letters to her from Gandhi[3] and, because many of the people in the story were still around, those she interviewed. Probably a softer picture of Mirabehn would have emerged if she had relied on Mira's telling of her own story. Obviously all of us want to paint ourselves in the best possible light for posterity. Mirabehn was no different. She barely mentions falling in love with Prithvi Singh in her autobiography (and leaves out all mention of him in her selection of Gandhi's letters). She does not go into the disagreements she had with Gandhi, or the times of estrangement between them, other than the ones caused by her attachment to him. In her collection of the letters, she did something similar. Not long after the Mahatma's death, at the stage she was compiling the volume, there was no indication that there would be a *Collected Works of Mahatma* Gandhi where all would be revealed. She could select at will. In the collection she leaves out letters, or the parts of letters, that detail damaging or private incidents such as the use of bhang at the Rewari ashram where she went to study Hindustani;[4] or that she was ostracised and treated like an untouchable at Sabarmati because she refused to go into seclusion during her menstrual periods;[5] that she believed that the ashram had lost its ideals and she dreaded the thought of returning there after Gandhi had sent her off to do village work;[6] that Chhaganlal Gandhi, one of Gandhi's earliest co-workers, was thieving from the ashram;[7] that the celibacy vows were breached by two young trusted ashramites;[8] or about her own period of estrangement from Gandhi in mid-1942. In her public writings she was not trying to criticise any aspect of the Gandhi community, in fact she was writing the most touching of epitaphs for her obviously increasingly doomed love. In her private letters to Gandhi, the depth of this love is revealed very clearly:

> I could not, even if I tried, be anything else but what I am before you, and that is why, however ashamed I am of my weakness, I have to lay my heart before my Bapu – Yes – you are indeed Father and *Mother* and what is more than all, you are Bapu, *my Bapu* – in whom I live and in whom I have that utter confidence that only boundless love can inspire – And it is Bapu alone who can make me what I

> should be. Oh! That I may learn to understand and serve, as I should. I will not pretend that I am alright. Nothing that bears the slightest shade of *untruth* can stand before you. And I know now, what infinite patience my Bapu has in spite of all my weakness. I cannot fear him – but I fear my own conscience which punishes me ever more severely every time I fall! So it will be that instead of fearing you in my moments of weakness I shall run to you like a frightened child to its mother's breast.[9]

A mere week before Gandhi's assassination, Mirabehn wrote that 'the richest and profoundest [memory of Gandhi] is the ever-recurring incident of his daily life', the measured and calm way that he did things:

> Whenever I am with Bapu I love to sit near him in silence for a while each day. Not when he is meeting people and carrying on discussions, but when he is alone, I know nothing more exquisitely gentle than the touch of Bapu's hand, and I am never tired of watching him handling his writing work. Nothing is ruffled or damaged by his hands, and nothing is wasted.[10]

But, of course, things were not always so straightforward.

## MADELEINE SLADE COMES TO GANDHI

Madeleine Slade was born into the tightly regulated world of the British elite in November 1892.[11] She was a headstrong rather compulsive girl who often felt an outsider among her peers. Although she had had no formal musical training, at age fifteen she heard a Beethoven sonata being played and it changed her life:

> I was finding something far beyond the music as such; I was contacting the spirit speaking through the sound, the spirit of Beethoven. Yes, I had found *him* … I threw myself down on my knees in the seclusion of my room and prayed, really *prayed* to God for the first time in my life. "Why have I been born over a century too late? Why hast Thou given me realization of him and yet put all these years in between?"[12]

Her father, who was often absent on duty, was Admiral Sir Edmund Slade, commander-in-chief in the East Indies Station. As a result, when she was sixteen, the family relocated to India for two years. India meant social functions and a formality that did not appeal to the young Madeleine, and following the visit to England by the women of the family for the Indian summer, she remained behind when they returned to Bombay. She unsuccessfully attempted learning the piano and went to concerts, especially of Beethoven's music. During the First World War she was sickened by the racial hate propaganda, not least because the music for which she lived came out of Germany and Austria. After the war, she registered herself as a concert agent in London and assisted the cause of racial tolerance by promoting Germanic music and artists, and travelled to Bonn and Vienna to Beethoven's birthplace and grave.

But she was restless. When books on Beethoven by the Swiss resident French writer and intellectual Romain Rolland came to her attention, she decided to meet him, but first she went to live in France so that she could master the language and read his books in the original. Madeleine Slade had no doubt in 1923, when she was finally going to meet Rolland in person, that something important in her life was about to change. She *knew* that through him she would find something that was the answer to her soul's longing: 'I had not the slightest idea *what*. I only knew that *all would be well*.'[13] Soon she had a copy of Rolland's newly published biography of Gandhi. She could not put it down: 'as I read the dawn in my heart glowed brighter and brighter, and by the time I had finished, the Sun of Truth was pouring his rays into my soul.' Some incredible yearning had been fulfilled and she arrived at the stage where 'the pure Light of Truth broke in upon my troubled soul and led me to my destination'.[14] Or what seemed to be her destination for well over forty years, before the wheel was to turn a full circle. But at *that* moment she *knew* that her life was dedicated to Gandhi: 'That for which I had been waiting had come, and it was this.'[15]

Immediately she left her Paris residence for London, to book her ship passage to India. On reading further about Gandhi and India, she realised that she needed some 'severe training' to get herself spiritually and physically ready, so she deferred her reservation for a year. Systematically she studied the rules of Gandhi's ashram, gave up alcohol, became a vegetarian, learned to sit cross-legged on the floor, learned to card, spin and weave, commenced learning Urdu, and subscribed to Gandhi's weekly paper *Young India*. When Gandhi had completed his twenty-one-day fast for Hindu-Muslim unity in September 1924, she wrote to him for the first time telling him of her plans and sent a twenty-pound donation. Gandhi replied that he was 'glad indeed that instead of obeying your first impulse you decided to fit yourself for the life here and to take time. If a year's test still impels you to come, you will probably be right in coming to India.'[16]

To prepare herself, Madeleine spent the summer months working with Swiss peasants in their hayfields to get herself into shape. When her training year was three-quarters completed, she wrote to Gandhi again thanking him for his reply, informing him of her progress, and asked whether she 'might dare to hope that I should be accepted by the Ashram'.[17] That second letter was already addressed to 'Most Dear Master,' and concluded pleadingly, 'Dear Master – may I come?'[18] Gandhi replied that she was welcome 'whenever you choose to come'.[19] From the receipt of this letter, her 'joy knew no bounds' and she 'lived in a state of inner ecstacy'.[20]

In the autumn of 1925, just a few weeks short of her thirty-third birthday, she farewelled her parents (never to see them again), and boarded an India-bound steamer in Marseilles. The voyage, she recalled, was 'one long dream of spiritual ecstacy' that was 'leading on and on towards the blessed goal'.[21] Twelve days later she was in Bombay and in the early morning of 7 November she reached Ahmedabad by train. She was met by leading nationalist politician and Gandhi co-worker Sardar Vallabhbhai Patel and Gandhi's secretary Mahadev Desai and was driven to the ashram at Sabarmati on the outskirts of Ahmedabad. At the ashram, she was ushered into Gandhi's room, where a 'small spare figure' rose to greet her: 'I knew it was Bapu, but, so completely overcome was I with reverence and joy, that I could see and feel nothing but a heavenly light. I fell on my knees at Bapu's feet. He lifted me up and taking me in his arms said, 'You shall be my daughter".'[22]

Although her disciplined childhood more than prepared her for the discipline of the ashram,[23] from the first she 'lived for the moments when I could set eyes on Bapu'[24] and her happiest times at the ashram were when she was 'lucky to be deputed to do all Bapu's personal service – cooking his food, washing his clothes, cleaning his room and so forth. Those were indeed, the happiest days of my life, for there is no greater joy for a disciple than the personal service of a beloved and revered Guru'.[25] Two weeks after her arrival, Slade wrote to Rolland: '... Ah, my father, I could never have imagined how divine he is. I had been prepared for a Prophet and I have found an Angel.'[26] The next day the fifty-six-year-old Gandhi cemented the mutual admiration circle by also writing to Rolland:

'What a treasure you have sent me! I shall try to be worthy of the great trust. … She shall be a fellow seeker with me and as I am older in years and therefore presumably in spiritual experience, I propose to share the honour of fatherhood with you. Miss Slade is showing wonderful adaptability and has already put us at ease about herself.'[27]

Although she kept her joining of the ashram a low key affair, her home press was interested in this strange woman who had joined the other side. Perhaps not unexpectedly, a London paper, *The Sunday Chronicle*, published 'fantastic things' about her that Gandhi termed a 'libel on Mira'.[28] When the article was reproduced in the *Indian Daily Mail*, Mira was forced to issue a clarification to 'disarm all criticisms' and deny 'many renunciations':

- I have not forsaken my relatives and friends. How could I ever give up my religion? The religion that was lying dormant within me for the last 33 years, has now revealed itself.
- I have not come to an Ashram that is a promiscuous medley of many races. I am living in a well-organised Ashram in which 200 of the best Indians including men, women, and children are gathered together. They all call Gandhiji not their *Guru* but '*Bapu*' (father) and regard him as a spiritual guide and social and moral reformer.
- I have not sold off my books, but have brought them in the Ashram for the use of the inmates. I have given up my private property.
- I was not dissuaded by my friends from coming over here. They knew that my coming here was a perfectly reasonable step.
- Gandhiji did not write to me, 'Come', immediately he knew of my desire to do so. He asked me to deliberate over my decision for one year and when he accepted me neither did he make me take the vow 'I will never swerve from the path,' nor did he demand that I should renounce everything I possessed. On the contrary, he had repeatedly warned me not to give a hasty promise and even though I gave up all that I had, he accepted it only as a deposited amount for one year.
- Neither was I given a grand reception when I came here, nor were the inmates here highly elated at my arrival. I was admitted in the simplest manner possible. I was not introduced to any radical brains. When I came here, I felt I came to my soul's real home and ever since my arrival I have been staying with everybody in peace and harmony. I do not go to listen to any speeches and am not studying any "situations". I am only learning carding, spinning, and Hindustani.[29]

Nevertheless, Gandhi had high hopes for Mirabehn. She was not to be merely a simple ashramite who occupied herself with spinning and carding. He saw a life of service for her. When Mahadev Desai decided that he would like to learn French from her, Gandhi admonished his faithful secretary for not only wasting his own time but also Mira's:

> Do you know that Miss Slade has come here, having burnt all her boats? Do you know that her sacrifice for our cause is greater than that of any one of us? Do you know that she is here to learn and study and serve and give all her time to the service of our people and thereby her own people, and that nothing that happens at her own home will swerve her from her appointed task here? Every minute of her time is therefore doubly precious and it is for us to give her as much as we can. She wants to know everything about us, she must master Hindustani. How else is she to do it unless we help her in making the best of her time? She may be quite willing to oblige us, but our duty is to give her as much as we can. Our own time is sacred enough. Hers is a more sacred trust. Rather than indulge in the luxury of learning French, I would expect you to give her an hour in Hindi, Sanskrit or such other thing.[30]

However, Mira's deepest desires did not quite correspond with Gandhi's vision.



## MIRABEHN AND GANDHI

It did not take long for the euphoria of their meeting to wear off. Although Mirabehn had been in the ashram for less than a month, Gandhi had to leave for a few days. This was their first separation, and it caused her great pain.[31] Gandhi assured her that she was constantly in his thoughts and then quickly added that 'This three days' separation is good discipline.'[32] This was to be the start of a pattern. Although she tried desperately to heed her master's voice and fight attachment, to concentrate on his work rather than his personality, it was futile. When she was away from Gandhi, her life lost meaning. Eventually even she came to see that a pattern had developed: 'Everytime I was separated from Bapu I used to suffer excruciatingly, and if the separation was long my health used finally to break down.'[33] Five months after the first, there was another separation. Looking back after Gandhi's death, she noted that in realising her pain

Gandhi had put before her the 'highest truth'; a truth which took her years to realise. Gandhi had written to her that she would get over her feelings of separation 'because it has to be got over. The few days' separation is a preparation for the longer separation that death brings.'[34]

Already, by early 1926, she could write to one of Gandhi's close followers that 'He is very strict with me … and will not let me do anything for him personally except to look after his spinning wheel. He says I must get on as fast as I can with my own work and I shall not be allowed to help him any more until I know Hindi, spinning, cooking etc. thoroughly well.'[35]

Although Mirabehn did not much like the communal life of the ashram, and thought that it was not ascetic enough, she disciplined herself and, although Gandhi was counselling caution, she soon wanted to cut off her hair and take a vow of celibacy. By this stage, Gandhi had long been addressing her in letters with the familiar 'chi Mira',[36] and was fulfilling his role of a father, requesting descriptions of her studies, meals and bowel movements,[37] and acknowledging receipt of her 'love letters' when they were separated.[38] He also commended her to the other ashram women: 'I send to Chi. Maganlal all the letters of Mirabehn. I want all you sisters to listen to them carefully, try to understand them and reflect over them. In my view she is at present the ideal woman worker among us.'[39]

However, by early 1927 he was telling her to 'throw off the nervousness' and not cling to him 'in the body' but to practise detachment.[40] At this stage Gandhi did not make it easy for her to follow his advice – there are what could be seen as mixed messages in his almost daily letters and perhaps he was simply demanding too much. When at one stage she suggested that the ill Gandhi should not feel the need to write to her, he replied that he could not deny himself the joy of writing weekly love letters to her.[41] Three weeks later he conceded that if the separation became unbearable for her despite the love of those around her, she 'must come without waiting for an answer or any prompting from me'.[42] A little over two weeks after that, he informed her that he did not want her to be what she was not, while trying to help her to be 'what you should be'.[43]

Mirabehn could see the logic of Gandhi's position but it was a struggle accepting it on a deeper level because it went against the advice of her heart. She wrote a cheerful letter to Gandhi with the words he wanted to hear, and he responded that he was pleased, noting that she had 'got the truth for the moment'.[44] But it was only a moment. Soon after, Mirabehn again wrote to him admitting that, as she put it later, 'In spite of the intellectual realisation the heart has failed me.'[45] Looking back on this time, a dozen years after Gandhi's death when she was re-evaluating her life, Mirabehn noted that she could see 'how I was progressively crushing my natural independence of nature and putting myself wholly under another's will, a thing I had never done in my life. It was the intense reverential love that I felt for Bapu which made me discipline myself in this way, but it increased the tension which was already there.'[46]

None of this is to imply that there were not times when Mirabehn was confident, self-assured and doing valuable village and community work, times when she was not at all obsessive or possessive. For example: 'I have just received your precious post-card and my heart is rejoicing – and I feel a special happiness to think that my Bapu has enough confidence in me now not to feel the necessity to write when he is busy.'[47] Unfortunately, these times were the aberrations.

Mirabehn knew that to be of use to Gandhi, in a way which allowed her to remain close to him, she had to learn Hindustani. And this, in turn, meant allowing Gandhi to send her from the Gujarati-speaking ashram at Sabarmati to the Bhagavad Bhakti Ashram at Rewari, in the Hindi speaking heartland just south of Delhi, where she could perfect her language skills. The separation was a heavy trial to her. Gandhi wrote to her about the return of her agitation[48] and discussed detachment at length.[49] Again Gandhi reminded her that generally one cannot give up a programme that has been voluntarily taken on, however, 'if you become highly emotional and your nerves remain under tension, you should come even though your course may not be finished' because he saw her health as more important than her studies.[50] Later, Mirabehn was able to comment that she grasped the truth of this ideal of detachment from the body of another with her intellect. However, she added that the 'heart lagged behind for still many years after this'.[51] In fact a great many years, until the unsatisfying break away from Gandhi following her infatuation with Prithvi Singh. In the meantime if Gandhi was sick, she felt an almost uncontrollable urge to nurse him, something Gandhi, who was not short of those ready to fulfill the role, did not want.[52] At times Gandhi lost his temper over this obsessiveness then had to apologise.[53] Mirabehn, later commenting on this state of affairs, noted that when she rushed to his sickbed she 'received a scolding, which in its turn, always broke my heart'.[54] In the meantime she clung to her dreams of settling with Gandhi, 'building ashrams in the air' where the 'pure' ashramites, such as her, could live the true ashram life and from where she could hope to draw Gandhi to her. 'Thus we dream and thus we long – How can we help it?'[55]

Towards the end of 1928, Mirabehn recalled how Gandhi had looked forward to her being an influence for good among women, making her 'fight for all I am worth with myself in order to try and serve you in this way.' The ashram was dispiriting her and her 'nervous outbreaks, and my Bapu's scoldings, became more and more frequent – and at last I said that I must go away, for I was not fit to be near you.' In her new life in the villages she claimed to have 'found my Bapu, and, *I have found myself*'. However, as this was a new stage in her life, she felt that she needed to talk to Gandhi about it and so requested his permission to visit him. In a pleading request to Gandhi (addressed to the Mahatma in the third person as she often did when matters were personal and centred on her possessiveness), who appeared not to be answering her letters, she noted that 'in Wardha, when he goes for morning and evening walks, there may now and then be a few moments when he can talk with me, without being unduly pressed.' She closed the letter, beseeching, 'So, my Bapu, can I come?'[56] Three days later she added that 'if you let me come to you, be assured that I shall not be coming with nervous trouble, and anxious questions. ... I no longer feel agitated now that I have not got to face living in the Udyog Mandir ['temple of crafts'][57] ... If I can be near my Bapu for a little (and above all in the quiet surroundings of Wardha) it would mean all the world to me and Heaven too!'[58] In order to be in his presence, she had to persuade him that she was doing what he wanted and that she no longer needed him. These letters are less than convincing. She was in a bind, as illustrated by a letter of early 1929, after she had received Gandhi's 'precious Monday card', where she wrote to him that 'in these hectic days' she does not want him 'to spend any time in writing letters to me'.[59] She tried to win his sympathy by describing her illnesses in graphic detail, but adding that he need not worry as 'this peculiarly wretched condition is probably the turning point';[60] or by writing to Naradas Gandhi, the then manager of the Sabarmati Ashram, about her ideas about how khadi work could be reorganised, how best to conduct village work, her ideas for improved carding tools etc., knowing that this would be reported back to Gandhi, perhaps prompting him to write to her, or even summon her for discussions.[61]

The love, the desperation, the longing to do her master's bidding are illustrated in a letter Mirabehn wrote Gandhi as she was about to commence work in an out of the way village with poor communications, just as Gandhi was about to begin a lengthy tour. She had to work out some form of communication so that she could maintain contact, to know how he was faring:

> I have tried not to think about it up till now – but as the time approaches my heart begins to bleed unbearably – my trouble is added to by the fact that Mahadev is not with you in these days – and I used to count on him with absolute confidence to send me immediate news if there was anything the matter. Bapu dearest – I have reasoned and argued with myself – but what can I do, there comes a time when love *will* have its way, and refuses absolutely to bend to philosophy!
>
> So might I dare to ask for this arrangement – that you tell Subbiah to send me a postcard twice a week? All he needs to write on it is my name and address and then the words – Bapu well – or Bapu fairly well – and then if it should ever have to be – Bapu ill – he must not keep me waiting for a postcard, but must send me a telegram!
>
> Will my Bapu allow that? I implore him not to force me too far in endurance – because I feel I should break – and I don't want to break! I want to be well and strong to work with all my might![62]

In a long and very blunt letter in mid-1929, Gandhi called Mirabehn's attachment to him a disease which he labeled 'idiolatry' and asked if it is not why she hankered after his company. He continued asking why she so helplessly relied on him, why she did everything to please him, why she had no independence. When he pointed out to her that she was capable of managing the symptoms of the disease but not its root causes, she broke down. He noted that others took his 'blows without being unstrung', while she was 'nerve-broken'.[63]

A Catch-22 situation was developing. At one stage, after a lengthy early separation, Mirabehn burst into tears of relief after seeing Gandhi again. When this came to Gandhi's attention, it made him 'still more convinced that I must accustom myself to separation.'[64] He sent her to Rewari. And while Gandhi insisted that she retain her individuality, if she acted in the way that was natural for her she displeased him. Once the first flush of excitement of the relationship had worn off, it became clear that they wanted different things from each other.[65]

In April 1928, Rolland wrote to a French friend, noting that Mirabehn was Gandhi's principal disciple. At the time he was having a disagreement with Gandhi over the Mahatma's explanations about his support for the British war effort back in 1914. Rolland commented on how important it seemed for Gandhi to make him understand his point of view. Perceptively, Rolland pointed out that 'He's infinitely more attracted by people who resist or criticize him than by those who acquiesce in his judgement.'[66] Mirabehn, being attracted by Gandhi the person, had no avenue to resist or criticise the Mahatma. She did acquiesce to his judgement (after all she had no choice) even when it was that she should be distanced from him. She tried to ease the pain of separation by pouring her heart out to Gandhi in letters. For example, from October 1928 till April 1929, she wrote him 53 letters. Nevertheless, this was no substitute for personal contact and she developed some defences against the separation, presumably at a deep psychological level, rather than a surface manipulative one – she got sick and had to be brought back.[67]

Mirabehn was sent to various small villages in distant parts of India to promote sanitation, carding and spinning, but she was back at Sabarmati for the lead-up to Gandhi's historic 1930 Salt March to Dandi which culminated in the breaking of British salt laws and the major Civil Disobedience movement which followed it. When he left, Gandhi vowed not to return to the ashram until he had achieved independence for his country. With Gandhi gone, the ashram was empty for her. However, after Gandhi had been released from his stint in prison in early 1931, she had the privilege to be with him during his peace negotiations with the Viceroy Lord Irwin, and to accompany him to London for the Second Round Table Conference on India's future constitutional status.[68] However, between these two periods of physical proximity, there was the usual struggle of negotiating their place in relationship to each other and the meaning of that relationship:

> You are on the brain. I look about me and miss you. I open the charkha [spinning wheel] and miss you. ... But what is the use? You have done the right thing [in going to the ashram]. You have left your home, your people and all that people prize most, not to serve me personally but to serve the cause I stand for. All the time you were squandering your love on me personally, I felt guilty of misappropriation. And I exploded on the slightest pretext. Now that

you are not with me, my anger turns itself upon me for having given you all those terrible scoldings. But I was on a bed of hot ashes all the while I was accepting your service. You will truly serve me by joyously serving the cause.[69]

Gandhi was perhaps the best-known person on the planet at this stage, and in London, because of her past and association with him, Mirabehn became one of the best-known women. She was interviewed and was the focus of countless newspaper articles. She became a press celebrity. One day, attending a large reception for Conference delegates at the prestigious Lyceum Club, when she handed her khadi shawl to the cloakroom attendant to be placed among the fur wraps of the other attending women, she noted to her new friend Agatha Harrison that 'the last time I was in this club, I was a member'.[70] On the way back to India, the Gandhi contingent visited Romain Rolland at his home in Villeneuve on Lake Geneva in Switzerland. Here, away from the hurly-burly of London, Mirabehn came to some dim realisation of what had happened to her life. In her autobiography she talked about



a feeling of coming back to the senses of my former free and independent life, but now under conditions of strictest discipline. In order to maintain that discipline I had, without realizing it, shut myself up in a self-imposed inner prison. It was when I met Romain Rolland again, and felt the influence of his penetrating blue eyes, that I vaguely knew something was wrong – wrong in the sense that I was not my full self. My spirit silently longed to reach out to him, but I could not emerge from that inner prison. ... So the days passed in a haze of inner sadness which I could not, at the time, explain to myself.[71]

Back in India, Mirabehn tried to put these thoughts behind her. Both she and Gandhi served various terms of imprisonment as negotiations with the British came to nought. Because of this, they had little chance of meeting in the early 1930s. When her letters could reach Gandhi, for example in mid-1933 during Gandhi's fast, they are still the love letters of a disciple. The almost daily letters end with sentiments such as 'I am so little worthy of you – but I will strive and strive'; 'Bapu, I embrace your feet – those feet at which I am sitting'; 'in prayer at your feet';

'Bapu, I will not keep you with many words. Having to come to your side for a minute, I will again sit at your feet in prayer till tomorrow'; and 'in prayer at your feet, your ever devoted daughter'.[72] The period of 'indefinitely long separation' meant that her nerves were 'getting a little bit over stretched' because of Gandhi's absence and because in prison she had no one to talk with in a way that exercised her mind. Nevertheless, she promised not to have a nervous breakdown 'or anything like that'.[73]

Regardless of her natural feelings, Mirabehn did have self-analytical insights. She understood her personal attachment and tried to explain it to Gandhi in terms of womanly instinct 'which is stronger than any amount of reason' and which can only be harnessed in a positive way 'if her nature is able to express itself'. In a lengthy letter, she informed Gandhi as to how this expressed itself for her in the rendering of personal service, and how it could be channelled constructively:

> When you are taken from us, as in jail, an instinct impels me to work with all my strength at outward service of your cause. I feel no doubt and no difficulty. When you are with us, an equally strong instinct impels me to retire into silent personal service; trying to do anything else, I feel lost and futile. The capacity for the former depends on the fulfilment of the latter. The one is the counterpart of the other, and something continually tells me that it was for fulfilment in that way that I was led to you.[74]

The debate over Mirabehn's attachment to his person had been a point of contention between her and Gandhi since she had arrived at Sabarmati Ashram seven years before. Now, finally, but in the end only temporarily, Gandhi seemed to give up the struggle to wean her from her clinging:

> I understand and appreciate all you say about yourself. Let me put you at rest. When I come out you shall certainly be with me and resume your original work of personal service. I quite clearly see that it is the only way for your self-expression. I shall no longer be guilty as I have been before in thwarting you in any way whatsoever. My only consolation in thinking over the past is that in all I did, I was guided by nothing else than the deepest love for you and regard for your well-being.[75]

Gandhi wanted workers and not devotees; however he well understood Mirabehn's psychological state and he realised that his reaction to her gave him greater insight into his own inner make-up. A few weeks before his letter of acquiescence, he had responded to another follower who had criticised Mirabehn:

> I may have spoken to you vehemently in defence of Mirabehn, but I have not made any man or woman weep as bitterly as I have made her. My hardness of heart, impatience and ignorant attachment were responsible for such conduct. I have felt Mirabehn's self-sacrifice to be beyond praise and, therefore, wish to see her perfect. The moment I see any imperfection in her, my ignorant attachment makes me impatient and I rebuke her sharply. The result is a flood of tears. These instances have opened my eyes to the presence of violence in me and, recalling them, I have been trying to reform myself.[76]

A few months later, the imprisoned Gandhi commenced a fast over the setting up of separate electorates for Harijans. Mirabehn was beside herself with concern but the authorities would not give her permission to visit him. Gandhi, in turn, refused to accept any visitors until she was granted permission to see him. She wrote a desperate letter to him: 'If only I would see you once more in your bodily form, once more hear your voice – somehow, without that human mercy, I feel as if the mind will crack ... I have nobody and nothing else in the world but you – no thought no care but you.'[77]

Soon she too was back in prison for being 'actively engaged in the furtherance of he Civil Disobedience Movement'. After Gandhi had been released he managed to visit her in Sabarmati jail on 21 July 1933, a year and a half since their last meeting. A week later he wrote her that he hoped she was 'not over-excited after the interview'. Then next day Gandhi was again back in prison and soon undertaking another fast, this time because of new jail rules that did not allow him to do scavenging work in solidarity with the 'untouchables'. Mirabehn was greatly disturbed by the news as Gandhi's health deteriorated rapidly and his death looked imminent. Hurriedly, she wrote to him that God had given her the 'light to recognise His messenger and servant in you. He will therefore give me the strength to go through anything and everything for the fulfillment of His word through you.' She added that 'My love would be a poor thing, if it failed at this supreme moment and gave way to misery and desperation.'[78]

After they were finally released from their respective rounds of imprisonment, Mirabehn in Bombay's Arthur Road and Ahmedabad's Sabarmati jails[79] and Gandhi in Yeravda Jail in Poona, they were united in Poona in late August and were together for a month until Gandhi had regained his strength and led his entourage to Wardha, as the first stage of his country-wide Harijan tour. Mirabehn travelled in south and central India with Gandhi. By June of 1934, with the walking tour over and the rushed vehicle and train tour about to begin, Mirabehn came to the realisation that she should be back in England to further Gandhi's cause by correcting misinterpretations of his mission that had emerged since they had left London following the Round Table Conference and to 'get in contact with the working classes'.[80] She sailed from Bombay on 19 June, and a week later Gandhi wrote to Sardar Patel that 'You must have read the news about Mirabehn. There is nothing more behind it. She suddenly felt that she herself should go and do something. I consented and she left. Her personality had become suppressed under me. I hope she will regain her former independence of character.'[81] In July she disembarked from her ship at Marseille and immediately went to visit Romain Rolland but 'again the longing to be myself, and the fact that I was not, weighed on me just as it had in 1931. Even more so, because this time I seemed more conscious of it.'[82]

In England as she chaired meetings, lectured and met government officials, she did not let any of her doubts show. She noted that she had been unhappy for years before she left England for India and things had been 'dark and futile' until she became a disciple of Gandhi. Next she sailed to the United States and in a two week-long lecture tour managed twenty-two gatherings and five radio broadcasts. She informed reporters in New York that 'You have your Christ. To me, Gandhi is Christ.'[83] How much her travels aided the nationalist cause or helped the world understand Gandhi is questionable and in late 1934 she was back in India. She went straight to Wardha and Gandhi where, in strained circumstances, she helped set the future geographical direction of the Mahatma's life.

Mirabehn stayed with Gandhi at Gandhi lieutenant Jamnalal Bajaj's property, Maganwadi, but found the conditions too confining. She tried to find relief by going for long solitary walks in the early mornings. To reach the open countryside she had to pass through the small nearby village of

Sindi. The insanitary conditions of the village appalled her and so, with the help of Mahadev Desai and other Maganwadi inmates and Gandhi's strong encouragement, she began a sanitation programme in the village. The success of efforts to discourage the villagers from defiling their environment, however, was minimal. Gandhi therefore instructed Mirabehn to take a contingent of Maganwadi residents and visitors who had come to see Gandhi to the village every morning to clean its roads.[84] Gandhi noted that although they were trying to become villagers, they were far 'from the thing'. Mira, however, was 'the hole-hogger among us all'.[85]

Towards the end of the year Gandhi's high blood pressure was troubling him and the cramped conditions at Maganwadi, along with the lack of progress in sanitation efforts in Sindi and other nearby villages visited, left him, in the words of a biographer, 'frustrated and contributed to his poor health'.[86] Mirabehn noted that 'his nerves were becoming severely strained.'[87] Gandhi decided to move to Sindi alone and work for and with the villagers while he was regaining his health. His associates at Maganwadi were shocked by the idea and he only agreed to remain where he could get adequate medical attention when Mirabehn offered to take his place in the village.[88]

A small one-roomed cottage was built for Mirabehn in Sindi. Although the village was occupied by low castes, even they had their strict hierarchy. When, on her first day there, Mirabehn accepted water from a man of the lowest caste in order to wash her hands, she was henceforth refused permission to take water from wells belonging to those of slightly higher castes.[89] Although she made some progress in the village, it was extremely slow and meagre. In reality, Sindi was little more than an outlying urban slum of Wardha and Mirabehn decided that she needed to experiment in a more typical Indian village. After a replacement was found for her in Sindi, she began the quest for a more suitable village within a five-mile radius. Eventually she settled on Segaon, east of Wardha as the least unsatisfactory of a poor lot. Although there was no connecting road and the village was built in a low-lying area between two water channels, and hence prone to malaria outbreaks, the advantage of Segaon was that the people 'were a little more responsive' and that it contained an orchard and farm belonging to Bajaj. Soon a hut had been built for her at the edge of the village and she had relocated there from Sindi. The population of the village stood at around 600 residents, two-thirds of whom were 'untouchables'.

In the meantime Gandhi's health broke down and he relocated to the nearby ashram of Vinoba Bhave, a long-standing and close disciple who had been in the area since the early 1920s. Mirabehn saw this as an opportunity for closer contact. She walked over to visit him but was barred from his presence with the words that the guard had orders to keep her away. The shock of the situation reduced her to tears and she 'did not get over it for years'.[90] When she was allowed to see Gandhi, it was for very short periods while others seemed to have free access to the Mahatma. She was informed that she had to remain in Segaon to help preserve Gandhi's health. A 'strange artificiality' arose between them, but Mirabehn could not talk about it for fear that Gandhi's blood pressure would rise. In the end it was she who broke down.[91]

Mirabehn later admitted her greatest longing was to live in a village *with* Gandhi. She had been torn between a love for the countryside (or was this at least partially a rationalisation when Gandhi sent her off to some distant rural area?) and desire for the physical proximity of the Mahatma. 'Now I had hoped that the time had come when the two longings could be fulfilled.' But living alone in Segaon 'meant perpetual separation from Bapu,' and that was something that her 'health and nerves would not be able to endure'.[92] When Gandhi learned that she was not up to staying at Segaon alone, he decided that he himself would go there and live alone. Besides the need for space and peace, it had become increasingly clear to Gandhi that he had to settle in a village and work alone because village co-workers had to be cultivated from within the village itself rather than imposed upon it from the outside.

Others in Gandhi's entourage were not particularly keen to live an out of the way rural existence and were concerned about deterioration in Gandhi's health if he took such a step. And to make matters worse, it appears that Mirabehn was 'openly criticised for having been the cause' of this new longing on Gandhi's part.[93] Eventually, in April 1936, Gandhi did settle in Segaon but if Mirabehn wanted any proximity with him she had to find another nearby village. This news 'nearly broke my heart'.[94] She prepared her old hut as his and settled in a cottage a mile away. Other coworkers eventually crowded in on Gandhi and Segaon became a new ashram, but one that seemed to have no place for Mirabehn.[95] Sushila Nayyar, a young trainee doctor and the sister of Gandhi's future secretary, Pyarelal, took over the personal nursing of Gandhi, once Mirabehn's privileged domain. Even though Gandhi recognised that Mirabehn 'cannot just live away from me', he laid down restrictions for her visits: she could go to Segaon once a week. In a letter to his chief woman disciple back at the Sabarmati Ashram he added, 'Let us see what happens now.'[96]

When, at the end of 1938, Mira was sent by Gandhi to the Frontier Province, she again started pining for his presence. He wrote to her that 'I am prepared to risk your death there rather than that you should return to Segaon to live'.[97] The prospect of never returning to live near Gandhi haunted Mira 'like a nightmare'.[98] Her consolation was that Gandhi was planning a trip to the Frontier. Her health did not allow her to wait for him and she returned to Segaon, and then, to fulfill his wishes that she work independently, she went to Bihar. Only then did Gandhi's long postponed trip to the Frontier materialise, and with this 'the sorrow in my heart became further accentuated'.[99] In response, she wrote Gandhi a stream of pleading letters. Although Gandhi assured her that she was not out of mind because she was out of sight and that he missed her,[100] he also hinted that she should restrict herself to one letter a week, or that a post card would be enough 'when you have no time'.[101]



## THE GROWING DISTANCE

The seeming loss of Gandhi because of his reluctance to have her physically near meant that Mirabehn was now free (or forced by an inner compulsion) to bestow her affections elsewhere. While she was in the Frontier Province, Prithvi Singh had presented himself to Gandhi. Prithvi Singh was a dashing character, a powerfully-built Punjabi nationalist revolutionary who was imprisoned by the British for ten years in 1915. In 1922 he staged a daring escape and since then had been 'underground' for sixteen years before apparently discovering nonviolence and turning to Gandhi for assistance.[102] Mirabehn got to know him when she was asked to polish up the English version of his remarkable life story for publication. They saw quite a lot of each other at Sevagram – village of service (as Segaon had been renamed in 1940). Mirabehn felt at ease with him and 'rejoiced in his frank and fearless manner' and she began to feel that 'Here at last is someone with whom I could perhaps work outside independently' as Gandhi had always wanted her to do.[103] She rechannelled her love for Gandhi to Prithvi Singh, who, in addition, held out the possibility of the fulfillment of her newly recognised sexual longing, something that could never even have been allowed to surface in her relationship with the Mahatma. She developed a passionate desire to marry Prithvi Singh, bombarding him with a dozen love letters in November 1939.[104] When Mirabehn shared the news of her love for Singh with Gandhi, she asked him for his blessings. He reportedly was quite happy to hand her on to Singh, saying: 'I should now like you to be guided entirely' by him.[105] However, Singh was not interested[106] and fled the complication of her love by suddenly taking a trip to visit family in Burma.[107]

Gandhi noted that

> Mirabehn looks upon him as her husband. She believes that her love for him is the result of her previous life. She has pledged her all to him. Prithvi Singh regards her as a sister. For this I am responsible. The moment he came here I told him that he should regard all the women here as his sisters. As a result he does not look upon her in any other way. Mirabehn is pining for him here. It is not that Prithvi Singh is not going to marry. I feel that if a woman whom one regards as a sister is really not one's sister and if there is no violation of morality, the brotherly sentiment is not binding. It is question of life and death for Mirabehn. Mirabehn is worthy in every way. She can be a great help to Prithvi Singh. Mirabehn does want a child and that too by Prithvi Singh. Under such circumstances it becomes my duty to persuade Prithvi Singh and if he has no religious objection it is his duty to marry her.[108]

Half a year later, Gandhi wrote to Singh that while Mira is cheerful and 'all right', she 'keeps harping on the same thing' and 'is hopeful and does not worry'.[109] It is obvious that Singh felt sorry for Mirabehn, and Gandhi tried to set him at ease by telling him a few days later that Mirabehn 'believes that she had the same relationship with you in a previous birth and it will be the same in future also. That you have forgotten it in this birth is a matter both for sorrow and joy for her.'[110]

How different would her life have been if he had acted on her approaches and Gandhi's encouragement? Her distance from Gandhi (in both the physical and, on Gandhi's part, emotional senses) and rejection by Singh caused an 'inner struggle' that had

> come to a crisis and such bewildering and delusive mists and fogs had enveloped my path that, in my anguish, I went into silence and seclusion that I might the better pray to God for help. The silence,

> with a few days' break for travelling, lasted 15 months. For part of the time my rule was to speak once a day for half an hour, if necessary, and for the rest of the time when I was in a cottage in the Sevagram fields, I spoke twice a week in the evening when I went to see Bapu.[111]

In a more brutal appraisal of her situation, mirroring her feelings at the times of her meetings with Rolland a decade before, she again was able to articulate the fact that her relationship with Gandhi came at significant personal cost. In a letter to Singh, she noted that when she originally came to the Mahatma, she had put herself in his hands,

> and he, with the fullness of his love, took complete possession of me, guiding not only my actions, but even my thoughts and feelings. It was a great disciplining and training out of which I learned a tremendous amount, but it also undermined my self-reliance and self-expression, and I became unable to do any sustained or independent work. Before I came to Bapu I was a person of free energy, enterprise and self-reliance. All this I somehow lost. Only when you came into my life did my natural strength re-awaken. When I went into that *tapasya* [penance] I was conscious of my real self coming back to life. I felt a new strength and freedom added to it, during those 15 months of silent prayers and readings. I gained spiritual riches which were unknown to me before. Having realized all this, what should I do?[112]



Of course, by this stage Prithvi Singh had long made it clear that he could not help her in this regard. But this was not the end of the story. Around this time, just over a year and a half after Singh first came to him, Gandhi wrote to Sardar Patel that Singh 'has lost faith in me, our relations have come to an end'[113] and a short while later he announced this in his newspaper.[114] This was soon after Singh had returned to India, and briefly the ashram and Mirabehn's renewed overtures of love.[115]

Two years later, Gandhi wrote to the estranged Singh about some unpleasant things he had learnt about his behaviour. He accused Singh of having calculatingly engineered his influence with him for personal gain until, no longer useful, he cast nonviolence aside and then 'clung to Mirabehn and tried to win me back through her'. In addition, he 'cast lustful eyes on two girls', who managed to evade him, but married another who he had lured away from her fiancé.[116]

Soon after, Gandhi wrote to Mirabehn informing her of the 'terribly disturbing' things he had been hearing from reliable sources about Prithvi Singh. Besides the issues raised in his letter to Singh personally, he added that 'He has been using questionable means to extort money' and that

> His profession of non-violence when he came to me and in his letters from the jail appears to have been a deep-laid plot to deceive me and through me some day or other to secure his release from the life of hiding which was worrying him. Thus, my prejudice is deepening. I should love to know from experience that the prejudice has no basis. It is generally believed that the Communist Party is exploiting you through him.[117]

Gandhi was warning Mirabehn and perhaps he was also trying to keep a hold on her. At the start of 1946, Gandhi mentioned Singh to Mirabehn for the last time: 'About P. I must not say anything. I am prejudiced. I only hope that God will be your guide in this, as in everything else.'[118]

Mirabehn's infatuation with Prithvi Sing was at a time of strong tension (possibly in part caused by her replacing Gandhi with Singh as the object of her affection) between her and Gandhi over financial matters concerning her money that was with the ashram[119] and accountability matters concerning the need for trustees to oversee her new plans to relocate to the Himalaya, and which of them was to blame for her relationship with Singh.[120] In mid-1944, Gandhi threatened to 'let the public know somehow or other that I am not at the back of any of your activities which are being undertaken in spite of my disapproval. This letter is my last warning. I shall trouble you no more. God be your only guide.'[121] Mirabehn pointed out what she saw as wrong interpretations of her position, and worse, the lack of fairness in this approach as it would stymie any venture of hers from the outset:

> Beloved Bapu,
> I have your letter. I had not realized the position regarding the fund kept in my name, and that my expenses were being drawn. I had the impression that the whole sum was being kept intact and that I was receiving food, clothing, travelling expenses, etc., like some others who gave their whole time to the cause according to their individual

capacity. But this was a misunderstanding. So, I will gladly put the matter straight at once. I cannot bear any bargaining in such matters. I, therefore, ask that Rs. 20,000 should be deducted from the total, which should cover the expenses incurred by the Ashram for me during these 20 years. The remainder can be transferred to my name.

I had understood that when I had this money, I should be free to do constructive national work without let or hindrance, so long as I made it clear that the scheme of work was entirely my own and without your personal approval. I did not realize that you would feel called upon publicly to express disapproval of my work.

You have given me my freedom with one hand and taken it away with the other. To give me my money and freedom, and at the same time to say that as soon as I begin to use them you will publicly disapprove, is to sabotage anything I may try to do. You at the same time sabotage any chance of my being able to prove to you that you are wrong.

You have brought up a whole lot of reports and prejudices against Sardarji. I have avoided discussing these matters with you because I could see that everything I said excited you. The result is that you have not understood my position. You have made up your mind that I am completely under his influence. It is you who have tried to urge me to that position, but as you know, I have protested all along. You said I should have to join the Communist Party. I said no. You said as a true Hindu wife I should have to follow him in everything. I said my opinion was the opposite, and that my whole instinct told me that I must resist him wherever necessary and live my own life according to the ideals in which I believe, by which means, he would some day know that I was right. If I had followed his advice, I should not have undertaken my scheme but I knew that I must resist him and I did. My faith in God is my guide. But now you propose to throttle, by the warning of public disapproval, any attempt on my part to put my ideals into practice. My ideals have not changed in the last few days. I am the same person that I was when we used to talk happily together.

Believing, as I did, that everything is finally settled I started the ball rolling. I have put out enquiries regarding co-workers, land, maps and other details. I have explained the scheme (as my personal idea) to many people. Must I now understand if I go on with my plans you

will feel called upon to disapprove. The fact that there will be Rs. 20,000 less does not worry me at all. I can start in a smaller way and make up with donations. But the possibility that you might broadcast public or semi-public disapproval of my work, which statement I should feel obliged equally publicly to answer, means that for decency's sake I must avoid any such catastrophe, and therefore cancel all my projects of work. I would, in that case, take the balance of the money after the deduction of Rs. 20,000, invest it somewhere, and go to live in seclusion until time as you revised your ideas.
Yours ever devoted daughter,
Mira

At this time three of Gandhi's very strained letters to Mirabehn were addressed to her with the 'coldness and correctness' of the English form of address as 'My Dear Madeleine'[122] and even 'Dear Miss Slade' instead of 'Chi Mira',[123] the address he had been using since 1926. However, he soon capitulated and was again using his usual address when the depth of her grief had been brought home to him: 'I must not cause dear ones grief when it is avoidable. This was and is avoidable. I know you forgave me long ago. But it is good to ask for forgiveness.'[124] This, of course, was at a time of the pending major nationalist struggle and Gandhi must surely have been impatient with minor personal matters.

## THE FINAL YEARS WITH GANDHI

Even during these strained times, Gandhi had included Mirabehn in the central workings of the nationalist struggle. In April 1942 she personally took Gandhi's 'Quit India' Resolution to Allahabad for the Congress Working Committee to consider. Then Gandhi sent her to Orissa to help prepare the masses for nonviolent resistance to the expected Japanese invasion, and in August he sent her to inform the Viceroy of the meaning of the resolution. This was useful and appreciated work and in August she had the privilege of being arrested with Gandhi and imprisoned in the Aga Khan's Palace in Poona for almost two years.

Earlier, when she was living at Segaon, Mirabehn could not admit to herself that the hand produced khadi cloth work she was engaged in 'was not a natural outlet' for her.[125] However, she pined for outdoor work with animals. The opportunity finally presented itself. Mirabehn decided that the time had come for her to set up her own small centre near the Himalaya where she could combine khadi and animal husbandry activities. While Gandhi agreed and provided the finances, the arrangements caused further tensions, as noted above. At the end of 1944, with her financial problems with Gandhi sorted out and the Gandhi desired trustees dispensed with, she ventured out alone to set up her own ashram between Haridwar and Roorkee in the northern United Provinces to work with the hill population. With the political struggles over the shape of an independent India raging, Gandhi had no opportunity to visit Kisan (farmer) Ashram.

The new Congress government appointed Mirabehn as Honorary Special Advisor to the U.P. Government as part of the newly launched 'Grow More Food' campaign. This had her working with government bureaucracy for the first time and she was given a secretary, a stenographer, some assistants and motor van to tour the province. The work, however, did not suit her temperament.

Back at her ashram she opened a well-patronised dispensary and her khadi work was bearing fruit with the locals. When she was asked by the government to aid with the planning of cattle development schemes at the foot of the Himalaya near Rishikesh, she left Kisan Ashram to the government and moved to the new area. She surveyed land from elephant back and decided upon her new home in a jungle area that was teeming with wildlife. She named the place Pashulok (Animal World).

Mirabehn harboured dreams of Gandhi eventually settling in the Himalaya, sentiments which Gandhi himself was wistfully expressing at this time. Of course, the political situation in the country, with the nearing of partition and independence and the communal rioting and mass killings that were occurring, meant that these thoughts remained distant dreams. In mid-1947, during the rainy season, when construction had to be suspended, she took up the Maharaja of Tehri-Garhwal's offer of the use of his guesthouse to edit a selection of Gandhi's letters to her for publication. Having finished at the guesthouse, Mirabehn heard news that Gandhi was preparing to spend the rest of his days in Pakistan. The news came as a shock and this may have contributed to her collapse on the journey back to her home. She did not want to be on the plains during the celebrations which accompanied the transfer of power from the British to independent India and Pakistan. However, before returning to Pashulok, in late 1947 she decided to go to Delhi for a medical examination.

She was staying at Birla House when she came down with a severe bout of malaria. At this stage Gandhi was in Calcutta bringing peace to the riot-torn city. He then went to Delhi to attempt the same miracle. Although Gandhi had intended to stay in an 'untouchable' colony, the government asked that he stay at Birla House. He agreed and consequently, after a long separation, Mira again found herself 'with Bapu and for over three infinitely precious months' she remained with him in New Delhi. When she asked Gandhi to open the Pashulok cattle centre when it was ready, he allegedly replied, 'What is the good of counting on a corpse'.[126] On 18 December, just six weeks short of his assassination she tore herself away and returned to Pashulok. Gandhi was fatally shot by a Hindu fanatic at Birla House on 30 January 1948.

A few days after news of Gandhi's death reached her, the fifty-five-year-old Mira wrote an article for the press which echoed Gandhi's oft-repeated message about bodies and physical attachment, titled 'They Have Become One':

> For me there were only two, God and Bapu. And now they have become one!
>
> When I heard the news something deep, deep down within me opened – the door to the imprisoned soul – and Bapu's spirit entered there. From that moment a new sense of the eternal abides with me.
>
> Though Bapu's beloved physical presence is no longer with us, yet his sacred spirit is even nearer. Sometimes Bapu had said to me, "When the body is no more there will not be any separation, but I shall be nearer to you. The body is a hindrance." I listened in faith. Now I know, through experience, the divine truth of these words.[127]

The realisation was relatively short-lived. In reality, for Mirabehn the body was not a hindrance but the object of desire. Now there was no more Gandhi, the bedrock of her life, no more letters, and 'no more building of cottages with the hope of Bapu coming to stay in them.'[128] The years after Gandhi's death were not happy ones spent in the semi-wilderness continuing the work of her master. In some sense she had been banished to nature while Gandhi was still alive, but there was always the hope that she could return to his side. Now a sense of disillusionment set in. She did not seem to find her place in the new India, people let her down, she did not have the drive and clout to make her projects work in an objectively measurable way, she bristled at government regulations and now, in her later years, with deep existential doubt, she was faced with important questioning as to who she really was.

Although her personal assistant between 1946 and 1952, Krishna Murti Gupta, remembered Mirabehn's love for her co-workers,[129] A.N. Seth, Mirabehn's government appointed Development Secretary at her Kisan ashram in the United Provinces, saw something different. In his recollections, he noted that the mountains attracted her as 'the abode of peace' because 'the affairs of men and women almost disgusted her'. He recorded how worried she was when one of her cows was sick, but was not seriously bothered when one of her ashramites took ill. When he asked her for an explanation, he recalled that 'At this she almost broke down and remarked, "Amar Nath, you do not know how much I have loved humans but I have been completely disappointed in them. With animals it is different".'[130]

Exactly twenty-three years to the day after she had first arrived at Gandhi's ashram and eight months after Gandhi's death, at her Pashulok ashram she looked back at her life with her master as she penned the preface for publication of Gandhi's letters to her. Towards the end of that piece, she wrote:



> I had reached my destination; the destination from which I was to begin. The old life was finished as if it belonged to a past birth, and I began life anew. And from now the real struggle began. In the old life I had groped my way through the mist and fog, led by an inner urge which I could not explain. But now I emerged into the bright sunlight, and the steep, narrow Path of Truth showed clear before me leading up and up; so beautiful, and yet so hard to climb.[131]

Of course it was not her final destination, but she was not to know that yet. She was still able to write that 'Bapu's love has at last led me out upon the upper pastures, where God's peace fills the sweet mountain air.'[132] But without Gandhi's presence the air could not hold her for long. After Gandhi's death, she moved from small ashram to small ashram, starting various animal husbandry and forestry projects in the Himalayan foothills. However, she was restless and local inertia and bureaucratic complications meant that little came of them and, according to one who came to know her intimately after she had returned to Europe, 'so her life in India seemed to have become purposeless'.[133]

In the concluding chapter of her autobiography, written in the late 1950s towards the end of the India period of her life, Mirabehn talked of a long 'period of suspense, a kind of hibernation', and waited for God's guidance as to the next step. She wondered whether being in the mountains was to escape a world of terrible political strains, but she saw no light and 'just went on living and waiting' and writing.[134] Then she rediscovered some of Romain Rolland's writings on Beethoven that he had given her in 1931 and started to read. Something fundamental stirred: 'it was the spirit of him from whose music I had been separated for over thirty years that I heard and felt, but now with new vision and inspiration. I became conscious of the realization of my true self.'[135] The former tensions and restlessness left her and she was finally ready to embark on the next phase of her life and find solace outside Gandhi's orbit.

It seems that while she had always needed another person to focus on, her relationship with Beethoven came through his music and had never depended on a physical presence the way the one with Gandhi (and indeed Prithvi Singh) had. Understanding the pattern of her obsessiveness and intellectually knowing the higher truth was not enough to bring peace to her life. Eventually, in 1959, eleven years after Gandhi's death, she returned to Europe and Beethoven, noting that the story in her autobiography was a prelude to this, the third period in her life.[136] Her life had gone the full circle. Beethoven had brought her to Rolland, who introduced her to Gandhi, and now that there was so little left for her in India where she spent over half her life trying to find a *modus vivendi* with the object of her love, she moved back to Europe and the forests where once Beethoven strolled. The 'native' had returned home. She died in Vienna in July 1982.

# The Difficult Disciples: Nilla Cram Cook and Margarete Spiegel

When one thinks about hippies on the Indian subcontinent, what comes to mind are youthful Westerners in Goa or Kathmandu in the late 1960s and 1970s who, in the name of personal freedom, disregarded local social and moral norms. In this sense, Nilla Cram Cook is an archetype. Strangely, she also came into contact with Gandhi who, instead of disregarding her as an eccentric or immoral nuisance, took her under his wing when she came to him seeking meaning for her life. She became the strangest of his Western women disciples, and, although not long in his orbit, the most controversial. Margarete Spiegel came to Gandhi at around the same time. We know less about her and she made less impression on Gandhi. She was perhaps a well meaning nuisance of the type that often attached themselves to the Mahatma, or perhaps a later version of Mirabehn, who did not quite have Mira's persistent obsession or dedication, which meant that she was able to free herself from her attachment before Gandhi's death. Although Cook and Spiegel were with Gandhi at the same time, they were very different personalities and did not get on well together.

## A BOHEMIAN BACKGROUND

Nilla Cram Cook's way of life is not entirely mysterious if one looks at her background. Her father was the Bohemian playwright, poet and novelist, best known for 'discovering' America's greatest playwright Eugene O'Neill after he had helped to establish the experimental theatrical organisation known as the Provincetown Players in 1915. George Cram Cook studied philosophy and literature at the University of Iowa and Harvard University (where he seems to have had mystical experiences of the 'oneness' of the universe) and had studied and taught at universities in Heidelberg, Geneva and Florence before returning to America to teach English at the University of Iowa. In 1898, he enlisted in the army during the war against Spain, following which he decided to concentrate on writing rather than teaching. He had no success getting his material published and was forced to return to teaching at Stanford University. After his first marriage and the eventual publication of his first novel, in 1903 he 'dropped out' to grow vegetables and to pursue his writing career. With the failure of his marriage he brought his new wife, the anarchist Mollie Price, to the farm in 1908. They had a daughter Nilla in 1910 and later a son Harl. Cook became a socialist and worked as a literary editor at the Chicago *Evening Post*. After living with Mollie for two and a half years, Cook turned to his soul-mate, Susan Glaspell, whom he married in 1913. They organised the amateur theatre group that has come to hold legendary status in American theatrical circles and they continued with the group in New York's Greenwich Village as the Playwrights' Theatre; however, Cook's disillusionment with American cultural life grew in direct proportion to the burgeoning commercial success of the theatre. The dreamer Cook had long been fascinated by ancient Greece. He moved there in 1921 with Glaspell to live as a poet and rural peasant and died at Delphi near the Temple of Apollo in January 1924. His local friends honoured him with the removal of a stone from the temple to be used as a marker of his grave.[1]

A less idealised version of Cram Cook's life than the one given by his third wife is provided by the American socialist and novelist Upton Sinclair, who thought that Cook's move to Greece had more to do with alcoholism which proved too expensive to maintain in prohibitionist America:

> The plain truth … is that poor Jig Cook, a poet who pinned his faith to Bacchus instead of to Minerva, was at the age of fifty a

pitiful white-haired sot, dead to the Socialist movement, dead to the whole modern world, wandering about lost among dirty and degraded peasants. He died of an infection utterly mysterious to his wife – who apparently knows nothing of the effects of alcohol in destroying the cells of the liver and breaking down the natural immunity of the body.[2]

Another observer put it in a slightly more romantic vein: 'He moaned and moaned for the beauty of the ancient Greeks. Finding it neither in Iowa, nor in Provincetown, and even less in Greenwich Village, he departed for the hills of Greece. There he donned the skirt of a Greek peasant and died in childish bliss'.[3]

Nilla's mother Mollie was 'a pretty Anarchist girl' who was working as a sub-editor at a magazine and living a Bohemian life in New York when she fell in love with the thirty-three year-old Cook. When he brought his new bride to the farm, she was 'a little girl with dark hair and a round face, twenty-two years old, happy and sparkling and delightfully talkative, much in awe of her godlike husband'.[4] To some disapproval she went around in overalls and bare feet. Her father was 'picturesque' and 'irresponsible', and in mid-adolescence 'she had found in succession the Vegetarian cult and other Nature and Health cults, and finally there in Chicago a brilliant Anarchist group'.[5] She had completed a year at college, posed nude for a famous sculpture by a great sculptor, and acted in a theatrical road company. According to Cook's close friend Floyd Dell, she was adventurous, had a 'boldness in facing the world, a courage born of poverty' and had the temperamental power 'for breaking the bars of circumstance and finding the riches of beauty and truth in an unpromising world'.[6] While marriage seemed to tame 'this wild bird', the marriage did not last when Cook realised that he had been in love with Glaspell all along. What could an Anarchist who believed in free-love do? Mollie gave him his freedom and took the children to California, where she taught school to support them.[7] Nilla and Harl shuttled between the two parents, spending the year with Mollie and most long summers with George and Glaspell. Nilla did not attend a conventional school until she was ten. At age twelve, she joined her father in Greece and learned the language. A year later, after Cook's death, she returned to America and her mother; and dreamed of India where she could 'become complete'.[8]

At the age of fifteen, she convinced her mother to allow her to go to India via Greece, where money from the Cook estate would provide her with an income to study at the University of Athens. Soon after arriving in Athens, not long after her sixteenth birthday, she married.[9] Leading a privileged life, sometimes in Athens with her husband a Greek poet, sometimes with friends in Delphi, she nursed her young son Sirios, read translations of Indian sacred texts, learned to spin, weave and make her own clothes, and became a vegetarian. In early 1932 she divorced her husband in order to retain her American citizenship and, when she decided it was time, with Sirios she set off 'to find the ancient origins of dreams, the source of the myths of beauty which remain the only reality out of the debris.'[10] She was twenty-two. On leaving the boat at Karachi, pretending to be fastening her sandals, she 'bent down to touch the earth of India. If there had been no one looking' she 'would have fallen down and kissed it'. As it was she could only 'pick up some gravel and kiss it on the sly.'[11] She set out for Srinagar in Kashmir. There, the free-spirited and naturally intoxicated Nilla intoxicated the men around her. She also rediscovered the Hinduism that she believed had governed her past lives, and was ceremonially reaccepted as Nila Nagini Devi.

Albert Parry's 1933 book on contemporary American bohemianism painted a picture of the life and reputation of Nilla, the 'beautiful young daughter' of George Cram Cook:

> though behaving most tomboyishly, does her caprices in lands far withdrawn from Greenwich Village. She is in India now, living on houseboats away from her Greek husband, adopting native dress and customs, admiring and following Gandhi, calling herself the Blue Serpent Goddess [that is, Nila Nagini Devi], creating scandal by entering temples closed to the likes of her, and being fined for it.[12]

Why did Nilla come to India and attach herself to Gandhi, who seems the opposite of everything she seemed to live for? Martin Green says that to understand Nilla we need to 'begin with her father, for in many ways her relationship to India and to other things was a continuation and fulfillment of his.' After all, George Cram Cook discarded 'an early transcendentalism for an erotic philosophy of life.' In Greece, 'he hoped to revive and adapt the ancient Greek theater', but he also 'began to make a cult of India, as a culture even older than Greece'.[13]

Nilla travelled India, plying her rosary, practicing yoga and taking various vows, having mystical experiences and imagining herself as one of Krishna's Gopis, visiting temples and swamis, living with a spiritual master in Mount Abu, mixing in the highest of princely society, making influential friends, lecturing at university on Greek theatre and philosophy, and producing plays. She also fell in love with the Maharaja of Mysore and lived on nothing but orange juice for three months because she did not know how to tell him. Later she admitted to Gandhi that this was not the Nilla of sacred pilgrimages, but the mere adventurer Nilla who wanted to marry for money and into royalty, the one who had sold her 'very soul to the devil'.[14] Then she did something perhaps even more dangerous: taking a vow of telling and living the truth. She gave away her possessions and moved to down-scale accommodation – which was prudent as most of her money had been used up and the bulk of her remittances from America had ceased. Nilla then became involved in the Untouchable temple entry agitation in Bangalore where she was staying. Gandhi's anti-untouchability campaign was in full swing and under the tutelage of Ramaswami, a young Brahmin student who had fallen under her spell, she read Gandhi's writings. Although Gandhi 'disapproved of the sensual world, and [she] had always adored it',[15] she fell under his spell. Then, with a group of youth who rapidly became infatuated with her, she and Ramaswami started doing the work of Untouchables, cleaning the streets of Bangalore. She wrote to Gandhi of her work. However, large sections of these early letters consisted of passionate New Age quasi-spiritual ramblings that mixed American Indian, Hindu and ancient Greek philosophy, and attempted to convey her ever deeper moral self-realisations. Around this time, even her brother thought of Nilla as being 'a bit goofy'.[16]



## NILA NAGINI: MOTHER, SPIRITUAL WIFE AND GOPI

Gandhi had fasted several times in his life before he met Nilla. Towards the end of his stay in South Africa, he had undertaken one and two week penitential fasts at Phoenix Settlement because of moral lapses of the inmates. In 1918 he had fasted for three days during the Ahmedabad textile workers' strike to help maintain the resolve of the striking workers. The following year he undertook a three day penitential fast at Sabarmati in response to anti-British mob violence. In 1921 he fasted for five days following rioting during the visit to India by the Prince of Wales, and in 1922 for five days because of violence resulting in the massacre of twenty-two policemen, by those claiming to be his supporters, at the village of Chauri Chaura. In 1924 he fasted for three weeks as penance for Hindu-Muslim violence and as a prayer for unity, and in September 1932, while in Yeravda Central Prison in Poona, he commenced his first 'fast unto death' against the British decision to award separate electorates to 'untouchables' (and, as he saw it, keep them from integrating into the Hindu mainstream). After six days a government communique on the issue satisfied him and he called off the fast. A little over two months later he undertook a sympathetic fast in protest against a fellow prisoner not being allowed to do scavenging work in the prison.

Nilla made contact with Gandhi soon after his September 1932 fast. In late November she wrote to Gandhi telling him about herself and her beliefs,[17] and in early December promised to visit him as soon as she could.[18] Just before Christmas, she wrote that she was disappointed that she could not come when she had hoped because she had realised that her 'means of living have not been right' and as she had determined to *live* the Truth, although it meant that she would come later, 'it will be a *truer* meeting when I can say that I have done my best and *have* begun to *live* the vow of poverty.' She informed Gandhi of the young men she was working with in the anti-untouchability campaign and how they would regenerate Hinduism.[19] Attacking the filth within herself seemed to have given her the motivation to tackle the filth of the outside world.[20] This allowed her to clean the drains and slums of Bangalore in an ecstasy and joy 'no other play or work has ever given me'.[21] In fact she was not merely cleaning streets, she was saving the world, and she was not just working on a perceived personal fault, she was recreating herself.

It is certain that Gandhi did not have too many correspondents like her. Although his earliest letters of reply are unavailable, from Gandhi's diary we know that he wrote to her about untouchability on November 22 and 29 and December 6 and 14. When Gandhi announced that he intended to fast in January on the issue of temple entry for untouchables, Nilla wrote to him that she would fast as well. Gandhi dissuaded her, but asked her for more information about herself. As their correspondence lengthened, he felt increasingly drawn to her and started entertaining hopes of her becoming 'an excellent member of the army of Harijan servants'.[22]

In mid-January, Gandhi replied to Nilla's letters,[23] commenting on the good work she was doing for the removal of untouchability by engaging, and encouraging others to take part, in street cleaning. He accepted the sincerity of her efforts and explained that he was surprised that anyone could criticise her endeavours, noting that he had often done similar work. He gave her permission to make public use of his letter of commendation and informed her that her letters whetted his appetite for seeing her face to face if she could be 'spared for a few days' from her 'great work': 'I confess that I am very stupid and I don't and I can't understand people merely through their correspondence. To know them I need to look at them and talk to them, and you have written so much to me about yourself that I do want to know you if I can.'[24]

Nilla Cram Cook was in Bangalore working at her new calling in life, but reports about her unconventional morals started to filter through to Gandhi. P. Kodanda Rao, a member of the Servants of India Society, heard unflattering allegations about Nilla when he visited Bangalore. On his return to Poona he 'confidently whispered a hint to Mahadev Desai that the Mahatma had rather be cautious in his estimate of N.'[25] He believed that she had been exploiting Gandhi's letters to her and warned that she was 'a mere adventurer of doubtful character'.[26] Gandhi wrote to her urgently explaining what he was hearing about her, and asked her to come at once to Poona, where he was still imprisoned. He was worried that the Harijan work could be endangered if the reports were true and if she was associated with the cause. Not only were there rumours, but the poetry of some of her letters was a little baffling for him (in early February she wrote to Gandhi addressing him as 'My Revered Son'[27]). Gandhi had decided that it was time to ask her some 'straight questions':



> Your way of addressing me as your son is very strange. I lost my mother years ago. I am fast making daughters and sisters. But mother I have not found. Age is no bar. If you can inspire me with mother-worship towards you nothing would please me better. But let me say that your letter before me has filled me with misgivings. It smells of the hysteric. Your judgment of the friend whom you have sent is not confirmed by my talks with him. He seems to me to be a youth of unbalanced mind....
>
> But more serious still is the attack upon your character that came to me yesterday from an unexpected source. The friend who gave me the warning is a man of great worth and has no end to serve by misleading me. He simply warns me against my playing into your hands; of course the friend has no first-hand information.

But it is against my nature to keep such reports from those of whom I have them and in whose welfare I may be interested as I am in yours. Your first letters prepossessed me in your favour and I thought that I could use you for the common service of Truth. This report coupled with your latest letter have created a doubt in my mind. I should hope that it has no solid foundation.[28]

Nilla complied and went to see the imprisoned Gandhi in Poona on 21 February. She visited him regularly for almost two weeks. On the strength of their talks, he was at first inclined to believe that the various allegations he had heard about her were baseless,[29] or that perhaps problems had arisen merely because she had 'failed to make allowances for the different social environment in India;[30] however, as the interrogation went on, he had increasing doubts about how much of her story to believe.[31] Mahadev Desai suspected that she could lose her balance before she made it back to Bangalore and one of his chief political lieutenants, Sardar Vallabhbhai Patel, asked Gandhi whether he expected a miracle from her. Gandhi had to admit that Nilla was 'totally rotten' but had wanted to come clean and make her past public. He saw that dealing with her was dangerous, and so did not ask her to stay in Poona. Gandhi and Mahadev Desai believed that if she could openly accept what she had done and make amends, there may be hope of reform.[32] To be absolutely clear about her, Gandhi took the opportunity to write to various contacts of hers for character references.[33] One of the referees wrote to Gandhi on the day Nilla left Poona, detailing her debts and neglect of Sirios.[34] However, it appears that by this stage Gandhi knew more about Nilla than his informant Ramachandra, and he was now less positive in his assessment:

She has been much worse than you have described her to be. She has led for years an utterly immoral and extravagant life and has been an utter stranger to truth. She has made that confession to me and has also definitely promised that she would make that confession publicly before the world and she has also promised to turn over a new leaf and lead henceforth a truthful, chaste life, and to that end she would retire from all public activity and live a beggar's life in Harijan quarters in the poorest possible style, living on charity, unknown to the world. Whether she has the strength to carry out this promise or not I do not know. Let's hope that she has. She thinks that she has that strength.[35]

Two days later, Gandhi wrote to another informant and friend of Nilla's, Mirza Muhammad Ismail, the Dewan of Mysore, about how the truth of Nilla's character emerged:

> I thank you for your letter about Nila. She was with me for a few days and I regret to have to report to you that her record is not what you describe. Bit by bit she made her confession and it made a ghastly story. She seems to have led a most extravagant and immoral life, even from tender years. She was open to the advances of practically any person, and she was no better after her acceptance of Hindu religion. She has debts amounting to nearly Rs. 10,000 spread over Europe and India. She has travelled under a false name. The only thing I am able to say in her favour is that she has been quite frank with me in her recital of her recklessness, though, as I have said, they came bit by bit in answer to my cross-examination. She has professed penitence and made me a definite promise to say good-bye to her past life. I have told her that I could not take her on trust but that if she proved true to her promise I would not hesitate to defend her and to guide her. I do not know what capacity she has still left for controlling herself and keeping her promises.[36]



On the same day, Gandhi wrote to Nilla that she had to 'realize the enormity of the past wrong', and 'shed all hysteria and unnaturalness', adding that she could only become his daughter if she was to 'be good as you have promised to me'.[37] Nilla moved into lodgings in the Harijan quarter in Bangalore to apply herself to the task Gandhi had set her. Her letters about her progress left doubts in Gandhi's mind that she would succeed – he noted that while he would love to own her as a child, it was too early for him to trust her. She had started to talk about a 'spiritual husband' and Gandhi felt that she was again falling into a trap: 'For a person who has dedicated himself or herself to the service of humanity there is no such thing as exclusive relationship. If, therefore, you will take my word, you will not travel from error to error, as you seem to me to be doing just now. Your promise is to have no exclusive or secret or private companionship. You are simply wedded to your work and nothing else.'[38] Gandhi also wrote to the intended 'spiritual husband', Ramaswami, that he was 'playing with fire and an echo of very subtle sensuality'. He urged him not to, consciously or unconsciously, prevent Nilla's moral progress which could easily result from her 'pliable nature'.[39] Soon Nilla was talking of Rudramani, an untouchable trainee 'priest' and of one of her Bangalore college student admirers as her 'spirit's companion', adding that sexual intercourse 'need not form a part of my "marriage to him".[40] That letter made Gandhi feel like crying.[41] Talk of 'spiritual marriages' greatly worried Gandhi. After all, a dozen years before, he had flirted with the idea in regard to Saraladevi Choudhurani, and had almost fallen and endangered his own marriage. He felt lucky to have been saved. Soon Nilla confessed her love affairs to Gandhi,[42] and informed him that she had 'completely recovered from most of the stupid ideas I expressed to you in letters about spiritual marriages.'[43]

The struggles with her past and her squalid living conditions lead to her physical breakdown. She expressed her desire to go to Chitaldrug village, to live with Rudramani's mother.[44] The temple where she was staying was within the grounds of the British military area of the Bagalore and around this time Nilla and Sirios were forced to leave. Eventually they relocated to Rudramani's Harijan village.[45] Nilla tried hard to follow Gandhi's injunctions, writing to him that she would 'follow through any trials the way you point out. There is no "guru" on the face of the earth or in the heavens – nothing for me now but Truth, which is the vast beautiful cosmos.'[46] Gandhi had approved of her sentiments and her plan to go to a village and live among its Harijans,[47] but warned her that good intentions would not be enough and that he would judge her 'in accordance with the actual results' that she demonstrated.[48] When she had set off for her selected village, Gandhi warned her that she would have to dress more conservatively than she was used to and to 'live like the village womenfolk do', to set a few hours aside a day for silence,[49] and asked her to keep him completely informed of her activities.[50] Gandhi seemed to be hoping that she would succeed as a simple villager, giving her tips about growing a vegetable garden and composting and about preparing appropriate clothes from her saris. However, he was still not yet ready to allow her into the most inner circle. 'As to your addressing me Bapu, you are wrong. You will address me as such when you have confidence in yourself that you will inspire me with trust in you and will never deceive me. I am trying to trust you by signing myself Bapu.'[51] But Gandhi still wanted close contact: 'For the last three days or four I have not heard from you. I have developed regarding you a mother's anxiety. I am sure it is unnecessary, but when I do not hear from you, I imagine all sorts of things. Could you have fallen ill? Or, could you have fallen from your resolution?You must not therefore fail in writing regularly as you have promised to do.'[52]

Nilla's letters from Chitaldrug in late March and early April are quite lucid and matter-of-fact. On the second of April she wrote a business-like letter to the President of the Chitaldrug Municipality informing him of the needs of the village. However, in a lengthy letter to Gandhi a few days later, it becomes clear that all is not well: she was starting to get boils, had asthma, and had been weak for some days. She asked Gandhi about how she should wash and oil her hair, informed him about how she hated clothes and how the problems of modesty only arose after they had been invented and here she could not go around naked even inside her own home. 'I look forward to the day when I will be permitted, through saintliness, to go about with a loin cloth. What more is necessary? But don't worry, Bapu dear, I have added some prudish little sleeves to my new garb which cover my arms to my elbows, and the rest of me is covered from collar bone to ankles.'[53]



Gandhi replied at length on 12 April giving Nilla advice on the treatment of the boils on her legs, the use of soap, and how much of a luxury it was in a poor country to use it to wash hair (he then instructed her to shave her head instead), on what to wear and how to wash her clothes, as well as on her diet. He also warned her against receiving gifts from those with whom she had had previous relationships and instructed her to control her temper.[54] He included a note to her son Sirios, thanking him for his 'lovely letter' and asked grandfatherly questions.[55]

In the following days Nilla added to her growing list of complaints: she had broken a tooth, Rudramani preferred to lecture others and give orders rather than do any work himself, she needed a co-worker who could speak the language,[56] she had chopped off her hair, much to the horror of Rudramani who now did not want to see her anymore and their working relationship seemed to be over,[57] she could no longer go out in the sun with her hair gone, more boils and illnesses.[58] Her physical deterioration was obvious, but her letters again started taking on a slightly hysterical edge.

Ramachandra recalled to Gandhi that in the early days he had set a period of strong discipline for Mirabehn, but that it was in the care of well-known friends and institutions, while 'now poor Nagini Devi is allowed to drift all by herself and to boot she is so easily susceptible and emotional.'[59] In the third week of April, realising that no one was adequately guiding her Harijan work in the village, Gandhi instructed Nilla to make a complete break with her past and associates, and to move back to Poona to be nearer to him.[60] For several days in his anxiety Gandhi sent someone to the station every morning to meet her. Finally, on the 22nd, she did come and Gandhi wondered whether she was capable of making the change he hoped she could make:

> I do not know, I suppose she herself does not know, whether the revolution has come to stay in her life. The break with the past is too sudden and yet I have known people to undergo such apparently sudden transformation. Looking back upon her letters I can trace the invisible working of her mind and the unconscious war between the forces of evil and forces of good that was going on within her. Let us hope that the forces of good have triumphed over those of evil.[61]

At this stage Nilla made a full confession in a 'statement' to Gandhi, detailing her unpaid debts of about Rs. 10,000, one-third in India and two-thirds overseas.[62] It also served as the basis for another concessionary letter to the Mahatma, where she requested that he make her mistakes public:

> I am writing to you because I have not succeeded in publishing in the papers the statement concerning my past life which I owe the world I would serve for Truth.[63] I want those who are aware of the impure and extravagant way I have lived up to only yesterday to know that I am sincerely striving to begin a new life, and I want the general public to know that as an aspirant to social service I have been a great hypocrite. Please do what you can to make it known that I have not only lived an impure life in the past but that I have been untrustworthy in my worldly dealings and sailed under false appearances. After squandering the capital of a small inherited income I recklessly and needlessly incurred debts. I was not even concerned about the payment of these debts until the implications of the new life I thought I had adopted began to dawn on me about six months ago. Even then, when, in order to discharge the obligation honourably, I had decided to earn by my own effort the amount I owed, I continued to incur new debts. Nor did I succeed in purifying my life even when I seemed to be leading a pure life.

> I thought at one time that I would discharge the obligations by writing and lecturing in America. But I saw that that would mean a continuation in another form of untruthful life. I, therefore, came to the conclusion that, if I were to be true to the new life, I must utterly break with the impure past and hope somewhat to repay at least the moral obligation, by serving the most despised of the community, with which I have thrown in my lot. As you know, I have, therefore, been trying for sometime to live among and serve Harijans to the best of my ability. I would gladly have toiled for my creditors as a common labourer if I could have thereby given them any satisfaction. But that could not be. I can only say to them that, if a single rupee comes to me in an honourable manner, it shall go to them. But the only honourable way open to me is to do what penance I can for the past through the silent service of Harijans.[64]



Gandhi, Mahadev Desai and Sardar Patel had lengthy debates about what to do with Nilla, what sort of supervision she would require to ensure that she did not relapse into her old ways. Desai thought that she had the strength to change, but he could still see 'impurity in her eyes'. Patel asserted that the ashram at Sabarmati should not be burdened with her.[65] Gandhi believed that as she had made all requested changes, she had to be looked after and believed that Nilla and Sirios should be sent to the Sabarmati Ashram if she was accepted.[66] He believed in her sincere efforts to change her life after she had realised her errors, however he warned Premabehn Kantak, who was in charge of the women's section of the ashram, not to ask her about her past but rather to discourage her from bringing it up as it is 'harmful to recall memories of sinful pleasures', and that if Nilla did take an interest in talking about her immoral past 'you may conclude that she is still not free from such desires'.[67] A week later he wrote to Narandas Gandhi, the manager of the ashram, that he was sending Nilla 'with great hopes' having 'cherished her like a daughter for the last three or four months', and a German woman Margarete Spiegel, to be trained for Harijan work. Gandhi added that while Nilla had hidden nothing from him and so had won his confidence, he 'could give no guarantee about her future conduct', noting that if 'she becomes proud of her ability or her noble intentions or good work, she will fall.'[68] Another week later, he asked Kantak to cultivate close contact with Nilla in the belief that 'sincere love will reform her and keep her on the right path.'

He added that, as he was the person who 'brought about this great and sudden change in her life', he hoped that she would 'be able to bear it'.[69]

Then a bombshell hit. Without warning, on 30 April 1933, Gandhi announced a twenty-one day fast to start on 8 May to purify himself and his associates 'for greater vigilance and watchfulness in connection with the Harijan cause'. The fast seemed to have come out of the blue; however his secretary Mahadev Desai reported that Gandhi had not slept the night before his announcement.[70]

Of all Gandhi's fasts to date, this one was the most puzzling. There did not seem to be any immediate cause and even in the case of previous penitential fasts there was no difficulty in pinpointing the actions of which he had disapproved. This fast was, in Gandhi's explanation, largely self-purificatory. But what did he need to be purified from? The reasoning behind this fast was far more amorphous than those for any previous fast; however it seems that Margarete Spiegel, and, especially, Nilla Cram Cook, played a large part in firming Gandhi's decision to take the step.

It appears that his thoughts were troubled by Nilla and Spiegel. Rather than send them away from his ashram, his inner voice told him to fast. In a letter to Narandas, Gandhi wrote that Margarete Spiegel and Nilla were 'certainly instrumental in persuading me to undertake the proposed fast. Among them Nila's share is probably greater.'[71] He attempted to explain himself, without any specific finger pointing, in a statement to the press:

> A tempest has been raging within me for some days. I have been struggling against it. On the eve of the "Harijan Day" the voice became insistent, and said, "why don't you do it?" I resisted it. But the resistance was vain. And the resolution was made to go on an unconditional and irrevocable fast for twentyone days, commencing from Monday noon the 8th May and ending on Monday noon the 29th May.
>
> As I look back upon the immediate past, many are the causes too sacred to mention that must have precipitated the fast. But they are all connected with the great Harijan cause. The fast is against nobody in particular and against everybody who wants to participate in the joy of it, without for the time-being having to fast himself or herself. But it is particularly against myself. It is a heart-prayer for the purification of self and associates, for greater vigilance and watchfulness....

> Let there be no misunderstanding about the impending fast. I have no desire to die. I want to live for the cause, though I hope I am equally prepared to die for it. But I need for me and my fellow-workers greater purity, greater application and dedication. I want more workers of unassailable purity. Shocking cases of impurity have come under my notice. I would like my fast to be an urgent appeal to such people to leave the cause alone. ...[72]

The explanation was not adequate for all, and many tried to persuade Gandhi to give it up. His son Devadas wept in frustration that 'So now it is Nilla and the Ashram Affairs.' Gandhi responded, 'Well, in a way.' Nilla and the ashram were supposed to be instruments to be used in the service of Harijans and both had let him down. Purity of character was needed. Devadas, however, thought that he was trying to defend the indefensible.[73] Nilla herself begged Gandhi not to go through with the fast, volunteering to take on any ordeal he prescribed for her as a substitute, and asked permission to stay with him if he was to undertake it. Instead, he sent her away to the Sabarmati Ashram, where she, but not Margarete, arrived towards the beginning of May.[74] After she had arrived at the ashram, but before the fast had commenced, Nilla challenged Gandhi: 'I read in the papers that you do not disclose the faults of those who were the last straw in your determination to fast. Why not? God helps us to be strong and preserve you.'[75]

Because Nilla was at what was still his official ashram, and because Gandhi did not want reports of Nilla's behaviour to taint his campaign (at the time Gandhi suspected that she was pregnant to the Harijan priest Rudramani[76]) and partly as a way to attempt an explanation for the fast, he decided to follow Nilla's request and make her story public and use it as a warning to other Harijan workers about the hard task ahead of them:

> Her life was one of lewdness, untruth and extravagance. The lewdness did not seem to repel her. She was brought up in a Bohemian family, where the very name Jesus was taboo. (Nila is only 24, was married in Greece at the age of 17[77] and has a son who is with her.) She seemed now to realize the amazing contradictions of her life. I put it to her that she was doing an irreparable damage to the faith of her adoption, injuring the Harijan cause and corrupting the morals of the youths who had gathered round her. I believe that she saw the

force of what I urged. She decided at once to break with the past, run the risk of being prosecuted by her creditors and to live among Harijans for their service and bring up her boy for the same work. She went back to Bangalore. She wrote a brief letter of confession for the Press, which the latter would not publish. She removed to Harijan quarters in Bangalore and, coming under the spell of a vicious man, fell again. She then went to a Harijan village near Chitaldrug. She was neglected by the person who took her there. She very nearly collapsed. During this period she was keeping up regular correspondence with me. She saw that it was impossible to serve Harijans or to hold herself together without proper guidance. I felt that it was my clear duty to work out the logical extent of the advice I had given and that if she was to live the life of service to the lowliest, she must go to the Ashram, where she had dreamt of going long ago. I could not possibly ask any friend or other institution to run the risk of taking a foreign young emotional girl with a black past hardly yet out of sight. With the consent of the manager of the Ashram, therefore, I have sent her there, though not without hesitation. Nor is it without hesitation that I am sharing her letter with the public. It is difficult to believe that all her terrible past is dead for ever. But sudden changes have happened in men's lives before. Let us hope that Nila will prove to be one more such case. What is impossible for man is possible for God.

... Let the youth of the country know that this Harijan service is the most difficult of all humane services. ... I do not publish one-tenth of what comes under my notice of the moral degradation to which the criminal neglect of caste Hindus has reduced them. The work, therefore, demands the highest purity and the greatest simplicity on the part of the workers. Let the young men and women who are working for the cause take heed from the example of Nila.[78]

In her first letter from the ashram, Nilla wrote to Gandhi that she had ceased menstruating and thought that she should have a medical examination because 'there is a danger of a conception from my error in Bangalore'.[79] The letters of the next few days indicated that she was enjoying herself, and included some constructive criticisms.[80] She milked cows and goats and even two weeks into her ashram stay she could still write how contented she was being there.[81] However, within a few days she confessed to Gandhi that she was having strong feelings for another resident:

> I have again felt a special liking for one being apart from the rest. And I don't know if liking describes it. I felt the same old unreasonable emotion as for those with whom this emotion led to so many falls and complications. Of course it was disguised – masquerading in a new form. But I do not wish to deceive myself, and so to be on the safe side I write to you that I did have special feelings for your doctor – Mr Sharma, when I met him.[82]

Her feelings for the doctor lingered on and so she went out of her way 'to avoid him and the temptations of glancing in his direction.'[83] She was relieved when he left the ashram.[84]

Gandhi appealed to Narandas to give more time to Nilla, to try to understand her heart. He also instructed him to read letters addressed to her before she received them[85] because 'she has little control over her mind', and admitted her role in his decision to undertake the fast: 'I see that she has had a large share in persuading me to undertake this fast. I did not know this. If there is anything which can give her strength, it will be this fast, and, if I have made any mistake in sending her there, the fast is the only thing which can undo it. I think that it will save many young men.'[86] Gandhi was, in effect, having her watched. He warned her to be on guard and asked her to report to him if the presence of someone she was previously attracted to excited her emotions, in which case 'I will have to see what can be done.'[87] He also wanted to ensure that she understood the moral necessity of avoiding an abortion,[88] believing that a birth could be redemptive for her and a test for the ashram.[89] Nilla insisted that she only wanted a medical examination to determine if she was pregnant and had never considered an abortion.[90] In any case she was not pregnant, and for the next two months she made strenuous efforts to fit in as an ashram member at Sabarmati.[91]

Her letters of this period, when she was trying to express her innermost thoughts rather than recount daily happenings, become a bit rambling and, as with Sonja Schlesin, even her hand writing deteriorates. Her moods swing. At times she expresses her joy with ashram life, at others she notes how unimpressed she is with the women's dormitory of the ashram, which reminded her of a Protestant boarding school, and considers leaving. She does not like the regimentation of the prayers and only goes because they are compulsory. She would rather dance in ecstasy (the way she sees the trees doing!).[92] A few days later she had changed her mind and attended prayers joyfully trying 'to forget the features of the function which seem forced to me and are not spontaneous, genuine human expression.'[93] She notes that the ashram facilities are locked to guard against thieves,[94] and questions why this is the case when they have all taken vows of poverty. They are hypocrites or thieves themselves if they are reluctant to part with their possessions. It is clear to her that they are better off than the masses, and 'We can counterbalance this *only* by the greatest detachment of the utmost willingness to give our coat to the man who steals our cloak.'[95] Nilla was a real challenge to Gandhi in many senses, however, in this narrow and immediate issue of ashram ethics she must really have forced the Mahatma to introspection. As she wrote to him, locking doors to go to prayers to recite the Gita 'is a mere sham to hide the lack of courage required to truly live the vows of fearlessness and non-possession.'[96]

Nilla Cram Cook, alias Nila Nagini, felt the world extremely strongly. For most people the sense organs block out much of the available information to prevent them from being overwhelmed. Nilla's senses were not good filters and she knew it, at times celebrating her cosmic awareness, at times cursing it. In mid-May she wrote to Gandhi that 'All is well with me physically, and let us hope – mentally, although – as I have said, I cannot trust my own judgement regarding my mental state.'[97] She shaved her head completely and observed periods of silence, speaking only to Sirios and the ashram children, so as to control potential angry or sarcastic remarks,[98] and she attempted to 'live the perfect day'.[99] When the monsoon came and the Sabarmati riverbed filled with water, the lights of the town on the other side reminded her of her longing for Kashmir so she began a fast of eating nothing but grapes. Her letters became more rambling, her hand-writing deteriorated, her 'oceanic feelings' became stronger, her self-analysis was relentless. Was she mad or exceedingly courageous? In any case, she was difficult for the other ashram members.

By early July, Sirios had become quite ill. Nilla wanted to take him to the mountains until he recovered. She asked Gandhi for a third-class fare to the Himalayas even though leaving the ashram, her 'true home', would be wrenching experience. She explained that she did not want more for her son than she wanted for other children because she did not like possessiveness or the concept of exclusive motherhood,[100] but thought that the roofless life of the sadhu or shepherd would be his only cure.[101] Gandhi responded:

> I do not deny the possibility of Sirios responding to the hills. But your *tapasya* [penance] lies in remaining where you are and risking his life. That is the price that faith has to pay. It is no faith that demands complete insurance against risk. Sirios will be all right if you will cease to worry about him and will simply do the nursing.
>
> If my argument or opinion does not appeal to you, you will not hesitate to tell me so. I do not want you to feel helpless or under any sort of compulsion. I want you to feel freer than you ever were. The only thing that binds you to me and the Ashram is love and acceptance of the common ideal. I guide you so long as you have confidence in my judgment. I have played sufficiently with the lives of the dearest ones on more occasions than one. But if you are to do likewise, you should do so [only] if you feel the truth of it. You must act out of strength, never out of helplessness. Therefore, you will not hesitate to tell me truly what you feel.[102]

Nilla and Sirios stayed in the ashram. Three weeks into her grape fast, Nilla collapsed with a violent fever and treated herself by reading poetry instead of taking the malaria medicine a Gandhi-appointed doctor had prescribed. While the Mahatma had been released from prison following the commencement of his fast, he could not spend the nights at the ashram because of the vow he had taken when he set off for Dandi on his famous Salt March in March 1930 not to return until India had achieved freedom. But now, as news spread that he was on his way to Ahmedabad, Nilla gave up eating completely until he arrived. For a week he visited the ashram daily and nursed the feverish Nilla. Then he dropped another bombshell.

Gandhi had to make a decision about the future of the ashram. As he could no longer use Sabarmati as his base without breaking his vow, and as the government was confiscating the property of those engaged in nationalist agitation, he felt that he had to sacrifice his home as well and had to find another location for his headquarters.[103] This meant a relocation of the inmates and the necessity to do something with the Westerners who were there because of him. He had decided to station himself in the centre of India, at Wardha, where Jamnalal Bajaj, one of his wealthy benefactors, provided for the Mahatma's future accommodation needs. Gandhi wrote to Bajaj in late July asking whether children could be taken at the women's Mahila Ashram in the area, noting that 'I have to solve the problem of Nila and Amalabehn [Spiegel]. I see no alternative to sending them there. Both of them should be given Harijan work. For the present, they are to be trained for the work. Nila should have as few contacts with men as possible...'[104] Gandhi arranged for Sirios to be looked after in Sharda Mandir, a Montessori school for well-to-do children in Ahmedabad. Nilla took a vow of silence for a week.

Besides Spiegel and Nilla, Mary Barr, another Gandhi devotee, was also sent to Mahila Ashram. Unfortunately in late September, not long after Gandhi had arrived at Wardha, she was hospitalised with malaria and Nilla accompanied her, as relatives often accompanied their own to hospitals that had little by way of nursing staff. Soon, however, Gandhi wrote to Barr that 'If you don't need Nila's help, let her come away. I know that the introduction of strangers disturbs doctors in a well-managed hospital.'[105] Barr particularly wanted Nilla near her and did not know why Gandhi was demanding the change. Gandhi's reasons did not sound overly convincing, especially given the usual practice in Indian hospitals. He was apparently being diplomatic. She immediately wrote 'a fretful little letter' to Gandhi asking for Nilla's return.[106] Gandhi replied the next day that he had 'made a stupid mistake in sending Nila in the very first instance' and asked Barr not to ask for her, assuring her that when she was well and back at the ashram he would convince her that he was right.[107] Barr remembered that the letter 'explained at length why it was not possible for Nila to stay'. However the explanation must have come in person when she was back in Gandhi's care two weeks later, and by that time Nilla was gone. Barr recalled that '"a soft answer turneth away wrath," and may even cause tears'.[108] In a period of madness (or probably some form of spiritual ecstasy in her own eyes[109]), Nilla had fled the ashram on the way to 'the mountains of China' and ended up in Bombay where Gandhi was staying before his arrival at Wardha. Accompanied by Mirabehn, he took her back to Wardha.

Only a few days before Barr's illness, Gandhi had written to Sardar Patel, that 'Nila and Amala are problems. The former is an emotional type, and the latter has no sense. She can't do any work. Both are something of a burden here. I will try to see if the burden can be lightened.' The two other Western ashramites, Duncan Greenlees and Mary Barr, were 'doing very well. Both are hard-working and upright'.[110] Sending Nilla into a hospital to relieve his burden, on reflection, seemed to be a bad move. Over three weeks before he had already observed that 'Nila is off the rails again', noting her 'unsettled mind in her letters' when she impulsively switched from Hinduism to Christianity in a way that Gandhi did not assess as a serious move. 'Her imagination tosses her from one thing to another. The vow of silence seems to have unsettled her mind all the more.'[111] On about 10 October, just after the prayer meeting, Nilla disappeared. Without a ticket, because she looked like a sadhu, she was allowed on a train for Delhi. There she called in at the home of Thakkar Bapa, a close friend of Gandhi's and General Secretary of the Harijan Sevak Sangh (Harijan Servants' Society), which had recently taken control of the Sabarmati Ashram, and then disappeared again, heading for Mathura, the birthplace of Krishna, the musician of the spirit she followed. A few days later, Gandhi wrote to Thakkar Bapa that Nilla's behaviour had been very strange of late ('Her brain has, undoubtedly, softened') and warned him not to 'waste any time over her and if she presses herself on your attention she may be reported to the police.'[112] Whatever it was that she did, it seems that finally Gandhi realised that he could not help her.

He made a statement to the press on 17 October:

> I regret to have to inform the public that Shrimati Nila disappeared suddenly from the Wardha Ashram about ten days ago. She had of late become more than usually unbalanced. All the affection that parents, brothers or sisters could show was shown to her, but evidently her fearful past proved too strong for her. It is likely that she is again leading the old thoughtless, untruthful and unclean life.
>
> I give this information to warn young men against tempting her, or being tempted by her. I would like those who may come in contact with her not to give any financial aid. She is hardly responsible for her actions, and it would be a deliverance for her, if some philanthropic institution would take charge of her. If she sees this notice, I would have her to recall all the promises she made to herself and to me, and in humility to ask God to exorcise the devil that has possessed her. She knows that if she asks truly, her prayer will not go in vain. She had such experiences in her sane moments.

She was last heard of in Delhi.[113]

Two days after the appearance of the article, Gandhi again wrote a letter to Thakkar Bapa, trying to explain his position on Nilla, about whom sensational items were again appearing in the press:

> What should I write about Nila? I have done my best for her. I think she did try honestly to restrain her passions. But she slipped during her attempts and ultimately ran away. If she drowns herself, I would neither be surprised nor sorry. If she is alive, I would not give up hopes for her improvement. I do not at all repent having readmitted her. It was my duty to do so. She was basking in affection not only here but at Sabarmati also. She used to write to me that she never experienced such affection even from her parents. All were content with whatever little restraint she voluntarily accepted. How can one be changed so suddenly, who remained unbridled for several years?[114]

Thakkar Bapa seems to have been annoyed by Gandhi's apparent indifference to Nilla's plight. Gandhi tried to explain his actions, noting that he was still anxious to have her back, 'But she is so unhinged that she might not come at all.' He telegraphed the American Mission about her case.[115] Thakkar was not satisfied and set out in search of Nilla, an action which deeply impressed Gandhi. The Mahatma noted that 'other friends have roundly blamed me for going out of my way to help her ... Where my love has failed, may yours succeed in melting her heart.'[116] The same day as his last letter concerning her was penned to Thakkar Bapa, a plea by Gandhi, under the title 'A Tragedy', appeared in his weekly paper:

> The longer I live the more do I realize that the happiness which I enjoy and which so many friends envy persists in spite of tragedies of which I have always had my due share. The latest is the disappearance of Nila. I have no doubt that her repentance was sincere. She struggled bravely against her past, but it did appear to me on my coming to Wardha that the struggle was getting too severe for her. She was becoming unhinged and losing control over herself. Previously, in one of her letters from Wardha, she had hinted that she might become insane. All the affection that could be shown to her was shown. She was never insensible to it. She was most responsive. But she was also most impulsive. She has gone away without any

> money or belongings. The reports published about her in the Delhi Press are sensational manufactures and do her grave injustice. She cannot be held responsible for her actions in her present mental state. Her proper place is in a philanthropic institution or in an asylum. Those who will throw a few silver pieces at her out of false compassion, or in order to get rid of her, will do her no kindness. Being irresponsible, she has been squandering what she has received. I would esteem it a favour if those who may come in contact with her will give me her address and show this writing to her.[117]

In her autobiography, Mirabehn summed up Nilla's life with Gandhi, and her disappearance, most poetically. She wrote that Nilla

> was a young woman from America, with a Greek background of dancing and poetry, the very opposite of my pupil in cooking and washing [Margaret Spiegel "an extremely earnest young woman from Germany who had fled Nazi persecution of the Jews"].[118] She had come to Bapu previously and had stayed at Sabarmati Ashram just before and during the disbandment of the place, after which she had come to Wardha for a time. So she was familiar with her surroundings. Bapu told me simply to look after her in a general way. This time the job was hard for me, because Nilla was a sprite, a spirit, dancing and singing her way through life like a bird. Earnest was she too, but it was an earnestness of exaltation, and one fine morning we found that she had flown from the nest, like the bird that she was. When we next heard of her she was in Brindaban [near Mathura, where the Gopis had danced for Krishna], where she had been taken to a missionary hospital with a poisonous thorn in her leg as a result of dancing all alone in the woods of Lord Krishna. Bapu did his best to extricate her from this predicament, but the Missionaries and the British Government combined to send her all the way back to America. Bapu was pained. It was clear to me that, in spite of the extraordinary escapades, he had seen much more in that passing spirit than the rest of us had at the time.[119]

And the news just seemed to get worse. Even a relatively unsensational news magazine like *Time* reported that in early December Gandhi was again embarrassed by Nilla's antics in New Delhi: 'A brand new automobile, ordered on approval, had gone roaring down the road 70 m.p.h., hit a bump, overturned. Out rolled Serpent Goddess Nilla, bruised, battered, but bitterly determined to lead her own life.'[120]

Three and a half months after her disappearance from the Wardha ashram, and one year after she had set out for Chitaldrug, Nilla and Sirios were repatriated to the USA. Just after she landed in New York she was married very briefly – she had promised a sick young no-hoper on the ship that she would marry him and now could not break her word. The marriage was annulled in 1936 and she did not marry again. Sensational newspaper articles carried scandalous, and largely untrue, articles about her. But she managed to put on a series of well-received Greek dance performances. In 1939 she went to Europe as a correspondent for *Liberty* magazine and covered the war from the Albanian front in Greece for American and Greek newspapers.

The brief but intense relationship with Gandhi was almost over, but not quite. Around the beginning of 1941 Nilla again made contact suggesting that she wanted to return. Gandhi replied that 'You will be welcome whenever you can come.'[121] Later in the year he wrote to a close associate that 'lately I had a letter from Nilla in which she has expressed her longing to come back to me. Because, she says, she found truth only with me.'[122] In the end she had to find her truth elsewhere, never making it back into Gandhi's orbit.

In 1941 she escaped to Turkey from war-torn Greece with Sirios and ended up in Iran as the Interior Ministry employed censor of theatres and cinemas. Between 1942 and 1943 she travelled and studied in Afghanistan before returning to Iran where she served as a United States cultural attache in Tehran (until 1947). During this time, the Ministry of the Interior engaged her to organise a Department of Theatres as well as the National Ballet and Opera. She converted to Islam, and in 1945 completed a translation of the Koran. In 1946 she left her directorships to found the Studio of the Revival of the Classical Arts of Iran, which in 1947 toured Mediterranean, Arab and Middle Eastern countries.[123] In 1950, very overweight, she turned up in Jerico announcing that she was annotating the Koran to make it 'comprehensible to every intelligent person who can read English.'[124] From then on, she vanishes except for a reported visit of several month's duration to Kashmir in 1953 and a return visit to India the following year to speak about the turmoil in Kashmir, the region from where her Indian spiritual journey that was to lead her to the Mahatma had commenced over twenty years before. Following a brief illness, she died at the age of seventy-three in October 1982, at her home in Aspang near Vienna.[125] Reportedly she is buried next to her father in Delphi.

## MARGARETE SPIEGEL: THE PROSPECTIVE DAUGHTER-IN-LAW

The little that is available in English on Margarete Spiegel's time with Gandhi comes from Gandhi's letters to and about her, the few letters of hers to him that have been preserved,[126] and from two short articles of her reminiscences of Gandhi.[127] There is not very much more in German.[128] She, even more than Nilla Cram Cook, is generally overlooked by Gandhi biographers, although one that does mention her in little more than passing assesses her as a 'German lady, who meant well but tended to be ill-tempered, impetuous and spiteful'.[129] What was she doing with Gandhi?

Born in October 1897 in Berlin into a merchant family, from a young age Margarete was interested in India and Indian philosophy and read the Nobel laureate Rabindranath Tagore as her favourite author. During the First World War she had been drawn towards pacifism. And, as with many others of Gandhi's European followers, she came to know about Gandhi through Romain Rolland's biography. After this, she read all the books by and about Gandhi that were available in the State Library in Berlin. She studied at various German universities, being awarded a Ph.D. by Bonn University in 1921. The following year, for her state examination, she wrote a paper on the alternative education system provided by the *Landerziehungsheime*, the German country boarding schools. Although her ambition was to become a teacher and join one of these schools, her teaching career was restricted to Berlin. She obtained a permanent teaching position in a government girls' highschool in 1929, where she taught European languages. Because there were no prescribed textbooks for higher classes in Germany at the time, in 1932 she chose a German edition of selections of Gandhi's writings for an advanced English class she was teaching.

In order to study the Gandhian movement first-hand, she obtained three months of unpaid leave from her job to visit India in October of that year. For two months she travelled around the country and spent three days at the Sabarmati Ashram from where Narandas Gandhi informed the imprisoned Mahatma that Margarete wanted to meet him. Gandhi replied that she could certainly write to him but doubted that she would be permitted to see him in person.[130] Nevertheless, in December she did meet Gandhi in Yeravda Central Prison. Decades later, Margarete Spiegel recalled that meeting: 'He was sitting in the court of the jail under a Mango-tree, surrounded by a host of men and women. I thought of Jesus or Socrates. This first meeting was the most impressive event of my life. I felt the magic aura which a truly great man emanates. He, the prisoner, was master; the prison warder bowed to him.'[131] Gandhi scolded her for having given up vegetarianism, and after she promptly promised to reinstate it into her life he allowed her the honour of washing up his crockery. After the meeting, Gandhi asked her to write to him and to come again.

Spiegel had written three letters from the ship on the way home, and, in mid-January 1933, Gandhi responded to her first 'love letter' saying that he was pleased that she had been able to stay at the ashram and take part in its service of Harijans. He commented on the many talents that she had been blessed with and concluded that: 'Next time we meet, if we do, you are not going to be "awed" by me, if you are to be a daughter to me', and invited her to write to him whenever she felt like it.[132] Of course, feel like it she did, and they continued a frequent correspondence (Gandhi penning ten letters to her from prison) until she returned to India and her master later in the year.

In the first ship-board letters, Spiegel had already written to Gandhi how she had felt Indian from childhood (in reply, Gandhi noted that this was an addition, not a substitute, for her German birth), and how she was struggling to choose between Tagore and him (Gandhi informed her that she could like both of them equally and that there should be no choice-making if she was to be 'a real daughter like Mira').[133] Soon after she had arrived home she was already thinking of returning, but Gandhi cautioned her that she should not consider obtaining a professorship in India that would give her the money to support her ageing mother. Instead, he advised, 'You will only come when the way is perfectly clear for you. Surely, it is possible for you to love India even from where you are and to do many acts of service. You have plenty of years before you. Go through the necessary training, keep India your goal, and some day you will gravitate here.'[134] By early March, Gandhi was noting that her regular letters were telling him nothing 'except about himself'. He requested information about her pupils, what and how she taught them (her syllabus included the writing of essays on Gandhi and teaching about *ahimsa* which, to her dismay, did not interest her students at all[135]), and wanted to know 'as a teacher what you would do to and for the Ashram children if you had them under your charge.'[136]

However, Margarete was having difficulty staying away. She wrote to Gandhi about coming on a short visit. He promptly replied:

> Why do you want to come here for three days or at the most a fortnight? If you have at all imbibed the central truth of the *Gita*, it will tell you that this kind of wish has got to be subjugated and sublimated into pure action, which for you consists in doing your duty there. You should hold on to your savings, and if you cannot restrain yourself from spending them somehow, you should send them here for the Harijan cause.[137]

The desire to come to India was not simply the pull factor of Gandhi. There was also a significant push factor in operation in Germany. Margarete Spiegel was Jewish and feared losing her job. From the end of January 1933, Hitler was chancellor and an air of anti-Semitism was becoming more apparent. She wrote to Gandhi that as a Jewess, she felt like a Harijan and informed him that a fellow teacher kept calling her an 'Asiatic subman', adding that she was 'honoured by that name, because you are an Asiatic too'.[138] To complicate matters, she was responsible for her ailing mother. Gandhi eagerly awaited news of her fate, but cautioned patience:

> ... your coming will be justified only when you are ready for the Ashram life. That clearly you are not. Your immediate duty is to be by your mother's side. ... If you are thrown out of employment and have to be in search of one, you have to courageously stand by your people and suffer the hardships that they will have to suffer, and if you have imbibed the fundamentals of the Ashram life, you might even render inestimable help to them. All your letters to 24 people in India, therefore, to get you a job should not have been written. You do not want a job in India, but you want to give your free service, the whole of yourself, to India. You cannot do two contrary things at the same time. I wish therefore you would give up the idea of the job, remain there by your mother's side and live the Ashram life there, so that if God wills it, He will send you some day to the Ashram.[139]

By this time Margarete was already on board a ship headed for India, her grieving mother having been left behind. New laws had been proclaimed on the first of April to restrict non-Germans in the civil service and to deprive Jews of their passports. Margarete immediately left Germany with her still valid visa for India. She set out for Venice from where she informed Gandhi that she was on the way. After waiting almost two weeks, she secured a berth for India. Gandhi promptly wrote to Narandas for permission for her to go to the Sabarmati Ashram, adding that 'She is a very good woman.'[140] In September, in *absentia*, she was officially dismissed from her German college teaching position.

After arriving in Bombay, Margarete went straight to Poona, arriving on 27 April. She asked Gandhi, again sitting under the same mango tree, if she could take the ashram vows and adopt an Indian name. Gandhi agreed, and gave her the Indian name of Amala, 'the pure one', because, according to Nilla, although she had wanted to marry and have many children, she had never even been kissed.[141] She joined Nilla in visiting Gandhi in jail as often and for as long as she could over the next fortnight, but seems to have been little impressed by Nila Nagini, who certainly had been kissed. In Spiegel's memory of those meetings, penned just before her death thirty-five years later, Nilla was a 'strange visitor' with her shaved head, 'gown of penitence' and 'illegitimate son' who was introduced to her by Gandhi with the words: 'She used to be a prostitute and has become a saint. She should be your model.'[142] Margarete angered Gandhi by physically manhandling Sirios when the youngster was climbing on Mahadev Desai. She responded by informing the Mahatma that that was how she treated her dog.[143] She further annoyed him by refusing to befriend Nilla, claiming that the saint was a hypocrite, adding that 'In the village of South India, where she allegedly lived as a saint, she is said to have seduced the male inhabitants of all races.' Later, Margarete wrote, she was deported from India 'for bringing white women into disrepute'.[144] She thought Nilla's silences to be idiotic.[145] Nilla was a little more kind in her assessment of Margarete: 'Margarete wanted to learn to milk cows inside of two seconds! She is a dear – but how hard it is for her to bear this joyless atmosphere. She told me that she cannot look at the children, for they never smile, and live in perpetual fear. She is much moved over it and because there is no singing along with spinning as in Europe.' She believed that Margarete had a sari-complex and so refused to dress sensibly, trying to look like Mirabehn but ending up dragging the inconvenient clothing through the mud and urine of the dairy, and then wearing it to meals. Her clothes were always dragging in the dust, and she 'never looks clean'. She had no time to dress or bathe properly as she was always rushing late, according to Nilla. 'She is a dear soul – so deep and sincere – if only she would not be so emotional and childish over simple things.'[146] Clearly, there was some serious 'sibling' rivalry between these two 'daughters'. Mahadev Desai's diary clearly shows that they did not get on.[147]

During the weeks at Poona, Spiegel wrote something of a will dedicating her life to the Mahatma: 'I leave the money and all the things I have got with me to Mahatma Gandhi's Ashram and for the Harijans' cause. The things they do not want are not to be destroyed, they are to be given to other people. In order to save the money for my burial, I leave my dead body for dissection to the Sassoon Hospital in Poona.'[148] As she desired, Gandhi made arrangement to send both her and Nilla to Ahmedabad as soon as he had finalised the matter with the ashram, warning Narandas that 'They and others who may join the Ashram should strictly follow the Ashram rules and you should see that they do so. If they do not observe the rules or become a source of trouble to you, I don't at all intend that you should still let them remain.' Gandhi gave a detailed description of how Nilla and Sirios were to be treated and noted his less than great hopes for Margarete. His attitude to her had changed since the months of love-letter writing. The visits and the contrast between her and Nilla, even given Nilla's major moral lapses, seem to have diminished Gandhi's earlier high regard for Margarete. The assessment of her that he sent Narandas was less than flattering:

> Margarete is of a different type. She is 35 years old and, therefore, her character is practically formed. She is a woman of great learning and is quick in learning things by heart, but she is not very intelligent. She is obstinate, but her motives are pure. I think her life has been blameless. She has great love for the Ashram. But she has no sense of proportion when she speaks. Ever since she has been here, she has been talking about the Ashram in season and out of season. She has left the country and come to India because of the movement in Germany against her but she has no plan before her. I am sending Nila there willingly and with great joy. I don't feel such joy in sending Margarete, but we cannot turn her away. She has come merely with the intention of living in the Ashram. What can we say to her? She

> will of course do whatever work she is physically capable of. She has been a teacher for some years and so you can immediately give her the work of teaching English. She is eager to do teaching. Even as a teacher, however, Nila is more capable.[149]

A few days later, Gandhi again wrote to Narandas noting that Margarete 'is very sincere, but has strong likes and dislikes. We should, however, support her as long as she observes the rules. If she shapes well, she will do very well indeed.'[150] Nilla went to join the ashram at Sabarmati; Margarete threatened to fast against Gandhi's fast in order to make him relent, and asked Rao to make arrangements for her counter-fast at the Servants of India Society Home where she was staying. When she was informed that 'the Home was open to the Mahatma's guests, but not for fasting either for or against him',[151] she went to Madras instead. Gandhi noted that 'If she fasts, that will certainly do her health good. She will lose some of the excessive fat on her body.'[152] Gandhi was adamant in his course and Margarete gave up her fast after two days. Gandhi sent her to Sabarmati Ashram and she wrote to him that 'I promise you to do my work so well in the ashram that you cannot but forget my shocking behaviour.'[153] The following day she added: 'If your doctors want to make a blood transfusion, a transplantation of glands or anything of the kind, *do* let me be the happy victim! I am *longing* to die for you so this would be a welcome substitute.' She added that she knew that she was nothing but a nuisance at the ashram, not being able to spin and her 'clothes are always dirtier after washing than before', but she pleaded, 'Bapu, if you really knew how I love you, you would not have been so cruel as to pack me off during your fast although I was wicked.'[154]

On the strength of her discussions with Gandhi in Poona, and probably as a result of discussions with others at the ashram, Margarete wrote an article on Gandhi and Indian women for the German professional journal of women teachers. There she described Gandhi as something of a saint and foreshadowed the role that women would play in the nationalist political struggle, noting that 'India's fate depends on her women, for in their hands lies the education of their children.' The final paragraph sums up her observation of Gandhi's attitude to women:

> No man has ever shown more understanding of women than ascetic Mahatma Gandhi. To him all women are sisters. As he is free from all

passions, he is able to discover the soul of a woman as no other man can. He holds the woman's intuition as more important than the superior knowledge of a man. In his eyes, a woman is the embodiment of devotion; he regards her as nobler than man. The Mahatma calls women "the better half of humanity, not the weaker sex".[155]

However, living at the ashram was not enough. She had no goal, no real desire to do Harijan work as an end in itself. Like her model Mirabehn before her, Margarete craved the physical presence of Gandhi. He chided her: 'You are with me when you are at the Ashram doing the Ashram work. I am sure you understand this very simple truth. There were many prisoners occupying the same yard, sharing the same verandah. Do you suppose that they were living with me?'[156] A few days later he had to remind her that it was not good to be constantly thinking of being with him instead of about the duty that was in front of her. He instructed her to 'become a wise woman of 35 instead of being a child of 5 years.'[157] He also wrote to Mirabehn that Amala 'is as mad as a mad-hatter. But what was one to do? She simply came and one had to take her. She is a good woman. But it remains to be seen how she shapes.'[158] A year later, he added, 'Amala is as mad as ever. But she is better with me than elsewhere.'[159]



Margarete was in turns grandmothering (questioning Gandhi's diet, presenting him with sermons on how he should do things) and demanding, and Gandhi periodically lost his patience:

My Dear Amala,
I have your two stupid and silly letters. I never knew that you were so unbalanced, suspicious and hypersensitive. What led you to think that I regarded you as a stranger? Or that you were less than a daughter to me? You, nowadays, sign yourself as a disciple. But do you not know that I claim nobody as my disciple? I have one disciple, too many, and that is myself. You suppose I would take additional burden and make my life a misery? I delight in owning sons and daughters, sisters and brothers. Therefore, you are either a daughter or nothing; certainly not a disciple, and what a disciple suspecting her own master at every step! Are you now surprised that I called you mad![160]

Gandhi was by now making plans to send his Western ashramites to Wardha. He informed the manager of the Wardha ashram and his principle disciple in the area, Vinoba Bhave, that they were coming to be trained to do Harijan work. He informed Vinoba that Barr and Greenlees would not be problems, that Nilla could be very useful if she maintained her health, but he had doubts about Margarete: 'I am not sure about Amalabehn. She is rather obstinate and her capacity is limited. Her intentions are very good but she is very slow in acting on them. She goes on making all kinds of plans.'[161]

Gandhi, with his being cruel to be kind philosophy, scolded Margarete, lectured her and tried to make her see the larger picture that was before him, as he had been, and still was, doing with Mirabehn. He wrote to her to shed her 'strange and embarrassing manners', pointing out that 'Effusiveness is no mark of true devotion. True devotion works stealthily'.[162] This, and perhaps the turmoil over reimprisonment and the disappearance of her fellow-ashramite Nilla, made her afraid of Gandhi, and this, in turn, resulted in another rebuke from the Mahatma after his release: 'You must shed this wretched fear of me. Whatever I said and did at the Ashram was said and done in pure love and for your good. Why should you fear me, if you believe what I say? You have therefore no need to avoid me or fear me.'[163] When Gandhi embarked on his Harijan tour at the end of the first week of November 1933, he took Mirabehn but left Margarete behind. However, her longing for him, regardless of her fear, did not diminish. That was part of the problem, and Gandhi saw it clearly:

> I have your letter. I call it good because it is truthful. I knew you were deceiving yourself and me. Will you now tell me what your nature demands? If it demands simply being in my presence, it cannot be satisfied. If it demands more teaching work and a life natural to most Europeans, I shall try to help you with hope of success. ... You ought to be steady and brave. To desire to die is cowardice. There is nobody about you who has any wish to repress you. You have built in front of you a mountain of difficulties. Make your choice resolutely and act.[164]

Such talk led to fears that Gandhi wanted her out of the ashram. He assured her that if life there suited her and she could conform to the discipline she was welcome to stay.[165] Nevertheless, Gandhi did want her to be a worker rather than a free-loader who was at the ashram to be near him when he was present. At this stage she was morbid, brooding, even a touch paranoid and suicidal.[166] He wanted her to find her deeper Self, to find purpose in her life, a purpose that was not totally dependent on him. Early in the new year, Gandhi took action regarding Margarete's future. He wrote to Parikshitlal Majumdar, President of the Gujarat Harijan Sevak Sangh, to try her for some time back at the Sabarmati (now Harijan) Ashram and retain her if she proved useful. Gandhi noted that she was extremely sincere, was proficient in eleven European languages, and was eager to 'serve Harijans personally', in fact 'dying to get to work'. He suggested that Majumdar could use her as an English teacher, although she was 'ready to do any work' without salary. If things did not work out, he was to feel free to send her back to Wardha.[167]

Margarete seemed to settle in relatively well at Sabarmati although Gandhi made things difficult for her, as he had done for Mirabehn, by giving her what may have seemed to be mixed messages. Earlier he had chided Margarete for playing the expert and advising him on health matters.[168] Now he complained that she relied too heavily on him for medical advice when she had to be a law unto herself.[169] Her letters at this stage were full of fears that Gandhi would drive her away, even that he hated her, about concerns over Gandhi's welfare, panics over his fasts, and that she was less than Mirabehn in his eyes. He explained to her that she should find satisfaction in doing his work and noted, discouragingly, that they would meet when God willed it.[170] Gandhi wanted to be allowed to stand on his own feet, and wanted her to do likewise. But that was a hard lesson to learn. After all, it was not why she was in India.

She struggled on at the ashram without Gandhi, teaching (or in Gandhi's observation imposing her will on) children. Gandhi again wrote to her in the middle of 1934 that he wanted to know her as she was rather than as she would be, asking her why she wanted to be like Mirabehn. He assured her that he loved her 'in spite of your faults', rather than hate her as she feared, and again told her not to fear him. He warned her not to let her imagination run away with her.[171] This was a letter to a troubled person. It soon became plain that Margarete was not happy. Gandhi wrote to her a month later that 'If you are finding life irksome there, tell me what you will have me to do. You have to settle down to something. Think hard and guide me.'[172] A few days later, he was more blunt. While Gandhi felt sorry that she was not at peace at Sabarmati, he asked her to make a choice, noting that she could not stay with him until he found a place to settle down, and that she would not be happy in Wardha either.[173] She opted for

Wardha even though that path was a gross neglect of duty according to Gandhi. To a young student associated with the ashram who had criticised Spiegel, Gandhi wrote that 'She is foolish, of course. If she were not, she would not cling to me,'[174] and yet again he reminded her that she was with him when she was doing his work even though physically they may have been far apart, and that she was not living with him even though they were physically in the same place if she was not doing his work.[175]

On 10 July, from Karachi, Gandhi announced that he would fast for a week from 7 August as a penance against intolerance following the attack on an opponent of his Harijan uplift campaign after he had promised his safety. When Margarete heard the news she announced that she wanted to serve Gandhi in his fast. Gandhi responded that she was unnecessarily alarmed and that a fast of a week would not kill him.[176] This, however, did not mollify her and on 20 July she left the ashram without money and without informing anyone. She was finally found at Nadiad station where Harijan workers bought her a train ticket so that she could join him.[177] Nevertheless, for all the problems she was causing, Gandhi rewarded her by allowing her to accompany him for over a week during his ongoing Harijan tour. She joined him in Kanpur and travelled to the holy city of Benares with him in late July 1934. Perhaps the close contact with Gandhi, perhaps her creeping age, meant that Amala was working on other plans than doing his work in some far off place, plans that may have helped to guarantee closer physical proximity. There is speculation that her reasons for leaving the Sabarmati Ashram might have included a desire to talk to Gandhi about the possibility of her marriage.[178]

Born in mid-1888, Gandhi's eldest son Harilal is perhaps the most tragic figure in the Gandhi narrative. In his earliest years his father was away from him in London and South Africa. When he finally could join his father, he felt that Gandhi's experiments were holding him back from a normal education and life. Although in his early years he had often been imprisoned as a satyagrahi, he also married against his father's wishes when he was eighteen and tried to make his own way in the world. His much loved wife died when he was thirty and his business dealings failed. He spiralled downwards into a life of drunkenness and hopelessness. In April 1933, Harilal wrote to his sister-in-law that he was tired of his lonely life and wanted to remarry.[179] In late 1934, Harilal tried to reconcile with his father and get his life back on track. For a while things looked good for the son and the relationship. Harilal wrote to his father about his changed life and about his desire to find a partner. Gandhi replied that he understood his son's desire, adding that he would 'not regard it as in the least blameworthy provided you find a suitable widow.'[180] Into this situation stepped Margarete Spiegel.

Margarete was uncertain about what it was that she wanted in life. On one hand Gandhi was feeling the responsibility of looking after her when it seems that she was contributing little by way of work and was losing weight dramatically, on another she was trying to make her own way in life by attempting to find a college job, which he supported but added that he could not 'recommend her to anybody'. Gandhi was worried 'that she will go off her head one day. She is hardly in her senses.' As he informed Narandas, the problem seems to have come from her desire to marry: 'And now she has become impatient to marry. I observe that she is not free from passion. In consequence of her trying to suppress it, it has become uncontrollable. She hopes to be mother of twelve children. She is 37 at present. Let us see what she does. I don't have the courage now to send her to you or somewhere else.'[181] A few days later Margarete learned that she had been appointed as the French instructor at Shantiniketan (where she would teach the teenage Indira Nehru, India's future Prime Minister). By late December she was in Tagore's institution and for a while seemed to be more settled in life.

Some months later, in another letter to Narandas, Gandhi noted that Harilal definitely intended to marry if he found a suitable wife, and added that while he may accept Harilal's marriage, he could not 'welcome or like it'. Adding: 'Still, I do wish that his marriage should be a happy one.'[182] Somehow the two desires came together. In April 1935, Gandhi wrote to Harilal that he understood his son's desire to remarry because he had not yet given up the craving for sex pleasure, but, given his own life philosophy, he could only help within his limits and could not have Harilal living with him while he was on this quest. It appears that Harilal asked Mahadev Desai to act as his go-between with Margarete. Gandhi, in a part of his letter that has been omitted from the published *Collected Works of Mahatma Gandhi*, added that he did 'not wish to interfere if Mahadev or somebody else wants to help you. You can write to Amla [sic] yourself. If you do so, disclose your previous life. Please do not mention my name, or even Mahadev's. I will never appreciate if Mahadev writes … If Mahadev writes on his own will, I will not stop him. If he will ask for my advice, it will go against …'[183]

Margarete must have met Harilal during this time[184] and may have known of his intentions from Gandhi if she had not received a direct letter from Harilal. However, there is little evidence as to what happened next. Harilal's great granddaughter and biographer believes that Harilal had written to Margarete and that Margarete had responded, although something in her letter put Harilal off. Harilal explained the situation to Gandhi, who replied:

> There is no need at all to be in a hurry to come to a decision about Amala's letter. I think you will have to drop the idea. You should write and tell her plainly that any children that may be born will have to be brought up in a simple manner. And whatever means of livelihood the Lord provides will probably be in Wardha. If you start going to women or drinking, she should be free to leave you immediately. And even this you may write only if you are sure that you wish to marry her. Amala's letter seems a good one to me, but I didn't know her as she reveals herself in it. I am, therefore, of the view that you will not be happy unless she comes to feel strongly that she cannot live without you.[185]



The Harilal chapter in Margarete Spiegel's life ends here.[186] Being away from Gandhi, at the school of her other mentor, Tagore, and with dreams of marriage finally behind her, she spent a happy time at Shantiniketan where she shaved her head but gave up wearing khadi, the influence of the Poet (as Tagore was known), a lover of beauty, winning out over that of Gandhi, the preacher of austerity and functionality. However, for reasons that are not clear, eventually it became obvious that she could not stay in Shantiniketan and she settled into a teaching position in Bombay where she received a good salary, saving up money to bring her mother out to be with her.

The lives of Gandhi and Spiegel diverged somewhat at this stage, Gandhi even noting that he would continue to call her Amala, 'But if you will have me to do otherwise, you will tell me.'[187] The letters became more relaxed, concentrating on her ability to write Gujarati, information about movements and friends, and general observations about health matters. Gandhi often inquired about her mother and pet dog. The possessiveness and suspicion disappeared. She even reverted to her former persona by signing her letters as Margarete Spiegel, even though Gandhi insisted that she would always remain Amala to him.[188]

During the war Gandhi's nonviolent approach to Nazism angered her.[189] After the war, it seems that she had some trouble earning money and had thoughts of returning to Germany. Gandhi advised her to stay in India, noting that she could give private tuition in Bombay rather than attempting to go abroad to earn more money. He added that her Semitic origin will be least resented in India.[190] It seems that he was right: her return to the country of her birth was brief.[191] Gandhi's last short note, in response to a postcard from Margarete Spiegel, remarked that 'I suppose one may say you have at last settled down now.'[192] At this stage she was the principal of the Maharani High School in Baroda.

Although she lacked Mirabehn's practical skills, drive and dedication, she had been a second Mira in her obsessions, but in the end she seems to have become relatively free of Gandhi's hold on her. She was in India, was earning money and had outgrown her life-preserver. She reverted from Amalabehn to Margarete Spiegel and became the middle-class immigrant she may have always wanted to be once the confusion of discipleship had evaporated. She died on 13 June 1968 in Bombay, without completing her reminiscences of Gandhi.



## GANDHI, MARY MAGDALENE AND AMALA

Ironically, when Nilla shaved her head at Wardha she was reminded of Mary Magdalene wiping the feet of Christ with her hair.[193] In the Bible, Mary was one of the women who followed Jesus and ministered to him. She was the one Jesus had 'healed of evil spirits and infirmities' (Luke 8:2), and from whom he 'cast out seven demons' (Mark 16:9). Although there is very little about her in the Bible, in Christian tradition she is seen as a sinner and prostitute who has been restored to purity by faith and penitence. Perhaps the imagery is apt, except that in the case of Nilla the demons were not cast out and she was not healed.

Green, who analyses Gandhi as a new-age revolutionary, notes that 'It is not possible to say how important the relationship with this woman was to Gandhi. Obviously, it was much briefer than many others, and tangential to the line of his practical activity. On the other hand, she represented to him an erotic-aesthetic version of the New Age more vivid than it seems likely he saw in anyone else.'[194] This is probably true, and it seems that it attracted him to her. However, she was not really tangential to his practical activities – when he came to know her she was engaging in anti-untouchability work with a creativity and passion he wished others, like

Margarete, could have had. The fact that she was a repentant 'fallen woman', or rather little more than a repentant fallen girl, still in her early twenties, must have given him hope for great things in her future. She seemed more interested in the work for a purified Hinduism than merely being attached to him. Here was perhaps another version of his belief that it was possible for a violent person to become nonviolent, there being no such hope for cowards.[195] Nilla was no coward, and perhaps she could become pure and take part in his very practical social (rather than narrowly defined political) work. Perhaps here was the ideal constructive work disciple who could serve as a model in a way that was just beyond the abilities of Mirabehn, and well beyond the abilities of Margarete Spiegel. Of course they were also beyond the abilities of Nila Nagini.

When she became ill, Gandhi took to his role of nurse as best he could given his busy schedule, fasts and imprisonments. Nilla commented that Gandhi had said that she 'has lost the tenant in her upper story', but he remained hopeful that 'we will be able to rent it out again soon'.[196] The upper story remained vacant for some time.

Nilla had come to Gandhi full of ideas, even if they were scatty. She had passion and was driven by ideals, even if they did not last long. Margarete came because she needed a place to stay and was looking for a job (and not the type of job Gandhi had in mind for her) and someone to cling to. Margarete would have been happy to die for Gandhi, Nilla wanted her old self to die 'asap' so that the new self could emerge.[197] While Margarete was obsessed with Gandhi, Nilla was intoxicated by life. Nilla mended and wore items of clothing that Gandhi gave her. Margarete believed that such actions were sacrilegious. She would have kept them as relics.[198] Nilla was seeking perfection and at one stage asked Gandhi 'to write to me only of my failings'.[199] One could strongly suspect that Margarete would have liked to have heard praise. It is not hard to see which of the two Gandhi preferred. Margarete rationalised this preference by noting that when Nilla, rather than she, got to stay in Gandhi's room at the Wardha Ashram, it was because the unstable Nilla, who found the strict discipline 'unbearable', had to be entirely under Gandhi's supervision. With seeming satisfaction, Spiegel noted later that in August 1934, during one of Gandhi's fasts, with a selected few (including Gandhi's wife and Mirabehn), she was allowed 'to live in his room and serve him'.[200]

Regardless of Nilla's spark, like her role-model Mirabehn, in the end it was Margarete who stayed for the longer haul and managed to centre herself through an evolutionary process, rather than through stages of psychotic turmoil. And like Mirabehn, although she managed it before the death of Gandhi, she drifted back to a previous mentor. Rabindranath Tagore seemed to break the spell of her Gandhi enthrallment. And this allowed her to have a relatively normal life, with the normal trappings of family (her mother and dog), financially renumerated work, and an appreciation of aesthetics, instead of a life obsessively devoted to one individual or to the remorseless and selfless task of Harijan uplift work.

# The Ideal Disciples: Mary Barr and the Khedi Workers

The village of Khedi, close to the town of Betul, which in turn is about 100 miles north of Gandhi's headquarters of Wardha, developed into a thriving centre of Harijan uplift and constructive work. This was Gandhi's dream – he wanted those who came to him to engage in the task of socially rebuilding India rather than be involved in the political freedom struggle, which was not their fight, and for which they would have been deported by the British authorities. Almost all of the Western women who came to Gandhi did so because they were attracted by his philosophy and because they were fascinated by him personally, the two being very hard to disentangle. Mary Barr and the other women who became her work colleagues were no different. However, somehow they managed to overcome their personal attachment to him, to focus on his work. At the time Barr was immersing herself in village work, Gandhi had asked Margarete Spiegel: 'Can you not see that it is impossible for all who love me to be physically with me?'[1] The Khedi workers managed to do rural reconstruction work in a positive spirit, not merely undertaking the daily grind of working in a poor village in order to be occasionally rewarded with a stay in the Mahatma's company.

## MARY BARR RENOUNCES GANDHI'S PERSON FOR HIS WORK

In his 1933 correspondence, Gandhi often mentions his various Western ashram visitors in one breath. While Nilla Cram Cook and Margarete Spiegel are often referred to as problems, Mary Barr and Duncan Greenlees are always praised as model workers. Barr had not come to India to be with Gandhi. Close Gandhi associate, Kishorelal Mashruwala, in his foreword to Mary Barr's book about Gandhi, noted that

> She desired to be as near him and as often as possible, but she did not wish to hang about him like a creeper clinging to a tree. On realizing that she could serve the cause for which he stood better by living at a distance, she did not hanker for staying near him. This robustness is rather rare in disciples with the result that when the Master is gone the disciples often become devitalised like paralysed limbs.[2]

In other words, for Gandhi she was in a real sense the ideal disciple. However, this meant that she was not easily noticed by those writing the story of Gandhi.

Before she met Gandhi, Mary Barr had already been in India for ten years in charge of a mission boarding school 'in a jungle station' at Karim Nagar in Hyderabad State. Although by 1930, Gandhi was possibly the most famous person on the planet, Barr was, by her account, so absorbed in her work that she knew very little of world events or even those unfolding in India. She barely knew anything about Gandhi, holding 'the average Britisher's feeling that he must be mis-guided, if not actually bad, to be in any way 'agin' the Government.'[3] On leave back in England before and during Gandhi's 1931 visit for the Second Round Table Conference, she began to take an interest in the Mahatma and reading about his life and thought. On her way back to India, Mary Barr found herself on the same ship, the *S.S.Pilsna*, which also carried Gandhi's party home.

Although Gandhi's group travelled 'steerage' and she was a second-class passenger, she soon became well acquainted with Gandhi and his travelling companions. Barr observed that while the captain invited Gandhi's entourage to take their meals in the second-class dining room (their meal times did not overlap with those of the other passengers) and that several people brought them chairs to sit on, none of these privileges were accepted because they had chosen to travel 'deck'. Also, observing the amount of laughter that emanated from the group surrounding Gandhi, she came to see him as an 'intensely human individual, and not the saintly but fanatical person of whom I had read'.[4]

On their arrival at Bombay on 28 December 1931, Barr's expected friends were not waiting for her so she went to Mani Bhavan, the home of a Gandhi supporter in a leafy suburb where the Mahatma was staying. She decided to spend the two remaining days of her leave at Sabarmati Ashram before returning to work in Hyderabad. Because she had a train to catch to Ahmedabad that evening, in the small time available to her, she did not expect to see Gandhi among the crowd welcoming him home. Nevertheless Gandhi sought her out at Mani Bhavan, made sure that she was fed, (this was the first time in ten years in the country that Barr ate a thali meal sitting on the floor), and arranged for someone to look after her on the trip to the ashram.

The days at the ashram whetted her appetite for a longer visit. A week after their return, Gandhi was back in Yervada Central Prison and now Barr avidly read newspapers to find out what was happening with him and the nationalist movement, and they started exchanging letters. In March 1932, a senior padre came to her remote mission station with a letter from the head of the mission informing her that because of her new associations she was in danger of being deported and reminded her that the mission could not spare her. She was requested to promise 'not to write to these political people any more'.[5] She knew that it would take months to get someone from England to replace her so she resolved not to write to Gandhi for three months after informing him of her decision. When the three months had elapsed, she again took up the correspondence without further consequences.

Barr's life had changed fundamentally as a result of her contact with Gandhi. She decided that she would leave the mission and serve 'Gandhi's India' in some village instead. In November, her replacement arrived and she set off to visit two Christian 'ashrams' in the south of India. One was Anne Marie Petersen's National Christian Girls' School at Porto Novo. She had met Petersen on the day she and Gandhi arrived back in Bombay from Europe and now they became firm friends.

After these visits, Barr wrote to Gandhi that she wanted to work under him and asked his permission to come and talk to him about her future plans. In his reply, Gandhi informed her that she should go to Shantiniketan because he did not want 'to harness you for untouchability work before you have gone through your touring'.[6] The anti-untouchability campaign was the focal point of Gandhi's life at this time, but he wanted Barr to be sure that both her 'head and heart' were ready for the task ahead. Her small savings did not allow her further travel (at this stage she did not know how cheap third-class travel could be) and, in any case, all she wanted at the time was to commence her training at the Sabarmati Ashram: 'The visits to the other Ashrams were intended to break me in gradually, and partly as a sop to some Christian friends who thought it rather terrible to be going to a *Hindu* Ashram'.[7]

In early 1933, she visited Gandhi in Yervada Central Prison and met Margarete Spiegel. By way of greeting 'from age to youth in India', Gandhi slapped her on the shoulder as she stooped to greet the seated Mahatma: 'This so surprised me that I automatically responded with a little slap on his ankle, showing how far away from Ahimsa is the "natural man" (and woman), even when interested in the subject'.[8] They both laughed at her instinctive retaliatory reaction. Gandhi advised her to spend what time she needed at Sabarmati to prepare herself before burying herself in village work. She visited Gandhi in jail three times and corresponded with him regularly on philosophical issues, Gandhi answering her questions about the Gita and idol worship. Following the visits, she wrote to him jokingly that although Gandhi was a prisoner, she felt like his guest. Gandhi replied that 'whatever you are, you are no guest. You are a member of the ever-growing family. Whether you are daughter, or sister or mother, matters little. In this strange family, each one makes his or her own choice of the position he or she would occupy. Therefore you understand you will be no guest to me wherever we meet'.[9] In her answer, she informed Gandhi that she chose the role of 'daughter'. He warned her that the role of daughter came with a high penalty, reminding her what it had cost Mirabehn to become a daughter: 'She is generally the Cinderella not however having the expectation of getting the golden slipper some day or other.'[10] Gandhi advised her to bury herself in a village after she learned what she needed to know for such work at Sabarmati.

By late January, Mary Barr, popularly known as Marybehn, was an inmate of the ashram. Gandhi worried about her asthma, diet, possibility of sunstroke, her ability to tolerate unboiled water, and insisted that she call a doctor if required. He added, 'You have chosen to be a daughter. Now you have the opportunity of proving one and quickly getting well by carrying out instructions.'[11] She practiced her Hindi and spinning, and in

April left Sabarmati to visit Kashmir with her exhausted friend, Petersen. Barr wrote to Gandhi asking whether the nine weeks she had already spent at Sabarmati qualified her to return for a longer period. Gandhi responded by saying that she would be welcome.[12] While they were away, Gandhi suggested a novel form of recreation to the women: 'In going about for your walks, make a search for all the Harijans you can find and add to your knowledge of Hindi by trying to make yourselves understood by them and in understanding them.'[13] He also instructed them to visit local spinning centres. Not long after leaving for Kashmir, they received news of Gandhi's twenty-one day fast. Gandhi wrote to Barr a week into his fast saying that he expected her 'to return to the Ashram refreshed for much concentrated work'.[14] Touched that he would remember her at such a time, she decided that she wanted to give her life to the ashram. In another letter, Gandhi told Barr that she 'must come again soon and finish your course and know much more of the Ashram than you do.'[15]

Mary Barr returned to Sabarmati, but the stay was not long. Soon, with Nilla, Margarete and Duncan, she was relocated to Wardha where she had trouble settling in and began to think seriously about burying herself in a village as Gandhi had requested months before.

Moving to a village was not easy – the right place had to be found and some villagers were reluctant to let a 'Gandhi-ite' such as her a house, fearing that the government might confiscate their property. Then she was offered 'a tumble-down verandah on one side of a cattle-yard' because she 'liked the simple life'.[16] She eventually settled on a house that was so damp that it was impossible to finally move into until the wet season had ended. In the meantime, in assessing this period of her life, Mary Barr was candid about her inner motivations concerning her eventual move to village life in Khedi Saoligarh about eight miles from the administrative capital of Betul:

> Looking back over that year I realize that my life did not contain the "hundred-per-cent truthfulness" about which Gandhi had written in one of his letters.[17] If I could have foreseen his early release and settling in Wardha, I feel sure I should not have left the Ashram within a month of going there, or chosen the beautiful but malarious village in Betul District which has been my home for several years. It is true I wanted eventually to work among village people, but more than all else, I wanted to be able to serve in Bapu's inner circle and near him. I did not realize at the time, but see now that it must

have been pride which prevented my suggesting a return to Wardha after having elected to go to a village. Yet I felt restless at a distance, so managed to make fairly frequent visits "on business".[18]

On one of these 'business' trips Barr caught up with Gandhi who had been recently released from prison and had taken up residence in Wardha. Barr fell ill, and on the third day of her fever she became bed-ridden and Gandhi came to nurse her. As her temperature was extremely high, Gandhi arranged for her to be examined by doctors. They originally thought that she was suffering from typhoid and Gandhi arranged for her to be admitted to the government hospital. It turned out to be malaria and she was looked after in the hospital by Duncan after Gandhi withdrew the services of the increasingly disturbed Nilla Cram Cook. As a result of her illness, Barr wondered if it was presumptuous on her part to try to 'go Indian'. Gandhi assured her that it was not, but warned her to take precautions with what she ate and drank. Now that her agreed one year of probation was up, she took the plunge, settling in Khedi and disciplining herself by not rushing to the station when trains carrying Gandhi were passing through. Gandhi visited the village in late November 1933.

In March 1934, Mary Barr returned to Hyderabad on a visit and some of her old friends were keen to meet Gandhi when he also arrived in the town on his country-wide Harijan tour. During an interview session at which she was present, she heard 'an obviously well-off missionary' who was working with outcaste villagers, many of whom had converted to Christianity, ask Gandhi for some practical suggestions about what could be done for 'untouchable' uplift. When Gandhi advised the interviewer that all workers should get off their pedestals and live with them, and share their burdens and shame, he responded that he wanted a specific programme of help, rather than 'mere platform talk'. Gandhi's stern response was that it was not at all 'platform talk', but that the best way to do away with all that untouchability meant 'in the way of dirt and degradation', was to live with the Harijans.[19] And this is exactly what Mary Barr had set out to do. At close to forty years of age she had decided on village life, sampled it before making a commitment and then stayed on in Khedi for eight years, leaving only briefly to tend her aged father.

In Khedi, during the holidays, Mary Barr had the company of a young boarding-school child she had adopted as a baby eight years before in Hyderabad. Work in the village was organised by her co-workers, who were recruited locally. With them, she had set up a spinning programme for the women and children so that they could earn some additional income. By the end of 1934 she had established a thriving cottage industry and turned her house into a casteless spinning centre with a flourishing vegetable garden.

Mary Barr travelled with Gandhi's entourage to the October 1934 Bombay session of the Indian National Congress. On the return journey to Wardha, she sought his opinion about a new proposal. She informed him that she had been invited to live in a tribal Gond hamlet near Khedi. Some had counselled her against the move, feeling that she would be unsafe among such 'primitive people'. Although Gonds were rarely interested in education, they had actually asked for her assistance. In good humour, Gandhi responded: 'Well, if I hear one day that the Gonds have taken a hatchet and chopped you up, I shall be quite happy about you.'[20]

## MARY CHESLEY COMES TO KHEDI

Soon after Mary Barr returned to Khedi, an unknown and unannounced Canadian Quaker, Mary Chesley, arrived. She was born in Nova Scotia in 1891, the daughter of a judge, the Reverend Robert Chesley, and a pacifist suffragist mother. She graduated with a B.A. from Mount Allison University, and following a further year of teacher training she taught school in Bridgewater, Nova Scotia, and in San Diego, California. Before the First World War she moved to Britain and after the war she worked for German children's relief, and later to raise money for Russian and Chinese famines. While in England, she graduated from the London School of Economics, earning a B.Sc. in Political Economy (with Honours in Public Administration), and then studied French at the Sorbonne. In London she had a motion recommending total disarmament put forward at the English annual Labour Party Conference in Birmingham in 1928. Needless to say, it was not carried. From 1926, with a Quaker friend, she conducted a small private school in London, carrying on alone until the early 1930s after her friend left. She then decided to devote her life to spreading 'the practice of Christian economics' and became a member of Neighbours, a group that restricted their personal spending to that of the average wage-earner of the country. In 1931 she became a Quaker. Her friends described her as a keen pacifist who never knew fear.[21] She had come to India to visit friends in the north of the country and to fulfill the desire to do some kind of village work if the opportunity presented itself. For Barr, she was a godsend. Not only did they get on extremely well, but she could carry on the Khedi work while Barr settled in the Gond hamlet. They visited Gandhi in mid-December 1934 and put the scheme to him. He merely told Chesley (affectionately called Tarabehn) not to promise anything 'precipitately' before she had visited her friends.

Barr returned to Khedi and undertook an experimental week with the Gonds. During this time she came to a realisation which she wanted to discuss with Gandhi. She knew that she sincerely wanted to work for villagers, but, she had to admit to herself, even more than that she wanted to be with the Mahatma, 'to serve in some capacity near him'.[22] Before dedicating herself to work with the Gonds, she wanted to determine if there was some niche for her in Wardha that would give her 'heart-satisfaction' as well as 'valuable mind-training'. Gandhi invited her to work with him at what was to become a Harijan training colony in Delhi. Barr observes that had the experiment been tried in a rural setting rather than Delhi she might have spent the rest of her time at his side. Perhaps it was Gandhi's genius to organise things this way, and Barr soon realised that in such a setting she had no ability to be of any use. After their month was over, she 'gladly returned to Khedi', noting: 'I now realise how wise he was then in his treatment of me, a sort of intuitive wisdom which I have noticed in his dealings with several individuals, but which is not always realised or appreciated at the time. Since those days, my love for him has grown rather than waned, but it does not now need the stimulation of being constantly with him.'[23]

During the Delhi interlude, after having seen her friends, Chesley arrived determined to join Barr at Khedi. Plans were discussed and Gandhi promised to send them a Hindu woman who could help them and teach them. Chesley became seriously ill before they left Delhi, but showed stubborn determination to push on, a determination that would later cost her her life.

The two Marys settled into Khedi along with Sumitra, whom Gandhi had sent to help them for six months. Chesley undertook the labour of building a mud wall and veranda to Barr's cottage without assistance, and limited her monthly expenditure to four rupees – the salary of better-off village coolies. Although they met infrequently, Gandhi informed them that they could rely on him for necessary finances[24] and guided their work. For example he instructed them on what their attitude to the dispensation of medicines should be:

...You cannot always make people pay for medicines. Always tell them that they ought to pay whatever they can, not, by way of fees, but in order that people who cannot afford anything might be helped. Where you find people are taking advantage of you, you should resolutely refuse to let them have any medicines without payment. Do not encourage people to come to you for medicines, but lead them to a natural life and point out to them household, nature-cure remedies.[25]

Around this time, Gandhi received a letter from Chesley that gives an idea of her values, and perhaps her pig-headedness. It is a letter about her work carrying headloads of mud in buckets from where she dug it up to make the verandah at the house in Khedi only eleven days after settling in the village:

M.B. and I had our first and only real disagreement about this as she wrote to you. She felt that I was likely to go wrong and do a lot of unnecessary work and that, therefore, we should have a coolie to tell me what to do. I thought that I enjoyed the work, that I did not want a coolie, that one should not have help for things one could do oneself and that in a village, where most people did their own building, one should be able to get enough free information not to go wrong.[26]

After receiving this letter, Gandhi described the work of Barr and Chesley in glowing terms in his paper:

A sister who in conjunction with another has just begun work in a little village in C. P. [the Central Provinces] writes a deeply interesting and earnest letter from which I take the following extract [about the manual labour of house construction and a desire to take up gardening.]. There is much more that is valuable in the letter before me. But I resist the temptation to quote more. I must not divide with other items the emphasis which I wish to lay on the necessity for village workers of labouring like the villagers, which the quotation so clearly recognizes. If these two sisters are blessed by God with health and can stick to their work for long, if not for life, they will certainly make of their village a model – not merely because they have begun with physical labour, but also because of the propriety of their whole scheme of work and the selfless love of the villagers which fires them.[27]

After a short time with Chesley and Sumitra, Barr went to live in the dharamshala (public rest house) about a mile from the Gond hamlet, until a hut could be constructed for her. However, within days she had come down with a severe bout of malaria and had to be hospitalised. Although she had been a complete vegetarian for three years, the doctors advised Barr to eat eggs, if she would not eat meat, to aid her recovery. She asked Gandhi if there was a substitute she could take. Although it is fairly certain that in such a case Gandhi would not have taken his own advice, such advice was never dogmatic, but tailored to the individual case before him. Mahadev Desai wrote on Gandhi's behalf that unfertilised eggs could possibly be procured, however 'Bapu says you must put on weight on milk and butter and eggs. The only substitute for eggs is eggs! Bapu says you must not worry about these things at present. You must take what the system needs and be done with it.'[28] He also suggested that she go to the Miraj Sanatorium, on the Western Ghats south of Poona, for examinations and treatment. Barr was able to get away in June, before the monsoon set in.[29]

During the three month absence of Mary Barr, another Mary turned up at Khedi. Mary Ingham had arrived from England at Chesley's suggestion that she come to India to do village work. Soon, however, the work at Khedi came to a halt. Barr was in hospital in Miraj, Sumitra was in hospital in Betul, and the newly arrived Ingham (who had taken the name Shantabehn) was in Mayo Hospital in Nagpur. As soon as she was well enough, Barr returned to Khedi via Wardha (the dharamshala having been washed away by a flood while she was in hospital) relieving Chesley of her post and, alone, tried to keep the Khedi work going as best she could. Chesley, who at first did not get on very well with Sumitra, now dedicated herself to looking after her colleague. When Sumitra had recovered enough to be relocated to Wardha hospital, Chesley went to look after her, spending several weeks tending her 'with an almost dog-like devotion'.[30] Chesley stayed on in Wardha well into 1936 helping Sumitra. In her time at the ashram, she became very friendly with some of the other ashramite women and decided to go with them on a pilgrimage to the Himalaya in the approaching hot season. In April, she returned to Khedi for a week to pack and left on the journey in early May, after rejoining her companions in Wardha.

Out of the blue, Barr received a letter bearing terrible news from Gandhi:

> I have just had a wire saying that Tara died at Hrishikesh. The news is stunning, unbelievable. I have no further particulars. I had warned her against braving the pilgrimage. But she had an iron will. Once it was made up it was immovable. I have wired for particulars. Perhaps you have them already. Her forgiving nature and charity had captivated me. Her belief in the goodness of human nature was beyond all praise. She has sacrificed herself for the cause she believed in. Shanta is here and she has given Miss Blythe's address. Miss B was her partner.[31] You will tell me all you know and I ought to know about Tara. ...[32]

From the Wardha ashram, Chesley and four Indian women had set out on their pilgrimage. They caught a train to Haridwar, and after a few days of rest, began their climb to the headwaters of the sacred river Ganges at Badrinath and Kedarnath. On the first day's walk the weather was hot and Chesley came down with a fever. Her companions suggested that they return to Haridwar, but she would not hear of it. For the following three days the women pushed on, covering about eight miles a day, Chesley subsisting on only small quantities of milk. On the fifth day the concerned women held a meeting and threatened to return to town without her if she did not voluntarily come. Chesley talked her companions into a compromise – she would continue on horseback and by bus to the next village, Devaprayag, where there was a local hospital. Although she rested for three Days, her condition did not improve. A car was sent for, and, accompanied by Vinoba Bhave's disciple Mahadevi Omma 'who adored Tarabehn as her own mother', she was taken back out of the hills. On the way she asked for the car to be stopped and on a piece of paper asked Mahadevi to write in Hindi for her: 'I leave all my property to Bapu', and she signed it, simply, 'Tara'. She died of pneumonia in Rishikesh, where the Ganges enters the plains, and was cremated in the nearby holy town of Haridwar according to Vedic rites.[33]

Gandhi penned a lengthy obituary for Mary Chesley in his paper *Harijan*:

> Miss Mary Chesley, an Englishwoman, came to India in 1934 when the Congress was in session in Bombay. As soon as she landed she

came to my hut in the Congress camp and told me she knew Mirabehn and had expected to come with her but somehow or other she had preceded her by a week or there-about. Her desire was to serve India through her villages. She did not prepossess me by her talk and I thought she would not stay in India many months. But I was wholly mistaken. She had come to know of Miss Mary Barr who had already commenced village work in Khedi, a village a few miles from Betul (C.P.). Miss Chesley found her way to Mary Barr. Mary Barr brought Mary Chesley to Wardha and we were together for a few days. Miss Chesley showed a determination that surprised me. She began work with Mary Barr in Khedi, adopted the Indian costume and changed her name to Tarabehn and toiled at Khedi in a manner that alarmed poor Mary Barr. She would dig, carry baskets full of earth on her head. She simplified her food as much as to put her health in danger. She had her own handsome income from Canada from which she kept only a paltry sum of about Rs 10 for herself and gave the rest to the A.I.V.I.A. [All-India Village Industries Association], or to Indians with whom she came in contact and who seemed to her to give promise of being good village workers and who needed some pecuniary help. I came in closest touch with her. Her charity was boundless, she had great faith in the goodness of human nature. She was forgiving to a fault. She was a devout Christian. She belonged to a Quaker family. But she had no narrowness about her. She did not believe in converting others to her own faith. She was a graduate of the London School of Economics and a good teacher, having conducted together with a companion a school in London for several years. She realized at once that she must learn Hindi and was regularly studying it. For being able to pick up conversational Hindi she lived for a few months in the Wardha Mahila Ashram and there with two members formed a plan of going to Badri-Kedar during summer. I had warned her against the adventure. But it was difficult to turn her from such adventures when once her mind was made up. So only the other day she started with her friends on her perilous pilgrimage. And I got a brief message on the 15th from Kankhal saying, 'Tarabehn expired'. In her love for India's villages she was not to be excelled by anybody. Her passion for India's independence was equal to that of the best among us. She was impatient of the inferiority complex wherever she noticed it.

She mixed with poor women and children with the greatest freedom. There was nothing of the patron about her. She would take service from none, but would serve anybody with the greatest zeal. She was a self-effacing mute worker whose left hand did not know what the right had done. May her soul rest in peace.[34]

She had become the epitome of the ideal, if a little headstrong, constructive worker. In letters to Mirabehn and Jamnalal Bajaj, Gandhi described her as an 'extraordinarily good woman' whose 'single-minded devotion, firmness of mind, purity, generosity and love of India baffle description.'[35] Following her death, he often used Mary Chesley's village work as an illustration of how such service should be undertaken, even as an example to himself when he was on the verge of leaving Wardha for the small nearby Harijan village of Segaon. For example, in a discussion with the German Jewish doctor Erika Rosenthal, who was doing welfare work in Mysore, Gandhi explained that prospective village workers had to follow Tarabehn's example. After narrating the story of her life and death in India, Rosenthal objected that she had been a rash adventurer who should not be imitated. Gandhi responded that he was talking of her spirit, 'the spirit in which she tried to identify herself with the poorest'.[36] He added that Mary Barr is more sensible because she makes allowances for her limitations while maintaining complete identification with the people.

Gandhi advised that Chesley's belongings should be left where they were until her relatives were traced and it was decided what could be done with her unusual will.[37] Gandhi was not sure that the unwitnessed will was valid under Indian law, and that even if it was he did not want to use her property, except for Indian village industries work if her relatives agreed.[38] She had left property in England and the newspaper of the Nova Scotia town of Bridgewater reported that the taxes on a property within the town limits that had been owned by Chesley had mounted to almost the assessed value of the land and that 'unless the Mahatma pays up soon, the land will be offered for sale by the town'.[39] In the end her relatives claimed her property and Gandhi received nothing from the Chesley estate.

## OTHER KHEDI WORKERS: PEARL MADDEN AND MARGARET JONES

In 1924, a Canadian missionary woman had written to Gandhi about how Christ could unify India and that Jesus was the only way.[40] Gandhi received countless letters with this message. However, when the retired Pearl Madden finally came into Gandhi's orbit a dozen years later, she was a greatly changed person.

Madden had heard of the work Barr and Chesley were doing in Khedi. She wrote to them asking if she could come to see them and stayed with them in April 1936, not long before Chesley set out on her fateful pilgrimage. Madden was an elderly retired missionary who had only worked in urban settings, and now she 'passionately', according to Barr, wanted to experience Indian village life. Although Chesley doubted her suitability, Barr concluded that 'such enthusiasm as she would obviously bring to the work would find a way out of all difficulties, an idea which proved correct'.[41] In mid-May she wrote asking if she could come and work with the two Marys for a year. This was providential, coming as it did just when Chesley died. In July she arrived in Khedi, remaining until her return to Canada in 1938.

During the two years that Madden stayed in Khedi she revolutionised the spinning and weaving industry, which Barr noted was not really worth the name 'industry' before she arrived. Barr wrote that 'She, with her business-like brain and tireless devotion, did more for the development of the work than Mary C. and I could have done together in a much longer time.'[42] In the village she became known as Motibehn, 'Moti' being the Hindi word for pearl, and a common name for girls.

Being cautious after Chesley's death, Gandhi wrote to Barr with instructions to Madden: 'She must go slow in making changes in her life. Europeans simply cannot make some changes. Each one has to recognise his limitations. ... You will take a lesson from Tara's life and not overdo things.'[43] A week later he wrote again informing Barr that he had heard from Pearl Madden: 'I am glad you have given me particulars about her. It is plucky at her age to come to village work. But faith can overcome mountains. I am writing to her.'[44] Gandhi's letter to 'Dear Sister' was most welcoming:

> Tara, who is the link between us, had written to me just before she set out on her fatal pilgrimage, that I must invite you to Wardha and cultivate your acquaintance much more fully. She had fallen in love with you. She was a great heart! I had fully intended therefore to write you on my return to Wardha, but you have anticipated me. ... Yes, we must meet and know each other better. For me Tara's death has made

it a sacred trust. There was a time when I used to pooh-pooh Tara's reading of people. But during my illness her persistence about some people and the truth of it made me revise my opinion of her judgements. Her reading of you therefore draws me towards you.

I am glad you are going to work with Mary Barr ... I must ask you to profit by Tara's example. You must not risk your health needlessly as Tara did. She thought she was leading a charmed life. You must recognise the limitations of your birth and age. You must give yourself the minimum comforts that you need for keeping your health. If the body is the temple of the Holy Ghost, it requires care – never pampering ...[45]

Gandhi finally met Madden in November.[46]

When Mary Barr had recovered from her illness, she left Khedi, having been roped into important work with the A.I.V.I.A. in Wardha. In early-August 1936, she floated the idea of taking a brief holiday back to England the following year, in part to get the country to accept a 'bigger share in helping India's poor'. Gandhi approved, but also informed her that even though she could seek funds to 'help our work here' she did not have to do it in order to support her livelihood because, 'You are a member of the family and are entitled to a wage as much as the rest of us.'[47] In the meantime, she spent the Christmas week in Gandhi's camp at the Faizpur annual Indian National Congress gathering, assisting in the exhibition book stall.

During her seven months in England, Mary Barr did not receive a single letter directly from Gandhi. Her explanation showed an unselfish generosity of spirit and a relaxed relationship that was not always apparent in Gandhi's other Western women disciples: 'He took for granted that, as I was with my parents and many old friends, I did not need his help – just as in the days of my exile in the Sanatorium he had taken for granted that I *did*, and wrote every few days.'[48] On her return to Khedi, via a visit to Gandhi in Sevagram, Barr remarked that 'It was, in many ways, a joyful homecoming – a pleasure as deep as had been greeting my own parents earlier in the year.'[49] She settled back into Khedi, which, because it had grown under Madden's guidance, occupied her fully, and even more so after Madden returned to Canada in March 1938.

Mary Barr met Gandhi infrequently now and when she did she apologised that even her letters were little more than dull business correspondence, Gandhi replied that 'Of course your letters are business letters, but business letters, when the business is the service of God's creatures, become love letters. Therefore there need be no apology for your letters being business letters.'[50]

In mid-1939, Barr's mother died and she was not sure as to whether to leave India to look after her father, or to bring him to India. Gandhi advised her that if she felt the call to go and serve her father, she should do it without hesitation after she had done what was possible to ensure the continuation of the work at Khedi, but he cautioned her that it would be risky to bring her father out as he would not stand the climate.[51] In 1940, on the way to joining her father in South Africa, Mary Barr spent a few days at Sevagram with Gandhi. During a brief discussion with him, she informed him that she wanted to greet him by touching his feet in the Indian fashion, but that her body was too stiff and that she was too self-conscious. Gandhi joked that really she was just not humble enough. On their evening walk, Barr came to the realisation that perhaps he was right and she was not humble enough to greet Gandhi the way it was appropriate in the country for a daughter to greet her father. While she was intellectualising her concerns to Gandhi, he remarked laughingly that 'you had better do it now.' As she stooped to grip his ankles, he again gave her the affectionate whack on the shoulders children received from adults, and they both laughed.[52]

Mary Barr started her South African sojourn with Gandhi's second son Manilal at Phoenix settlement.[53] Soon, however, she realised that for harmony with her widower father she would have to make some changes in her life. Barr, who had been a vegetarian for nearly nine years, decided that to continue with her diet would cause a barrier to develop between her and her father. She wrote to Gandhi about her decision to again eat meat and fish. Barr noted that some Hindus would have been horrified at such backsliding, but Gandhi's response, characteristically, was quite different. Through a secretary, he replied that regarding the meat-eating 'he says that you are *absolutely* correct, and you should have no qualms about it. If he were in your place he would do exactly as you have done.'[54]

She returned to India in August 1941, visiting Gandhi on her way back to Khedi.

Another English woman, Margaret Jones (who took the Indian name Kamala – lotus flower – on her first day in the village), came to Khedi not long before Barr left for South Africa. Kamala and a young and very capable Indian male worker, Chandel, who had been in charge of the spinning centre, continued the work at Khedi. When the two of them visited Sevagram for two weeks, Gandhi urged Jones to stay for three months. However, she felt that there was nothing useful for her to do there and plenty to do in Khedi, so she returned with Chandel.

Jones had come to the conclusion that midwifery training would be useful to her work and, so, in November 1940 she broached the subject with Gandhi. The following March, she went to Bombay to commence her course. Soon, however, she became disappointed with the 'general unsatisfactoriness of the atmosphere there'[55] and communicated her feelings to Gandhi. He reminded her that she was there to train herself and therefore should persevere 'unmindful and undistracted by what may be going on around'.[56] In September she came top in her first examination.

While the women were away, Chandel was in full charge of the Khedi centre which was by then in a rented house rather than in the small room and the verandah that Mary Chesley had built onto Mary Barr's cottage, and was more than covering its own costs. By the end of following year, two further buildings had been constructed, one for village industry and another as a dwelling and dispensary for Jones who had completed her midwifery training.

In January 1942, Gandhi asked Mary Barr to take the temporary post of warden of the girls' hostel at Shantiniketan. Rabindranath Tagore had asked Gandhi to suggest someone, Gandhi suggested Barr and Tagore approved of the choice. When the ailing eighty-year-old Tagore passed away in early August the assistance became even more crucial. Barr took on the post for some months until a suitable permanent replacement could be found. Family responsibilities took her back to South Africa in 1943, and Mary Barr never saw Gandhi again. Kamala happily continued the work at Khedi.

In June 1946, Mary Barr was arrested as part of the South African Indians' renewed struggle against discriminatory laws. Before going to prison she informed Gandhi of the struggle. Through one of his secretaries, Gandhi blandly acknowledged her letter. The reply noted that she may have been already released, hoped that she was well, and that she would soon return to Sevagram.[57] Initially she was disappointed by the response. But then she had an important realisation:

> On first reading this I felt almost hurt that there was not some word of appreciation of my help to the Nonviolent resisters. But it was not many moments before it dawned on me that the lack of congratulatory comment was due to the fact that Bapu and his friends accepted me as one of themselves; and I rejoiced, for the highest honour I could ever crave is to be at one with those who, through the ages, have fought for peace with the weapons of peace.[58]

Following the death of her father, Mary Barr, now a Quaker, returned to India in 1951 and eventually settled in Kotagiri in the Nilgiri Hills in South India as one of the Quaker trinity with Marjorie Sykes and Alice Barnes. She edited the Indian Quaker magazine, *The Friendly Way* with Barnes. She died suddenly on 4 December 1968.[59]

## THE KHEDI WORKERS AS WORKERS

Most of Gandhi's other disciples who craved his presence did not volunteer to go far away from him to work, or somehow, if they were sent, managed to end up in situations which ensured that they had to be brought back to be under the Mahatma's care. But then, Mary Barr had been in India doing social work for a decade before she met Gandhi. Pearl Madden, likewise, was a long-term missionary who wanted to work in a rural village more than she was interested in the persona of Gandhi. Gandhi, the man, was perhaps more than merely a senior colleague on the quest for a better educational system, but he was certainly no object of fixation.

For less obvious reasons, Mary Chesley, Mary Ingham and Margaret Jones also became ideal working disciples. While many came to Gandhi, they all came to serve the poor. Mary Barr must take some credit for attracting such colleagues. Still, even she was strongly tempted. Those who came to the Mahatma had great trouble transferring their allegiance to the work.

As the years of their relationship wore on, the personal contact between Gandhi and Marybehn gradually diminished, but had done so for all the best Gandhian reasons: Mary Barr 'began to realise the burden and strain it must be always to have people around him. Now I should make way for others, of whom some are new – a constant stream of people being attracted to him – and some are old friends.'[60] The other Khedi workers and, later, Marjorie Sykes and Saralbehn seem to have had the same insight.

# Other European Disciples: Antoinette Mirbel, Francisca Standenath and Helene Haussding

Besides his best know female disciples, many other women visited and stayed with Gandhi. He had strong enough impact on several of them that, while they may not all have spent years living as natives, they could be called disciples. Unfortunately, those of them that did not come from English backgrounds have tended to escape the attention of most Gandhi biographers. Some of them provide interesting and even important insights into the mind of the Mahatma, in particular into his thoughts on celibacy, and deserve to have their place recorded among the family of Gandhi followers.

### ANTOINETTE MIRBEL, FRANCISCA STANDENATH AND BRAHMACHARYA

Around the time Madeleine Slade joined Gandhi at the Sabarmati Ashram, several other European women would-be disciples, who, like her, had read Romain Rolland's biography of Gandhi, made their way to Ahmedabad to become disciples of the Mahatma. Sometime in late 1924 and early 1925, a thirty-six year-old married French woman, Antoinette Mirbel, wrote two letters to Gandhi insisting on being accepted as his disciple. It seems that he, as was his want, was equivocal in his replies. In mid-January she wrote again: 'I think I understand that I am not worthy of this favour, but the steps that one must ascend in order to hear the master say "I accept you as my disciple", I wish to climb them, I wish to (will).' In the meantime she asked the Mahatma to take her and some selected others under his spiritual direction.[1]

A little over a week later she wrote a lengthy letter describing herself (giving her zodiac sign 'with mystic Uranus as the governing planet') to Gandhi. She explained that Catholicism directed her childhood and youth but her frustration at the bigotry of the 'narrowness of the spirit' of her religion made her an atheist. There was darkness in her life until she came across Theosophist literature, 'but that which filled my mystic soul with joy was "The faith in the Guru", the master.' She started a regime of self-purification: becoming vegetarian, giving up wine, control of desires, and meditation. She made efforts for eleven years to search out the true path, but her heart would 'remain sad so long as the benediction of the guru will not be obtained.' She added that 'I don't know how to write you these things O master of compassion; I feel so unworthy of you; but I would desire – to die for it – if I fail to have the pleasure of being your disciple.' As the financially-dependent wife of a lowly-paid engineer, she could not afford to make the journey without his permission: 'But O master if you do not wish to receive, it will be a death of my soul. I shall feel this want all my life if O master you condescend to receive me, I shall respectfully ask you to appoint the date and the place where I may meet you.[2]

It took a while for the letter to reach Gandhi, and when he replied towards the middle of the year, his response to his 'Dear Friend' was still not overly encouraging: 'I was delighted to receive your letter. But I must not encourage you to undertake what is a long and expensive journey for the mere purpose of seeing me. Nor is it necessary for you to see me for your spiritual progress. It comes through service rendered in the name of God'.[3] In her next letter she informed Gandhi that she had been reading his writings and realised that her thoughts and his were one and so wanted to make him her 'Master and Guru'. She added that she has 'good Karma' and that 'My husband, who loves me like a brother, is also anxious to help me in this sojourn towards you, and would resign himself to the pain of separation which my absence might produce'.[4] To this 'most touching letter', Gandhi responded that she could come but not get her hopes up too high about him. However, he noted that at times physical nearness may be useful and if she gained by being near him it would be 'because of your marvellous faith and not because of any superhuman powers that I possess.' He told her that, if she came, she would be met at the docks in Bombay and put on a train for Ahmedabad.[5] She responded that his letter made her 'shed tears of joy' because 'In order to boldly stand in your presence, with all our weaknesses, and moral and spiritual poverty, it is absolutely essential that we should know you to be human. We come unto you, because you understand us'.[6] In her next letter she informed Gandhi that she was to set sail from Marseilles on 9 October and reach Bombay later that month.[7] She duly arrived, but it seems that there was no one to meet her. Romain Rolland, in a letter to a friend, noted that he could not imagine how, knowing no language but French, 'she arrived in the depths of that huge country (Ahmedabad is a good way from the coast, a whole night's train journey from Bombay, and Sabarmati is some way from Ahmedabad on foot)'.[8]

From what little information is available, Mirbel arrived at the ashram a few days before Madeleine Slade did[9] and stayed for about a month.[10] As no one at the ashram could speak French, after she arrived, one of Mirabehn's first jobs was to act as the interpreter between Mirbel and Gandhi. From Mirabehn's letters to him, Rolland deduced that Mirbel, a woman of 'no great social rank', had 'studied theosophy in a confused sort of way, and her thoughts were disturbed; she longed to see the Mahatma so that he could soothe the troubles of her soul.' Gandhi's approach to Mirbel gave Mirabehn 'an impressive vision of light and peace gradually returning into this lost soul under the Mahatma's words and calm gaze.' Mirbel 'found the answer that her restless mind was seeking, and she set off again alone, at peace with herself, to return to France'[11] after a few days 'just as she came, alone, in silence and at peace. Isn't it a great thing?' He added that 'There must be countless others about which we shall never know! …'[12]

Following her return home to Lille, she kept up a steady correspondence with Gandhi. She seemed to have had doubts about whether she was worthy of being Gandhi's disciple (he reassured her that she was not unworthy, but that he was too imperfect to have disciples rather than co-workers). He instructed her to engage in selfless action in the service of God as such work 'always clears difficulties in front of us and shows us also whenever we err', and assured her that his advice will always be at her disposal. He hoped that she was at peace with herself and her neighbours.[13] She sent money to the ashram regularly[14] and it seems that she was trying very hard to listen to Gandhi's advice, but what it did for her marriage we can only guess. Three years after her brief stay with him, in response to a letter from her 'in such good English' that he had no difficulty understanding what she wrote, Gandhi replied that 'I am glad that you are trying to observe *brahmacharya*.'[15]

In August 1925, forty-year-old Frederic Standenath wrote to Gandhi that he and his forty-two year-old wife Franziska (known to Gandhi as Francisca) were learning English so that they could read Gandhi's writings, writings that had changed them, in an untranslated form. He was an academic physician who was troubled by the contradictions of Western medicine, who had come to realise that only natural therapies offered real cures, and who hated vivisection and the cruelty to animals that seemed to go with his profession. The split between mind and body in Western science, a science which did not question the meaning of existence, also concerned him. He dabbled in occultism and Theosophy, but fortunately his wife guarded him against mystical extremism and helped him to distinguish right from wrong, teaching him 'that nothing is obtained by theories, but only by practical morality in life.' For years they had been reading sacred Hindu texts, and German translations of Gandhi's writings, especially his *Guide to Health*. In Gandhi he had found the satisfaction he had not found in Western science. Now he and his wife were trying to live by the principles of Gandhi's health guide:



> Also in the most difficulty [sic] seeming – in the total sexual abstinence, what I have heard by so many men as impossible to do. That is even Europe. And so steady in this belief, that we living only in a mental fellowship – as my wife would – yet have married in order to not have to fear, our pure mental life would be pulled in the dust. Nobody would think as possible, that we live as brother and sister, or if believing he would take us to be lunatics.[16] Total sexual abstinence is really possible as our life demonstrates, though the abstinence were hard of me in the first time. Also to my wife I have to thank.
>
> How much misery would disappear out of the world, when the men were so thinking and in sexual abstinence living as we, except when they desire a child. But what a misuse of the sexual force in

Europe! The government of the sexual demonstrates – I mean – the degree of evolution of the human being.[17]

Frederic's letter was accompanied by one from Francisca detailing her life story. Here she makes it clear that sexual abstinence is 'natural' for her and that she is the driving force behind their *modus vivendi*, however she noted that Frederic esteemed her standpoint. Her father had died when she was three and she did not like parties or dancing lessons as a child. Her mother had remarried and her step-father had married her off as it was not possible for a girl of a well-to-do family to study and have a profession. She had been home schooled, and had no friends before her marriage; in fact, till then, she had never spoken to another man and hardly even with other girls. Her marriage was a terrible ordeal for her, entailing 'unspeakable sufferings' and the 'badest ill-usage' from the first day. She could not 'and cannot give way to sensuality in my life'. After almost eight years of suffering she obtained her majority and divorced her husband. She went to live in Vienna for studies but the war intervened. After that she studied in grammar school and attended medical college. She married Frederic before he was called up for the navy shortly after the end of the war. She was sorry for him because she knew that abstinence was difficult for him, but was consoled by the fact that Gandhi's writings were good for his evolution. Although he was away during the war, they organised to read spiritual tracts at the same time and she learned the value of silence. When Frederic returned home after the war, they had to leave their home, which was occupied by the Italians, to take up residence in Graz. While her husband went to university, she gave singing lessons to make ends meet. She gave up the idea of studying medicine, seeing Western science as godless. She hated the materialism of Europe, the hypocrisy of a religion which was only practiced on Sundays, cruelty to nature, alcoholism and the 'inordinate love of pleasure'. Three years before her first letters to Gandhi, she had discovered the *Bhagavad Gita*, and for a year and a half, she and her husband had read a chapter together each night. Since reading Gandhi's *Guide to Health*, she had given up the tea, spices and even drugs, weathering a serious illness without them. With Frederic, she had become a vegetarian and started experimenting with fasting. She and her husband seemed to be demonstrating that a Gandhian way of life was possible in the West.[18]

Two months later Francisca wrote to the Mahatma worrying about her mail from India and copies of *Young India* being opened before they reached her.[19] Gandhi warned her against suspicion and advised her to show the authorities all her correspondence if this could induce them to deliver it promptly.[20] In March of the following year she informed him that she 'joined' his ashram prayers at 3.30 (which would be 7 pm in India) being a 'ray for me in the midst of my day.' She also informed him of the drunkenness and anti-animal callousness of Germans, and that she was learning Hindustani and Sanskrit.[21] A few days later, Frederic added that for years his wife had been 'obeying the principles of *Guide to Health* and looks years younger than she is ... I thank to Mrs Standenath the encouragement to strive for Brahmacharya.'[22]

Although they were soon wearing khadi, Francisca requested more and asked specific permission to wear it and for a spinning wheel to be sent to her.[23] She received the cloth and the permission.[24] Her correspondence with Gandhi covered topics such as the deeper meaning of spinning, of the relative value of spun cotton and wool, about people misrepresenting Gandhi in the press and about his health, and of her efforts to learn Sanskrit.[25] She also told him that his proposed but not undertaken trip to Europe could, by the power of his word alone, put the continent 'on the right track and protect it from the dark path on which it is treading now'. She added that she thought that he was the 'greatest man on the earth' and despite his modesty, the trip was really about delivering Gandhi's 'great message to the World'.[26] These were the types of letters Gandhi received by the score, and while he sent friends who were visiting Europe to see their authors (including the Standenaths), his answers were also relatively pro-forma. However, he finished a letter to Francisca and her husband with an invitation to visit India and him:

> Whenever you can spare some money, you should both come to India, if only for a season and see things for yourself. You will then perhaps get a true perspective and probably be enabled to modify some of the exaggerated notions you might have about India in general and the Ashram and myself in particular. I am anxious that you should know things as they are, or at least as they appear to you at close quarters and not as they seem to you from a distance.[27]

In another letter, Gandhi, noting their poverty, went further, informing the Standenaths that 'If you will accept donation please inquire and let me know what will be the cost of two return-passages. You may also consider whether you could think of settling in India.'[28]

Gandhi had advised the Standenaths to come in November or December, when the hot season was over.[29] They were overjoyed at the invitation, but could not wait that long as Frederic could only leave his post at the medical department of the university where he was lecturing during the long vacation (and for the extra month or so after this period that they hoped to be away he had to pay for someone to substitute for him at the laboratory out of his own pocket, a sum which amounted to half his salary.) Further, the fare to India was cheaper in the summer and Frederic assured Gandhi that 'We rather crave for the heat and are sure to endure the temperature during the months, September to November.'[30]

The trip could not go ahead until August of 1928 and may have had to wait until 1929; they thought that they would only be able to remain until the end of October. Frederic informed Gandhi that second-class return tickets in the off season (January to August) were £80, and during the main season (September to December) £94 from Trieste, with an extra charge for cabins as Europeans are not allowed to travel steerage beyond Suez.[31] Franscica added, in her letter written the same day,[32] that they would like to settle in India where she could work the way Mirabehn was doing. She felt bad about depriving India of the money they would use for the trip, but noted that Frederic's salary was small and that her parents' wealth, and thus her inheritance, was lost with the breakup of the old Austro-Hungarian empire in 1919. By this time she was corresponding with Mirabehn about mistakes in Rolland's book about Gandhi and was angry that they were not being corrected and that Mira was not pushing the issue. She also expressed criticism of Helene Haussding's article on Gandhi.[33]

In 1928 the trip became possible. Francisca wrote to Gandhi informing him that they needed a written invitation from him that he was prepared to guarantee their expenses for visa purposes.[34] Gandhi's letter offered his official invitation and guarantee to support them throughout their stay as well as paying for their passage. It cleared the way with the British Passport Control Office in Austria, which issued their visas in only ten minutes. Gandhi noted that he was happy to do this because they were 'most deserving' and had to be 'acquainted with the country'.[35] Gandhi's chief financial backers, the wealthy industrialists G.D. Birla and Jamnalal Bajaj, covered their costs while they were in India.[36] Early in July Gandhi arranged for Rs 2,600 to be sent to them through Lloyds Bank, 'being somewhat larger than that mentioned by you in your letter'. Gandhi was now awaiting their arrival and directed them to 'come directly to the Ashram'.[37] The Standenaths received a draft for £193-12-11 from Bajaj later in the month and immediately started making preparations for the journey.[38]

One of Gandhi's most able lieutenants, Rajendra Prasad, who had been in London working on a legal case, decided to attend a No-War Conference outside Vienna. Following the conference, with a letter of introduction from the Mahatma, he visited the Standenaths en route to calling in on Romain Rolland during a longer Europe trip. A few days into August, not long before the Standenaths set out for India, the couple met Prasad at the Graz railway station, took him home for refreshments and then took him to a nearby hall where Prasad had hoped to 'do anti-war propaganda' at what he thought was going to be a Women's International League for Peace and Freedom meeting. A gang of Austrian nationalist thugs attacked Prasad at the pub where he attempted to speak and Frederic and Francisca were injured trying to protect their guest.[39] They returned to the Standenaths' home 'bleeding profusely'. Doctor Standenath dressed Prasad's wounds, then his wife's and finally his own. Prasad noted that they 'spoke very little English and were not able to express themselves well'.[40] This did not seem to come in the way of their communicating with Gandhi.

Frederic and Francisca sailed from Trieste on 31 August aboard the *S.S. Cracovia*, arriving in Bombay on 17 September. They joined Gandhi at the Sabarmati Ashram soon after. By early October the couple had learnt to card cotton insisting on showing him all their finished slivers, further overloading his busy schedule.[41] During the celebrations for Gandhi's fifty-ninth birthday (celebrated a week after the actual date in Indian custom), Francisca swapped her Punjabi outfit for a full sari.[42] In the course of their almost three month stay, Francisca asked Gandhi to give her an Indian name. The Mahatma had trouble coming up with anything suitable. On Thursday 25 October, after evening prayers, she asked again and he informed the crowd around him that because Francisca had asked, and because the ashramites, and especially the children, were having difficulty pronouncing her name, he was giving her a name that would have meaning for all. Frederic had been debilitated by a bad attack of malaria and this prompted the Mahatma to call the Austrian couple Savitri and Satyavan, mythological figures from the Hindu epic the Mahabarata.[43] Gandhi announced that the name Savitri was not quite adequate because

Francisca had done more than Savitri, the ideal wife, had done in saving the life of her husband. After the evening prayers when he visited Frederic, Gandhi told him he must call his wife Savitribehn (sister Savitri).[44] The first time that Francisca saw herself addressed as Savitri in print was in a farewell postcard sent by Gandhi to her at Mani Bhavan just after they had left Sabarmati Ashram for Bombay from where they were to board ship back to Europe: 'My Dear Savitri, just a line to send you my love. The parting was sad but I hope both of you are now composed. I hope you had a good journey and no difficulty at the station in Bombay. Love to you both Bapu'.[45]

Gandhi had given Francisca his sandals as a parting gift, and as the day of their departure was a Monday, the Mahatma's day of silence, he wrote them a small farewell note: 'don't cry, stay healthy and come back whenever you want'.[46] They left India two days later on 21 November, and by early-December they were sailing off the coast of Crete on the way home.[47] The couple felt the separation from the ashram keenly and dreaded going back to their old lives. On the return voyage, Francisca wrote that she knew that separation is just from the body, and that for the soul there could be no separation, but she could not help weeping at having to leave.[48] Frederic added a note about the 'heart-coolness and not understanding of our countrymen "at home". No, Bupuji, please to allow that we are taking the Ashram, India, for our real home.' He added what amounts to a promise to continue in their practice of celibacy, self-restraint and self-control: 'In the beginning is this a hard work as I have made the experience myself. Savitriben has saved not only my bodily life but also my spiritual life. The man is – as Bapuji says – put in this world in order to overcome the difficulties and to master oneself, to know Lord and to serve him.'[49] Gandhi wrote to them when they had arrived back in Graz that he understood their pain as a result of their separation from the ashram, but instructed them to compose themselves and 'go on steadily' with their mission.[50] He gave Francisca his blessings to translate any of his writings and praised her for repudiating and correcting misrepresentations about him and his movement, but also warned her to 'let them not disturb you'.[51] In mid-October 1929, Gandhi noted that 'I know that you are advertising me for all you are worth. Only I hope that you are not consciously or unconsciously exaggerating anything. Remember it is always best to under-rate the merits of friends.'[52] By April 1931, Francisca had completed her book on their stay at the Ashram and of Gandhi's Salt Satyagraha.[53]

Many people wanted to visit Gandhi. Generally he tried to dissuade them, but if they turned out to be more than merely curious, he often invited them to come. This was the case here, but in this case he also offered to pay their expenses. Why this extra desire to have the Standenaths with him? It was surely not enough that they could become future possible advocates of his cause, as they did in fact become. It seems that the reasons had more to do with their practice of celibacy within marriage and the fact that they were demonstrating that his philosophy was not something that was only applicable in the East but was universal, as confirmed by their example in Europe.

In September 1929, Gandhi penned an article on marriage where he expressed his views that wedded union did not need to imply a decision to have children and could be conducted 'despite the absence of any sexual desire'. He noted that Olive Schreiner had such a relationship[54] and that 'there is a couple in Austria whose relationship today is of such a kind and was also like that from the very outset.' Gandhi then asked,

> Why cannot the purity of conjugal love imply the supreme striving towards the unity of all living beings? Cannot that which appears to be an impossibility today become possible tomorrow? Can there be any limits to self-control? Let us not set any restriction to higher states to which a human being can reach, by looking at the example of creatures other than human beings.[55]

In the detailed German language book she wrote on Gandhi's Civil Disobedience campaign (which included translations of may of Gandhi's speeches and articles of the time), Francisca noted that for the past ten years she had been unwittingly trying to live by the same rules as Gandhi's ashramites by refraining from taking meat, alcohol, nicotine and other toxic substances, and by practicing celibacy even in her married state. She explained that these rules had to be abided by anyone, Europeans included, who wanted to join the ashram for one and a half years before admission and that she and Frederic had no trouble with this as they had already fulfilled the conditions, having lived as brother and sister for a decade.[56]

After Gandhi left London for the continent on his return to India in 1931, Francisca Standenath managed to catch up with him in Geneva (Frederic could not get away from his university duties). The meeting was not a happy one. Francisca was judgmental of others and was overly proud in her righteousness.[57] Whether this had anything to do with her practice of celibacy (or the fact that she had just had her book on Gandhi published) is not recorded; however it is clear, Frederic's many supportive comments notwithstanding, that this practice was causing problems in their marriage:

> I think Satyavan's problem is simple. No person can go beyond his or her limits. You cannot force anyone to be chaste. He or she must have the inner conviction. You can give him the fullest freedom to separate himself from you and get a divorce decree if necessary. He must be at liberty to marry some other woman of his choice. It is most dangerous to have a carnal mind constantly brooding over satisfaction of animal passion. You must surround him with all the affection you can give him and not judge him harshly. It is to his credit that he has striven all these years to control himself. Of course if you have the slightest desire to satisfy his craving, you should regard yourself at liberty to do so. For you both came to a joint conclusion about self-control. If now one party wishes to revise the agreement, the other may also, if there is the desire. Whereas if you are satisfied that you have no craving at all, you must resist every entreaty from Satyavan as lovingly as possible, but with the utmost firmness. Let him read this letter. Let him think over it and pray to God for light. And if he finds that he cannot bring his passion under subjection, he must take another wife if you have no wish to surrender. You should part as friends. If you have to part, what happens to you is a matter of little concern. If you have the strength, as I know you have, you will earn your bread by your own labour.[58]

Two months later, towards the end of November 1932, Gandhi was again reminding Francisca that celibacy was no merit for someone like her who was without 'passion', but that if Frederic could control his passion then this was a real achievement:

> The key to Satyavan's purity is perhaps in your own hands. You have to be patient like the Himalayas and have the charity of the ocean. You must not irritate him on any account whatsoever nor sit in judgment upon him if he yields to his animal passion. You do not need to go through the struggle because you are a stranger to that

> passion. Your brahmacharya therefore is no merit in you, but Satyavan's is. All the time he is struggling against the Devil and if he finally subdues it, it would be indeed a great merit and a singular triumph. Let us all therefore pray for him that he may have the necessary strength to overcome the enemy.[59]

The problems seemed to continue. In mid-January 1933, Gandhi wrote to Francisca that,

> I am glad you have entirely seen my point. You will therefore become more and more tolerant and generous towards Satyavan. I know that that very fact would steady him and protect him from falling. You should induce him and ask him on my behalf to write to me more often than he does. Let him pour out his heart to me.[60]



In July 1935, Francisca informed Gandhi of Frederic's long illness,[61] and two months later notified the Mahatma of his death. By way of consolation, if she was not engaged in anything important, Gandhi asked, 'will you not come here and settle down to humanitarian service?'[62] She did not venture back to India and the letters from Francisca became more infrequent. In mid-1936 Gandhi received a letter from her complaining that nobody was interested in her writings. Gandhi responded that 'The wonder is that they have so long tolerated what you had to say about me. The whole thing is so outside their experience', that truth would eventually win out regardless of what they did.[63]

Although at this time the few letters exchanged between Gandhi and Francisca revolve around her sorrow and Gandhi's reassurances that she was doing valuable service in promoting an understanding of work,[64] the memory of the experiment that she and Frederic had been engaged in was not forgotten by Gandhi. In a letter to his daughter-in-law Nirmala, he appears to refer to the erstwhile ashram visitors and possibly to the mythological couple they were named after,[65] explaining that the 'snake that bit Satyavan was not a snake in the physical sense; the snake was lust. Savitri got the venom out by her purity and love. That is the mystery of the story of Savitri. A person whose purity can overcome lust in another can overcome anything.'[66] Four days later Gandhi seems to have reconciled himself to the fact that Nirmala wanted to be with her husband, Gandhi's son Ramdas, however he reminded her that he had already explained to her what it was Savitri saved Satyavan from and instructed her to 'Save Ramdas in the same way'.[67]

Correspondence between Gandhi and Francisca ceased during the war. In a reply to Francisca's first letter in years, in April 1947, Gandhi remarked that he did not know that she was still alive, and asked her what she was doing for a living.[68] In a further exchange of letters a month later, Gandhi expressed delight that Francisca had reappeared and asked her about what she had endured and about conditions in Austria.[69] Some months later, in her following letter to Gandhi, Francisca explained all that she has gone through since they were in contact a decade ago, detailing the scarcities of post-war Europe. Gandhi commented on her cheerfulness in spite of everything and asked her how she passed her time, whether she earned anything, and wanted to be reminded of her age.[70] Unsurprisingly, it appears that she never remarried and lived in Graz until her death in August 1971.

Unfortunately we have no more of the story of the relationship between Francisca Standenath and Gandhi or even a greater knowledge of the relationship between the married partners themselves. Going native can mean more than physical relocation. In this case it was a moral relocation. Here we have a woman who 'lacked passion' finding a moral justification for her feelings (or lack of them) in Gandhi's philosophy. The issue of celibacy is something that troubled several of Gandhi's close Indian colleagues, but it was generally not of great concern to his Western women disciples who were either what were then called 'spinsters' who had dedicated themselves to the work of peace or with the poor, or who were seemingly happily married and had children (or wanted to be married and have children). Antoinette Mirbel and Francisca Standenath were the main exceptions.



## HELENE HAUSSDING: 'MY DEAR SPARROW'

As already noted, during the mid-1920s, there was a steady stream of European women who wanted to meet, and even devote themselves to, Gandhi. The German Buddhist, Helene Haussding was another of this brigade. She was only in India for a relatively short time and had, until recently, more or less disappeared from the Gandhi story. Lately she has been resurrected in a novel about the relationship between Gandhi and Mirabehn. In the novel, Haussding is described as a tiresome, clinging woman who annoyed Gandhi with her constant self-promotional prattling.

In this fictional narrative she so frustrated the Mahatma that in a fit of annoyance she was slapped by him, to the utter horror of both of them.[71] The description of her behaviour seems to be a closer representation of Margarete Spiegel, Gandhi's other German disciple and the slapping incident, if it ever occurred, has escaped credible documentation. Gandhi spoke highly of Helene Haussding and had high hopes for her; however she only spent a relatively brief time at Gandhi's ashram, and for much of this the Mahatma was absent. Probably they did not have enough personal contact for a very close relationship to have formed before she fled India in poor health.

In April 1925, Haussding wrote to Gandhi asking him what she should bring to India in the way of clothes.[72] Later, on the same day after receiving a post card from the Mahatma, she again wrote: 'I feel so happy, for coming to you means to me coming home at last ... Your people will be my people and I shall toil with you to the end of my days.' She believed that Gandhi's ideals mirrored her own and she wanted to go to India to work with him, rather than to be with him because she was personally enamoured of the saintly Mahatma.[73] She had hopes of being with him before the end of the year, and before then she had planned to sell her house and all her furniture, pack what she wanted in India in two boxes (one to send and one to bring with her), and planned to minimise any problems with obtaining a visa by saying that she was going to go to Gandhi.



Three months later, Haussding informed Gandhi that her aunt had died and so she had no further responsibilities and was ready to go. She requested a language book so that she could prepare herself and asked whether she could be a teacher in the ashram school. She also had to inform Gandhi that she was having visa difficulties with many forms and currency declarations and the problem that Germans would generally not be allowed to go to India for another year. She agonised that every day she remained home was a wasted day: 'I am beating the wings of my soul sore against the bars of conventionalities.'[74] Finally, in March of the following year she received her visa and wrote to Gandhi asking if she should bring her sewing machine.[75]

Her persistence was rewarded. Gandhi was pleased that she would soon be with him, adding 'I am not going to discourage you any longer now, nor give you any warning. I am hoping that you will be able to retain your health here and that you will have no cause for disappointment. I shall try my best to make you comfortable and to keep you employed.' He asked her to bring her sewing machine, musical instruments and library, and to come to the Sabarmati Ashram.[76] To one of his sons he wrote that Haussding 'looks as if she is Mirabai's double'.[77]

Helene Haussding had obtained her visa for India in March 1926 and was expected in India early in June. As it turned out she did not arrive until the 25th and Gandhi had one of his Bombay acquaintances meet her boat and arrange her trip to Ahmedabad.[78] All went according to plan and Haussding arrived at the Sabarmati ashram on 26 June. The initial meeting was warm and light-hearted and Gandhi's sense of humour instantly put her at ease.[79] She participated fully in ashram life, cleaning latrines, learning Hindi and sewing. She seemed to have settled in well, even though the singing at prayer meetings offended her delicate sense of music. It appears that she was secure enough in her surroundings that she had no desire to infringe on the Mahatma's time with meaningless questions as far too many of his followers did. Gandhi, in turn, found Haussding 'very courteous and goodnatured'.[80] However, within a month he was writing to his friend Mathuradas Trikumji that the warm weather of Gujarat was not suiting her and that he wished to send her to 'some cool place' for a month. He asked Trikumji if he had room in his Panchgani (in the mountains about sixty miles south of Poona) bungalow for her, assuring him that 'she will not be a burden to anyone', that she was a 'very simple lady, with a fine sense of humour'.[81]

Following that, for the next few months, she stayed with Gandhi's son Devdas in the Himalayan hill station of Mussoorie.[82] There she seemed to settle in, despite feeling guilty about neglecting her teaching duties at Professor J.B. Kripalani's Gujarat Vidyapith college near the Sabarmati ashram. Gandhi assured his 'Dear Sparrow', as he had nicknamed her, that 'I would like that distant chirp from Mussoorie rather than your boilful, constipated chirp from close quarters. I believe in the Latin proverb *mens sana in corpore sano* ["a healthy mind in a healthy body"].'[83] Somewhere along the line she adopted a son in Lucknow, but Gandhi advised her to not to go to visit him until cooler weather had settled in on the plains.

By early December she was back with Gandhi, travelling to Wardha, and then, a month later, was involved in a temple entry scandal. On 9 January, she was with Gandhi in a procession from the Benares Gandhi Ashram to Dashashwamedh, the main bathing ghat on the banks of the holy Ganges river, to pay homage to the Sanskrit educator, Swami Shraddhanand, who had been assassinated by a Muslim fanatic two weeks before. Following the ritual dip in the river, the party walked through the narrow lanes of the town to Kashi Vishwanath, one of the main Hindu temples. Haussding removed her shoes (and said good-bye to them, fearing that they would be stolen), but felt uneasy about entering as a Westerner. Because of the crowd, she had no way out. Suddenly, Gandhi put his arm around her and, as he later explained to the ashram women at Sabarmati, 'It was doubtful whether she would be permitted to enter. She is a Buddhist and hence can be regarded as a Hindu. How could she be denied admittance? *I had decided that if she was stopped, I too would not go in.* But the priest kept quiet when he was told that she was a Hindu.'[84] The following day the priests had to cleanse both of the temples they had entered of her polluting presence, and the town was in uproar over the incident. The newspapers debated Gandhi's actions and a month and a half later, in the town of Pandharpur, those in charge of the temple were 'terribly exercised' over what to do if Gandhi was to enter their temple with his 'European friend'. They must have breathed a sigh of relief, for Haussding had by then long left the tour; however, in his speech, Gandhi reminded his audience that he would not have visited the temple without her (or his 'untouchable' adopted daughter) if she had been there with him.[85] In an ironic twist, Gandhi's sandals, which he had left outside the temple during his Pandharpur visit, were stolen.[86] After he had read some of the articles about her presence at Kashi Vishwanath, Gandhi wrote to Haussding that he was happy that some blows were directed at the superstitious belief in human uncleanliness.[87]



Soon after the Benares visit, they were parted again and Haussding spent her last month in Ahmedabad as a superintendent in a hospital attached to a textile factory. But all was not well. Gandhi wrote to his old Ahmedabad colleague Anasuyabehn Sarabhai,[88] asking about 'Sparrow', noting that her letters had shocked him.[89] In distress, he wrote to Haussding, however the letter seems to be lost.

Unexpectedly Haussding's health had collapsed and the next preserved letter by Gandhi was sent to her in Germany in early June. It noted that it was 'disturbing to think that you are not yet well'. Gandhi then shared his theory of disease with her: 'I regard it as a result of some conscious or unconscious sin' or 'breaches of Nature's laws', adding that 'When you lose mental equanimity, be it ever so little, it sets up terrible agitations in the body, and these latter produce visible effects upon it.' He admitted that he was not free from such problems, allowing overwork and strain, even if done in the best of causes, to lead to his own physical collapses. He explained that individuals who had attained equanimity know when to work and when to rest. He concluded by pointing out that his 'confession is merely a preface to tell you that you must not hug your disease to yourself and from your philosophic height blame the doctor, the weather, the food and everything and everybody else but yourself. Let us call a spade a spade.'[90] Three weeks later he insisted: 'You must not prolong your sickness beyond certain limits and those limits have been crossed already.'[91] She promised not to hug her disease to herself any longer.[92]

Apparently someone had written something about what Haussding allegedly said on her journey back to Germany. It had greatly upset her:

> You agitate yourself unnecessarily over the translation that was sent to you. Surely you have humour enough to take all such stuff lightly. I merely passed it on to you so that you might see what is written by your fellow-passenger about you. Why should we take notice of such writings especially when strangers write? So far as I am concerned, your repudiation is quite enough. I am not going to send your repudiation to the Press. I don't suppose that anybody now remembers the writing. Are you now perfectly all right?
>
> ... I want your assurance that you will never worry about it. All the nasty things that may be said about you need not worry you; for, after all the chief thing with which we should be concerned is to know what the inner voice tells us about ourselves.[93]

Not long before Christmas, Gandhi again wrote to her that 'I expect to hear from you any day that you have now thrown into the Danube all the weakness of the flesh that you took away from India and that your chirp is as vigorous as it was before you reached this land of sorrows'.[94]

A few months later she was back in Ahmedabad, but it seems that again illness had laid her low. She wrote to Gandhi from the Calico Mill Hospital in April 1928. She explained her bluntness to Gandhi and the fact that this will make her enemies, but notes that 'there are those who love me in spite of all my faults and I know you are one of them, and you know that my love for you is not based on sentimentality, but it is strong like a rock and you can build on it. I may not see you often – though I only need to lift my eyes to look at you for the only two photos that decorate my room are yours and my mother's...'[95]

In his last recorded letter to Haussding, written in mid-1929, Gandhi responded to her complaint at being neglected in his correspondence by pointing out that he was very busy and by noting that,

> Letters are bridges of love no doubt but no bridge is needed if we live on the even plateau. You are wrong in thinking that I am disappointed. Loneliness is not bad but I cannot say I feel lonely. That you feel my surroundings to be alien to you and not me betrays something wrong. Find it out. When we quarrel with our surroundings the wrong is in us, not in them. I trust you receive my general weekly letter.[96]

Haussding may have taken to complaining the way Mirabehn (or Spiegel) did on occasions when they did not feel they were getting what they needed from their master, however, she did not manage to survive India in the hot season, or have the dogged determination of Mirabehn, to stay on regardless of the vicissitudes of life. The potential of her becoming another Mirabehn was not fulfilled. Before the fact, 'going native' may have greatly appealed to her, but physically she was not up to it and her discipleship did not last. It is interesting to speculate what would have happened had her health not given way, after all her letters to Gandhi are full of love but they also radiate a confidence, a willingness to work, rather than the blind devotion of Antoinette Mirbel's correspondence.

# Disciples after Gandhi: Marjorie Sykes and Catherine Mary Heilemann

Many women followers came and went during Gandhi's life. Following his death, Mirabehn managed to last another ten years in India trying to live the life of a disciple, but in the end even she returned to Europe. Some of the best-known Gandhian workers (as opposed to disciples) came relatively late into Gandhi's life, at a time when the place of Western women in Gandhi's orbit was largely replaced by Indian women. Two of them, Marjorie Sykes and Catherine Mary Heilemann, who became known as Saralabehn, did most of their influential Gandhian constructive work after the death of the Mahatma. Saralabehn stayed in India for the rest of her life; and Sykes stayed until late in life, when, following much world travel in the Quaker cause, she finally retired in England. Because they came late into Gandhi's life and because they were workers rather than devotees, unfortunately there are no available lengthy or significant letters from Gandhi to them, or from them to Gandhi.

## MARJORIE SYKES AND NAI TALIM

Gandhi and the Quakers had a natural affinity through beliefs concerning the importance of nonviolence and the presence of God in everyone, as well as their practical approach to social problems. It is no mystery why they were drawn to each other and why the Quakers were among Gandhi's closest supporters in Europe and America. Marjorie Sykes has been called a Quaker Gandhian because of the way she lived her Quaker beliefs, and a Gandhian Quaker because of the way she practiced Gandhian philosophy.[1] Of Gandhi's significant Western women disciples, she came as the last into his orbit, but continued his work for decades afterwards.

Marjorie Sykes was born to not overtly religious schoolteacher parents in May 1905 in Yorkshire. The children of the family were expected to take their share of daily chores, cooking and cleaning, and Marjorie learnt much from her father who had a firm belief that children learned by doing things – the basis of Gandhi's own education system. During the First World War, a well-liked teacher was taken from her school because she was German and hence an 'enemy alien'. Her father, who had spent a year studying in Dresden and had made many friends there, was appalled at the peace settlement imposed on Germany, seeing in it the seeds of a future war. In 1923 Marjorie entered Newnham College at Cambridge University with a scholarship to study English.[2] At the university she mixed with Indian students and came to know something about Gandhi through them, and also started to seriously read the Bible under the influence of some of her teachers. After graduating with honours in 1926, she spent another year earning her Cambridge Teacher's Diploma and then placed her name on a list for those interested in teaching in Africa as some of her student friends had done. No position was immediately available and she was advised to gain further experience at home first, so she took a junior teaching post on the outskirts of Liverpool. In May 1928 Marjorie received an urgent request to go and teach at the Bentinck School for Girls, run by the London Missionary Society in Madras. In October the twenty-three year-old teacher set sail for India.

With only about 350 pupils, Bentinck School was relatively small and seemed more like a family than an impersonal institution, and, although it was under Christian management, broached no religious or caste barriers. The school favoured the use of the children's mother tongues, favoured cooperation over competition, and encouraged practical work around the institution by the children themselves. Early on, Marjorie displeased her superiors by riding her bicycle around the streets, travelling on 'ordinary native buses' and starting to wear khadi.[3] She also became a vegetarian. Soon after her arrival at the school, a fellow teacher attended a meeting at the Sabarmati Ashram, coming back deeply impressed with Gandhi.

Marjorie became lifelong friends with the principal of the Bentinck School, Alice Varley, who in 1930 married the Quaker Ted Barnes and left the institution. Soon Marjorie was principal of the school, which remained her home for ten years. She learnt Tamil (later she was also to master Hindi and Bengali), and, through Alice, became involved with the Madras International Fellowship that attempted to bring together Indian and British people regardless of their religious or political beliefs so that they could learn to understand each other. When the Fellowship held a weekend conference with the Gandhian social reformer Chakravarti Rajagopalchari as the main speaker, Marjorie attended. They became firm friends and he introduced her to the Gandhian way of life and the politics of the national struggle. She visited his ashram at Thiruchengode and observed Gandhian philosophy being put into action. As a result of what she was learning, she made changes at Bentinck. Competition was replaced by cooperation, student prizes were abolished, the bright were encouraged to mentor the slow, and students took on tasks of school cleaning.

Although Bentinck had been an ideal home for Marjorie, by the mid-1930s, she was starting to have second thoughts about the entire educational system: it was partially financed by revenue derived from alcohol sales, much of it was irrelevant to India's real needs, and with the passing of education portfolios to local, usually nationalist-controlled government after the 1937 elections, there were often accusations that 'communal' institutions were guilty of proselytising, with the result that 'the former easy, frank intercourse was shadowed by suspicion.'[4] Marjorie started to wonder whether 'she could not make a contribution as a teacher in a more independent and more fully Indian setting.'[5]

Through the Fellowship, Marjorie first met Quakers and soon felt that this was where she belonged. Alice attended meetings in private homes with Ted Barnes, and it was not long before Marjorie was attending as well. During a trip to England in 1936, she formally became a member of the Religious Society of Friends. Back in India, in August of 1937, she read a short article by Gandhi on his vision for the educational system that he wanted for Indian children.[6] He championed an education system based on active scientific and socially and culturally appropriate work related to basic human needs, such as the provision of food and clothing, undertaken jointly by the school community of children and adults. Here was 'someone talking real sense about education at last!'[7]

In 1938 a British Quaker, who had recently met Rabindranath Tagore, came to Madras and informed Marjorie of the poet's desire to have a representative of English culture on the staff at Shantiniketan, his experimental international university one hundred miles north-west of Calcutta. During the Christmas holidays she went on a pilgrimage to visit Gandhi's school at Sevagram (where she met the Mahatma for the first time) and then Shantiniketan where Tagore invited her to join his staff. She became aware of the similarity in the educational ideals of the two institutions and of the frequent exchange of personnel between them. She secured funds from the London Quakers and accepted Tagore's offer, arriving at Shantiniketan in early July 1939.

At Shantiniketan, Marjorie Sykes set to learning Bengali and became a close friend of C.F. Andrews, who returned to be with Tagore after a long absence (he died there in April 1940). She again met Gandhi when he visited Shantiniketan in February 1940. In the following May, she took a vacation in the south with Ted and Alice Barnes, arriving as Ted came down with malaria and pneumonia. She was able to help nurse Ted during his last weeks and comfort Alice when he died. As her language skills improved she became Tagore's translator until his death in August 1941.

The Women's Christian College in Madras was in desperate need of an English teacher, but, because the war had made travel between Britain and India very difficult, could not get a replacement. They asked Marjorie to fill the gap, and Shantiniketan agreed to loan her to the college for two years from mid-1942. Marjorie went on the condition that she could live off-campus in a slum area of the city. She lived an extremely simple life, waking at four in the mornings, getting her own water from a nearby hand pump, her small home having no plumbing, and doing her cooking on a firewood stove. She started a local nursery school for the children of working mothers.

Sykes visited Sevagram several times during 1944/45 for educational conferences as Gandhi was becoming increasingly interested in the development of appropriate education after his release from prison in 1944. At the end of the school year in 1944, she returned to Shantiniketan to write a biography of Andrews. The following year she visited Gandhi to consult the files at Sevagram which contained Andrews' letters to Gandhi. While she was there, Gandhi asked her to consider coming to the ashram to help with the basic education program. She agreed to do so after the biography was finished. By that time, Gandhi was dead and India had achieved independence. Sykes was now forty-four years-old. She decided to stay on in India as a citizen of the newly formed republic and joined Sevagram with the responsibility for training Gandhian teachers in 1949.[8] She was based at Sevagram for the next ten years as the head of the Teacher Training Section.

Marjorie Sykes did much more Gandhian work in her years in India. In 1957 Vinoba Bhave had founded the Gandhian 'peace army', the Shanti Sena, to ensure peace without the necessity for state intervention. In mid-1958 he established a committee to oversee the work of the fledgling organisation under the leadership of women with Marjorie Sykes as convenor.[9] She found the hot weather debilitating and, as she craved to do educational work in a smaller-scale setting, in 1959 she joined Alice Barnes and Mary Barr in Kotagiri in the Nilgiri Hills, built a house and started month-long nonviolence training programs for small groups. Following an invitation from the North American Regional Council of the World Peace Brigade, she visited the United States in 1964, helped organise nonviolence training camps and met leading pacifists. On her return to India in September, she attended the Madurai session of the Gandhian umbrella organisation, the Sarva Seva Sangh, where the great Gandhian activist Jayaprakash Narayan was reporting on the troubled situation in Nagaland. Following his invitation, for three years from the mid-1960s, she was one of the key figures in the Shanti Sena's Nagaland Peace Mission.[10]

Sykes spent the rest of her life writing, travelling and teaching, dividing her time between various Quaker centres in India and England. With advancing age, Marjorie Sykes settled into the Quaker retirement community 'Swarthmore' near London in 1991 where she died in August 1995 at the age of ninety.

## SARALABEHN AND WORK IN THE MOUNTAINS

Catherine Mary Heilemann was born on Good Friday, 5 April 1901, in London. Her father was a Lutheran jeweller and property owner of German-Swiss background. Her mother was English and died when Catherine was only seven years old. As a child she attended a Congregational church and developed a deep reverence for Christian missionaries who served in 'heathen countries' seeing the possibility of such a vocation for herself. Although her father had never visited Germany, due to an irregularity in his birth certificate, he was interned at the start of World War I as an enemy alien. This proved to be a traumatic experience for the young Catherine, and as she could not reconcile her knowledge of Christian teachings[11] with the support of the organised churches for the war, she stopped attending church and started thinking for herself:

> The new inhuman conception of total war, the spirit of reprisals, all struck home as sheer stupidity to one who could not accept current theories of economics and politics as gospel, but weighing them in the balance of common sense and finding them wanting was therefore categorised as an enemy of the nation. People were prepared to accept that if on a certain day, the rulers of two countries sign documents declaring themselves at war, it is the bounden duty of citizens of both countries to set about killing one another, even if until yesterday they had regarded themselves as friends. ... Is it good sound common sense? It didn't seem so to me.[12]

Although a bright student, she failed to receive a scholarship in part because of her lack of support for the war and so she left school at the age of sixteen. Social ostracism led her to seek peace in nature and fostered her love of wandering in the woods. Her first job was as a clerk for a merchant company; however her employer, who had sons serving in the war, was not overly keen about having an 'enemy' in his business. At the end of the war, Catherine's father Otto was released from detention. Soon the daughter was at loggerheads with her traditional father, and, following an argument over whether washing could be hung outdoors to dry on the Sabbath, she left home.[13]

She came to know of Gandhi from Indian students who were staying at or visited the cosmopolitan boarding house in London where she had taken lodgings in the 1920s. She took a concerned interest in the growing nationalist movement. Gandhi's 1930 Dandi Salt March inspired her to the point where her childhood dream of becoming a missionary had been overtaken by one to go to India and be part of the nationalist movement by joining in Gandhi's constructive activities. When the Mahatma was in London for the Round Table Conference she made attempts to meet him. A friend of hers who was working at Kingsley Hall with Muriel Lester had arranged a meeting; however another important engagement kept Gandhi away. A few days later Gandhi was to address students in Oxford. Catherine made the journey in heavy rain, but again she was to be disappointed. While she was in the reading room warming herself by the fire, Gandhi had come and gone without her being called on his arrival as had been arranged.

One day, while walking in the woods of Surrey, Catherine decided that she had to go to India to meet Gandhi. She wrote to him of her plans, asking permission to visit his ashram. He replied that many Westerners had come to India and tried unsuccessfully to live as Indians and had to return. He advised her against making the trip. She then contacted other Indian organisations, but they were all discouraging. This led her to realise that she had to learn a useful skill, so that she would have something to offer India. She underwent training in midwifery, took a correspondence course in commerce and also read sociology, politics and psychology. At this time she came to know some Quaker and Fabian peace workers who, while encouraging her intellectual efforts, were a little less encouraging of her idea of going to India. Eventually, a letter came from Udaipur, in the Rajputana grouping of princely states in what is now Rajasthan in India, informing her that a new progressive school was being established there and that she was being invited to join the staff. Catherine left her midwifery training and undertook a three-month course in child education.

Following some difficulty in obtaining a passport, in early January 1932, at the age of thirty-one, she set out for India to be part of the struggle, never again to return to her homeland. On board ship Heilemann witnessed her first instances of racial discrimination when she noted that Indian passengers were shunned by the whites, and when she interacted with the Indians, she too was shunned. At the school in Udaipur, she read about Gandhi's constructive program and experiments with education, and during the school vacations she toured north India, visiting various educational institutions. The fact that the school catered to middle-class children and because of the general backwardness of the state of Rajputana, Heilemann felt that she was making more compromises than she was comfortable with; after all she had come to India to work with the masses in Gandhi's constructive program. In the vacation for the ten-day Dussera festival in October 1935, she decided to visit Gandhi's women's ashram and girls' school (Mahila Ashram) at Wardha for guidance in her work. Gandhi was present at Wardha during this time and she decided that she should attempt to pay the Mahatma a visit. She wrote to the manager of the ashram, but received no reply and assumed that the letter had been intercepted by the police Criminal Investigation Department. Although she was sure that she would not get to see Gandhi, she telegrammed that she was coming, and went anyway. When she arrived, she was met by someone wearing only a dhoti who proceeded to take her straight to Gandhi. At Maganwadi, where the Mahatma and his entourage were staying, almost everyone was asleep when she arrived. While she was having her late dinner she realised that the only other light on in the establishment was the one in the room of the late-working Gandhi. The following morning she got up early and met Gandhi during his early morning walk. This was their first meeting. Gandhi was very affectionate in the way he went about ascertaining her intentions. She informed Gandhi that some people called her Saralabehn and that she had hoped to stay for around ten days. He asked her if he could make use of her during that time: for two days she was to be his guest, then she had to work and wash her own utensils. She informed him that this would be no hardship as such domestic chores were part of her daily routine.

After morning prayers on the third day of her visit, Saralabehn informed Gandhi that she had a complaint: she had not been given any work to do. Gandhi responded that she had mixed in with the ashramites so well that there was little more he could ask of her. She responded that that was her nature, and so what she was doing could not be considered work. Gandhi then asked her to join the scavenging work team in the nearby village that Mirabehn had organised. She also learnt the art of spinning cotton with Mary Barr, who Gandhi had appointed her teacher.

In 1936 Saralabehn finally left Udaipur and found her way into Gandhi's Nai Talim basic education scheme. She desired to go to Ahmedabad to work in a girls' school. She requested permission from Ahmedabad and when no reply came she again suspected the CID. Only later was she to realise that in India generally no replies indicated a refusal. She went regardless. In Ahmedabad she tried to learn Gujarati and worked with the children of spinning mill employees. The ever-present noise of the urban slum was more difficult for her than even the heat. Later, she was asked to help a doctor at the local hospital. Not only was the doctor rude to the patients but the hospital was dirty and she became so ill that she had to be hospitalised. She contacted Jamnalal Bajaj in Bombay, and, after telling him of her predicament, received permission to go to Wardha until she recovered. As she approached Gandhi slowly, he insisted that she had to run and told her how happy he was, not because she was well enough to run, but because she had come to work with them. She walked to Sevagram (to where Gandhi had relocated by this time) with the Mahatma. They discussed her health and diet. She spent time at the Mahila Ashram and at Vinoba's Nalwadi Ashram and continued her spinning practice. The heat troubled her and she contracted malaria. Her condition deteriorated steadily while she was at Sevagram. In January 1937, she went to Poona for naturopathy treatment. Gandhi, who was in the city for discussions with the mill owners and labourers, sent his secretary Pyarelal to enquire about her health and then his personal physician, Pyarelal's sister Sushila Nayar, to look after her. Saralabehn was instructed that she had to take quinine, but instead she treated herself by wrapping her body in wet sheets in order to break the fever. Later she teased Sushila about the value of Western trained doctors like her as opposed to those skilled in naturopathy. She decided to return to Udaipur to affect a complete cure.

After Udaipur, she returned to Sevagram to work for the Talimi Sangh but again came down with malaria. One day a friend informed her that she had just returned from the Gandhian woollen khadi-producing ashram at Chanauda near Almora, and how beautiful the setting was. Saralabehn asked Gandhi's permission to go and he agreed on the condition that she took a year of rest to regain her health. He instructed her to mix freely with the local population and the Gandhian workers, without engagement in political activities. Saralabehn arrived in Chanauda in the late summer of 1941. She took part in the selling of khadi from house to house, and in this way came to meet the local women. She also undertook a trip on foot deep into the hills with other workers for the annual purchasing of Tibetan wool. Her experiences convinced her that her work would be more effective if she stayed in one place and did one task well rather than dissipating her energies in a wider range of activities. Her chosen task was to work with girls from mountain villages. A friend provided her with a four-roomed building to live in and use for her work in nearby Kausani. It was named after the wife of the benefactor, a Gandhi-supporting civil servant. Eventually the name Lakshmi Ashram stuck. Saralabehn promised that her activities, in line with Gandhi's wish that constructive workers, especially European ones, would not be of a directly political nature as long as she could maintain her self-respect.[14]

In August 1942, following the passing of the 'Quit India' resolution, Saralabehn learned that the Chanauda ashram workers had been arrested. Her mission now became clear to her: as she had come to know the local population she would stand between them and the ongoing oppression. Although she was placed under house arrest, Saralabehn (or Saraladevi as she had become known) regularly snuck out to visit isolated areas on foot in order to understand the situation of the families of imprisoned activists and to determine how they could best be assisted. Eventually she was arrested. When the judge, a man from the local community, hinted that she should be ashamed of her illegal activities, she replied immediately that it was he, as an Indian, who should be ashamed for assisting the British.

Before her first term of imprisonment, Saraladevi discovered communities of strong women who were continuing to maintain households and had taken on the running of farms in the absence of their imprisoned and otherwise absent men-folk. Nevertheless, the women she found did not seem to be aware of their inner strength and so she decided to take on the task of empowering the hill women. At the time of her release from prison in mid-1944, she learned that Gandhi was also free and in Bombay, and she visited him there before returning to the hills to collect funds and continue mobilising people for the nationalist cause. Her resumed tours of the countryside resulted in her second imprisonment in mid-1945. Gandhi wrote to 'Shri Sarala Devi, Political Prisoner, District Jail, Almora' instructing her to come and see him as soon as she was able.[15] After her release from Almora jail, she was informed that Gandhi was spending several weeks based at the Poona clinic of the well-known nature cure specialist Dr Dinshaw Mehta, and she joined him there. Meeting Gandhi for the first time since the death of Kasturba, she instinctively touched Gandhi's feet in salutation – something she had never done before – to be rewarded by the customary hard slap on the back. One day, while on a walk with Gandhi, a Parsi woman asked the Mahatma why he liked the English woman so much. She was sure that he would respond by praising her work in Almora, but instead Gandhi answered that he liked the way that she opposed his instructions to take quinine while she was suffering a bout of malaria. At this stage in his life, Gandhi was placing emphasis on his newly awakened passion for nature cure. Saralabehn was concerned that Gandhi would ask her to remain in Poona to work in the clinic, so she continually attempted to steer their conversations back to the issues of the hills and especially Kausani. She accompanied Gandhi from Bombay to Wardha. It was to be their last time together.

Saralabehn had lengthy periods of living with Gandhi at Sevagram, however she has written surprisingly little about it (her autobiography is about her life generally rather than merely an account of her life with the Mahatma). When she was not with Gandhi, she did not seem concerned with keeping in touch. She remained one of those relatively rare followers who were more interested in constructive work than Gandhi the person.

In 1946, with the Mahatma's encouragement and the support of the local freedom fighters, Saralabehn set up the Kasturba Mahila Utthan Mandal (Kasturba Association for Women's Uplift), in Kausani, and for twenty years served as its secretary. The core activity of the KMUM remained the running of the Lakshmi Ashram. The institution trained young women in Nai Talim, with emphasis on agriculture, animal husbandry, craft production and health. Sarala Devi also took her students to neighbouring villages as a practical exercise in understanding the difficulties in the life of the villagers. In short, her ashram was not merely providing an academic education and empowerment for women, but was also training social activists. Some of the young women who had grown up under her tutelage went on to form their own service centres in the hills from where they continued their social activities independently. In 1961 Sarala Devi founded the Uttarkhand Sarvodaya Mandal (Uttarkhand Welfare of All Association) dedicated to the uplift of the hill population and the protection of the hill environment.

Her various programmes continued quietly for almost twenty years and then started showing considerable results with the women's movement to picket liquor shops, a campaign that lasted into the early 1970s. Not only did the cadre of women who came up under her care take leading social work roles in this campaign, which mobilised thousands of women with around one hundred being arrested, but the influence of Saralabehn was also one of the determining forces of the tree-hugging Chipko movement of the 1970s which eclipsed the prohibition campaign and gained world-wide attention.[16]

During his famous land redistributing Bhoodan movement in the 1950s,[17] Vinoba Bhave had asked Sarala Devi to lead the campaign for women's empowerment in Uttar Pradesh state (the state that then contained the region where the Lakshmi Ashram was situated). She responded that such a responsibility would require her to close the ashram. However, as Vinoba did not want this to happen, and in line with her preference for local educational constructive work, she had no regrets in refusing his offer. However, when at a conference of Bhoodan workers it was decided to begin Bhoodan activities in the Almora district, as no one else was willing to take on the responsibility, although untrained for such work Sarala Devi volunteered to undertake the task of local campaigning. Later, when Vinoba wanted to close down all Gandhian ashrams so that the workers could be freed up for work in the Bhoodan movement, she could not agree not only because of the amount of time that had gone into hard Gandhian work at Kausani, but because she saw a closure as a way of thwarting Gandhi's challenge to devote twenty years to the task. She decided that she had to talk to Vinoba about the issue. He agreed that the ashram should not be closed as it was an important symbol of the empowerment of women.

Following the brief Indo-Chinese border war in 1962, the government increased development in the hill areas. Roads were cut, towns grew and workers arrived from the plains. The new roads opened large areas of forest to exploitation for the first time. Sarala Devi pointed out that while the development was justified in terms of national defence, 'In the border areas the main defence measure is a satisfied and prosperous local population.'[18] Twenty years of work completed, in a rapidly changing social climate, in 1967 Sarala Devi, a wanderer by nature, relinquished management of the Lakshmi Ashram to her ex-student and ashram co-worker, Radhabehn Bhatt. She then spent time touring India as part of Vinoba Bhave's Bhoodan and later village-gift Gramdan movements,[19] and worked with the wives and children of renegade bandits in central India's Chambal valley who had surrendered to senior Gandhian Jayaprakash Narayan.[20] Her peripatetic life led her to Marjorie Sykes and Mary Barr in the Nilgiri Hills in the south of India – but after the grandeur of the Himalaya the Nilgiris were of little appeal. The last years of her life were spent in a small cottage at the isolated village of Dharamghar in Pithoragarh district near the Nepalese border, in sight of the snow-capped Himalaya. She occupied those years writing on the ecological problems confronting the mountains and fighting the commercialisation of mountain forestry. In January 1982, a few months before her death, Sarala Devi established the Parvatiya Paryavaran Sanrakshan Samiti (Society for the Protection of the Mountain Environment), dedicated to environmental protection, and donated all her belongings to aid the new institution and its work. She, like Mirabehn the other mountain crusader, died in July 1982. From Almora, her body was taken to Kausani, the place of her most significant work in India. She was cremated at the Lakshmi Ashram which continues her most cherished projects.

# V

# Conclusion
## Gandhi and Western Women

Gandhi's intense political activism absorbed much of his time, however, when time allowed, and even frequently when it did not, Gandhi engrossed himself in traditional womanly occupations such as nursing the ill, discussing small intimate details of daily life, preparing and serving food, spinning and tending to guests. Not surprisingly, Gandhi revelled in the company of women and surrounded himself with them. After all, he felt at home with them (as they did with him) because he was among his own.

The relationships between Western women and Gandhi demonstrate that he had an astonishing talent for attracting people from around the world to himself, and in many cases these people were outstanding individuals. Although they may have exhibited many of the usual human weaknesses, the stories of these women hopefully give some sense of what can be achieved through courage and the power of the will, and inspirational characters are of value simply because they are just that – inspirational. And certainly they should not be written out of the Gandhi story as they tend to have been in the past. Without them, that story is diminished to one focussing on a diminished Gandhi, a great statesman who was chiefly concerned with a narrowly defined political struggle. These Western women friends and disciples not only give the Gandhi saga more life and colour, but they are also important from a broader view of history, a less masculinely constructed one, one that does not privilege power politics over smaller-scale social reform and the social and spiritual dimensions of a more whole approach to being in the world.

## WHY THESE WESTERN WOMEN CAME TO GANDHI

As often happens at the end of a century, New Age movements flourished in the West at the end of the nineteenth. And this time the ferment occurred while Gandhi was maturing politically and spiritually. Green reminds us that during this period, 'A number of interests, in diet, reformed clothing, nature cure, sunbathing and so on – in opposition to city life and scientific medicine and factory production – came together to form a cult of nature and simplicity'.[1] Gandhi was caught up in this romantic reaction to the Enlightenment and its belief in the inevitability of human progress, and the seeming sterility of the industrial world.[2] So were others, and to many of them he would become a beacon.

This period was closely followed by a time of disillusionment during and immediately after the Great War. In a time of spiritual questing, the Theosophists and other esoteric religious movements popularised quasi-Hindu spirituality. Their largest audience was women. With colonialism, and the upswing in globalization it engendered, an opportunity was provided to visit the source of this new spiritual yearning – one could now get to India. And there was no shortage of those wanting to make the journey – relatively young, highly educated people with independent minds, often coming from religious backgrounds (the types who are still attracted to new religious movements), many of them women.

In 1913, dressed in flowing white robes, the mystical-looking long-bearded sage, Rabindranath Tagore became the first non-European to win a Nobel Prize. The literature prize went to the poet, till then unknown in the West, for *Gitanjali*, his collection of prose poems that the author himself had translated from the original Bengali. As his fame spread and he was feted in literary and learned circles, Tagore helped to further popularise the spirituality of the East at the very time that the war had shaken faith in Christianity for many disillusioned Europeans. The economic disaster wrought by the war, Tagore's visits and 'the sense of frustration and the consciousness of the failure among middle-class intellectuals' were 'some of the factors that shaped the response of the West towards India between 1920 and 1940'.[3] Tagore's lectures (along with esoteric religious and mystical groups) helped to acquaint Europeans and Americans with an India that assisted those 'who had lost their way in the aftermath of war to find back their lost spirituality'.[4] Into this desire for knowledge about eastern spirituality came a book that would offer Europeans a Jesus-like Hindu – Romain Rolland's book, *Mahatma Gandhi: The Man Who Became One With the Universal Being*.

Rolland's book on Gandhi made a great impression on many European women and directly led several of them to the Mahatma. In England there was knowledge of India (and some awareness of its exotic swamis and gurus) as the 'jewel in the crown' of empire, and in Germany there was a long-standing intellectual interest in India and Hinduism. Rolland's book provided something more. He described a spiritual figure who held not only a basic Christlike goodness, but who also seemed to understand the mysteries of the universe. Here was someone who must have been very appealing for those with a questing soul and who were dissatisfied with their own religion. Here was the promise of something more than could be obtained from joining a local branch of the Theosophical society or mystical group. Here was a potential flesh-and-bone spiritual saviour.

Rolland was a French intellectual and, like Tagore, a Nobel literature laureate. As a pacifist, in self-imposed exile, he settled in neutral Switzerland during World War I to devote himself to writing. During the early 1920s, he met leading Indians, such as Tagore, and Western friends of Gandhi, including C.F. Andrews, who introduced him to Gandhi's philosophy and writings. Although he could not read English and had no personal contact with Gandhi until after the London Round Table Conference in 1931, Rolland was impressed by the Gandhi-led nonviolent struggle for Indian independence. In early 1923 he penned an essay on Gandhi's life and message which appeared as three instalments in the Parisian monthly *Europe*. The following year it was released in book form, selling at least 100,000 copies in the first year of publication. By the end of 1924, it had been translated into Russian, German, Spanish and English.[5] During his travels on the continent in 1928, Gandhi's lieutenant Rajendra Prasad met and heard of Gandhians in Switzerland and Germany, which led him to 'realise to what an extent Romain Rolland's book on Gandhiji had made him known in that part of the world'.[6]

In Rolland's book, Gandhi comes across as more than a nationalist fighter. He is portrayed 'in the context of man's search for permanent peace'[7] and is compared, amongst others, to Saint Francis of Assisi. Even more impressively, after spelling out Gandhi's message of strength, self-sacrifice and nonviolence, in the concluding pages of the book Rolland notes that 'the only thing lacking is the cross'.[8] In March 1924, Romain recorded in his diary that the many editions and translations of the book were 'making a deep impression in the religious world, particularly among Protestants. It reawakens the sleeping Christ in them. The Mahatma himself almost seems Christ reborn'.[9] Some years later, Gandhi admitted that 'All the reputation that I enjoy in the West is borrowed from him [Rolland].'[10]

It was through Rolland's book that Mirabehn, Margarete Spiegel, Antionette Mirbel and, almost certainly, Francisca Standenath and Helene Haussding first came to know of Gandhi, and the book greatly influenced Muriel Lester and Agatha Harrison.

Sudhir Kakar notes that many of Gandhi's closest women disciples had come to him seeking the equivalent of a therapist. In the case of Madeleine Slade, he notes that she was like the client of the psychoanalyst Ralph Greenson 'who came to analysis not to seek insight but to enjoy the physical proximity of the analyst.'[11] This may be true for some of the other devotees besides Mirabehn, for example, Francisca Standenath, Helene Haussding and Margarete Spiegel. The bonds were ones of love and obsession (at times from Gandhi's side as well as from theirs), but they also often lead to frustration and impatience. Whatever they were seeking, and whether they understood it or not, Nilla Cram Cook and Antoinette Mirbel needed the insights of an analyst, not mere proximity.

Martin Green, the best interpreter of Gandhi's New Ageism, notes that although Nilla was 'in most ways' unlike Mirabehn, 'she too had psychological problems relating to her father, and found in Gandhi, at least temporarily, a solution to those problems. She was, however, a less-dignified figure by ordinary moral standards. She carried with her the aura of scandal, of sexual and other kinds.'[12] While it is certain that Nilla had unfinished business with her dead father[13] and that there was a whiff of scandal about her, Gandhi was still strongly drawn to her because of her passions and chance for a great reformation which only a great sinner could provide. Mirabehn could become a valued co-worker of the highest order if she overcame her obsessions with him; Nilla however could become an example to the world if she overcame her obsessively sinful ways and channelled her passions into constructive work as she had shown that she could do with her self-initiated street cleaning efforts in Bangalore. However, in the end, in both her case and Mirbel's, Gandhi was not up to the task of bringing about this reformation.

On analysis, it can be seen that the women who were drawn to Gandhi as more than supporters were not all obsessive devotees like Mirabehn and Nila Nagini, and that they can roughly be divided into three categories. Those who felt the spiritual vacuum prevalent in Europe after the War, who may have been seeking answers in New Age spiritualism, and who were often led to Gandhi by Romain Rolland's book, were only one group. They became disciples and some went 'native'. However, except in the case of Mirabehn, they generally did not stay for an overly long time because insanity (Cook and Mirbel), bad health (Haussding) or the need to return to work (Standenath) drove them away. Others (for example Spiegel) managed to outgrow their obsession with Gandhi and did not remain under his influence. Those who came to Gandhi for other reasons than the search for spiritual solace are perhaps more interesting, and certainly more in keeping with Gandhi's desires for co-workers rather than devotees.

Guru-disciple relationships are usually analysed in terms of Max Weber's theories on the attractiveness of charismatic leadership.[14] It seems that this strong attraction can even be felt when the charismatic leader is distant. Most of the women in this narrative had only read about Gandhi when they embarked upon journeys to the ends of the world to be at his feet. While the needs that were driving them may be recognisable, through the work of Elizabeth Puttick we get a glimpse into the personality types of the women who seem to most strongly feel these needs. Puttick studied women who are attracted to new, often eastern, religions. She notes that those who joined these religious movements, for example the one that was led by the Indian guru of free-expression Swami Bhagwan Shri Rajneesh, tended to be middle class, well educated, professionally qualified, divorced, had suffered a personal crisis, and were in their thirties. Often they were also rebels, who had dabbled in left-wing politics, did voluntary work and had experimented with communal living. They had a spiritual or philosophical ideal, and many were feminists.[15] This sounds like a close profile of many of those who can be classed as first category disciples who 'went native' to join Gandhi; but it also applies to several of those who did not become geographically close devotees, but returned home and continued with their social work. Many of the women in this second group came from England, were feminists, pacifists and socialists, often Quakers, and often unmarried, with fathers who were men of the cloth. They realised that Gandhi was doing in India on a large scale what they were doing on a small one at home. They went to visit a kindred soul, although perhaps a more advanced one (in their eyes), to share ideas, to learn. They returned home to continue the work they were already engaged in with new inspiration and a new ally. This group includes Muriel Lester, Agatha Harrison, Maude Royden, and Ellen Hørup. They felt no need to relinquish their own autonomy to that of a charismatic leader.

The third category is made up of those who were already in India, generally as teachers, usually in mission schools. They may originally have come to fulfill what they saw as the civilizing mission of empire or Western culture but some of them lost the certainty of the validity of that mission. They gradually came to the realisation that they were more part of a problem than part of the solution. The questioning led them to explore alternatives, such as the ones offered by Gandhi. They became anti-imperialist, threw in their lot with the Mahatma and started their own institutions doing Gandhian constructive and educational work in villages. They went 'native' and often stayed doing the work for the rest of their lives. Mary Barr, Mary Chesley, Mary Ingham, Margaret Jones, Marjorie Sykes, and Catherine Mary Heilemann are the obvious examples. Those who came as missionaries had similar aims. After meeting the Mahatma, although never doubting the rightness of their faith, some of them (for example Esther Færing, Anne Marie Petersen, and Pearl Madden) started to question its exclusivity or at least the notion that it had to be cloaked in European garb. Their spiritual mission could take on the flavour of local idioms, and local co-workers or converts could be seen as equals rather than as mere assistants.

Perhaps this tells us no more than that women came into the orbit of the Mahatma for many varied reasons. For some, paradoxically, the attraction may have had to do with the unattractiveness of sexuality. While Margaret Sanger claimed that Gandhi did not understand women, perhaps her view of the heart and mind of women was not universal. It seems from other close Western women friends of the Mahatma, at least the social worker 'spinsters' (and the rare happily married friend such as Millie Graham Polak), that he did understand them admirably. As Gandhi's own attitudes against sexual relations even between married couples hardened, those who had turned their backs on any physical expression of sexuality, or had never faced it for whatever reason (for example Mirbel and Standenath), felt a deep spiritual affinity with him. Although they may have admired him, those who celebrated sexuality (like Margaret Sanger and Margaret Bourke-White) did not. This raises the further question of whether Gandhi tended to attract women who were not interested in sex and therefore for whom celibacy was a positive rather than a negative force in their involvement with a spiritual group or master. Cook's pervasive sexuality caused her great problems in trying to fit into Gandhi's sexually sterile environment. She served as the example of the fallen in need of redemption, not as the selfless spinster who could be held up as a model to be emulated.

The women interviewers of Gandhi, not surprisingly, were concerned with the position of women in India, and came to Gandhi ostensibly to learn about his attitude to various issues surrounding women and to obtain his support for their campaigns. Two of them were greatly concerned with apparent obscenity. (Sanger noted that Indian women generally seemed to be in favour of birth control, the only ones against it being 'converted Eurasians'; mothers were for it and those against it 'were unmarried'. It was the unmarried who were also the ones who most often talked 'of the lusts and passions of men'.[16]) Whether their published views represented genuine feelings or merely expediency in furtherance of their political agenda, of the four interviewers, the two prudes were the unmarried Mayo and (the unmarried?) Kendall. On the other hand, the sexually liberated Bourke-White and Sanger seemed not to notice phallic symbols and erotic carvings on temples, or focus on stories of temple prostitution and general licentiousness the way that the two sensationalist writers did.

Looking at the women themselves in a little more detail provides some valuable insights into their relationship with Gandhi. Millie Graham Polak came quite early into Gandhi's life. He was not yet a Mahatma and she had a strong personality of her own, one that could stand up to any man, even the charismatic Gandhi. This allowed for an equality in their relationship that the Western women who came later into his life could no longer achieve. She did not place Gandhi on any guru pedestal. She was simply too equal to be disciple. The compromise, to ensure that their bond did not become more intimate than one that the Gandhi-Henry Polak relationship could bear, became that of a brother/sister relationship.[17] In this way the relationship could be controlled and channelled into a less problematic direction. Gandhi obviously liked strong spirited women. His fulsome praise of the young Sonja Schlesin makes this clear. After Millie he seems to have had something of a crush on Esther Færing. Esther was young and naive and her innocence seems to have protected both of them. Saraladevi Chaudhurani was far more Gandhi's equal and the relationship was sexually charged and as emotionally intertwined as the one he had with Millie; however it seems that no mechanism was created to take the passion out of the relationship in the way that it had with the Polaks where Henry became the brother and his wife Millie the sister. Without an avenue for the channelling of the relationship to a less problem-fraught configuration, Gandhi almost fell. After his infatuation with Chaudhurani ended, his closest relationships with women were never again with equals. Although the letters to Nilla Cram Cook, and especially Mirabehn, were love letters by another name, the women nevertheless remained disciples of the master.

Sonja Schlesin was a proud and often cantankerous person, but she was never overawed by Gandhi. Like Millie, she came to him while he was still a young barrister setting out on his career, and at the time that he was commencing his first 'passive resistance' campaign. She started off as an employee and developed into a very competent co-worker. She may have liked Gandhi rather strongly as a person (and hence the seeming feeling of abandonment when Gandhi left South Africa and the love/hate relationship demonstrated in her later letters) but she did not worship him as the guru that he became to many who followed her. Even twenty years after their physical separation, long after Gandhi had become a world-revered Mahatma, Sonja Schlesin did not elevate him to any particularly lofty position. In fact she often did the opposite. She actively pointed out his faults, and did so with extreme bluntness. It may have been easy for Gandhi to say that she was 'as mad as ever', but in reality there were few who would have dared to talk to him the way she did in his Mahatma phase. Does this make her mad (she was certainly crabby, and probably miffed that the Gandhi she knew and respected and looked up to had moved on and become something of a stranger to her), or did Gandhi really not know how to handle such a strong, independent and opinionated woman – especially at a time in his life when such female associates had become rare?

Perhaps against expectations, even the women who came as dedicated disciples in the long run proved to be more than unthinking followers. And even young and impressionable Esther Færing questioned Gandhi's army recruiting efforts in India towards the end of the First World War. One wonders how convincing she found Gandhi's rather tortuous justification. Perhaps Gandhi betrayed some of his own doubts as shown by his response to her query:

> I know I have put the argument most clumsily. I am passing through new experiences. I am struggling to express myself. Some things are still obscure to me. And I am trying to find words for others which are plain to me. I am praying for light and guidance and am acting with the greatest deliberation. Do please write and fight every inch of the ground that to you may appear untenable. That will enable me to find the way.[18]

To the degree that Gandhi was sincere in expressing these sentiments, and we have no reason to doubt that he was, several of his Western women friends and disciples 'pushed' him in this way: Cook questioned his ashram practices; Schlesin questioned his use of others to further his own ends; she and Florence Winterbottom told him that he was losing something of his joyous humanity with his growing asceticism; Besant, and especially Olive Schreiner, questioned his continuing support of British war efforts at a time when it seemed quite contradictory to his otherwise pacifist teachings; later Millie Polak questioned his large-scale anti-British campaigns; Harrison, Schlesin, and especially Royden, questioned his continued pacifism in the face of the atrocities of Nazism; Hørup questioned his patriarchy and lack of class analysis (although these criticisms probably did not reach him personally); Sanger pushed him very hard on his attitude to sex and sexuality; Bourke-White questioned his glorification of rural simplicity in a country that could have benefited from modern technology; and Catherine Mayo challenged him in ways that left him obsessed with her criticisms for years to come. The fact that Gandhi engaged with such criticisms, instead of dismissing the critics out of hand, tells us something very positive about him and may also explain why many of these empowered women were drawn into substantial relationships with him and why he may have encouraged them.

By way of summary, Martin Green notes that Nilla took her place in the sequence of remarkable women who came close to Gandhi, listing her with Saraladevi Chaudhurani, Mirabehn and Amrit Kaur. 'Nilla was different because hers was a brief episode, because she did less for him, and because of the more obvious instability that always threatened her; but she belongs in the sequence because of her gifts and the impression of moral and intellectual size she gives. These women were all queens or princesses. Amrit Kaur was a literal princess, and the others deserve the title if it is used freely.'[19] Reading accounts of the lives of many of the Western women Gandhi had close relationships with reveals the aptness of Green's characterisation. Nevertheless, this analysis is really about Gandhi rather than the Western women. Although their lives deserve a fuller account, I have only provided a brief glimpse of their lives before and after their encounters with the Mahatma, and in essence in this narrative they serve as a vehicle to allow us to better understand Gandhi.



## WHY GANDHI ENCOURAGED THEM

More interesting than why the women were caught up in Gandhi's orbit, perhaps, is why he let them in. The reasons why they were attracted to him may be fairly obvious, but why did he find them so attractive? Gandhi did not seem to actively want to make disciples of these women in a way that would help to spread his message to the West. While he was trying to make converts to the cause of India's struggle for freedom, he was not looking for missionaries for his own spiritual beliefs. He was engaged in a dialogue with co-workers (who, as Lester did, could point out that possibly he had as much to learn from the West as Westerners had to learn from him). The encounters encouraged them to continue *their* own work when they went home. He was certainly not looking for disciples in India who would take a leading role in his movement. After all, he did not want to found a movement and there were already many extremely talented and dedicated Indian women (in the most part whose story is yet to be adequately told) in his close circle who could have fulfilled that role had he wanted successors.[20] He wanted constructive workers, and many of the Western women who threw in their lot with him served as conspicuous models.

As the preeminent political figure in the country, and indeed from 1930 a major world figure, how did Gandhi find the time for this Western women disciples (and they took up a great deal of time), or even find the time to take their voluminous correspondence with him seriously? What was in it for him? Why did he go to such lengths to get them to come or allow them to stay? Was he flattered that the daughters of the Empire or races who considered themselves superior had come to take him as their master? Surely, he could not have missed the propaganda value in such relationships. However, there must have been more to it than this as, with some of them, the propaganda value was limited or even negative. Were some of them important because he could hold them up as unselfish and unmarried models as an ideal of womanhood to his Indian sisters? The question of whether Gandhi was attracted to Millie Polak, Esther Færing or Mirabehn because of some latent or repressed sexuality, or in the case of Nilla or Mirabehn as proof to himself that he had conquered his desires (as he admitted was the case with Manu later on), must be left to those with greater psychological analytical skills.

Early on in his career, Gandhi often used Western sources to give credibility to his ideas. He would provide reading lists of important British, and other European and American works that backed up positions he held.[21] Partially, this may have been the legacy of a colonial mentality on his part where he felt compelled to show that his ideas could be taken seriously because important people from among the ruling races also held similar views. Later, he must have recognised the symbolic value of having Western disciples, particularly women who completely threw their lots in with him. And what could be more symbolic in a freedom struggle against the British than having the daughter of an English admiral sitting at his feet and fetching his food the way a servant does, while he was negotiating with the Viceroy, the King's representative in India? This is not to say that Gandhi deliberately used Mirabehn in this blatant political manner. However, such matters run at deep psychological levels and he may have had some feelings of satisfaction. He may also have had such feelings when Esther Færing first came to him. It must have served as a signal of his importance to his own followers that people would come from far away to be his disciples. (To this day many well-known Indian gurus seem to make a great deal of having Western, and especially Western celebrity, disciples). And in wanting legitimacy for some of his spiritual practices, particularly those that seemed perverse to Westerners, such as his insistence on celibacy even within marriage, Western examples were more than welcome. Probably this goes more than just part of the way to explaining why he not only encouraged the Standenaths to visit him in

India, but also paid their expenses to ensure that they could come and so become ambassadors for his vision of abstinence among a sceptical audience in the West.

The young Gandhi, before he attracted disciples because of his spiritual reputation, was obviously already very attractive to Western women. While he was still in London as a law student, young women showed interest in him. From the South Africa days we have Millie Polak's testimony about his attractiveness to women, and Henry Polak's sisters, especially Maud, had clearly fallen in love with him. And Gandhi was certainly not blind to his attractiveness. Conversely, at least initially, until the burdens became too great, he seemed to be attracted to Western women whom he saw as having something to offer him intellectually or emotionally. He tried to form a father/daughter relationship with Sonja Schlesin, but she would not submit to the role. While she may have been strongly attracted to him, she was a trusted co-worker, not surrogate family. Millie was his equal. She argued with him rather than sit worshipfully at his feet and she carved out a place in his pantheon of relationships as a well, respected and close-younger sister. But she was to be the last. With the exception of the episode of infatuation with Saraladevi Chaudhurani, his relationships with his closest women associates, including Western ones, were of Bapu and daughter, with the Bapu at times being as much a mother as a father.



It is clear that until the last, busiest decade and a half of his life, Gandhi particularly admired and was drawn to strong-willed independent Western women. In 1906, observing the campaigning of the English suffragettes, Gandhi noted that 'it is no wonder that a people which produces such daughters and mothers should hold the sceptre.'[22] The Western women he befriended and lauded in his writings were worldly-wise, had travelled, and were independent. They were very different from his simple and semi-illiterate wife (who at times resented their presence) or the ashram women who were there because their husbands had decided to join the Mahatma. And when he did meet a comparable Indian woman, severe problems followed. Gandhi admired Western women for their freedom and ability to act unhindered by tradition. His closest friends, those who were fellow workers for the causes of social justice and peace – rather than the personal devotees – provided something of a model that he held up to the Indian women who moved in his orbit. And, in turn, several of those women who became more than mere ashramites and disciples (for example Sarojini Naidu, Sushila Nayar, and Rajkumari Amrit Kaur) were westernised. Needless to say, most of his Western women associates were unmarried – something he believed allowed for a full life of service and so again he could hold them up as models for his more conservative Indian women followers. Perhaps his ideal was a blend of self-sacrificing Indian women and their strongly independent Western social activist sisters. This is reflected in a letter to Esther Menon:

> You tell me how desolate Bajaj's house looked for want of the woman's touch. I have always considered this a result of our false notions of division of work between men and women. Division there must be. But this utter helplessness on the man's part when it comes to keeping a household in good order and woman's helplessness when it comes to be a matter of looking after herself (*more here than in the West*) are due to erroneous upbringing. Why should man be so lazy as not to keep his house neat, if there is no woman looking after it, or why should a woman feel that she always needs a man protector? This anomaly seems to me to be due to the habit of regarding woman as fit primarily for housekeeping and of thinking that she must live so soft as to feel weak and be always in need of protection. We are trying to create a different atmosphere at the Ashram. It is difficult work. But it seems to be worth doing.[23]

Some religions that see sex as being inconsistent with moral progress (generally of men) tend to segregate the sexes, and some individuals (again usually men) who have an abhorrence of sex try to ensure that there is no close contact with the causes of temptation (generally seen as women). While Gandhi may have been repulsed by sex, he certainly did not extend that horror to the company of women, as many sex-renunciants afraid of temptation do. He surrounded himself with women, they massaged him, talked with him when he was in the bath, he walked with his arms around their shoulders and they discussed the most intimate matters with him. While he was occasionally criticised for his ease of relationship with women, for his relaxed physical contact with them, and, more reasonably, for his Noakhali and earlier brahmacharya experiments, they were as comfortable with him as he was with them. As Millie Polak had noted, he simply was 'untouched by any play of sex-emotion'.[24] Tagore added that Gandhi's 'tenderness for women is one of the noblest and most consistent traits of his character.'[25]

Gandhi believed that true spiritual power, in fact self-realisation, came from suppressing sexuality. He struggled with his own 'lust' almost from childhood and came to see sex, when it was not for the purpose of procreation, as not only undignified, but as harmful and even disgusting. He conducted lifelong experiments in trying to purge himself of lust and to prove to himself that he had succeeded. While his brahmacharya was not pure, as his occasional nocturnal seminal emissions demonstrated, his battle to achieve it was constant and often embarrassingly public.[26] Margaret Sanger saw the problem when she talked with him in 1935: '… his state of mind would not change. After reading his Autobiography, I thought I saw the cause of his inhibitions. He himself had had the feeling which he termed lust, and now he hated it. It formed an emotional pivot in his brain around which centered everything having to do with sex.'[27]

The young Gandhi was highly sexed and later he tried desperately to expunge the lustfulness in himself. He attempted to make himself into a eunuch, a sexual neuter, and probably more than the negative of overcoming sexuality, he wanted to attain the positive virtues of nonviolence and self-suffering, the qualities, he believed, that women had in far greater abundance than men. In that sense, he wanted to make himself into a woman. He believed (Sanger's protests notwithstanding) that women did not have the sex-drive of men. They were passive, the victims of male lust. He saw his spiritual development tied in with brahmacharya, an overcoming of the passions, a total control of the senses. How things tasted did not matter, how he appeared physically to others did not matter, but most importantly he had to overcome the incubus of sex. What the gender of the people around him was did not matter as they were all people. If he could overcome any feeling of arousal in the company of women, he was on the way to the brahmacharya ideal.

Enter Nilla Cram Cook, the complete sensualist, the passionate, wanton woman. While Mirabehn took up most of Gandhi's time and was possibly his longest-standing female close-quarters disciple, Western or otherwise, Nilla was probably the most challenging and consequently perhaps the most important. She was an unashamedly sexual being with unbounded optimism in her own abilities. When she did something, she did it without reservation. While, on the surface, Gandhi should have totally rejected her, she fascinated him. If she, the 'fallen woman', could be cleansed and could demonstrate a living example of brahmacharya, a triumph of the individual will would have been demonstrated. And when she decided to become a brahmacharin she did that full-tilt too. If she could succeed then anyone could. Even him. How could he not be drawn to this amazing woman who not only challenged him and his ability to heal, something Gandhi the carer took great pride in, but also operated at the level that fed into his own sexual preoccupation and could potentially prove the maxim that 'if it exists, it is possible'? He had high hopes for himself and his hopes were a little higher when his hopes for Nilla appeared to be bearing fruit.

When Nilla decided to become an asexual being, her menstrual cycle ceased. Gandhi believed that she was pregnant; however the truth seemed to be that the hiatus came from her starving herself, leading to a condition where her body was simply too run down to menstruate. Nilla announced it as a sign of spirituality, having willed her menstruation to stop. What if she had achieved what she claimed? Perhaps this was not a matter for science but Gandhi, without any scientific evidence, believed that a true brahmachari could control their bodily functions and a genuine woman brahmacharin would simply not have monthly periods.[28] Gandhi reminded Nilla that while a complete brahmachari, who is pure in thought as well as action will reach such a state, she was not yet there. Nevertheless, he assured her (and probably hoped for her), 'That you can do so, I have not a shadow of doubt. You have in you the making of such a woman.'[29] Nilla's internal struggle may have been a more open and immediate version of his own. But then of course, at the time, Nilla was mad and the episode ended in disaster.

After her failure, Gandhi was alone and had to conquer his own passions without the role model of sorts that Nilla could have provided. In a letter of April 1933, Gandhi replied to one of Nilla's associates who had written to the Mahatma that while he was with Nilla, he was unmoved by any animal passion whatsoever (something Nilla disputed). Gandhi responded: 'This is impossible for any person who is not utterly impotent or who is not a God, and I suppose that you are neither the one nor the other. You should get rid of this self-deception altogether, if you will be a true man.'[30] Almost fifteen years later, Gandhi, who knew he was no God, and needed to know if he was deceiving himself, had to test the strength of his own impotence. It is not difficult to see why he cared so much about the sensualist Nilla, someone whom others warned him against because of the damage she could do to him and his cause, as they would later warn him against his own actions in Noakhali, again because of the damage they could do to him and his cause. For the greater quest of spiritual development he was willing to take the risk with Nilla and later with Manu.

Stanley Wolpert, in his analysis of what he sees as Gandhi's infatuation with a young Esther Færing, notes that 'Gandhi was completely unconscious of Freud's luminous work, he had read no psychoanalytical literature, and would for the rest of his life remain virtually unaware of his own sexual passions towards a number of Western women drawn to him as disciples and for several virginal Indian women who lived in his ashrams as well.'[31] Esther Færing was Gandhi's first Western woman total-ashramite. She did not come to Gandhi after reading Romain Rolland. She was already in India and had thrown in her lot with Gandhi many years before the book had come out. She was in love with Gandhi as a great spiritual figure, but there is no indication that she was romantically infatuated with him. Perhaps, as Wolpert states, the reverse is a little less straight forward. She was young, tall, blond and blue-eyed, a daughter of Europe. It must have been a personal ego-satisfying coup to have someone like her hanging on his every word. After all, as Gandhi continually reminded his audiences (although many refused to listen), he was human, with all the faults that that entailed, and he was very passionate. However, even if Wolpert is right, and he did fell in love with Færing a little more than a father loves a daughter, he did not avail himself of even any possible propaganda opportunity that may have been afforded by having her at his feet. He wanted her to fulfill her obligations to her mission society, and he could not give her the time or guidance she may have wanted because he was rarely at the ashram when she was, instead he was trying to possess Saraladevi Chaudhurani (and vice versa). How would it have been with Esther if Saraladevi had not been on the scene? Would his infatuation with Chaudhurani have come about if Esther had not woken something in him? Again more speculation. In any case there seems to be little indication that the youthful Esther saw herself as anything but a daughter to him.

Madeleine Slade came on the scene after Gandhi's infatuation with Chaudhurani had run its course. He was never again to put himself in a position where he 'could lose his anchor' and possibly 'fall'; however Mirabehn's early obsession with him, before it became a burden, was reciprocated in fair measure. Even when her clinging became too obsessive and demanding and he sent her away in desperation to do constructive work far from his presence, he was often overcome with remorse at her pitiable reactions and his hardness of heart. He would quickly regret his harsh actions and follow them up with consoling love letters.[32] This developed into something of a pattern that revealed contradictory messages. There were parallels in his relationship with Spiegel, who had an obsessive desire to overtake Mira as the chief disciple.

Rosetta Spalt, a friend who helped care for the aging Mirabehn in Austria, recounts in her reminiscence that while 'being near Bapu, serving him, accompanying him on tours, was for Mira the greatest happiness, not so easy were the separations, which Gandhi insisted upon, and which caused her great distress.'[33] She went on to note that Mirabehn saw India through Gandhi's eyes, and experienced it through his feelings, her activities being inspired by his principles. There were hints that later she became aware 'of her utter dependence on him during the years she spent at his side, the crushing of her own strong nature and personality. She once admitted, "I only became a free person after I left India".'[34] Spiegel became emancipated from the hold of Gandhi in a more evolutionary way. On the positive side, it goes to Gandhi's credit that he allowed such distancing without showing any obsessive attachment on his part when the women were ready to leave him. He inquired after them, when he remembered he tried to maintain contact, but he was not grasping as they moved from his circle. On the negative, he could be quite brutal in his detachment, as he was with Mirabehn during their troubled time in the mid-1940s. Did he abandon friendships too easily when there were no immediate benefits for him, or was he merely too busy for formal relationships and unnecessary physical contact?

Kakar notes that in the case of the relationship between Gandhi and Mirabehn, the relationship was not as one-sided as Mirabehn's obsessive clinging would have it. She came directly to him, rather than to India first followed by some later realisation and attachment. And there is more than enough evidence that she was romantically infatuated with him. He tried to keep her at a comfortable distance – at least a distance that was comfortable for him. Following her communications of distress, did he offer his frequent consoling and, to an outside observer (and probably to Mirabehn), contradictory messages because he realised that he was hurting her, or was there something deeper? He could not let her go completely. He wanted her to remain in his comfort zone, while she, clearly, wanted to be in hers. And as the two did not match, there was a constant struggle and many tears. Kakar observes that 'As with his other women, Gandhi could not let Mira get away further than the distance he unconsciously held to be the optimal for his own feelings of well being.'[35] Perhaps until his latter years he needed the attention of his Western women disciples as much as they needed him.

## A FINAL WORD ON GANDHI AND HIS RELATIONSHIP WITH WESTERN WOMEN

Over and above Gandhi's immediate relationship with Western women, there is one other dimension of the Gandhi/Western women nexus that could possibly provide the basis for further useful exploration. Gandhi had many Indian ashramites staying with him at any given time. The Western women were fewer and tended to come at greater intervals (although, probably through serendipity, there was a cluster of them present in the 1933–34 period). The relationships between them would make a fascinating study. We know of the close and fruitful relationship of the Khedi workers; of Marjorie Sykes, Mary Barr and Alice Barnes; and of Muriel Lester, Agatha Harrison and Maude Royden in England. On the other hand, Francisca Standenath complained about the writings of Helene Haussding, Mirabehn seems to have had a disagreement with Agatha Harrison and Muriel Lester,[36] and there was no love lost between Margarete Spiegel and Nilla Cram Cook. Given that Mirabehn and Saralabehn lived close to each other in the Himalayan foothills after the death of Gandhi, it is somewhat puzzling that there is no mention of Saralabehn in Mirabehn's autobiography, and the passing references to Mirabehn in Saralabehn's are somewhat unflattering. Did they ever meet in those long years without the Mahatma? And if they didn't, why not? Perhaps coincidentally, Mirabehn and the admittedly much younger Nilla Cram Cook died in Vienna within three months of each other in 1982. There does not appear to be any record of contact. Nor does there seem to be any record of contact between Mirabehn and Francisca Standenath, who was much closer to her in age, and who, throughout the 1960s, lived less than 200 kilometres away in Graz.

Muriel Lester met Mirabehn during her first visit to Gandhi's ashram in 1926. They were to be in close contact during Gandhi's stay at Kingsley Hall for the Round Table Conference in 1931 and during the continental trip following it. Mira again stayed at Kingsley Hall in 1934. When she left India for Europe for the final time in 1959, Mirabehn called in on Lester in London. Although after the first meeting Lester noted that she was 'getting quite fond of her', it is perhaps surprising that 'no particular friendship ever developed between the two women'.[37] Lester's biographer thinks that this 'was partly because their paths tended not to cross very often in India but partly also because each, albeit unconsciously, tended to be rather possessive of her friendship with Gandhi.'[38] Lester set herself up as the guardian of the Mahatma's time, rationing visitors to him at Kingsley Hall. This may have irked Mira when she was supplanted from this role as another guest of Lester's and may have led to tensions on the continent when Lester was no longer obviously the gatekeeper and roles may have been reversed. This was probably the cause of Rolland's harsh description of Lester rather than of his protégée Mira. Perhaps there were jealousies and competition for the master's attention among the devotees (they were after all human and the existential stakes were large). This did not seem to occur among the mutually supporting Gandhi-influenced social workers in England and in India.

While it is not possible to say more about these relationships here, and indeed there may not be enough available sources to do the topic adequate justice in any case, perhaps the relationships that the Western women had with each other can tell us a little more about the types that are attracted to gurus as disciples and the types that become less attached active workers in causes.

• • •

Of course, most of Gandhi's many women friends, associates, and devotees were Indian. This book merely deals with the Western women in his life. This is not to imply that they were the most important or necessarily the most favoured by him. In fact, in the totality of Gandhi's life, most of them play a relatively small part. It is only because they are central to this narrative that their significance for him, or indeed in many cases his significance for them, appears to be as large as it is. In order to come to a satisfactory understanding of the 'whole' Gandhi, one needs to read about Gandhi's constructive programme and his spiritual quest, and not merely his activities in a more narrowly defined political sphere; as well one would also need to read political biographies, rather than rely on books such as this one, to provide an important context so that a fuller picture of the Mahatma emerges.

In examining Gandhi's relationships with his Western women friends and co-workers, and especially with his disciples, and in seeing Gandhi through their eyes, we get a more nuanced view of Gandhi than is often presented. We see not only a compassionate and loving Gandhi, but also one who could appear to be a demanding and even angry person at times. He gave out mixed signals, discouraged and sometimes fought with those he originally welcomed so openly. It is of course true that at many stages in his life Gandhi carried a superhuman burden on his frail shoulders. Too often he was incredibly busy with the demands of his various projects and campaigns, yet people did not cease coming to him in large numbers for their own benefit, to ask questions that had been asked countless times before, to take up his valuable time with little tangible benefit to him. However, there are consistent comments from visitors to Gandhi's ashrams about how generally they were places of joy, permeated by the laughter of children. And comment on his own gentleness, consideration of others' feelings and sense of humour is a typical refrain from those who knew him or came into contact with him. If the picture presented here is too one-sided and these positive attributes do not adequately come across in these pages, it is not the fault of Gandhi. Perhaps the subject matter has downplayed these elements, or perhaps I simply did not manage to convey skillfully enough the generally underlying feeling that prevailed in his communities, or the underlying essence of his nature.

When reading individual chapters about particular Western woman disciples, it may appear that they were the central focus of his life. They were often a central focus, but just one of many overlapping ones: for example in the year (late 1933 to late 1934) that Nilla seemed to be dominating his life,[39] Gandhi was also having one of his relatively tumultuous times with Mirabehn, was trying to discover what to do with Margarete Spiegel, was hosting Duncan Greenlees and Mary Barr (who he was advising about settling in a village) and was winding up the affairs of the Sabarmati Ashram. In addition, Gandhi spent a large portion of the year in prison holding discussions with individuals and delegations that visited him, kept up a steady stream of correspondence with fellow ashramites, nationalist colleagues and government officials, and wrote articles for his papers. He undertook two lengthy and debilitating fasts. His only time of freedom in 1933 was from May (when he was still fasting) until the end of July, spent in Poona and Ahmedabad, and from September onwards. He managed to spend the month of October with his ashramites in Wardha before setting off on his extended Harijan Tour which would not see him back at Wardha for a year. This year in his life could be described by focussing on his relationships with the women discussed, or focussing on Gandhi's prison life, his fasts or his anti-'untouchability' campaign. It must be borne in mind that all these things were happening simultaneously when considering the accounts of his relationships with the selected women.

On close examination, his relationships with his Western women friends also clearly showed Gandhi's humanity, consideration and willingness to compromise on principles, if they were not of a most fundamental nature, in the name of friendship. For example, even though it is fairly certain that he would not have made the exceptions for his own benefit, at times of illness he instructed Mary Barr to eat eggs and for Catherine Heilemann to take quinine. Esther Menon, reflecting on her close relationship with Gandhi, noted that 'It was wonderful how he could spare the time to write so often to me, an ordinary woman, while he had the burden of the country on his shoulders. I often think of this and marvel. I cannot understand why he was so kind and good to me.'[40] Should she really have been so surprised? Although Gandhi was a busy person who did many things at once, he valued his friends. He always seemed to find time for his constructive worker women associates, and devotees who had the potential to become valuable constructive workers, especially those who had come from afar and had given up so much to be with him.

# Notes

### Introduction: Gandhi, the Feminine and the West

1 In this regard, see in particular Ved Mehta, *Mahatma Gandhi and His Apostles*, London: Andre Deutsch, 1976, pp.190-213.

2 I say reasonably well researched because while Kakar has used Gandhi's letters to Mirabehn, he has somehow overlooked the large collection of letters from her to Gandhi that have been preserved.

3 See Thomas Weber, *Gandhi as Disciple and Mentor*, New Delhi: Cambridge University Press, 2007, pp.120-26.

4 Narayan Desai, *My Gandhi*, Ahmedabad: Navajivan, 1999, pp.51-90.

5 I have used the word 'disciple', and at times 'devotee', to characterise those who saw Gandhi as their leader, and especially spiritual master, rather than as a co-worker or as a teacher they could learn from to help them in their own (as opposed to his) work.

6 'Mahatma' literally means 'great soul'. It is a title of enormous respect.

7 M.K. Gandhi, *To the Women* (Anand T. Hingorani ed.), Karachi: the author, 1941.

8 M.K. Gandhi, *Women and Social Injustice* (Bharatan Kumarappa ed.), Ahmedabad: Navajivan, 1942.

9 M.K. Gandhi, *Women* (Bharatan Kumarappa ed.), Ahmedabad: Navajivan, 1958.

10 M.K. Gandhi, *Women's Role in Society* (R.K. Prabhu comp.), Ahmedabad: Navajivan, 1959.

11 M.K. Gandhi, *The Role of Women* (Anand T. Hingorani ed.), Bombay: Bharatiya Vidya Bhavan, 1964.

12 M.K. Gandhi, *Gandhi on Women* (Pushpa Joshi comp.), Ahmedabad: Navajivan, 1988.

13 Often these sections are somewhat ironic. For example in Prabhu and Rao's compilation *The Mind of Mahatma Gandhi*, women are discussed under the heading of *Brahmacharya* (celibacy); and in Nirmal Kumar Bose's *Selections from Gandhi*, the relevant heading is 'Women's Problems'. Perhaps even more ironically, the one book where the plain heading 'women' appears is in the collection titled *All Men Are Brothers*.

14 'Women in the Smritis', *Harijan*, 28 November 1936. See also Barbara Southard, 'The Feminism of Mahatma Gandhi', *Gandhi Marg* (1981), vol.3, no.7, p.407.

15 'A True Congressman', *Young India*, 19 November 1925.

16 'What is Woman's Role?', *Harijan*, 24 February 1940.

17 'To the Women of India', *Young India*, 10 April 1930.

18 'Obscene Advertisements', *Harijan*, 14 November 1936.

19 'Speech at Prayer Meeting', *Harijan*, 23 March 1947.

20 'Discussion with Representatives of Municipalities and Local Boards', *Harijan*, 18 February 1939.

21 'What is Woman's Role?', *Harijan*, 24 February 1940.

22 'Implications of Constructive Programme', *Harijan*, 18 August 1940.

23 'Position of Women', *Young India*, 17 October 1929.

24 'Discussion with Representatives of Municipalities and Local Boards', *Harijan*, 18 February 1939.

25 'Talks to Ashram Women', 1926.

26 In its broader sense *brahmacharya* meant the search for Brahma, the Truth. As Gandhi put it '*brahmacharya* means control in thought, speech and action of all senses, at all places and at all times.' See 'Brahmacharya', *Navajivan*, 25 May 1924.

27 David Hardiman, *Gandhi in His Time and Ours*, Delhi: Permanent Black, 2003, p.110.

28 Madhu Kishwar, *Gandhi and Women*, Delhi: Manushi, 1986, p.34.

29 Kishwar, *Gandhi and Women*, p.45.

30 M.K. Gandhi, *From Yeravda Mandir: Ashram Observances*, Ahmedabad: Navajivan, 1932.

31 Gandhi, *From Yeravda Mandir*, p.7.

32 F. Mary Barr, *Bapu: Conversations and Correspondence with Mahatma Gandhi* (Second Edition), Bombay: International Book House, n.d., pp.125-26.

33 Gandhi to Hermann Kallenbach, 12 April 1914.

34 'Swaraj Through Women', *Harijan*, 2 December 1930.

35 'Speech at Second Gujarat Educational Conference', 20 October 1917.

36 'What is Woman's Role?', *Harijan*, 24 February 1940.

37 'Not Man's Work?', *Young India*, 11 June 1925.

38 Kishwar, *Gandhi and Women*, p.29.

39 'The Hindu Wife', *Young India*, 3 October 1929.

40 'What is Woman's Role?', *Harijan*, 24 February 1940.

41 Kishwar, *Gandhi and Women*, p.31.

42 For Gandhi's changing conception of the character and role of women, see Sujata Patel, 'Construction and Reconstruction of Woman in Gandhi', *Economic and Political Weekly*, 20 February 1988, vol.23, no.8, pp.377-86.

43 For women's engagement in the nationalist struggle, see Anup Taneja, *Gandhi, Women, and the National Movement, 1920-47*, New Delhi: Har-Anand, 2005; and Bharti Thakur, *Women in Gandhi's Mass Movements*, New Delhi: Deep & Deep, 2006.

44 Southard, 'The Feminism of Mahatma Gandhi', p.406.

45 Devaki Jain, 'Gandhian Contributions Towards a Feminist Ethic', in Diana L. Eck and Devaki Jain (eds), *Speaking of Faith: Cross-Cultural Perspectives on Women, Religion and Social Change*, New Delhi: Kali for Women, 1986, p.268.

46 Kishwar, *Gandhi and Women*, p.36.

47 See Patel, 'Construction and Reconstruction of Woman in Gandhi'.

48 Hardiman, *Gandhi in His Time and Ours*, p.116.

49 Millie Graham Polak, 'Gandhi and Women', in Chandrashanker Shukla (ed.), *Gandhiji as We Know Him by Seventeen Contributors*, Bombay: Vora, 1945, p.47.

50 John C. Vine, 'Interview with Mrs Millie Graham Polak', 2 May 1960, in S. Durai Raja Singam, 'They Were Ready to Talk About Gandhi', unpublished manuscript, (n.d.), p.18.

51 Chandrashanker Shukla, *Gandhi's View of Life*, Bombay: Bharatiya Vidya Bhavan, 1968, p.165.

52 'Discussion with Representatives of Hindustani Talimi Sangh', *The Hindu*, 29 October 1944.

53 Gandhi to Sarojini Naidu, 17 September 1932.

54 Erik H. Erikson, *Gandhi's Truth: On the Origins of Militant Nonviolence*, New York: W.W. Norton, 1969, p.111, and see in general pp.103-12. For the different approaches to the concept of 'masculinity' in the West and in India, in a way that places Gandhi's identification with the feminine in both a social and political context, see Lloyd I. Rudolph and Susanne Hoeber Rudolph, *The Modernity of Tradition: Political Development in India*, Chicago: University of Chicago Press, 1967, pp.192-216.

55 'Speech at Women's Meeting Colombo', 22 November 1927.

56 Gandhi to Krishnachandra, 28 October 1939.

57 Gandhi to Amrit Kaur, 18 March 1947.

58 Discussion of these 'experiments' can be found in Nirmal Kumar Bose, *My Days with Gandhi*, New Delhi: Orient Longman, 1974, especially at pp.163-78; and Pyarelal, *Mahatma Gandhi, volume IX: The Last Phase, Part I, Book II*, Ahmedabad: Navajivan, 1956, pp.209-44. For a general discussion of Gandhi's striving for *brahmacharya*, see Vinay Lal, 'Nakedness, Non-Violence, and the Negation of Negation: Gandhi's Experiments in *Brahmacharya* and Celibate Sexuality', *South Asia* (1999), vol.22, no.2, pp.63-94; and the essay 'Gandhi and Women' in Sudhir Kakar, *The Essential Writings of Sudhir Kakar*, New Delhi: Oxford University Press, 2001, pp.221-61 at pp.221-42.

59 Manubehn Gandhi, *Bapu – My Mother*, Ahmedabad: Navajian, 1949, p.3.

60 Rajkumari Amrit Kaur, 'Foreword', to M.K. Gandhi, *Women and Social Injustice* (Bharatan Kumarappa ed.), Ahmedabad: Navajivan, 1942, p.iii.

61 On this see Kakar, *The Essential Writings of Sudhir Kakar*, pp.252-56; Sudhir Kakar, *Intimate Relations: Exploring Indian Sexuality*, New Delhi: Penguin, 1989, p.118; Erikson, *Gandhi's Truth*, p.404; Anthony J. Parel, *Gandhi's Philosophy and the Quest for Harmony*, Cambridge: Cambridge University Press, 2006, pp.137-56; and D.A. Gangadhar, *Mahatma Gandhi's Philosophy of Brahmacharya*, Bangalore: ISPCK, 1984. For Gandhi's own writings on *brahmacharya* see M.K. Gandhi, *The Law of Continence* (Anand T. Hingorani ed.), Bombay: Bharatiya Vidya Bhavan, 1964; M.K. Gandhi, *Self Restraint vs. Self Indulgence*, Ahmedabad: Navajivan, 1947; and M.K. Gandhi, *Conquest of Self* (R.K. Prabhu and U.R. Rao comps.), Bombay: Thacker and Co., 1943.

62 'General Knowledge About Health [- XVII]', *Indian Opinion*, 26 April 1913. See also Gandhi's letter to Hermann Kallenbach, 16 June 1912, quoted in James D.Hunt and Surendra Bhana, 'Spiritual Rope-Walkers: Gandhi, Kallenbach, and the Tolstoy Farm, 1910-13', *South African Historical Journal*, (2007) vol.58, p.176.

63 See Mahadev Desai, 'Weekly Letter', *Harijan*, 22 February 1936. There may of course be a deeper meaning in this, one alluded to by Ashis Nandy when he noted that the colonialism Gandhi struggled against was one based on a strong sense of masculinity that characterised Indians as feminine and therefore weak and inferior. It could be argued that through Gandhi, the colonised came to reject the 'cultural consensus' surrounding this superiority and,

rather than 'trying to redeem' their masculinity, they become 'counterplayers of the rulers according to the established rules' and discovered 'an alternative frame of reference within which the oppressed do not seem weak, degraded and distorted men trying to break the monopoly of the rulers on a fixed quantity of machismo.' In short, femininity can be turned into a powerful force through the proclamation of its superiority. And if this happens, 'the colonizers begin to live with the fear that the subjects might begin to see their rulers as morally and culturally inferior, and feed this information back to the rulers. Colonialism minus a civilizational mission is no colonialism at all. It handicaps the colonizer much more than it handicaps the colonized.' Ashis Nandy, *The Intimate Enemy: Loss and Recovery of Self Under Colonialism*, Delhi: Oxford University Press, 1983, p.11. See also Nandy's chapter 'Final Encounter: The Politics of the Assassination of Gandhi', in Ashis Nandy, *At the Edge of Psychology: Essays in Politics and Culture*, Delhi: Oxford University Press, 1980, pp.70-98.

64 'Painting' the world as he found it 'from experience' for his son, Gandhi admitted: 'I cannot imagine a thing as ugly as the intercourse of man and woman'. Gandhi to Manilal Gandhi, 17 March 1922. He added in his political manifesto that 'A man who is unchaste loses stamina, becomes emasculated and cowardly. He whose mind is given over to animal passion is not capable of any great effort.' M.K. Gandhi, *Hind Swaraj or Indian Home Rule*, Ahmedabad: Navajivan, 1939, p.84.



65 'Talk with Bhai Paramanand', *Harijan*, 20 January 1940.

66 Gandhi to Narandas Gandhi, 10 January 1911.

67 M.K. Gandhi, *Satyagraha in South Africa*, Madras: Ganesan, 1928, p.5.

68 'Speech to Inmates of Shantiniketan', *Navajivan*, 26 September 1920.

69 Pyarelal, *Mahatma Gandhi*, p.134.

70 See discussion with A.V. Thakkar, 24 February 1947, quoted in Pyarelal, *Mahatma Gandhi*, p.225.

71 Bose, *My Days with Gandhi*, p.177.

72 'Since resistance through satyagraha is offered through self-suffering, it is a weapon open pre-eminently to women.' See 'Speech at Meeting in Lausanne', 8 December 1931.

73 Amrit Kaur, 'Foreword', p.iii.

74 Amrit Kaur, 'Foreword', pp.iv-v.

75 Rameshwari Nehru, 'Gandhiji and Women', in Shukla, Chandrashanker (ed.), *Incidents of Gandhiji's Life, by Fifty-Four Contributors*, Bombay: Vora, 1949, p.212.

76 Muriel Lester, *Gandhi: World Citizen*, Allahabad: Kitab Mahal, 1945, p.52.

77 Barr, *Bapu*, p.126.

78 Rajkumari Amrit Kaur, 'Gandhiji and Women', in Kshitis Roy (ed.), *Gandhi Memorial Peace Number*, Shantiniketan: Visva-Bharati Quarterly, 1949, p.171.

79 Margaret Sanger, *An Autobiography*, New York: Dover, 1971, p.470.

80 M.K. Gandhi, *An Autobiography or The Story of My Experiments With Truth*, Ahmedabad: Navajivan, 1940, p.4.

81 Mahadev Desai, *The Diary of Mahadev Desai*, Navajivan: Ahmedabad, 1953, vol.1, p.52.

82 'Discussion with Christian Missionaries', *Harijan*, 24 December 1938.

83 'My Life', *Harijan*, 4 November 1939.

84 Fatima Meer, 'Gandhi on Women – A Critique', in Fatima Meer (ed.), *The South African Gandhi: An Abstract of the Speeches and Writings of M.K. Gandhi, 1893-1914*, Durban: Madiba, 1996, p.998.

85 See Gandhi to Hermann Kallenbach, 10 August 1920; and Gandhi to Saraladevi Chaudhurani, 17 December 1920.

86 See his letters to Esther Færing, 16, 24 and 25 January 1920; and Gandhi to Narahari Parikh, after 25 January 1920.

87 See his diary extract for 16 March 1947; and Gandhi to Amrit Kaur, 18 March 1947.

88 See his discussion with Margaret Sanger, below.

89 For Gandhi's relationship with Saraladevi Chaudhurani, see Martin Green, *Gandhi:Voice of a New Age Revolution*, New York: Continuum, 1993, pp.223-26, 273-85; and Girja Kumar, *Brahmacharya, Gandhi & His Women Associates*, New Delhi: Vitasta, 2006, pp.215-41.

90 Bose, *My Days with Gandhi*, pp.165-66.

91 'Nothing without Grace', *Harijan*, 29 February 1936.

92 Bose, *My Days with Gandhi*, p.167. For Gandhi's horror at the death of his father when he was making love to his wife instead of massaging the old man, as he should have been, see Gandhi, *An Autobiography*, pp.21-23.

93 'Interview to the *Vegetarian* - I', *The Vegetarian*, 13 June 1891.

94 For the early influences on Gandhi, especially Western ones, see Thomas Weber, *Gandhi as Disciple and Mentor*, New Delhi: Cambridge University Press, 2007, pp.26-33, 36-45.

95 See the chapter titled 'The Magic Spell of a Book' in Gandhi, *An Autobiography*, pp.219-21.

96 Pyarelal, *Mahatma Gandhi, volume 1: The Early Phase*, Ahmedabad: Navajivan, 1965, p.707.

97 See Gandhi, *Hind Swaraj*, chapter VI 'Civilization', chapter IX 'The Condition of India: Railways', chapter XI 'The Condition of India: Lawyers', and chapter XII 'The Condition of India: Doctors'.

98 Gandhi, *An Autobiography*, p.28.

99 Gandhi to H.S.L. Polak, 26 October 1906.

100 See Gandhi to Millie Graham Polak, 14 November 1909; and to H.S.L. Polak, 15 November 1909.

101 James D. Hunt, 'Suffragettes and Satyagraha', *Indo-British Review* (1981), vol.9, no.1, p.65.

102 Hunt, 'Suffragettes and Satyagraha', p.75.

103 Hunt, 'Suffragettes and Satyagraha', p.65; and James D. Hunt, *Gandhi in London*, New Delhi: Promilla, 1978, p.102.

104 'Deeds Better than Words', *Indian Opinion*, 24 November 1906.

105 'Transvaal Asiatic Ordinance', *Indian Opinion*, 30 March 1907.

106 'When Women are Manly, Will Men be Effeminate?', *Indian Opinion*, 23 February 1907.

107 'London', *Indian Opinion*, 28 August 1909.

108 'London', *Indian Opinion*, 9 October 1909; see also 'London', *Indian Opinion*, 23 October 1909.

109 Hunt, *Gandhi in London*, p.141; Hunt, 'Suffragettes and Satyagraha', p.74; and 'London', *Indian Opinion,* 13 November 1909.

110 'London', *Indian Opinion*, 30 October 1909.

111 Latter, when he had clarified the terminology, he was to characterise the actions of the suffragettes as 'passive resistance' but not satyagraha. See 'Satyagraha – Not Passive Resistance', written about 2 September 1917; and 'Satyagraha', *Navajivan*, 14 September 1919.

112 Hunt, 'Suffragettes and Satyagraha', p.73.

113 See for example 'Brave Women', *Indian Opinion*, 28 December 1907.

114 See for example 'London', *Indian Opinion*, 28 August 1909; 'London', *Indian Opinion*, 6 November 1909; and 'London', *Indian Opinion*, 4 December 1909.

115 Hunt, *Gandhi in London*, p.103.

116 See Thomas Weber, 'Claiming Credit for Gandhi', *Gandhi Marg* (2005), vol.27, no.2, pp.165-78.

**Western Women Contacts: Friends, Supporters and Critics**

1 M.K. Gandhi, *An Autobiography or The Story of My Experiments With Truth*, Ahmedabad: Navajivan, 1940, p.34.

2 Gandhi, *An Autobiography*, p.47.

3 And, in a creative novel, the friendship with the young lady also. See Keith Heller, *The Woman Who Knew Gandhi*, Boston: Mariner, 2003.

4 Gandhi, *An Autobiography*, p.52. See also 'The Late Miss Manning', *Indian Opinion*, 16 September 1905.

5 See James D. Hunt, *Gandhi and the Nonconformists: Encounters in South Africa*, New Delhi: Promilla, 1986, pp.29-30; and Thomas Weber, *Gandhi as Disciple and Mentor*, New Delhi: Cambridge University Press, 2007, pp.31-32.

6 Gandhi, *An Autobiography*, p.88.

7 See Gandhi, *An Autobiography*, pp.139-140; M.K. Gandhi, *Satyagraha in South Africa*, Madras: Ganesan, 1928, pp.93-95; 'Mr Gandhi and the Lady', *The Natal Mercury*, 18 January 1897; and 'Mr Gandhi Ashore: Mobbed – Stoned and Kicked', *The Natal Advertiser*, 14 January 1897.

8 Muriel Lester, *Gandhi:World Citizen*, Allahabad: Kitab Mahal, 1945, p.53.

9 Gandhi, *Satyagraha in South Africa*, p.275.

10 See Weber, *Gandhi as Disciple and Mentor*, pp.55, 70.

11 See Gandhi, *Satyagraha in South Africa*, pp.268-71; and Gandhi, *An Autobiography*, pp.217, 220-24.

12 Gandhi, *Satyagraha in South Africa*, p.272. A few years after Gandhi's stay, Ada West was back in London working as the resident cook in Muriel Lester's Kingsley Hall.

13 Gandhi to Hermann Kallenbach, 27 August 1911.

14 See Gandhi's letters to L.W. Ritch, 27 February and 15 April 1928.

15 Joseph J. Doke, *M.K. Gandhi: An Indian Patriot in South Africa*, London: The London Indian Chronicle, 1909 (and reprinted in several Indian editions).

16 Gandhi, *Satyagraha in South Africa*, p.263.

17 See Gandhi's letters to Olive Doke, 15 December 1910, and 3 March 1911; and Olive C. Doke, 'Reminiscences of M.K. Gandhi', in Chandrashanker Shukla (ed.), *Incidents of Gandhiji's Life, by Fifty-Four Contributors*, 1949, Bombay: Vora, p.45.

18 See 'A Fruit of Passive Resistance', *Indian Opinion*, 28 October 1911.

19 Gandhi to Hermann Kallenbach, 11 November 1911.

20 See 'Address to Mrs Vogl', *Indian Opinion*, 25 November 1911.

21 Gandhi to Millie Graham Polak, 17 February 1912. See also Sonja Schlesin to Manilal Gandhi, 1 October 1928.

22 Gandhi to Chhaganlal Gandhi, 27 May 1912.

23 Prabhudas Gandhi, *My Childhood with Gandhiji*, Ahmedabad: Navajivan, 1957, p.181.

24 Sushila Nayar, *Mahatma Gandhi, volume IV: Satyagraha at Work*, Ahmedabad: Navajivan, 1989, pp.482-83.

25 Gandhi to Hermann Kallenbach, 25 February 1914.

26 For the life of Emily Hobhouse, see John Fisher, *That Miss Hobhouse*, London: Secker and Warburg, 1971; Emily Hobhouse, *Emily Hobhouse: A Memoir compiled by A. Ruth Fry*, London: J. Cape, 1929; Brian Roberts, *Those Bloody Women: Three Heroines of the Boer War*, London: John Murray, 1991; and Heloise Brown, *'The Truest Form of Patriotism' Pacifist Feminism in Britain, 1870-1902,* Manchester: Manchester University Press, 2003.

27 For the life of Smuts and his relationship with Gandhi and Hobhouse, see W.K. Hancock, *Smuts: The Sanguine Years 1870-1919*, Cambridge: Cambridge University Press, 1962.

28 See 'Some Remarkable European Women Who Helped Gandhiji in South Africa', available on the ANC website: *www.anc.org.za/ancdocs/history/people/gandhi/6.html*

29 Emily Hobhouse to Jan Christiaan Smuts, 29 December 1913, quoted in William Hancock and Jean van der Poel, *Selection from the Smuts Papers*, Cambridge: Cambridge University Press, 1966, vol.3, pp.152-56, at pp.154-55.

30 Quoted in 'Some Remarkable European Women Who Helped Gandhiji in South Africa' (however, it does not come from the source claimed, that is C.F. Andrews, 'Mr Gandhi at Phoenix', *Modern Review* (Calcutta), May 1914, pp.563-66).

31 Gandhi to Emily Hobhouse, 5 January 1914.

32 Gandhi to Hermann Kallenbach, 24 February 1914.

33 Gandhi to Elizabeth Mari Molteno, 27 February 1914.

34 Emily Hobhouse to Jan Christiaan Smuts, 23 April 1914, quoted in Hancock and van der Poel, *Selection from the Smuts Papers*, vol.3, pp.172-74, at pp. 173-74.

35 'A Great Heart', *Young India*, 15 July 1926. See also Mahadev Desai's description of her life: 'Brave Woman Passes Away', *Navajivan*, 11 July 1936.

36 For the life of Olive Schreiner see Ruth First and Ann Scott, *Olive Schreiner*, New Brunswick, NJ: Rutgers University Press, 1990; Vera Buchanan-Gould, *Not Without Honour: The Life and Writings of Olive Schreiner*, London: Hutchinson, 1946; S.C. Cronwright-Schreiner, *The Life of Olive Schreiner*, London: T. Fisher Unwin, 1924; and Claudia Roth Pierpont, *Passionate Minds: Women Rewriting the World*, Melbourne: Scribe, 2000, pp.3-31.

37 'Deputation's Voyage [ – 1]', *Indian Opinion*, 31 July 1909. See also Gandhi to H.S.L. Polak, 14 July 1909.

38 Eleanor Morton, *The Women in Gandhi's Life*, New York: Dodd, Mead & Co., 1953, p.63.

39 Morton, *The Women in Gandhi's Life*, p.63.

40 Morton, *The Women in Gandhi's Life*, p.77.

41 Gandhi, *Satyagraha in South Africa*, p.61.

42 Gandhi, *Satyagraha in South Africa*, p.281.

43 Gandhi reminded his readers of Schreiner's views on human unity regardless of colour or race. See for example, 'Olive Schreiner on the Unity of Races', *Indian Opinion*, 3 June 1911.

44 She told Gandhi's friend, the great Indian poet Sarojini Naidu that Gandhi was the 'greatest spirit that has ever come to South Africa', and named him the 'Mazzini of the Movement.' Reported in *Indian Opinion*, 30 September 1914.

45 Morton, *The Women in Gandhi's Life*, p.76.

46 Olive Schreiner, *Dreams*, London: T.Fisher Unwin, 1894, p.175.

47 Speech on Resolution on South African Indians, Kanpur Congress, *Young India*, 7 January 1926.

48 Gandhi to W.H. Wiser, 28 July 1926.

49 Letter in the South African Library, Cape Town, quoted in 'Some Remarkable European Women Who Helped Gandhiji in South Africa'. For a detailed discussion of the contradiction between Gandhi's nonviolence and his support of British war efforts in South Africa and during the Great War, see Manfred Steger, *Gandhi's Dilemma: Nonviolent Principles and Nationalist Power*, New York: St Martin's Press, 2000, pp.141-55; and Peter Brock, 'Gandhi's Nonviolence and His War Service', *Gandhi Marg* (1981), vol.2, no.11, pp.601-16, reprinted in a slightly expanded form in Peter Brock, *The Mahatma and Mother India [Essays on Gandhi's Non-Violence and Nationalism]*, Ahmedabad: Navajivan, 1983, pp.50-74.

50 James D. Hunt, *Gandhi in London*, New Delhi: Promilla, 1978, p.100; and 'Notes: A Good Englishwoman', *Young India*, 27 January 1927.

51 See Gandhi to Miss F. Winterbottom, 13 November 1906; and 'Deputation Notes – II', *Indian Opinion*, 15 December 1906.

52 'Ritch's Speech at East India Association', *Indian Opinion*, 29 December 1906.

53 'Johannesburg Letter', *Indian Opinion*, 21 September 1907.

54 Florence Winterbottom to Gandhi, 9 September 1920.

55 Florence Winterbottom to Gandhi, 14 October 1920.

56 'Notes: A Good Englishwoman', *Young India*, 27 January 1927.

57 Gandhi was admitted to the Transvaal bar on 14 April 1903, and it is safe to assume that he would have needed secretarial help some months later, when work had 'piled up'. Further, in his autobiography, Gandhi notes (p.210) that 'The appointment of Miss Dick was not enough for my purpose. I needed more assistance.' He then acquired the services of Louis Walter Ritch as an articled clerk in his legal practice. Ritch became articled to Gandhi sometime in 1903. While Miss Dick's full name seems to be lost to history,

she witnessed some legal documents for Gandhi, for example a Power of Attorney certificate on 26 May 1904, as J.S. Dick. I thank Charles DiSalvo for this information.

58 Gandhi, *An Autobiography*, p.208. We do not know the date of her departure, but by this time he knew her well enough 'to give her away in marriage.'

59 Gandhi, *Satyagraha in South Africa*, p.275.

60 Almost two decades later, Sonja Schlesin was to recall that she started working with Gandhi in November 1906. Gandhi refers to Sonja Schlesin as being 'only sixteen years of age' (*Satyagraha in South Africa*, p.276), or 'about seventeen' (*An Autobiography*, p.209), when she joined him.

61 Gandhi, *Satyagraha in South Africa*, pp.275-76.

62 When Gandhi, Kallenbach and Henry Polak were arrested in November 1913, Gandhi wrote to Polak's wife Millie asking her to continue the struggle by assisting Sonja Schlesin 'who knows the struggle almost like Henry' and whom he had asked to 'assume full control'. See Gandhi to Millie Graham Polak, 12 November 1913.

63 For the most detailed account of the life of Sonja Schlesin, see George D. Paxton, 'Sonja Schlesin, Gandhi, and South Africa', *Gandhi Marg* (1999), vol.21, no.3, pp.325-38. Much of the information in the article is reproduced in George, Paxton, *Sonja Schlesin: Gandhi's South African Secretary*, Glasgow: Pax, 2006.

64 Gandhi, *Satyagraha in South Africa*, p.275. In the account in Gandhi's autobiography, Gokhale also comments on her fearlessness and adds that 'Amongst your co-workers, she takes the first place in my estimation.' Gandhi, *An Autobiography*, p.209.

65 Gandhi, *Satyagraha in South Africa*, p.277.

66 In the original edition of *Satyagraha in South Africa* (p.277) these words are also attributed to Doke. In the version in Gandhi's *Collected Works*, only the first sentence is not Gandhi's own.

67 'Johannesburg Letter', *Indian Opinion*, 11 January 1908.

68 Gandhi, *Satyagraha in South Africa*, p.277. During 1912, Schlesin twice refused to move from compartments reserved for 'Coloured persons' when she was travelling with her Indian co-workers in the Transvaal Indian Women's Association and challenged the railway administration to prosecute her. See 'Railway Travelling in the Transvaal', *Indian Opinion*, 31 August 1912.

69 Gandhi to Sonja Schlesin, 15 August 1924. Schlesin had similar digs at Gandhi, for example when, as early as 1911, she commented on Gandhi's growing typing abilities in spite of the anti-machinery injunctions of a certain book they were both aware of – Gandhi's own *Hind Swaraj*! See Schlesin's addition to Louis Ritch to Gandhi, 15 April 1911.

70 Enclosure, Gandhi to Sonja Schlesin, 15 August 1924.

71 Gandhi, *Satyagraha in South Africa*, pp.277-78. See also Gandhi, *An Autobiography*, p.209.

72 See Gandhi to Manu Gandhi, 6 June 1946; and Nayar, *Mahatma Gandhi*, p.465.

73 Gandhi, *Satyagraha in South Africa*, p.276.

74 Gandhi, *An Autobiography*, p.209.

75 Gandhi, *An Autobiography*, p.209.

76 *Schlesin* v *Incorporated Law Society of the Transvaal* [1909]TS 363. See also'Ladies as Attorneys. A Supreme Court Application. The Judge's Decision', *The Star* (Johannesburg), 23 April 1909; and 'Female Attorneys. The Supreme Court Application', *The Star* (Johannesburg), 24 April 1909.

77 See 'Indian Women as Passive Resisters', *Indian Opinion*, 10 May 1913.

78 See Gandhi to Hermann Kallenbach, 12 August 1911; and Gandhi to H.S.L. Polak, 13 and 26 August 1911.

79 Gandhi to Hermann Kallenbach, 2 September 1911.

80 Sonja Schlesin to Gandhi, 25 March 1911.

81 Sonja Schlesin to Gandhi, 29 March 1911.

82 See Prabhudas Gandhi, *My Childhood with Gandhiji*, pp.152-53, 165-66.

83 Sonja Schlesin to Gandhi, 31 July 1913.

84 Quoted in Paxton, 'Sonja Schlesin, Gandhi, and South Africa', p.330.

85 Sonja Schlesin to Gandhi, 3 November 1915.

86 Sonja Schlesin to Gandhi, 25 December 1915.

87 Millie Graham Polak to Gandhi, 23 January 1916.

88 'Talk with Teachers of the National School', Ahmedabad, 23 June 1917.

89 Gandhi to Ramdas Gandhi, 28 August 1917.

90 Gandhi to Sonja Schlesin, 2 June 1919. See also Gandhi to Sonja Schlesin, 23 June 1918, and 23 February 1919.

91 See Gandhi to Sonja Schlesin, 23 February 1919.

92 Paxton, 'Sonja Schlesin, Gandhi, and South Africa', p.332; and Paxton, *Sonja Schlesin*, p.33.

93 Gandhi to Sonja Schlesin, 2 June 1919. Ahmad Mohammad Kachalia and Shapruji Adajania Sorabji were leading colleagues of Gandhi's in the South African struggle, while Parsi Rustomji was a wealthy businessman who helped finance the struggle.

94 Gandhi to Hermann Kallenbach, 29 September 1921.

95 Sonja Schlesin to Gandhi, 2 July 1924.

96 Sonja Schlesin to Gandhi, 11 September 1924.

97 Sonja Schlesin to Gandhi, 3 December 1925.

98 Gandhi to Devi West, 21 December 1927.

99 Sonja Schlesin to Gandhi, 4 May 1928.

100 Sonja Schlesin to Gandhi, 2 June 1928.

101 See for example Sonja Schlesin to Gandhi, 3 January 1927, where in a neat hand she discusses Biblical interpretations, whether anger is allowable if there is a just cause, and Stanley Jones' recently published book, *The Christ of the Indian Road*.

102 Sonja Schlesin to Gandhi, 15 May 1928.

103 For the intensely close relationship Kallenbach shared with Gandhi, see Weber, *Gandhi as Disciple and Mentor*, pp.69-83.

104 Quoted in Paxton, *Sonja Schlesin*, p.37.

105 Gandhi to Manilal and Shushila Gandhi, 15 July 1928.

106 This instalment appeared on 11 August 1927. In the final published version of the book the section reads 'She is at present a teacher in one of the High Schools in the Transvaal.' See Gandhi, *An Autobiography*, p.209. The error however remained in *Satyagraha in South Africa*, which was published at about the same time. See p.278.

107 'A Correction', *Young India*, 28 June 1928.

108 Gandhi, *An Autobiography*, p.209.

109 Sonja Schlesin to Manilal Gandhi, 1 October 1928.

110 Gandhi to Sonja Schlesin, 2 February 1930.

111 Gandhi to Sonja Schlesin, 18 August 1931.

112 Gandhi to Sonja Schlesin, 20 January 1945.

113 Quoted in Pyarelal, *Mahatma Gandhi; The Last Phase, Part I, Book I*, Ahmedabad: Navajivan, 1956, p.102.

114 Gandhi to Sonja Schlesin, 1 November 1947.

115 For Schlesin's later teaching and post-teaching career, see Paxton, 'Sonja Schlesin, Gandhi, and South Africa', pp.334-37.

116 Morton, *The Women in Gandhi's Life*, p.87.

117 In fact he addressed his first letter to her after he left South Africa to 'My Dear Daughter' (see Gandhi to Schlesin, 16 January 1916), but this was a one-off and the rest of his correspondences were more formally addressed to 'Dear Miss Schlesin'.

118 Geoffrey Ashe, *Gandhi: A Study in Revolution*, London: Heinemann, 1968, p.329.

119 See Maureen Swan, *Gandhi: The South African Experience*, Johannesburg: Ravan Press, 1985.

120 There have been many biographies of Annie Besant, including Gertrude Marvin Williams, *The Passionate Pilgrim: A Life of Annie Besant*, New York: Coward – McCann, 1931; Arthur H.Nethercot, *The First Five Lives of Annie Besant*, Chicago: The University of Chicago Press, 1960; Arthur H. Nethercot, *The Last Four Lives of Annie Besant*, Chicago: The University of Chicago Press, 1963; Anne Taylor, *Annie Besant; A Biography*, Oxford: Oxford University Press, 1992. Annie Besant also published her own life story as *An Autobiography*, London: Unwin, 1908; and a later Indian edition in 1939.

121 From a letter to the *Times*, quoted in Jyoti Chandra, *Annie Besant: From Theosophy to Nationalism*, Delhi: K.K. Publications, 2001, p.31.

122 Annie Besant, *India, Bond or Free? A World Problem*, London: Putnam's, 1926, p.26.

123 See Raj Kumar, *Annie Besant's Rise to Power in Indian Politics 1914-1917*, New Delhi: Concept, 1981.

124 'Message on Annie Besant's Birthday', 1 October 1919.

125 Gandhi, *An Autobiography*, pp.48-49.

126 Gandhi to Dr Pranjivan J. Mehta, 8 May 1911.

127 Pyarelal, *Mahatma Gandhi, volume I: The Early Phase*, Ahmedabad: Navajivan, 1965, p.259; Hunt, *Gandhi and the Nonconformists*, p.6.

128 Hunt, *Gandhi and the Nonconformists*, p.7.

129 Pyarelal, *Mahatma Gandhi, volume III: The Birth of Satyagraha*, Ahmedabad: Navajivan, 1986, p.25; Joseph J. Doke, *M.K. Gandhi: An Indian Patriot in South Africa*, London: The London Indian Chronicle, 1909, p.8.

130 Gandhi to Mrs A.M. Lewis, 4 August 1894.

131 Gandhi to Annie Besant, 13 May 1905.

132 'How to Build a Nation', *Indian Opinion*, 9 February 1907.

133 Gandhi, *An Autobiography*, pp.177-78.

134 'A Message of Hope From Annie Besant', *Indian Opinion*, 27 March 1909.

135 Gandhi to Dr.Pranjivan Mehta, 8 May 1911.

136 G.A. Natesan, 'Reminiscences', in D.G. Tendulkar and others (eds), *Gandhiji: His Life and Work*, Bombay: Keshav Bhikaji Dhawale, 1944, pp.213-14. Needless to say, Besant saw the visit somewhat differently. She claims that it was 'very enjoyable', that Gandhi visited the Panchama school adjoining the headquarters grounds and that he had inspected the Theosophical press. See Annie Besant, *An Autobiography*, Adyar: Theosophical Publishing House, 1939, p.561.

137 At least one author sees this incident as a deliberate ploy on Gandhi's part to assert his claim to Indian leadership at the expense of Annie Besant who was blocking his way. This is the thrust of I.M. Muthanna's anti-Gandhi book *Mother Besant and Mahatma Gandhi*, Vellore: Thenpulam, 1986. For the 'Benares

incident' see pp.157-74. For Gandhi's explanation of what had happened, see 'Interview to A.P.I. on Benares "Incident"', *The Bombay Chronicle*, 10 February 1916; and 'Reply to Mrs Besant', *The Hindu* 17 February 1916. For Besant's explanations, see 'Annie Besant's Explanation Regarding Benares Incident', *New India*, 10 February 1916 and 17 February 1916; and 'In Defence of M.K. Gandhi', 19 February 1916.

138 Annie Besant to Gandhi, 7 June 1917.

139 'Speech at Gujarati Political Conference', 3 November 1917.

140 'Speech at Ahmedabad Meeting', *Prajabandhu*, 17 March 1918. See also 'Speech at Annie Besant Felicitation Meeting, *Bombay Chronicle*, 2 October 1919.

141 Gandhi to Private Secretary of Viceroy, 7 July 1917. A few months before, when Besant was prohibited from entering the Bombay Presidency, Gandhi made similar protests. See 'Speech on Defence of India Act', *Bombay Chronicle*, 24 October 1916.

142 Mahadev H. Desai, *Day-To-Day With Gandhi [Secretary's Diary]*, Rajghat, Varanasi: Sarva Seva Sangh, 1968, vol.2, p.34.

143 Annie Besant to Gandhi, 10 May 1919.

144 Gandhi to Annie Besant, 10 May 1919.

145 Annie Besant to Gandhi, 11 May 1919.

146 See 'Speech at Calcutta Congress', *Amrita Bazar Patrika*, 5 September 1920; 'Some Difficulties', *Navajivan*, 7 November 1920; and 'Difficulties in Our Way', *Young India*, 10 November 1920.

147 See Gandhi to Devadas Gandhi, 12 August 1926.

148 Catherine Lowman Wessinger, *Annie Besant: And Progressive Messianism (1847-1933)*, New York: Edwin Mellen Press, 1988, pp.247-48.

149 Annie Besant, *The Future of Indian Politics: A Contribution to the Understanding of Present-Day Problems*, Adyar: Theosophical Publishing House, 1922, pp.256-57.

150 'The Parting of the Ways', *New India*, 1 January 1921.

151 *New India*, 21 March 1919.

152 Quoted in Martin Green, *Gandhi: Voice of a New Age Revolution*, New York: Continuum, 1993, p.259.

153 See 'Discussion Aboard the "Gurkha"', *Navajivan*, 29 December 1920: 'Mrs Besant was right when she once said that I wanted a political revolution. Only, the revolution should not be a simple revolution but an evolutionary revolution. But a revolution, I think, there must be. There is no alternative.'

154 See Gandhi to Annie Besant, 18 September 1924.

155 'Message on Annie Besant's Birthday', *New India*, 2 October 1924. See also, 'Tribute to Annie Besant', 6 August 1924, on the occasion of the completion of fifty years of her public service.

156 For Gandhi's assessment of the consequences of this, see 'An Appeal to Madras', *Young India*, 21 January 1920.

157 'Tribute to Annie Besant', *The Bombay Chronicle*, 21 September 1933.

158 Quoted in Chandra, *Annie Besant*, p.192.

159 Vera Britain, *The Rebel Passion: A Short History of Some Pioneer Peace-makers*, London: Allan and Unwin, 1964, p.85.

160 For the story of Lester's life, see her autobiographical volumes, *It Occurred to Me*, New York: Harper and Brothers, 1937; and *It So Happened*, New York: Harper and Brothers, 1947; as well as the biography by Jill Wallis, *Mother of World Peace: The Life of Muriel Lester*, Enfield Lock, Middlesex: Hisarlik Press, 1993.

161 Lester, *It Occurred to Me*, p.49.

162 Lester, *It Occurred to Me*, p.41.

163 Muriel Lester, *Entertaining Gandhi*, London: Nicholson and Watson, 1932, p.3.

164 Hunt, *Gandhi in London*, p.198.

165 Lester, *Entertaining Gandhi*, p.2

166 Gandhi's closest friends in England at the time, C.F. Andrews and Henry Polak, wanted him to stay in the West End in more convenient and comfortable surroundings, pointing out that Kingsley Hall was too far from St James' Palace, the site of the Round Table Conference. Lester countered: 'Isn't it time some one broke through the old custom of letting diplomats and ambassadors confer only with diplomats and ambassadors? The people of Bow can understand the suffering of the people of India better than even the most sympathetic and sensitive dinner-out. Will peace ever come until it's based on the will of ordinary people? Let Mr Gandhi be the first plenipotentiary from a foreign land, summoned to an imperial city, who throws in his lot with the working-people.' Lester, *It Occurred to Me*, pp.167-68. Soon the eight mile trip proved to be too time-consuming and a house in Knightsbridge near Hyde Park was rented as an office and headquarters. However, Gandhi returned to Kingsley Hall each night to sleep. For a lengthy account of the wrangling over Gandhi's residence-to-be, see Lester, *Entertaining Gandhi*, pp.23-26; and for a glimpse into the work at Knightsbridge, see Agatha Harrison, 'Knightsbridge, London', in Chandrashanker Shukla (ed.), *Gandhiji as We Know Him, by Seventeen Contributors*, Bombay; Vora, 1945, pp.82-93.

167 Lester, *It So Happened*, p.51.

168 Muriel Lester, 'Gandhiji: 1926-39', in Shukla (ed.), *Incidents of Gandhiji's Life*, p.143.

169 See, John C. Vine, 'Interview with Miss Muriel Lester', 26 February 1960, in S. Durai Raja Singam, 'They Were Ready to Talk About Gandhi', unpublished manuscript, (n.d.), p.13.

170 The Fellowship of Reconciliation was formed in the early days of the First World War to resolve human conflict through the power of love and truth. It is a non-sectarian but spiritually-based organisation that opposes war and works towards a just and peaceful world community with full dignity and freedom for all human beings. Muriel Lester had attended FoR meetings since 1915, and between 1920 and 1924 she had been chairperson of the London branch of the FoR (known as the London Union).

171 Lester, *It Occurred to Me*, p.135; and see also Muriel Lester, *My Host the Hindu*, London: Williams and Norgate, 1931, pp.49-55.

172 Vine, 'Interview with Miss Muriel Lester', p.13.

173 Lester, *My Host the Hindu*, p.55.

174 Lester, *Entertaining Gandhi*, 1932, p.12. For a copy of the leaflet see pp.198-204.

175 Muriel Lester to Gandhi, 29 March 1927.

176 Lester, *It Occurred to Me*, pp.139-40; also Lester, 'Gandhiji: 1926-39', p.145.

177 Francis Watson and Hallam Tennyson, *Talking of Gandhi*, New Delhi: Sangam, 1976, p.78.

178 Gandhi to Muriel Lester, before 5 July 1931.

179 See Gandhi to C.F. Andrews, 16 July 1931.

180 'A Retrospect', *Young India*, 31 December 1931.

181 Gandhi, however, noted that by his standards they were quite wealthy, some even having pianos (see 'Interview to *The News Chronicle*', 17 September 1931); and Romain Rolland strongly suspected that Lester's British sense of pride may have led her to hide the real poverty from Gandhi (see Publications Division, *Romain Rolland and Gandhi Correspondence (Letters, Diary Extracts, Articles, Etc.)*, New Delhi: Publications Division, Ministry of Information and Broadcasting, Government of India, 1976, p.216). Lester gives the impression of attempting the opposite, and thus hoping for publicity that would help her cause. See Lester, *Entertaining Gandhi*, 1932, pp.54-55.

182 Lester, *Entertaining Gandhi*, 1932, p.126.

183 'A Retrospect', *Young India*, 31 December 1931.

184 'Letter to Ashram Sisters', 25 January 1932.

185 Lester, *Entertaining Gandhi*, 1932, pp.187-88.

186 Publications Division, *Romain Rolland and Gandhi Correspondence*, p.173.

187 Dorothy Hogg, *Memories for Tomorrow*, London: Regency Press, 1981, p.19.

188 Muriel Lester to Gandhi, no date, quoted in Ghanshayam Das Birla, *Bapu: A Unique Association*, Bombay: Bharatiya Vidya Bhavan, 1977, vol.1, pp.464-67; and Gandhi to Lord Willingdon, 15 March 1934.

189 'Wanted: A Manifestation of Christ in Daily Life', *Harijan*, 30 March 1934.

190 See Mahadev Desai, 'Weekly Letter: Our Village', *Harijan*, 25 January 1936.

191 Gandhi to Mirabehn, 9 December 1938.

192 Her report was published in the *Hindusthan Standard* on 8 November 1946, and is quoted in Pyarelal, *The Last Phase*, Part.1, Book 1, p.281.

193 Quoted in Pyarelal, *The Last Phase*, Part.1, Book 1, p.301.

194 See for example, Muriel Lester to Gandhi, 10 January 1927.

195 Horace Alexander, *Gandhi Through Western Eyes*, Bombay: Asia, 1969, p.83.

196 Hugh Tinker, *The Ordeal of Love: C.F. Andrews and India*, Delhi: Oxford University Press, 1979, p.250.

197 Quoted in Irene Harrison, *Agatha Harrison: An Impression by Her Sister*, London: Allen & Unwin, 1956, p.68.

198 Quoted in Irene Harrison, *Agatha Harrison*, p.18.

199 See Tinker, *The Ordeal of Love*, p.259.

200 Alexander, *Gandhi Through Western Eyes*, pp.132, 137.

201 Irene Harrison, *Agatha Harrison*, p.77.

202 Irene Harrison, *Agatha Harrison*, p.77.

203 For example after the very popular Gandhi left London, during his visit to Italy a local reporter fabricated a story that the Mahatma had felt that the Round Table Conference was a waste of time and that he was returning to India to restart an economic struggle against an already economically depressed Britain, leading to a surge of bitterness against him among the English masses. On this and other similar occasions, Harrison worked overtime to set the record straight or give Gandhi's side of a contentious report.

204 Irene Harrison, *Agatha Harrison*, p.78; and Agatha Harrison, 'Knightsbridge, London', p.85.

205 Agatha Harrison to Gandhi, 5 May 1938, quoted in Birla, *Bapu*, vol.3, pp.162-67.

206 Agatha Harrison, 'Some Impressions', in Shukla (ed.), *Incidents of Gandhiji's Life*, p.64.

207 Agatha Harrison, 'Some Impressions', p.64.

208 Irene Harrison, *Agatha Harrison*, p.80.

209 For Harrison's notes of the tours, see 'Notes of Agatha Harrison', in Birla, *Bapu*, vol.1, pp.357-63.

210 Agatha Harrison to Gandhi, 14 July 1934, quoted in Birla, *Bapu*, vol.1, pp.399-400.

211 Agatha Harrison, 'Some Impressions', p.69.

212 Gandhi to Agatha Harrison, 11 April 1940.

213 Tinker, *The Ordeal of Love*, p.313.

214 Agatha Harrison, 'Some Impressions', p.70.

215 For example, just a few days before Gandhi's assassination, she sent him a clipping from the *Times* of London informing him that the rumours of a rift between Nehru and Patel had spread to Britain, that it was a bad omen, and that he should do something to set matters right. See Sudhir Ghosh, *Gandhi's Emissary*, London: Cresset, 1967, p.224.

216 'Note on letter from Horace Alexander', 3 August 1942, quoted in Alexander, *Gandhi Through Western Eyes*, p.206.

217 'Discussion with Agatha Harrison', 3 June 1939.

218 Pyarelal, *Mahatma Gandhi; The Last Phase, Part I, Book I*, p.160.

219 'Talk with Agatha Harrison', *Harijan*, 7 April 1946.

220 Gandhi to Agatha Harrison, 22 October 1941.

221 Irene Harrison, *Agatha Harrison*, p.131.

222 Alexander, *Gandhi Through Western Eyes*, pp.83-84.

223 Irene Harrison, *Agatha Harrison*, p.73.

224 Quoted in Brian Heeney, *The Women's Movement in the Church of England 1850-1930*, Oxford: Clarendon Press, 1988.

225 For a view of the three-way relationship see Maude Royden, *A Threefold Cord*, London: Gollancz, 1947.

226 For Royden's life, see Sheila Fletcher, *Maude Royden: A Life*, Oxford: Basil Blackwell, 1989; Martin Ceadel, *Pacifism in Britain 1914-1945: The Defining of a Faith*, Oxford: Clarendon Press, 1980; and her entry in Virginia Blain, Patricia Clements and Isobel Grundy (eds), *The Feminist Companion to Literature in English*, London: Batsford, 1990, pp.928-29.

227 Maude Royden Shaw, 'Master Christian?', in Kshitis Roy (ed.), *Gandhi Memorial Peace Number*, Shantiniketan: Visva-Bharati Quarterly, 1949, p.130.

228 See Maude Royden to Gandhi, 4 and 7 December 1925.

229 Fletcher, *Maude Royden*, p.251.

230 Mahadev Desai, 'Letter from Europe', *Young India*, 31 December 1931.

231 Hunt, *Gandhi in London*, p.192.

232 Fletcher, *Maude Royden*, p.258.

233 Royden, 'Master Christian', p.131.

234 Gandhi to Maude Royden, 30 September 1931.

235 'Speech at Students' Meeting', 1931, *The Bombay Chronicle*, 17 October 1931.

236 'Reminder to Youth,' in *The New World*, November 1931, p.7. The journal states that the extracts are 'from a sermon recently delivered.'

237 Gandhi to Ashram Women, 30 January 1932.

238 See the leaflet, 'The Peace Army: A Sermon by A. Maude Royden, C.H., D.D., preached at the Guildhouse, Eccleston Square, W.W.1, on Sunday evening, February 28, 1932.' For a history of the Royden's Peace Army, see Thomas Weber, 'Gandhi's "Living Wall" and Maude Royden's "Peace Army"', *Gandhi Marg* (1988), vol.10, no.4, pp.199-212.

239 Fletcher, *Maude Royden*, p.259.

240 For a history of these attempts, see Thomas Weber, 'From Maude Royden's Peace Army to the Gulf Peace Team: An Assessment of Unarmed Interpositionary Peace Forces' *Journal of Peace Research* (1993), vol.30, no.1, pp.45-64.

241 Albeit ones who would go to the front weaponless in order to die rather than kill, see 'Speech at Khandhali', *The Bombay Chronicle*, 3 June 1918.

242 A. Maude Royden, 'The Peacemaker', in William Paxton, Philip Inman, C.B. Alderton, J.W. Tuffley, A. Maude Royden, Charles G. Ammon, J.G. Beaumont, and Hugh Redwood (eds), *Dick Sheppard: An Apostle of Brotherhood*, London: Chapman and Hall, 1938, p.76.

243 Royden, 'Master Christian', p.132.

244 Gandhi to Maude Royden, 26 April 1932.

245 See Weber, 'Gandhi's "Living Wall" and Maude Royden's "Peace Army"', p.207; Royden, 'The Peacemaker', p.78; and Royden, 'Master Christian', p.133.

246 Royden, 'Master Christian', p.133.

247 Royden, 'Master Christian', p.133.

248 Fletcher, *Maude Royden*, p.269.

249 Maude Royden, 'An Englishwoman's Faith', in S. Radhakrishnan (ed.), *Mahatma Gandhi: Essays and Reflections on His Life and Work*, Bombay: Jaico, 1956, p.206.

250 Royden, 'An Englishwoman's Faith', p.209.

251 Fletcher, *Maude Royden*, p.274.

252 'On its Trial', *Harijan*, 15 March 1942.

253 See for example, 'How to Combat Hitlerism', *Harijan*, 22 June 1940; and 'Is Non-Violence Impossible?', *Harijan*, 11 August 1940.

254 Royden, 'Master Christian', p.132.

255 'Interview to Ralph Coniston', before 25 April 1945.

256 See Holger Terp 'Mohandas Gandhi and Ellen Hørup', available at FRED.DK Peace on the Net, *www.fred.dk/peace/hoerup5.htm*; E.S. Reddy and Holger Terp

(editors and publishers), 'The Danish Peace Academy: Gandhi and Nordic Countries: Notes on People in Nordic Countries who Corresponded with Gandhi', available at *www.fredsakademiet.dk/library/nordic/bionotes.htm*; and E.S. Reddy and Holger Terp (eds), *Friends of Gandhi: Correspondence of Mahatma Gandhi with Esther Færing (Menon), Anne Marie Petersen and Ellen Horup*, Berlin and Copenhagen: Gandhi-Informations-Zentrum and The Danish Peace Academy, 2006, p.21.

257 Anne Marie Petersen to Gandhi, 15 January 1929.

258 See Gandhi to Esther Menon, 25 January 1929.

259 Ellen Hørup to Gandhi, 2 May 1929. The rest of this letter is a rambling account of Italian politics and an anti-Catholic diatribe.

260 Ellen Hørup to Gandhi, 6 June 1931. For an account of this meeting see the Appendix to Reddy and Terp, *Friends of Gandhi*, pp.417-26.

261 Edward Holton James, *I Tell Everything: The Brown Man's Burden (A Book on India)*, Geneva: Imprimerie Kundig, c1931, p.196.

262 See Thomas Weber, *On the Salt March: The Historiography of Gandhi's March to Dandi*, New Delhi: HarperCollins, 1997, p.459.

263 Ellen Hørup, *Gandhis Indien*, Copenhagen: H. Hagerups, 1931.

264 Ellen Hørup to Gandhi, 6 February 1933.

265 The journal was suspended in 1935 when the Indian National Congress decided that it had to win independence by its own efforts. Hørup wrote that 'Because of the decision ... we have decided to suspend the publication of our magazine for the time being. We will take it up again as soon as the Indian organizations themselves recognise the necessity of a propaganda campaign in foreign countries.' Quoted in Reddy and Terp, 'The Danish Peace Academy: Gandhi and Nordic Countries: Notes on People'.

266 I am grateful to Holger Terp of the Danish Peace Academy for much of this information.

267 This is a reference to a violinist who played Bach and Beethoven for Gandhi when he, Muriel Lester and Mirabehn visited Romain Rolland in Switzerland during the second week of December 1931.

268 Ellen Hørup to Gandhi, 6 February 1933.

269 Gandhi to Ellen Hørup, 23 February 1933.

270 In fact the organisation was not a member of the small select group, that includes members of the Norwegian Parliament, that has the power to nominate potential laureates. The nomination came from the influential Norwegian labour politician Ole Colbjörsen whose wife was the vice-president of Lasson's Indiens Venner.

271 For the history of Gandhi's 1937 nomination for the Nobel Peace Prize, see Thomas Weber, 'Gandhi and the Nobel Peace Prize', *South Asia* (1989), vol.12, no.1, pp.29-47.

272 The address was published in the November 1936 issue of *Indiens Venner*, quoted in Terp, 'Mohandas Gandhi and Ellen Hørup'.

273 Quoted in Holger Terp, 'Introduction' to Reddy and Terp, 'The Danish Peace Academy: Gandhi and Nordic Countries'.

274 Terp, 'Introduction' to Reddy and Terp, 'The Danish Peace Academy: Gandhi and Nordic Countries'.

**Western Women Interpreters: Constructing an Image**

1 See for example, Maureen Swan, *Gandhi: The South African Experience*, Johannesburg: Ravan Press, 1985.

2 See T.K. Mahadevan, *The Year of the Phoenix: Gandhi's Pivotal Year*, New Delhi: Arnold-Heinemann, 1982, pp.159-64.

3 For a brief sketch of Mayo's life, see Harry H. Field, *After Mother India*, New York: Harcourt, Brace and Company, 1929, pp.275-86; Mary F. Handlin, 'Mayo, Katherine', in Edward T. James, Janet Wilson James, and Paul S. Boyer (eds), *Notable American Women, 1607-1950: A Biographical Dictionary*, volume 2, Cambridge: Belknap Press, 1971, pp.515-17; and Mrinalini Sinha, 'Editor's Introduction', to Katherine Mayo, *Selections from Mother India*, New Delhi: Kali for Women, 1998, pp.1-61.

4 Handlin, 'Mayo, Katherine' at p.516.

5 See Sinha, 'Editor's Introduction', p.17.

6 See Sinha, 'Editor's Introduction', p.16.

7 Sinha, 'Editor's Introduction', p.17.

8 See 'To American Friends', *Young India*, 17 September 1925.

9 See William W. Emilsen, 'Gandhi and Mayo's Mother India', *South Asia* (1987), vol.10, no.1, pp.69-81.

10 Gandhi to Katherine Mayo, 4 March 1926.

11 Katherine Mayo, *Mother India*, London: Jonathan Cape, 1927, p.20.

12 See Gandhi to Katherine Mayo, 26 March, 9 April, and 7 July 1926.

13 'Interview to Katherine Mayo', 17 March 1926. Gandhi's replies to her questions were truncated in *Mother India* in a way that made him look like a sharp politician or foolish, when her own notes indicate far lengthier and nuanced replies. See Manoranjan Jha, *Katherine Mayo and India*, New Delhi: People's Publishing House, 1971, pp.89-90.

14 See Emilsen, 'Gandhi and Mayo's "Mother India"', p.72; C. Seshachari, *Gandhi and the American Scene, An Intellectual History and Inquiry*, Bombay: Nachiketa, 1969, p.51; and Sinha, 'Editor's Introduction', p.4. For the impact of *Mother India* in America, see Manoranjan Jha, *Civil Disobedience and After: The American Reaction to Political Developments in India During 1930-1935*, Meerut, Meenakshi, 1973, pp.30-33.

15 Nilla Cram Cook, *My Road to India*, New York: Lee Furman, 1939, p.264.

16 Sonja Schlesin to Gandhi, 4 May 1928.

17 Seshachari, *Gandhi and the American Scene*, p.53.

18 Gandhi to Katherine Mayo, 13 September 1927.

19 See Field, *After Mother India*, pp.14-26.

20 Even Margaret Sanger, who was affected by the book, charged Mayo with disingenuousness in regard to her use of statistics: 'For example, when she discussed the age of marriage she made sweeping statements and quoted on page so and so of such and such a report; you turned there and they were correct, and that was the reason for the astounding acceptance of her book. Nevertheless, she had violated the spirit, because two pages further in the same report followed an explanation of, or exception to, her conclusions.' See Margaret Sanger, *An Autobiography*, New York: Dover, 1971, p.489.

21 'Drain Inspector's Report', *Young India*, 15 September 1927. Gandhi supporter, the French intellectual Romain Rolland summed up Gandhi's critique by asking, 'Suppose I come to London and visit nothing but the slums, the brothels and the clinics catering for serious illnesses, and then say, "This is England!" Would that be honourable?' See Rolland to Renée Thiesson, 2 October 1927, in *Romain Rolland and Gandhi Correspondence (Letters, Diary Extracts, Articles, Etc.)*, New Delhi: Publications Division, Ministry of Information and Broadcasting, Government of India, 1976, pp.406-8, at p.407.

22 Six years after the publication of the book, Gandhi was still writing critically about it and Miss Mayo. See for example 'An American Criticism', *Harijan*, 22 July 1933.

23 See L.F. Rushbrook Williams, 'Indian Unrest and American Opinion', *Asiatic Review*, (1930) July, pp.479-96 at p.491.

24 Negley Farson, 'Indian Hate Lyric', in Eugene Lyons (ed.), *We Cover the World: By Sixteen Foreign Correspondents*, London: Harrap (1937), p.139.

25 Something Edward Holton James, the US lawyer who visited Gandhi in Allahabad with Hørup, makes much of in his book *I Tell Everything: The Brown Man's Burden (A Book on India)*, Geneva: Imprimerie Kundig, c1931. See in particular pp.139-77. Nilla Cram Cook, the free-spirited one-time Gandhi follower, who was an active participant rather than outsider looking in on Hindu culture, called her a foreign pornographist. She noted that no one who 'gained real access to Hindu domestic life, and not merely to hospitals' could have written in the way Mayo had. See Cook, *My Road to India*, pp.231-32.

26 See Jha, *Katherine Mayo and India*; Sinha, 'Editor's Introduction', pp.19-24; and P. Athiyaman and A.R. Venkatachalapathy, 'Debate: On Gandhi, Mayo and Emilsen', *South Asia* (1989), vol.12, no.2, pp.83-86.

27 Who had earlier written a lengthy twelve part refutation of *Mother India*. See C.F. Andrews, 'The Facts About India: A Reply to Miss Mayo', *Young India*, 17

May, 24 May, 31 May, 7 June, 14 June, 21 June, 28 June, 5 July, 12 July, 19 July, 26 July and 2 August 1928.

28 Gandhi to C.F. Andrews, 29 November 1928.

29 C.F. Andrews to Gandhi, 6 November 1928.

30 See 'Notes: A Visit to Miss Mayo', *Young India,* 21 March1929.

31 'Notes: A Visit to Miss Mayo', *Young India,* 21 March1929.

32 Sinha, 'Editor's Introduction', p.27.

33 Patricia Kendall, *Come with Me to India!: A Quest for Truth Among Peoples and Problems*, New York: Scribner's, 1931.

34 Mayo claimed that while she was in Guinea, an East Indian saved her life and that was one of the reasons why she was interested in India. See Jha, *Katherine Mayo and India*, p.19.

35 Kendall, *Come with Me to India!*, p.427.

36 Kendall, *Come with Me to India!*, pp.329-30.

37 Kendall, *Come with Me to India*!, p.328.

38 The description of Gandhi and the scene in his room seems to be a close paraphrase of Mayo's book, which, surprisingly, is not mentioned by her. See Mayo, *Mother India*, p.201 and Kendall, *Come with Me to India!*, p.328.

39 Morton, in commenting on Kendall's quoting of Gandhi having told her that in India if one wants to be a politician, they must be a saint first, notes that 'Gandhi however had neither the naivete nor the lack of common sense to have spoken these words.' Eleanor Morton, *The Women in Gandhi's Life*, New York: Dodd, Mead & Co., 1953, p.163.

40 See his article 'Position of Women', *Young India*, 17 October 1927; his speeches at Tralsa (*Bombay Chronicle*, 26 March 1930) and Dhaman (*Prajabandhu*, 6 April 1930) only days after the alleged interview; and his letter to Amrit Kaur, 2 February 1935, where he explicitly refers to the *Act* as 'a wise step.'

41 Kendall, *Come with Me to India!*, p.343.

42 Kendall, *Come with Me to India!*, p.418.

43 Kendall, *Come with Me to India!*, p.332.

44 Kendall, *Come with Me to India*!, p.427.

45 In fact information about her is scarce. She does not make it into biographies of American writers and her work is not referred to in any major source. Two years after the publication of her book she is recorded as giving a lecture that followed 'no exact plan' in the 'Arts 100' class at the University of British Columbia. In the lecture, the 'noted speaker' declares 'British rule beneficial to India.' The tone of her lecture could be guessed, but the pettiness is illustrated by the report of her attempt to denigrate the Mahatma: 'A note of humour was sounded by the statement that Gandhi purchased a new set of false teeth the day before he began his "starve-

to-death diet".' See 'Problems of India Unsolved by Gandhi Says Noted Speaker', *The Ubyssey*, 1933, vol.15, no.32.

46 For biographical details of Margaret Sanger's life, see Margaret Sanger, *An Autobiography*, New York: Dover, 1971; Lawrence Lader, *The Margaret Sanger Story and the Fight for Birth Control*, Westport, Con.: Greenwood Press, 1955; Ellen Chesler, *Woman of Valor: Margaret Sanger and the Birth Control Movement in America*, New York: Simon and Schuster, 1992; and Madeline Gray, *Margaret Sanger: A Biography of the Champion of Birth Control*, New York: Richard Marek, 1979.

47 Gandhi to N.S. Phadke, 20 March 1924.

48 Gandhi to Margaret Sanger, 8 July 1925, referred to in Chesler, *Woman of Valor*, pp.356-57.

49 Sanger, *An Autobiography*, p.461.

50 Quoted in Emily Taft Douglas, *Margaret Sanger: Pioneer of the Future*, New York: Holt, Rinehart and Winston, 1970, p.233.

51 Sanger, *An Autobiography*, pp.465-66.

52 Sanger, *An Autobiography*, pp.468.

53 Sanger, *An Autobiography*, pp.468-70; and Margaret Sanger 'A Summit Meeting on Birth Control', in Norman Cousins (ed.), *Profiles of Gandhi: America Remembers a World Leader*, Delhi: Indian Book Company, 1970, pp.35-41. Gandhi may have had some forewarning of what was to come. Almost a year before, Gandhi had given 'long hours' to British birth control advocate Edith Howe-Martyn, who, although she could not convince him, had reportedly said, 'but wait until Mrs Sanger talks to you.' See 'Gandhi and Sanger Debate Love, Lust and Birth Control', *The Margaret Sanger Papers Newsletter*, no.23, Winter 1999/2000, available on line at *www.nyu.edu/projects/sanger/gandhi_debate.htm*

54 The introductory paragraphs to Sanger's article in Cousins' book *Profiles of Gandhi*, note that 'Fortunately, Mrs. Sanger was accompanied by her secretary, who took down a verbatim account of the historic meeting. The following dialogue represents the interview exactly as it took place, in addition to a few introductory passages from Mrs Sanger's diary' (p.34).

55 For accounts of the interview, see Mahadev Desai, 'Mrs Sanger and Birth Control', *Harijan*, 25 January 1936 (in Gandhi's *Collected Works*, the interview appears under the title 'Interview to Margaret Sanger'); *Margaret Sanger Papers Newsletter*, 'Gandhi and Sanger Debate Love, Lust and Birth Control'; Sanger 'A Summit Meeting on Birth Control', pp.36-41; and Sanger, *An Autobiography*, pp.470-71.

56 Sanger, 'A Summit Meeting on Birth Control', p.36.

57 *Margaret Sanger Papers Newsletter*, 'Gandhi and Sanger Debate Love, Lust and Birth Control'.

58 Gandhi to Mathuradas Trikumji, 2 December 1935.

59 Gandhi to Mathuradas Trikumji, 6 December 1935.

60 Sanger, *An Autobiography*, p.470.

61 Sanger, *An Autobiography*, p.471; and Sanger 'A Summit Meeting on Birth Control', p.41.

62 'Discussion with Edith Howe-Martyn', *Harijan* 1 February 1935.

63 The article appeared to mock Gandhi for his 'appalling fear of licentiousness and over-indulgence' – and probably not unreasonably. Interestingly, the article was vetted by Muriel Lester before publication. See Desai, 'Mrs Sanger and Birth Control'.

64 Gandhi was open about the debate. A month after the report of the interview, his paper *Harijan* carried a rejoinder by Margaret Sanger in its 22 February 1936 issue. See Mahadev Desai, 'Weekly Letter'. There was some debate here about whether Desai had in fact gone further than the Mahatma had in the interview on this point. Desai rejected this pointing out that Gandhi was trying to see her point of view.

65 Martin Green, *Gandhi: Voice of a New Age Revolution*, New York: Continuum, 1993, p.336.

66 Green, *Gandhi*, p.336.

67 See Green, *Gandhi*, pp.273-85, and Girja Kumar, Brahmacharya, *Gandhi & His Women Associates*, New Delhi: Vitasta, 2006, pp.215-41.

68 'Birth-Control [1]', *Harijan*, 14 March 1936.

69 Gandhi to Margaret Sanger, 27 November 1936.

70 They were more interested in securing the vote than women's contraceptive issues which they felt would follow female suffrage.

71 The biographical details of Bourke-White's life come from her autobiography: Margaret Bourke-White, *Portrait of Myself*, New York: Simon and Schuster, 1963; and her leading biography: Vicki Goldberg, *Margaret Bourke-White: A Biography*, London: Heinemann, 1986.

72 Bourke-White, *Portrait of Myself*, p.11.

73 Margaret Bourke-White, *Halfway to Freedom*, New York: Simon and Schuster, 1949, p.12.

74 Bourke-White, *Halfway to Freedom*, p.12.

75 See Bourke-White, *Portrait of Myself*, pp.273-78; and Bourke-White, *Halfway to Freedom*, pp.83-86. Her writing on Gandhi were drawn together from these two sources and published as 'Mahatma Gandhi', in Will Yolen and Kenneth Seeman Giniger (eds.), *Heroes For Our Times*, Harrisburg, Pa.: Griniger, 1968, pp.88-109. A section from *Portrait of Myself* was published as 'The Last Days with Gandhi', in Norman Cousins (ed.), *Profiles of Gandhi: America Remembers a World Leader*, Delhi: Indian Book Company, 1970, pp.85-92.

76 Bourke-White, *Portrait of Myself*, p.278.

77 Goldberg, *Margaret Bourke-White*, p.308.

78 Bourke-White, *Portrait of Myself*, pp.272-73.

79 There appears to be some confusion as to the date of the final formal interview. Bourke-White insists that her interview with Gandhi occurred only a few hours before his assassination (see *Portrait of Myself*, p.297; and *Halfway to Freedom*, p.185), and this is backed up by Gandhi's secretary (see Pyarelal, *Mahatma Gandhi, Volume X: The Last Phase, Part III*, Ahmedabad: Navajivan, 1958, p.771). However, in Gandhi's *Collected Works* the date of the interview is given as 29 January, and the diary of Manu Gandhi, the Mahatma's closest associate during his last years of life, confirms this date (see Manu Gandhi, *Last Glimpses of Bapu*, Delhi: Shiva Lal Agarwala, 1962, p.284). Regardless of the mention of the 'few hours', Bourke-White herself provides this date in 'The Last Days with Gandhi', p.90 and *Halfway to Freedom*, p.178.

80 Bourke-White, *Halfway to Freedom*, p.179.

81 Bourke-White, *Portrait of Myself*, p.294. See also Bourke-White, *Halfway to Freedom*, pp.183-84.

82 Bourke-White, *Halfway to Freedom*, p.128. See also Bourke-White, *Portrait of Myself*, p.295.

83 Bourke-White, *Portrait of Myself*, p.295-96; and Bourke-White, *Halfway to Freedom*, p.184. For an account of the interview see 'Interview to Margaret Bourke-White', *Harijan*, 22 February 1948.

84 Bourke-White, *Portrait of Myself*, p.296-297. For a slightly different version, that of Gandhi's secretary, see Pyarelal, *Mahatma Gandhi,* volume X, pp.808-09.

85 Goldberg, *Margaret Bourke-White*, p.313.

86 Some reports have her attempting to pull off one of the photo-journalistic scoops of the century by producing a hidden camera to photograph Gandhi's body. Amid great indignation the film was removed from the camera and she was evicted from the building. See Goldberg, *Margaret Bourke-White*, p.313.

87 Goldberg, *Margaret Bourke-White*, p.309.

88 Goldberg, *Margaret Bourke-White*, p.313.

89 See Stephen Murphy, 'Constructing the Mahatma: The Evolution of Gandhi's Image in his Western Biographies, 1909-1954', unpublished Master of Arts dissertation, Department of Politics, La Trobe University, 1992.

**Western Women Disciples: Going Native**

1 Margaret MacMillan, *Women of the Raj*, n.p.: Thames and Hudson, 1988, p.200.

2 Mirabehn to Gandhi, 29 January 1929

3 MacMillan, *Women of the Raj*, p.210.

4 MacMillan, *Women of the Raj*, p.217.

5 Sudhir Kakar, *The Essential Writings of Sudhir Kakar*, New Delhi: Oxford University Press, 2001, p.243.

**Too Equal to be a Disciple: Millie Graham Polak**

1 See Thomas Weber, *Gandhi as Disciple and Mentor*, New Delhi: Cambridge University Press, 2007, pp.54-68.

2 'Talk with Mahadev Desai', 31 August 1917.

3 H.S.L. Polak,, 'Some South African Reminiscences', in Chandrashanker Shukla (ed.), *Incidents of Gandhiji's Life, by Fifty-Four Contributors*, Bombay: Vora, 1949, p.232.

4 Polak, 'Some South African Reminiscences', p.233; and Albert West, 'In the Early Days with Gandhi', *The Illustrated Weekly of India*, 3 October 1965, p.31.

5 Polak, 'Some South African Reminiscences', p.239.

6 M.K. Gandhi, *An Autobiography or The Story of My Experiments With Truth*, Ahmedabad: Navajivan, 1940, p.221; West, 'In the Early Days with Gandhi', p.33.

7 Gandhi, *An Autobiography*, p.225.

8 Gandhi, *An Autobiography*, p.227.

9 Millie Graham Polak, *Mr Gandhi: The Man*, London: Allen and Unwin, 1931, pp.17-18.

10 Gandhi to Millie Graham, 3 July 1905.

11 Gandhi, *An Autobiography*, p.227.

12 M.G. Polak, *Mr. Gandhi*, p.18.

13 Gandhi, *An Autobiography*, p.228.

14 See, John C. Vine, 'Interview with Mrs Millie Graham Polak', 2 May 1960, in S. Durai Raja Singam, 'They Were Ready to Talk About Gandhi', unpublished manuscript, (n.d.), p.17.

15 M.G. Polak, *Mr Gandhi*, p.23.

16 M.G. Polak, *Mr Gandhi*, pp.18-19.

17 M.G. Polak, *Mr Gandhi*, p.49.

18 Gandhi to H.S.L. Polak, 15 November 1909. See also, M.G. Polak, *Mr Gandhi*, pp.117-19.

19 M.G. Polak, *Mr Gandhi*, p.55.

20 This was the so-called 'Zulu Rebellion'. There was a large rebel encampment not far from the settlement and the tension of the situation began to affect the white settlers.

21 See Millie's account in Francis Watson and Hallam Tennyson, *Talking of Gandhi*, New Delhi: Sangam, 1976, pp.34-35.

22 M.G. Polak, *Mr Gandhi*, p.160.

23 M.G. Polak, *Mr Gandhi*, p.11.

24 M.G. Polak, *Mr Gandhi*, p.97.

25 M.G. Polak, *Mr Gandhi*, pp.44-46.

26 M.G. Polak, *Mr Gandhi*, p.98.

27 M.G. Polak, *Mr Gandhi*, p.109.

28 M.G. Polak, *Mr Gandhi*, p.100.

29 Gandhi to Millie Graham Polak, 14 November 1909.

30 See S. Durai Raja Singam, 'The Polaks and Gandhiji', *Indian Review* (1964), vol.63, May and June, p.175.

31 Vine, 'Interview with Mrs Millie Graham Polak', p.18.

32 Gandhi to Millie Graham Polak, 26 December 1909.

33 Gandhi to Millie Graham Polak, 31 December 1909.

34 Gandhi to Millie Graham Polak, no date.

35 H.S.L. Polak, 'Some South African Reminiscences', in Shukla, *Incidents of Gandhiji's Life*, p.246.

36 Polak, 'Some South African Reminiscences', pp.246-47; see also H.S.L. Polak, H.N. Brailsord and Lord Pethick-Lawrence, *Mahatma Gandhi*, London: Odhams Press, 1949, p.94; and M.G. Polak, *Mr Gandhi*, pp.168-72.

37 M.G. Polak, *Mr Gandhi*, p.172.

38 Homer A. Jack, 'Henry S.L. Polak', *Gandhi Marg* (1959), vol.3, no.4, p.291.

39 M.G. Polak, *Mr Gandhi*, p.174.

40 See Millie Graham Polak to Gandhi, 18/19 November 1918.

41 Gandhi to Millie Graham Polak, 16 January 1918.

42 Mahadev H. Desai, *Day-To-Day With Gandhi [Secretary's Diary]*, Rajghat, Varanasi: Sarva Seva Sangh, 1973, vol.1, p.242.

43 Millie Graham Polak to Gandhi, 7 December 1921.

**The First Disciples: The Danes Esther Færing and Anne Marie Petersen**

1 The biographical details of Esther Færing's life are based on Alice Barnes' 'Introduction', to Esther Færing's edited collection of Gandhi's letters to her: *'My Dear Child': Letters from M.K.Gandhi to Esther Færing*, Ahmedabad: Navajivan, 1956, pp.xii-xix; Tine Elisabeth Larsen, *Anne Marie Petersen: A Danish Woman in South India: A Missionary Story 1909-1951*, Chennai: Lutheran Heritage Archives, 2000, pp.27-43, 179-86; E.S.Reddy and Holger Terp (editors and publishers), 'The Danish Peace Academy: Gandhi and Nordic

Countries: Notes on People in Nordic Countries who Corresponded with Gandhi', available at *www.fredsakademiet.dk/library/nordic/bionotes.htm*; and E.S. Reddy and Holger Terp (eds), *Friends of Gandhi: The Correspondence of Mahatma Gandhi with Esther Færing, Anne Marie Petersen and Ellen Horup*, 2006, Berlin and Copenhagen: Gandhi-Informations-Zentrum and The Danish Peace Academy.

2 In the middle of 1917 the ashram relocated several miles upstream to a rural area, near Sabarmati Jail, where farming and orchards could be established. Færing and Petersen visited the proposed site when they were with Gandhi. See Færing to Gandhi, 20 May 1917.

3 Quoted in Larsen, *Anne Marie Petersen*, p.28.

4 Quoted in Reddy and Terp, 'The Danish Peace Academy: Gandhi and Nordic Countries: Introduction'. This is an English translation of the original Danish, and allowance needs to be made for this.

5 Gandhi to Esther Færing, 11 January 1917. See also Gandhi to Esther Færing 15 January 1917.

6 Quoted in Barnes, 'Introduction', p.xiv.

7 Gandhi to Esther Færing, 13 May 1917.

8 Esther Færing to Mahadev Desai, 24 March 1919.

9 Esther Færing to Gandhi, 22 June 1917.

10 Gandhi to Esther Færing, 15 April 1917.

11 See for example Gandhi to Esther Færing, 3 August 1917.

12 Gandhi to Esther Færing, 6 September 1917.

13 Gandhi to Esther Færing, 13 January 1918.

14 Esther Færing to Gandhi, 25 January 1919; and Gandhi to Esther Færing, 25 January 1919.

15 Quoted in Larsen, *Anne Marie Petersen*, p.32.

16 Gandhi to Esther Færing, 13 May 1917.

17 Gandhi to Esther Færing, 30 June 1917

18 Gandhi to Esther Færing, 12 December 1917.

19 Gandhi to Esther Færing, 22 July 1918.

20 Gandhi to Esther Færing, 22 July 1918.

21 See Gandhi to C.F. Andrews, 6 January 1919.

22 Esther Færing to Gandhi, 22 May 1919. She took the *swadeshi* vow on her 30th birthday 22 June 1919. See Esther Færing to Gandhi, 20 June 1919.

23 Gandhi to Esther Færing, 28 May 1919.

24 Esther Færing to Gandhi, 29 April 1919.

25 Esther Færing to Mahadev Desai, 4 May 1919.

26 Esther Færing to Gandhi, 20 June 1919.

27 Esther Færing to Gandhi, 30 June 1919.

28 See Esther Færing to Gandhi, 15 and 21 September 1919.

29 Esther Færing to Gandhi, 28 September 1919.

30 Gandhi to Esther Færing, 27 June 1919.

31 Esther Færing to Sundaram, n.d., forwarded by Sundaram to Gandhi, 22 August 1919.

32 See for example Gandhi to Esther Færing, 14, 16, 17, 18, 19, 21 and 22 March 1920.

33 Quoted in Larsen, *Anne Marie Petersen*, p.35. This is a clarification of the translation of the published letter, communication from Tine Elisabeth Larsen, 19 May 2005.

34 Quoted in Larsen, *Anne Marie Petersen*, p.36.

35 Gandhi to Esther Færing, 24 August 1919.

36 Esther Færing to Gandhi, 25 August 1919.

37 Emilie Bjerrum to Gandhi 2 October 1919.

38 See Esther Færing to Gandhi, 20 January 1920.

39 Gandhi to Esther Færing, 22 October 1919.

40 See Gandhi to Anne Marie Petersen 13 January 1920.

41 Gandhi to Esther Færing, 7 December 1919.

42 See Gandhi to Narahari Parikh, 31 January 1920; the two letters from Gandhi to Færing, 1 February 1920; and Gandhi to Maganlal Gandhi, 1 February 1920.

43 Stanley Wolpert, *Gandhi's Passion: The Life and Legacy of Mahatma Gandhi*, New York: Oxford University Press, 2001, p.104.

44 Gandhi to Esther Færing, 15 April 1920.

45 Gandhi to Esther Færing, 2 September 1920.

46 This seems to be a slip in her writing, or in the translation. It should read 1921.

47 Quoted in Larsen, *Anne Marie Petersen*, p.40.

48 Quoted in Larsen, *Anne Marie Petersen*, p.41. Their wishes would later come true when, on 6 June 1924, Kuhni Menon was baptised at Porto Novo.

49 Quoted in Larsen, *Anne Marie Petersen*, p.42.

50 Esther Menon to Gandhi, 30 September 1924.

51 Gandhi to Esther Menon, 5 October 1925.

52 Gandhi to Esther Menon, 26 March 1927.

53 Gandhi to Esther Menon, 11 November 1932.

54 See Gandhi to Esther Menon, after 25 February 1935.

55 Quoted in Reddy and Terp, *Friends of Gandhi*, p.35.

56 Named after the Danish philosopher and educator, Niels Frederik Severin Grundtvig who had founded the folk high school movement which added agricultural training and a study of current affairs to the normal educational curriculum.

57 This section is based on Larsen, *Anne Marie Petersen*; Reddy and Terp, 'The Danish Peace Academy: Gandhi and Nordic; and Reddy and Terp, *Friends of Gandhi*.

58 This was essential because even though Løventhal had been in India for forty years, he had never built a mission, church or school. He saw his calling as walking from village to village preaching the gospel in a way as to allow a church to come from the people when they were ready. See Larsen, *Anne Marie Petersen*, p.53.

59 Quoted in Larsen, *Anne Marie Petersen*, p.17.

60 Quoted in Larsen, *Anne Marie Petersen*, p.20.

61 Quoted in Larsen, *Anne Marie Petersen*, p.64.

62 Larsen, *Anne Marie Petersen*, p.67.

63 Quoted in Larsen, *Anne Marie Petersen*, p.69.

64 An article in Gandhi's Gujarati language paper the following day, seems to give at least the flavour of the speech, if not its exact text. See 'Courts and Schools', *Navajivan*, 15 August 1920.

65 Quoted in Larsen, *Anne Marie Petersen*, p.75.

66 Anne Marie Petersen to Gandhi, mid-August 1920.

67 'The Inwardness of Non-Cooperation', *Young India*, 8 September 1920.

68 Gandhi to Esther Færing, 2 September 1920.

69 Quoted in Larsen, *Anne Marie Petersen*, p.78.

70 Larsen, *Anne Marie Petersen*, p.87.

71 Larsen, *Anne Marie Petersen*, pp.105-106.

72 Quoted in Larsen, *Anne Marie Petersen*, p.119.

73 Quoted in Larsen, *Anne Marie Petersen*, pp.135-36.

74 Quoted in Larsen, *Anne Marie Petersen*, p.173.

75 Quoted in Larsen, *Anne Marie Petersen*, p.168.

76 Quoted in Larsen, *Anne Marie Petersen*, pp.179-80.

77 Anne Marie Petersen to Gandhi, 14 March 1933.

78 Gandhi to Esther Menon, 24 March 1933.

79 Gandhi to Mary Barr, 26 April 1933.

80 Larsen, *Anne Marie Petersen*, pp.195-96.

81 Quoted in Larsen, *Anne Marie Petersen*, p.196.

82 For a glimpse of what went on at the conference, see Marjorie Sykes, *The Story of Nai Talim: Fifty Years of Education at Sevagram 1937-1887*, Sevagram: Nai Talim Samiti, 1988, pp.42-44.

83 See Larsen, *Anne Marie Petersen*, pp.199-200.

84 Quoted in Larsen, *Anne Marie Petersen*, p.204.

85 Gandhi to Anne Marie Petersen, 23 August 1945.

86 Gandhi to Anne Marie Petersen, 23 August 1945.

87 Gandhi to Anne Marie Petersen, 2 October 1945.

88 Rajkumari Amrit Kaur to Anne Marie Petersen, 6 October 1945

89 Quoted in Larsen, *Anne Marie Petersen*, p.214.

90 Quoted in Larsen, *Anne Marie Petersen*, p.219.

91 See for example Gandhi to Esther Menon, 11 November 1932.

92 Esther Færing to Mahadev Desai, 23 April 1919.

93 Esther Færing to Gandhi, 29 April 1919.

94 Esther Færing to Mahadev Desai, 24 March 1919.

95 Esther Færing to Gandhi 20 January 1920.

96 Esther Færing to Gandhi, 14 August 1926.

97 See Gandhi to Esther Menon, 13 April 1932.

98 Gandhi had attempted to convince her that 'God and Christianity can be found also in institutions that do not call themselves Christian and that truth is the same in all religious [sic] though through refraction it appears for the time being variegated even as light does through a prism.' See Gandhi to Esther Færing, 7 December 1919. Some years later he added that he did not see any fundamental distinction between Jesus and other great teachers. He informed Esther that he could understand her exclusive position because of her upbringing. He added that while he had no desire to change her conviction, she should 'understand and appreciate the other inclusive position.' See Gandhi to Esther Menon, 17 September 1926.

99 Anne Marie Petersen to Gandhi, 29 January 1924.

100 Gandhi to Petersen, 16 August 1931. See also Gandhi to Mary Barr, 4 June 1932.

101 Anne Marie Petersen to Gandhi, 23 September 1924. See also Anne Marie Petersen to Gandhi, 15 January 1929, where she notes that 'it is only wasting your time and energy writing to you when I have nothing particularly to write about.'

102 Anne Marie Petersen to Gandhi, 24 September 1924.

103 See for example Anne Marie Petersen to Gandhi 15 January 1929.

104 See Anne Marie Gandhi to Petersen, 2 October 1945 and 16 October 1945.

105 Gandhi commented that, 'When you and Esther came to me, it was, I think, common between us that conversion from one faith to another was needless and created heart-burning.' Gandhi to Anne Marie Petersen, 16 October 1945.

**The Ultimate Disciple: Mirabehn**

1 Mira Behn [Madeleine Slade], *The Spirit's Pilgrimage*, London: Longmans, 1960.

2 Eleanor Morton, *The Women in Gandhi's Life*, New York: Dodd, Mead and Co., 1953.

3 Mirabehn (ed.), *Bapu's Letters to Mira [1924-1948]*, Ahmedabad: Navajivan, 1949.

4 See Mirabehn to Gandhi 15 May, and 3, 6 and 8 June 1927; and Gandhi to Mirabehn, 23 and 28 May, and 3 June1927.

5 See Gandhi to Mirabehn, 25 July and 14 August 1927.

6 Mirabehn to Gandhi 2 November 1928. See also Mirabehn to Gandhi 27 October 1928, and 15 November 1928.

7 See Gandhi to Mirabehn, 1 April 1929.

8 See Gandhi to Mirabehn, 24 March and 6 April 1933.

9 Mirabehn to Gandhi, 15 May 1927.

10 Mirabehn, 'His Daily Life', in Chandrashanker Shukla (ed.), *Incidents of Gandhiji's Life, by Fifty-Four Contributors*, Bombay: Vora, 1949, pp.186-187.

11 This biographical sketch comes from Mira Behn, *The Spirit's Pilgrimage*; Mirabehn, *Bapu's Letters to Mira*; 'Autobiographical Note' in Krishna Murti Gupta (ed.), *Mira Behn: Gandhi's Daughter Disciple: Birth Centenary Volume*, New Delhi: Himalaya Seva Sangh, 1992, pp.295-98; and Morton, *The Women in Gandhi's Life*.

12 Mira Behn, *The Spirit's Pilgrimage*, p.31.

13 Mirabehn, *Bapu's Letters to Mira*, p.3; and see also Mira Behn, *The Spirit's Pilgrimage*, p.58. For Rolland's view of the meeting, see 'Extract from Romain Rolland's Diary', *Romain Rolland and Gandhi Correspondence (Letters, Diary Extracts, Articles, Etc.)*, New Delhi: Publications Division, Ministry of Information and Broadcasting, Government of India, 1976, pp.46-47.

14 Mirabehn, *Bapu's Letters to Mira*, p.3.

15 Mirabehn, *Bapu's Letters to Mira*, p.4; and see also Mira Behn, *The Spirit's Pilgrimage*, p.60.

16 Gandhi to Mirabehn, 31 December 1924.

17 Mirabehn, *Bapu's Letters to Mira*, p.5.

18 Madeleine Slade to Gandhi, 29 May 1925.

19 Gandhi to Mirabehn, 24 July 1925.

20 Mirabehn, *Bapu's Letters to Mira*, p.5.

21 Mirabehn, *Bapu's Letters to Mira*, p.5.

22 Mirabehn, *Bapu's Letters to Mira*, p.6; and see also Mira Behn, *The Spirit's Pilgrimage*, p.66.

23 Mirabehn, 'The Blessings of Discipline', *Harijan*, 30 November 1947.

24 Mira Behn, *The Spirit's Pilgrimage*, p.69.

25 Mirabehn, 'How Bapuji Trained his Followers', *Bapu Raj Patrika*, June 1952, reproduced in Gupta, *Mira Behn*, p.285.

26 Madeleine Slade to Romain Rolland, 12 November 1925.

27 Gandhi to Romain Rolland, 13 November 1925.

28 See Gandhi to Nargis D.Captain, 9 February 1926.

29 Mahadev Desai, 'Miss Madeline Slade', quoted in Mahadev H.Desai, *Day-To-Day With Gandhi [Secretary's Diary]*, Rajghat, Varanasi: Sarva Seva Sangh, 1973, vol.8, pp.83-84. Some years later the English press were again reporting that Mirabehn had embraced Hinduism. Gandhi responded that she had not, and that hopefully 'she is a better Christian than when four years ago she came to the Ashram. She is not a girl of tender age. She is past thirty and has travelled all alone in Egypt, Persia and Europe befriending trees and animals. ...We have in the Ashram today several faiths represented. NO proselytising is practiced or permitted. ... Miss Slade bears not a Hindu name but an Indian name. And this was done at her instance and for convenience.' See 'Notes', *Young India*, 20 February 1930.

30 'Our Time a Trust!', *Young India*, 26 November 1925.

31 Mirabehn, *Bapu's Letters to Mira*, p.11.

32 Gandhi to Mirabehn, 4 December 1925.

33 Mirabehn, *Bapu's Letters to Mira*, p.12.

34 Gandhi to Mirabehn, 15 May 1926.

35 Mirabehn to Jamnalal Bajaj, 18 January 1926.

36 'Chi', short for chiranjiv ('long lived') is the usual Gujarati form of address in a letter to a child by a parent.

37 See for example Gandhi to Mirabehn, 11 December 1926.

38 See for example Gandhi to Mirabehn, 27 December 1926; and 14 January 1929.

39 Gandhi to Ashram Women, 20 December 1926.

40 Gandhi to Mirabehn, 23 March 1927.

41 Gandhi to Mirabehn, 4 April 1927.

42 Gandhi to Mirabehn, 25 April 1927.

43 Gandhi to Mirabehn, 12 May 1927.

44 Gandhi to Mirabehn, 27 April 1927.

45 Mirabehn, *Bapu's Letters to Mira*, p.45.

46 Mira Behn, *The Spirit's Pilgrimage*, p.88.

47 Mirabehn to Gandhi, 21 October 1928.

48 Gandhi to Mirabehn, 2 May 1927.

49 Gandhi to Mirabehn, 27 April 1927. Six years later he was still writing about the same issues. See Gandhi to Mirabehn, 3 June 1933.

50 Gandhi to Mirabehn, 8 May 1927.

51 Mirabehn, *Bapu's Letters to Mira*, p.41. This struggle was encapsulated in her letter to Gandhi, written on 4 May 1933, where she claimed that 'God will help me to bring the heart and intellect together.'

52 See Gandhi to Mirabehn, 8 May 1927.

53 See Gandhi to Mirabehn, 20 November 1929.

54 Mirabehn, *Bapu's Letters to Mira*, p.96.

55 Mirabehn to Gandhi, 1/2 November 1928.

56 Mirabehn to Gandhi, 15 November 1928.

57 As the Satyagraha ('truth force') Ashram at Sabarmati was renamed because of the failings of the ashramites.

58 Mirabehn to Gandhi, 18 November 1928.

59 Mirabehn to Gandhi, 11 January 1929.

60 Mirabehn to Gandhi, 19 January 1929.

61 Mirabehn to Narandas Gandhi 25 November 1929.

62 Mirabehn to Gandhi, 14 January 1929. Gandhi granted her request for the postcards, enabling her to 'live and work with a peace of mind, which I could not otherwise have succeeded in imposing upon myself. (Forgive me Bapu, I will ever strive to try and do better).' Mirabehn to Gandhi, 21 January 1929.

63 Gandhi to Mirabehn, 24 June 1929.

64 Mira Behn, *The Spirit's Pilgrimage*, p.92.

65 For a fictionalised account of the relationship that is based on reasonably solid research and maintains the ring of authenticity, see the book by Indian psychoanalyst and writer, Sudhir Kakar, *Mira and the Mahatma*, New Delhi: Penguin, 2004.

66 Romain Rolland to Marcel Martinet, 12 April 1928. Quoted in *Romain Rolland and Gandhi Correspondence*, p.412.

67 See Gandhi to Mirabehn, 23 March 1936.

68 Neither Gandhi nor other representatives of the Indian National Congress attended the first RoundTable Conference, held a year before from November 1930 to January 1931.

69 Gandhi to Mirabehn, 24 June 1931.

70 Agatha Harrison, 'Knightsbridge, London', in Chandrashanker Shukla (ed.), *Gandhiji as We Know Him, by Seventeen Contributors*, Bombay; Vora, 1945, p.90.

71 Mira Behn, *The Spirit's Pilgrimage*, pp.146-47.

72 See Mirabehn's letters to Gandhi in early May (for example the 8th, 11th, 12th, 14th and 15th)1933, during his fast.

73 Mirabehn to Gandhi, 29/30 April 1933.

74 Mirabehn to Gandhi, before 8 April 1932, quoted in Mahadev Desai, *The Diary of Mahadev Desai*, Navajivan: Ahmedabad, 1953, vol.1, p.63.

75 Gandhi to Mirabehn, 8 April 1932.

76 Gandhi to Premabehn Kantak, 25 February 1932.

77 Mirabehn to Gandhi, 4 May 1933.

78 Quoted in Morton, *The Women in Gandhi's Life*, p.202.

79 Mirabehn served 15 months in prison, nine in Arthur Road Gaol in Bombay and the rest in Sabarmati Central Gaol. For her own account of her jail experiences, see 'Arthur Road Prison', *Harijan*, 10 October 1933.

80 Mira Behn, *The Spirit's Pilgrimage*, p.183.

81 Gandhi to Vallabhbhai Patel, 25 June 1934.

82 Mira Behn, *The Spirit's Pilgrimage*, p.183.

83 Quoted in Morton, *The Women in Gandhi's Life*, p.218.

84 Gandhi, *Bapu's Letters to Mira*, p.273; Mahadev Desai, 'Weekly Notes: A Sanitation Campaign', *Harijan*, 15 March 1935.

85 Gandhi to Agatha Harrison, 25 April 1935.

86 Mark Thomson, *Gandhi and His Ashrams*, Bombay: Popular Prakashan, 1993, p.187.

87 Mira Behn, *The Spirit's Pilgrimage*, p.194.

88 Mira Behn, *The Spirit's Pilgrimage*, p.194; and Mirabehn, *Bapu's Letters to Mira*, p.275.

89 Mira Behn, *The Spirit's Pilgrimage*, p.194.

90 Mira Behn, *The Spirit's Pilgrimage*, p.197.

91 Mira Behn, *The Spirit's Pilgrimage*, p.198.

92 Mirabehn, *Bapu's Letters to Mira*, p.277.

93 Mira Behn, *The Spirit's Pilgrimage*, p.201.

94 Mirabehn, *Bapu's Letters to Mira*, p.277.

95 See Gandhi to Mirabehn, 13 and 14 February 1936.

96 Gandhi to Premabehn Kantak, 12 September 1936.

97 Gandhi to Mirabehn, 27 December 1938.

98 Mirabehn, *Bapu's Letters to Mira*, p.310.

99 Mirabehn, *Bapu's Letters to Mira*, p.317.

100 Gandhi to Mirabehn, 9 February 1940.

101 Gandhi to Mirabehn, 18 May 1940.

102 For Prithvi Singh's story, see 'Statement to the Press', *Harijan* 28 May 1938; 'The Old Revolutionary', *Harijan*, 30 September 1939; Kakar, *Mira and the Mahatma*, pp.221-27; and Prithvi Singh, *Baba Prithvi Singh Azad, the Legendary Crusader: An Autobiography*, Bombay: Bharatiya Vidya Bhavan, 1987.

103 Mira Behn, *The Spirit's Pilgrimage*, p.216.

104 See Mirabehn's two letters to Prithvi Singh, both written 11 November 1939, quoted in Kakar, *Mira and the Mahatma*, pp.236-37; and her letters to him dated 18 November 1939 and 19 January 1941, quoted in Singh, *Baba Prithvi Singh Azad*, pp.330-31, 336.

105 Mirabehn to Singh, 11 November 1939, quoted in Kakar, *Mira and the Mahatma*, p.237.

106 In fact, later Singh recalled explaining to Gandhi in quite blunt terms that while he was not averse to the idea of marriage, it would be to a young woman and not 'a lady who would want to make me her slave for the fulfilment of her sexual urge.' Singh, *Baba Prithvi Singh Azad*, p.236.

107 Singh, *Baba Prithvi Singh Azad*, p.231.

108 Gandhi to Nrisinhprasad K.Bhatt, 9 August 1940.

109 Gandhi to Prithvi Singh, 8 March 1941.

110 Gandhi to Prithvi Singh,12 March 1941.

111 Mirabehn, *Bapu's Letters to Mira*, p.321. See also Mira Behn, *The Spirit's Pilgrimage*, p.219.

112 Mirabehn to Prithvi Singh, no date, quoted in Singh, *Baba Prithvi Singh Azad*, pp.333-35, at p.333.

113 Gandhi to Vallabhbhai Patel, 23 May 1942.

114 See 'Sardar Prithvi Singh', *Harijan* 7 June 1942. For Singh's account of this loss of faith, see Singh, *Baba Prithvi Singh Azad*, pp.253-54

115 See her love letters to Prithvi Singh, and his distancing responses in Singh, *Baba Prithvi Singh Azad*, pp.235-39; Kakar, *Mira and the Mahatma*, pp.251-58; and Girja Kumar, *Brahmacharya, Gandhi & His Women Associates*, New Delhi: Vitasta, 2006, p185.

116 Gandhi to Prithvi Singh, 23 June 1944. On Singh's version of his attraction to women and his marriage, see Singh, *Baba Prithvi Singh Azad*, pp.261-67.

117 Gandhi to Mirabehn, 11 June 1944.

118 Gandhi to Mirabehn, 1 January 1946.

119 See Gandhi to Mirabehn, 11 June 1944; and Gandhi to Rameshwardas Birla, 12 August 1944.

120 See Mirabehn to Gandhi, 12 June 1944. Included as an appendix to the relevant volume of the *CWMG.*

121 Gandhi to Mirabehn, 11 June 1944.

122 Gandhi to Mirabehn, 6 June 1944.

123 See Gandhi to Mirabehn, 12 and 14 June 1944.

124 Gandhi to Mirabehn, 18 July 1944.

125 Mira Behn, *The Spirit's Pilgrimage*, p.209.

126 Mira Behn, *The Spirit's Pilgrimage*, p.290.

127 Mirabehn, *Bapu's Letters to Mira*, p.366.

128 Mira Behn, *The Spirit's Pilgrimage*, p.293.

129 Gupta, *Mira Behn*, pp.21-22.

130 A.N.Seth, 'Mira Behn – Some Reminiscences', in Gupta, *Mira Behn*, pp.257-59, at p.258.

131 Mirabehn, *Bapu's Letters to Mira*, pp.6-7.

132 Mirabehn, *Bapu's Letters to Mira*, p.6.

133 Rosetta Splat, 'Retracing Mira Behn's Path', in Gupta, *Mira Behn*, p.229.

134 Mira Behn, *The Spirit's Pilgrimage*, p.314. This is not to say that this final period of her Indian sojourn did not involve important contributions on her part. During her time in the mountains she did remarkable and ground-breaking (and much before its time) work trying to push governments to protect the Himalayan environment. She wrote about the degradation of nature and the dangers of nuclear power. But at the time no one was listening. Later Sunderlal Bahuguna, one of the leading figures of the celebrated Indian environment-protecting, tree-hugging Chipko movement did. See Thomas Weber, *Hugging the Trees: The Story of the Chipko Movement*, New Delhi: Penguin, 1989, pp.25-29.

135 Mira Behn, *The Spirit's Pilgrimage*, p.316.

136 Mira Behn, 'Author's Note' in Mira Behn, *The Spirit's Pilgrimage*, p.7. For her life in Austria see Gupta, *Mira Behn*, pp.18-30, 33-38; and the recollections of friends and helpers in Gupta, *Mira Behn*, pp.225-67. For a less than sympathetic account of her life there, see Ved Mehta, *Mahatma Gandhi and His Apostles*, London: Andre Deutsch, 1976, pp.223-29.

## The Difficult Disciples: Nilla Cram Cook and Margarete Spiegel

1 For the life of George Cram Cook, see Susan Glaspell, *The Road to the Temple*, London: Ernst Benn, 1926; and Allen Churchill, *The Improper Bohemians: A Re-creation of Greenwich Village in Its Heyday*, London: Cassell, 1959, pp.190-218.

2 Upton Sinclair, *Money Writes!*, New York: Albert and Charles Boni, 1927, p.169.

3 Albert Parry, *Garrets and Pretenders: A History of Bohemianism in America*, New York: Dover, 1960, p.301.

4 Floyd Dell, *Homecoming: An Autobiography*, Port Washington, N.Y.: Kennikat, 1969, pp.171-72.

5 Dell, *Homecoming*, p.173.

6 Dell, *Homecoming*, p.174.

7 Dell, *Homecoming*, p.255.

8 Nilla Cram Cook to Gandhi, 25 November 1932.

9 For Nilla's account of her life, see Nilla Cram Cook, *My Road to India*, New York: Lee Furman, 1939. She gives her age at the time of her marriage as sixteen at p.56.

10 Cook, *My Road to India*, p.104.

11 Cook, *My Road to India*, p.105.

12 Parry, *Garrets and Pretenders*, p.348. The temple fine incident seems to be a figment of the imagination of the American press that relished making up stories about Nilla, including one that she had been baptised by Gandhi in the river Ganges long before she had met the Mahatma, accompanied by pictures of the event showing her in white robes that had actually been taken years earlier in Greece. See Cook, *My Road to India*, pp.189 and 218-19.

13 Martin, Green, *Gandhi: Voice of a New Age Revolution*, New York: Continuum, 1993, p.331.

14 Nilla Cram Cook to Gandhi, 5 June 1933.

15 Cook, *My Road to India*, p.307. In a letter to Gandhi she noted that while her father 'died from drinking excessive wine', she had a weakness for emotional intoxicants. See Nilla Cram Cook to Gandhi, 21 March 1933.

16 Harl Cook to Nilla Cram Cook, 23 March 1933.

17 Nilla Cram Cook to Gandhi, 25 November 1932.

18 Nilla Cram Cook to Gandhi, 11 December 1932.

19 Nilla Cram Cook to Gandhi, 23 December 1932.

20 Nilla Cram Cook to Gandhi, 6 January 1933.

21 Nilla Cram Cook to Gandhi, 14 January 1933.

22 Gandhi to Mirza Muhammad Ismail, 9 March 1933.

23 And there were many letters. From the time of her first letters to Gandhi, until she joined him in Ahmedabad in mid-July, Nilla Cram Cook produced an output of letters that would have done Mirabehn proud. Gandhi had asked her to write daily (see Gandhi to Narandas Gandhi, 6 May 1933) so that he

could keep check on her progress and, although she did not comply strictly, in that half year there is a record of forty-five letters from her to Gandhi.

24 Gandhi to Nilla Cram Cook, 18 January 1933. In the versions of the letters reproduced in Gandhi's *Collected Works*, Nilla (or Nila [blue] as he wrote it) is generally only given as N. and Sirios is given as S.

25 P. Kodanda Rao, 'As I Knew Him', in Chandrashanker Shukla (ed.), *Incidents of Gandhiji's Life, by Fifty-Four Contributors*, Bombay: Vora, 1949, p.112.

26 'A Confession and a Warning', *Harijan*, 6 May 1933.

27 Nilla Cram Cook to Gandhi, 9 February 1933.

28 Gandhi to Nilla Cram Cook, 12 February 1933. After her return south from Poona, she wrote to Gandhi, this time addressed to 'My Revered Father'. It appears that again there was something peculiar in her untraceable letter of 4 March: 'First I must say that the signature on my last letter to you ... must have made you despair of all the time you have given me! It seems as though the male being a superior species I was posing as a male!' Nilla Cram Cook to Gandhi, 8 March 1933.

29 See Gandhi to Shantivijayji, 24 February 1933.

30 Rao, 'As I Knew Him', p.113.

31 See Mahadev Desai, *Mahadevbhai ni Diary*, vol.3, Ahmedabad: Gandhi Smarak Sangrahalaya, 1993, pp.170-71.

32 Desai, *Mahadevbhai ni Diary*, pp.173-74.

33 See, for example, Gandhi to Mirza Ismail, 24 February 1933; Gandhi to Ramachandra, 24 February 1933; and Gandhi to K.Ramachandra, 3 March 1933.

34 Ramachandra to Gandhi, 4 March 1933.

35 Gandhi to Ramachandra, 7 March 1933.

36 Gandhi to Mirza Muhammad Ismail, 9 March 1933.

37 Gandhi to Nilla Cram Cook, 9 March 1933.

38 Gandhi to Nilla Cram Cook, 17 March 1933.

39 Gandhi to Ramaswami, 18 March 1933. Ramaswami denied ever broaching the subject of spiritual or any other type of marriage with Nilla, adding that in his twenty-three years he had 'not wasted one drop of seminal fluid on any woman', that their physical relationship was confined to kissing with 'not the slightest lust motive behind it.' See Ramaswami to Gandhi, 23 and 24 March 1933. Nilla implies otherwise, see Nilla Cram Cook to Gandhi 25 March 1933.

40 Nilla Cram Cook to Gandhi, 14 March 1933.

41 Desai, *Mahadevbhai ni Diary*, p.198.

42 Nilla Cram Cook to Gandhi, 20, 25, and 26 March 1933.

43 Nilla Cram Cook to Gandhi, 23 March 1933.

44 Nilla Cram Cook to Gandhi, 19 March 1933.

45 For details of her relationship with Rudramani and of her various residences, see Rudramani to Gandhi, 17 April 1933.

46 Nilla Cram Cook to Gandhi, 21 March 1933.

47 Gandhi to Nilla Cram Cook, 23/24 March 1933.

48 Gandhi to Nilla Cram Cook, 24 March 1933.

49 Gandhi to Nilla Cram Cook, 31 March 1933.

50 Gandhi to Nilla Cram Cook, 29 March 1933.

51 Gandhi to Nilla Cram Cook, 6 April 1933.

52 Gandhi to Nilla Cram Cook, 10 April 1933.

53 Nilla Cram Cook to Gandhi, 7 April 1933.

54 Gandhi to Nilla Cram Cook, 12 April 1933.

55 Gandhi to Sirios Cram Cook, 12 April 1933.

56 Nilla Cram Cook to Gandhi, 13 April 1933. The same sentiments were expressed by a Gandhi trustee who had visited her. See B.K. Rama Chandra Rao to Gandhi, 13 April 1933.

57 Nilla Cram Cook to Gandhi, 17 April 1933.

58 Nilla Cram Cook to Gandhi, 18 April 1933.

59 Ramachandra to Gandhi, 20 April 1933.

60 See Gandhi to Nilla Cram Cook, 18 April 1933; Gandhi to B.K. Ramachandra Rao, 18 April 1933; and Gandhi to Ramachandra, 23 April 1933.

61 Gandhi to Ramachandra, 23 April 1933.

62 Nilla Cram Cook to Gandhi, 15 April 1933. About a month earlier, Ramachandra had already written to Gandhi about Nilla's hard pressed Indian creditors. See Ramachandra to Gandhi, 11 March 1933.

63 It appears that Mirza Ishmail prevented the *Daily Post* from publishing anything about or by Nilla. See Nilla Cram Cook to Gandhi, 8 March 1933. This is possibly because it appears that he was also a sexual partner of Nilla's. See Nilla Cram Cook to Gandhi, 25 March 1933.

64 Nilla Cram Cook to Gandhi, 24 April 1933.

65 Desai, *Mahadevbhai ni Diary*, p.240.

66 Gandhi to Narandas Gandhi, 28 April 1933.

67 Gandhi to Premabehn Kantak, 23 April 1933.

68 Gandhi to Narandas Gandhi, 29 April 1933.

69 Gandhi to Premabehn Kantak, 7 May 1933.

70 Desai, *Mahadevbhai ni Diary*, p.255. Gandhi was released from jail immediately he commenced his fast on 8 May, however he remained in Poona and continued to fast for the full twenty-one days.

71 Gandhi to Narandas Gandhi, 3 May 1933. Spiegel certainly thought that the blame for the fast lay with Nilla: 'Bapu fasted for three weeks for Neela's sins, saying officially that it was for "self-purification".' She believed that the fast was useless as Nilla was unredeemable. See Margarete Spiegel, 'My Recollections of Mahatma Gandhi', *Indo Asia:Vierteljahreshefte fur Politik, Kultur und Wirtschaft Indiens* (1968), vol.10, no.4, p.365; and also Rao, 'As I Knew Him', p.114.

72 'Statement on Fast', *Harijan* 6 May 1933.

73 Sushila Nayar, *Mahatma Gandhi, volume VII: Preparing for Swaraj*, Ahmedabad: Navajivan, 1996, p.113.

74 Duncan Greenlees, who was staying at the Sabarmati Ashram, reported that 'Only *one* girl has turned up; was the other lost in transit or does she continue her threatened 'satyagraha' at your bedside?' See Duncan Greenlees to Gandhi, 5 May 1933.

75 Nilla Cram Cook to Gandhi, 6 May 1933.

76 Gandhi to Narandas Gandhi, 8 May 1933. For Gandhi's thoughts on the priest see Gandhi to P.S. Rudramani, 23 April 1933.

77 By Western reckoning Nilla was twenty-three at this time and she gives her age of marriage as sixteen. In India, following a birthday an age has been completed and the person is in their next year, so Nilla would have been twenty-three complete and in her twenty-fourth year.

78 'Confession and a Warning', *Harijan*, 6 May 1933.

79 Nilla Cram Cook to Gandhi, 2 May 1933.

80 See Nilla Cram Cook to Gandhi, 2, 3, and 4 May 1933.

81 Nilla Cram Cook to Gandhi, 7 and 13 May 1933. For a description of the ashram and its daily routine at this time, see Duncan Greenlees, *Gandhi Ashram*, Phalghat (Kerala): Scholar Press, 1934.

82 Nilla Cram Cook to Gandhi, 5 May 1933. See also her letter to Gandhi 12 May; and Gandhi's warning to Sharma, who excited Nilla's 'animal passion', Gandhi to Hiralal Sharma, 9 May 1933.

83 Nilla Cram Cook to Gandhi, 14 May 1933.

84 Nilla Cram Cook to Gandhi, 21 May 1933.

85 Gandhi to Narandas Gandhi, 7 May 1933.

86 Gandhi to Narandas Gandhi, 8 May 1933.

87 Gandhi to Nilla Cram Cook, 9 May 1933.

88 Gandhi to Nilla Cram Cook, 10 May 1933.

89 Gandhi to Narandas Gandhi, 7 May 1933.

90 Nilla Cram Cook to Gandhi, 11 May 1933.

91 See Gandhi to Nilla Cram Cook, 9 June 1933; 20 June 1933; 30 June 1933; and 4 July, 1933; and Cook, *My Road to India*, pp.361-74.

92 Nilla Cram Cook to Gandhi, 11 May 1933.

93 Nilla Cram Cook to Gandhi, 14 May 1933.

94 Duncan Greenlees informs us that at this time the ashramites stood guard duty at night, two at a time, for three and a half-hour stints because of 'the nearness of a camp of 'thieves', who occasionally raided us and stole away our few possessions.' See Greenlees, *Gandhi Ashram*, p.20.

95 Nilla Cram Cook to Gandhi, 16 May 1933.

96 Nilla Cram Cook to Gandhi, 16 May 1933.

97 Nilla Cram Cook to Gandhi, 14 May 1933.

98 Nilla Cram Cook to Gandhi, 23 May 1933.

99 Nilla Cram Cook to Gandhi, 19 May 1933.

100 Nilla Cram Cook to Gandhi, 3 July 1933.

101 Nilla Cram Cook to Gandhi, 5/7 May 1933.

102 Gandhi to Nilla Cram Cook, 5 July 1933.

103 For the history of the disbandment of the ashram, see Thomas Weber, *On the Salt March: The Historiography of Gandhi's March to Dandi*, New Delhi: HarperCollins, 1997, pp.501-7; and for some of the possible deeper reasons for the abandonment of his home of thirteen years, see Thomas Weber, *Gandhi as Disciple and Mentor*, New Delhi: Cambridge University Press, 2007, pp.84-101.

104 Gandhi to Jamnalal Bajaj, 22 July 1933.

105 Gandhi to Mary Barr, 28 September 1933.

106 F.Mary Barr, *Bapu: Conversations and Correspondence with Mahatma Gandhi*, (Second Edition) Bombay: International Book House, n.d., pp.54-55.

107 Gandhi to Mary Barr, 29 September 1933.

108 Mary Barr, *Bapu*, p.55.

109 Cook, *My Road to India*, pp.388-92.

110 Gandhi to Vallabhbhai Patel, 24 September 1933.

111 Gandhi to Jamnalal Bajaj, before 4 September 1933.

112 Gandhi to Amritlal V. Thakkar, 12 October 1933.

113 *Amrita Bazar Patrika,* 18 October 1933.

114 Gandhi to Amritlal V. Thakkar, 20 October 1933.

115 Gandhi to Amritlal V. Thakkar, 25 October 1933.

116 Gandhi to Amritlal V. Thakkar, 27 October 1933.

117 'A Tragedy', *Harijan*, 27 October 1933.

118 When Nilla was taken from her side at her hospital bed, the ill Mary Barr asked Gandhi to send Mirabehn in her place. Gandhi replied that 'I am not sending Mira because she has to give nearly four hours daily to Amala. She is wasting her time.' Gandhi to Mary Barr, 29 September 1933.

119 Mira Behn [Madeleine Slade], *The Spirit's Pilgrimage*, London: Longmans, 1960, pp.179-80.

120 'India Runaway Disciple', *Time*, 11 December 1933, p.24. How much was exaggeration we do not know. She did not mention the incident in the autobiography of her India days. In any case, it seems that she was just too good as copy even for respectable weeklies. The article continued with her claiming that: 'I don't care what others say. My heart is leaping for thrills. I want speed. I want to fly. I want to attend orchestra dances. ... One day Gandhi stated that he had not put a fence around the cantonment and any girl could leave, so I took the hint. ... I have written to Gandhi fully concerning my change of heart including the flutter caused in meeting a man with beautiful eyes and brows.'

121 Gandhi to Nilla Cram Cook, 21 January 1941.

122 Gandhi to Sushila Nayar, 10 September 1941.

123 See Nilla Cram Cook, 'The Theater and Ballet Arts of Iran', *The Middle East Journal* (1949), vol.3, no.4, pp.406-20.

124 'Comings and Goings', *Time*, 20 February 1950.

125 See Nilla Cram Cook's obituary in the *New York Times* on 13 October 1982; and 'Cook, Nilla Cram: Wanderer Cook loved adventure', *Des Moines Register*, 21 March 2007.

126 See the *Spiegel Papers*, in the Nehru Memorial Museum Library in New Delhi.

127 Margarete Spiegel, 'How he Taught Through Letters', in Chandrashanker Shukla (ed.), *Reminiscences of Gandhiji, by Forty-Eight Contributors*, Bombay: Vora, 1951, pp.212-16; and Spiegel, 'My Recollections of Mahatma Gandhi'.

128 What there is has been used in Johannes H. Voigt, 'Under the Spell of the Mahatma: Dr Margarete Spiegel', in Anil Bhatti and Johannes H. Voigt (eds), *Jewish Exile in India: 1933-1945*, New Delhi: Manohar, 2005, pp.150-60.

129 Nayar, *Mahatma Gandhi, volume VII: Preparing for Swaraj*, p.112.

130 See Gandhi to Narandas Gandhi, 19 December 1932.

131 Spiegel, 'My Recollections of Mahatma Gandhi', p.363.

132 Gandhi to Margarete Spiegel, 12 January 1933.

133 Gandhi to Margarete Spiegel, 14 January 1933.

134 Gandhi to Margarete Spiegel, 17 February 1933.

135 Margarete Spiegel to Gandhi, 27 February 1933.

136 Gandhi to Margarete Spiegel, 2 March 1933.

137 Gandhi to Margarete Spiegel, 17 March 1933.

138 Margarete Spiegel to Gandhi, 27 February 1933.

139 Gandhi to Margarete Spiegel, 13 April 1933.

140 Gandhi to Narandas Gandhi, 25 April 1933.

141 Cook, *My Road to India*, p.369.

142 Spiegel, 'My Recollections of Mahatma Gandhi', pp.363, 365.

143 Desai, *Mahadevbhai ni Diary*, p.254.

144 Spiegel, 'My Recollections of Mahatma Gandhi', p.365.

145 Nilla Cram Cook to Gandhi, 19 May 1933.

146 See Nilla Cram Cook to Gandhi, 16, 19 and 21 May 1933.

147 Desai, *Mahadevbhai ni Diary*, p.254.

148 Margarete Spiegel, 'Testament of Dr Margarete Spiegel', Poona, Servants of India Society, 2 May 1933. *Spiegel Papers*, in the Nehru Memorial Museum Library in New Delhi.

149 Gandhi to Narandas Gandhi, 29 April 1933.

150 Gandhi to Narandas Gandhi, 3 May 1933.

151 Rao, 'As I Knew Him', p.114.

152 Gandhi to Narandas Gandhi, 8 May 1933.

153 Margarete Spiegel to Gandhi, 15 May 1933.

154 Margarete Spiegel to Gandhi, 16 May 1933.

155 Quoted in Voigt, 'Under the Spell of the Mahatma', p.154.

156 Gandhi to Margarete Spiegel, 6 June 1933.

157 Gandhi to Margarete Spiegel, 9 June 1933.

158 Gandhi to Mirabehn, 7 June 1933.

159 Gandhi to Mirabehn, 16 August 1934.

160 Gandhi to Margarete Spiegel, 22 June 1933.

161 Gandhi to Vinoba Bhave, 7 July 1933.

162 Gandhi to Margarete Spiegel, 1 August 1933.

163 Gandhi to Margarete Spiegel, 16 September 1933.

164 Gandhi to Margarete Spiegel, 1 December 1933.

165 Gandhi to Margarete Spiegel, 7/9 December 1933.

166 See Gandhi to Margarete Spiegel, 2 and 15 December 1933; and 2 February 1934.

167 Gandhi to Parikshitlal L. Majumdar, 23 January 1934.

168 See Gandhi to Margarete Spiegel, 22 and 30 June 1933.

169 Gandhi to Margarete Spiegel, 28 February 1934.

170 Gandhi to Margarete Spiegel, 29 March 1934.

171 Gandhi to Margarete Spiegel, 4 June 1934.

172 Gandhi to Margarete Spiegel, 9 July 1934.

173 Gandhi to Margarete Spiegel, 14 July 1934.

174 Gandhi to Puratan J. Buch, 9 July 1934.

175 Gandhi to Margarete Spiegel, 20 July 1934.

176 Gandhi to Margarete Spiegel, 20 July 1934.

177 Chandulal Bhagubhai Dalal, *Harilal Gandhi: A Life* (Tridip Suhrud ed. and trans.), Chennai: Orient Longman, 2007, p.95.

178 Dalal, *Harilal Gandhi*, p.95.

179 Harilal Gandhi to Balibehn (Jivibehn Vora), 17 April 1933; quoted in Nilam Parikh, *Gandhiji's Lost Jewel: Harilal Gandhi*, New Delhi: National Gandhi Museum, 2001, p.163.

180 Gandhi to Harilal Gandhi, 19 September 1934.

181 Gandhi to Narandas Gandhi, 8 September 1934.

182 Gandhi to Narandas Gandhi, 5 May 1935.

183 Gandhi to Harilal Gandhi, 12 April 1935. The latter section is quoted in Parikh, *Gandhiji's Lost Jewel*, p.77.

184 There were opportunities: they were both in Poona visiting Gandhi on 14 and 15 May 1933; and their paths may have crossed at the Sabarmati Ashram in July 1934. See Dalal, *Harilal Gandhi*, pp.94-95.

185 Gandhi to Harilal Gandhi, 22 April 1935.

186 Harilal's life was soon again in a mess. His business ventures failed, he relapsed into alcoholism and debt, temporarily converted to Islam, railed publicly against Gandhi, turned up drunk at his mother's deathbed, and died, ill, in poverty and alone at the age sixty, half a year after Gandhi's assassination.

187 Gandhi to Margarete Spiegel, 9 April 1936.

188 Gandhi to Margarete Spiegel, 5 and 12 December 1938.

189 Gandhi to Margarete Spiegel, 15 November 1940.

190 Gandhi to Margarete Spiegel, 15 August 1946.

191 Voigt, 'Under the Spell of the Mahatma', p.158.

192 Gandhi to Margarete Spiegel, 4 October 1947.

193 Cook, *My Road to India*, p.381.

194 Green, *Gandhi*, p.331.

195 See 'Hindu-Muslim Unity', *Young India*, 16 June 1927.

196 Cook, *My Road to India*, p.403.

197 See Nilla Cram Cook to Gandhi, 28 March 1933.

198 See Nilla Cram Cook to Gandhi, 21 May 1933.

199 Nilla Cram Cook to Gandhi, 6 May 1933.

200 Spiegel, 'My Recollections of Mahatma Gandhi', p.367.

**The Ideal Disciples: Mary Barr and The Khedi Workers**

1 Gandhi to Margarete Spiegel, 29 March 1934.

2 K.G. Mashruwala, 'Foreword' to F. Mary Barr, *Bapu: Conversations and Correspondence with Mahatma Gandhi* (Second Edition), Bombay: International Book House, n.d., p.v.

3 Barr, *Bapu*, p.1.

4 Barr, *Bapu*, p.6.

5 Barr, *Bapu*, p.15.

6 Gandhi to Mary Barr, 30 November 1932.

7 Barr, *Bapu*, p.23.

8 Barr, *Bapu*, p.26.

9 Gandhi to Mary Barr, 17 January 1933.

10 Gandhi to Mary Barr, 26 January 1933.

11 Gandhi to Mary Barr, 12 February 1933.

12 Gandhi to Mary Barr, 8 April 1933.

13 Gandhi to Mary Barr, 26 April 1933.

14 Gandhi to Mary Barr, 7 May 1933.

15 Quoted in Barr, *Bapu*, p.46.

16 Barr, *Bapu*, p.51.

17 See Gandhi to Mary Barr, 5 March 1933.

18 Barr, *Bapu*, p.52.

19 Barr, *Bapu*, p.75.

20 Barr, *Bapu*, p.106.

21 See Mahadev Desai, 'Tarabehn Chesley', *Harijan*, 1 August 1936; and 'Notes: A Villager's Humanity', *Harijan*, 18 July 1936.

22 Barr, *Bapu*, p.125.

23 Barr, *Bapu*, pp.126-27.

24 Mahadev Desai to Mary Barr, 17 February 1935.

25 Gandhi to Mary Barr, 17 March 1935.

26 The letter is reproduced in the newspaper *Harijan* but not in the *CWMG*, where only Gandhi's reflections on it are printed.

27 'Well Begun', *Harijan*, 8 March 1935.

28 Mahadev Desai to Mary Barr, 4 May 1935; Barr, *Bapu*, p.144.

29 Barr, *Bapu*, p.144. See also Gandhi to Mary Barr, 26 April, 9, 16 and 24 May 1935.

30 Barr, *Bapu*, p.151.

31 Miss P. Blythe was Chesley's friend in London and Gandhi wrote to her at length about the fate of Mary Chesley. See Gandhi to Mary Barr, 24 May 1936.

32 Gandhi to Mary Barr, 15 May 1936.

33 The details of the final trip of Mary Chesley come from Mahadevi Omma's note, 'Concerning Mary Chesley (Tarabehn)', which was sent to her relatives in Canada; and Mahadev Desai, 'Weekly Letter: Tarabehn Chesley', *Harijan*, 30 May 1936. I thank Sharon MacDonald for sharing Mahadevi Omma's letter with me. A newspaper story, 'The Passing of Miss Mary Chesley in India', based on the letter, appeared in the *Bridgewater Bulletin*, 4 November, 1936.

34 'In Memoriam', *Harijan*, 23 May 1936.

35 Gandhi to Mirabehn, 21 May 1936; and Gandhi to Jamnalal Bajaj, 21 May 1936.

36 'Discussion with Dr Erika Rosenthal', *Harijan*, 6 June 1936.

37 See Gandhi to Mary Barr, 7 June 1936.

38 'Notes: About Tarabehn Mary Chesley', *Harijan*, 19 September 1936.

39 'Mahatma Gandhi of India, Local Property Owner', *Bridgewater Bulletin*, 16 September 1936.

40 Pearl Madden to Gandhi, 8 October 1924.

41 Barr, *Bapu*, p.152.

42 Barr, *Bapu*, p.153.

43 Gandhi to Mary Barr, 15 May 1936.

44 Gandhi to Mary Barr, 24 May 1936. Unfortunately Barr's letter about Pearl Madden has not been preserved. We know very little about her beyond what appears in Barr's book.

45 Quoted in Barr, *Bapu*, pp.154-55.

46 See Gandhi to Mary Barr, 20 November 1936.

47 Mahadev Desai to Mary Barr, 14 August 1936. See also Gandhi to Mary Barr, 20 November 1936.

48 Barr, *Bapu*, pp.172.

49 Barr, *Bapu*, pp.173.

50 Gandhi to Mary Barr, 7 January 1939.

51 Gandhi to Mary Barr, 4 July 1939.

52 Barr, *Bapu*, pp.179-83.

53 Gandhi asked Manilal to keep in touch with her, noting that she was a 'fine woman' who had 'done excellent work here.' Gandhi to Manilal and Shushila Gandhi, 19 July 1940.

54 Quoted in Barr, *Bapu*, p.206.

55 Barr, *Bapu*, p.191.

56 Quoted in Barr, *Bapu*, pp.191-92.

57 Letter to Mary Barr, 26 September 1946, quoted in Bar, *Bapu*, p.221.

58 Bar, *Bapu*, p.221.

59 Mary was not the only family member who 'went native'. Her younger sister Margaret was a member of a small English group known as the Friends of India. She first met Gandhi on an India visit in 1933 when she was on route to Calcutta to take up a teaching position. He told her that she should be doing village work. She worked in a town for many years, until after a few months in Sevagram in 1948 she finally handed her school over to the government and started her own village school which later became the Kharang Rural Centre in the Khasi Hills of what is now Meghalaya state. See Margaret Barr, 'A Gandhi Centre in the Hills', in G. Ramachandran and T.K. Mahadevan (eds), *Gandhi: His Relevance for our Times*, New Delhi: Gandhi Peace Foundation, 1964, pp.230-37.

60 Barr, *Bapu*, pp.107-8.

### Other European Disciples: Antoinette Mirbel, Franisca Standenath and Helene Haussding

1 Antoinette Mirbel to Gandhi, 17 January 1925. Mirbel's letters to Gandhi are available in both French and English translations. Whether they were sent together in duplicate, the French in her own hand and English translation in someone else's hand, or whether the English translations were done in India after the letters had reached Gandhi, is unclear.

2 Antoinette Mirbel to Gandhi, 26 January 1925.

3 Gandhi to Antoinette Mirbel, 15 June 1925.

4 Antoinette Mirbel to Gandhi, 6 July 1925.

5 Gandhi to Antoinette Mirbel, 13 August 1925.

6 Antoinette Mirbel to Gandhi, 6 September 1925.

7 Antoinette Mirbel to Gandhi, 29 September 1925.

8 Romain Rolland to Henri Hisquin, 14 January 1926, in *Romain Rolland and Gandhi Correspondence (Letters, Diary Extracts, Articles, Etc.)*, New Delhi: Publications Division, Ministry of Information and Broadcasting, Government of India, 1976, pp.401-2 at p.402.

9 Gandhi to Romain Rolland, 13 November 1925.

10 Gandhi to Chhaganlal Joshi, 13 May 1929.

11 Romain Rolland to J.Taupin, 10 December 1925, in *Romain Rolland and Gandhi Correspondence*, pp.398-400 at p.400.

12 Romain Rolland to Henri Hisquin, 14 January 1926, in *Romain Rolland and Gandhi Correspondence*, pp.401-2 at p.402.

13 Gandhi to Antoinette Mirbel, 12 February 1926.

14 Gandhi to Chhaganlal Joshi, 13 May 1929.

15 Gandhi to Antionette Mirbel, 7 December 1928.

16 In a March 1929 letter to the couple, Gandhi lamented the 'false position' they have to live because they cannot speak their opinions for fear of Frederik losing his teaching position at the university. Presumably Gandhi was referring to matters such as this. See Gandhi to Francisca Standenath, 7 March 1929.

17 Frederic Standenath to Gandhi, 23 August 1925.

18 Francisca Standenath to Gandhi, 23 August 1925.

19 Francisca Standenath to Gandhi, 21 October 1925.

20 Gandhi to Francisca Standenath, 17 September 1926.

21 Francisca Standenath to Gandhi, 18 March 1926.

22 Frederic Standenath to Gandhi, 21 March 1926.

23 Francisca Standenath to Gandhi, 26 June 1927.

24 Francisca Standenath to Gandhi, 23 September 1927.

25 See Gandhi to Francisca Standenath, 9 December 1926, 26 May 1927, and 27 July 1927.

26 Francisca Standenath to Gandhi, 21 May 1928; reproduced in Ghanshayam Das Birla, *Bapu: A Unique Association*, Bombay: Bharatiya Vidya Bhavan, 1977, vol.1, pp.98-99.

27 Gandhi to Francisca Standenath, 27 July 1927.

28 A part of this letter, without a visible date, appears with other photographs at the back of Franziska Standenath, *Vier Monate Gast Mahatma Gandhis: Indiens Freiheitskampf 1930, Gefängnisbriefe des Mahatma*, Graz: Leuschner & Lubensky, 1931. The original of the letter, dated 3 October 1927, is the Austrian National Library's Handschriftensammlung (Manuscripts Section), in Vienna. I thank Laurie Cohen for sharing the Standenath's letters from this source with me.

29 Gandhi to Frederic and Francisca Standenath, 27 April 1928.

30 Frederic Standenath to Gandhi, 20 May 1928; and see also Fracisca Standenath to Gandhi, 21 May 1928. Gandhi gave these two letters to Birla (see Gandhi to G.D. Birla, 18 June 1928) and they are reprinted in Birla, *Bapu*, pp.98-99.

31 Frederic Standenath to Gandhi, 6 November 1927.

32 Given the repetition in their letters, one wonders whether they read each other's notes or whether they lived completely independent lives.

33 Francisca Standenath to Gandhi, 6 November 1927.

34 Francisca Standenath to Gandhi, 28 March 1928.

35 Gandhi to G.D. Birla, 18 June 1928; and Gandhi to Frederic and Francisca Standenath, 27 April 1928.

36 Gandhi to G.D. Birla, 18 June and 2 July 1928; and Standenath, *Vier Monate Gast Mahatma Gandhis*, p.8.

37 Gandhi to Frederic and Francisca Standenath, 7 July 1928, in the Austrian National Library.

38 Francisca Standenath to Gandhi, 24 July 1928.

39 See Francisca Standenath to Gandhi, 7 and 14 August 1928; Romain Rolland to James H.Powers, 11 August 1928, in *Romain Rolland and Gandhi Correspondence*, pp.414-15; 'Europe-Goers Beware', *Young India*, 30 August 1928; and Rajendra Prasad, *Autobiography*, Bombay: National Book Trust, 1957, p.280.

40 Prasad, *Autobiography*, p.280.

41 See Gandhi to Mirabehn, 8 October 1928.

42 Standenath, *Vier Monate Gast Mahatma Gandhis*, pp.51-52.

43 The story of Satyavan and his devoted wife Savitri is told in a number of Sanskrit versions including the Hindu epic, the Mahabarata and several Puranas. On Satyavan's death, Savitri's love and piousness induced Yama, the god of death, to grant her boons other than restoring her husband to life. Savitri outwitted Yama by requesting children, forcing him to return her husband to the land of the living. This has been interpreted as more than just love conquering death. It may be seen as an allegory where Satyavan ('the soul of truth') represents a soul that carries the divine truth within but descends into ignorance and death. Savitri (the sacred verse and daughter of the sun) is the 'goddess of the supreme Truth who comes down and is born to save.' Sri Aurobindo, *Savitri: A Legend and a Symbol*, Pondicherry: Sri Aurobindo Ashram Trust, 1972, p.817.

44 Standenath, *Vier Monate Gast Mahatma Gandhis*, pp.175-76.

45 Gandhi to Francisca Standenath, 19 November 1928. Reproduced at the back of Standenath, *Vier Monate Gast Mahatma Gandhis*. The original is in the Austrian National Library.

46 Standenath, *Vier Monate Gast Mahatma Gandhis*, pp.179-80.

47 Francisca Standenath to Gandhi, 4/5 December 1928.

48 Francisca Standenath to Gandhi, 23/24 November 1928.

49 Frederic Standenath to Gandhi, 23 November 1928.

50 Gandhi to Frederic and Francisca Standenath, 18 January 1929.

51 Gandhi to Francisca Standenath, 2 May 1929. The original is in the Austrian National Library.

52 Gandhi to Francisca Standenath, 12 October 1929. This is from the original in the Austrian National Library, the version reproduced in the *Collected Works* is slightly different.

53 However, not being able to read German, and so verify the account, he turned down the offer to write a foreword. Gandhi to Francisca Standenath, 28 April 1931. The original is in the Austrian National Library.

54 Schreiner and her husband in fact had a daughter (who did not live through her first night), however her many illnesses and at times hysterical eccentricities may have resulted in long periods of celibacy for the couple.

55 'Marriage and Its Rites', *Navajivan* 15 September 1929.

56 Standenath, *Vier Monate Gast Mahatma Gandhis*, pp.13, 430.

57 Gandhi to Francisca Standenath, 21 December 1931.

58 Gandhi to Francisca Standenath, 15 September 1932.

59 Gandhi to Francisca Standenath, 25 November 1932.

60 Gandhi to Francisca Standenath, 14 January 1933. The original is in the Austrian National Library.

61 Gandhi to Francisca Standenath, 15 August 1935. The original is in the Austrian National Library.

62 Gandhi to Francisca Standenath, 9 October 1935. The original is in the Austrian National Library.

63 Gandhi to Francisca Standenath, 17 June 1936. The original is in the Austrian National Library.

64 See Gandhi to Francisca Standenath, 26 October 1936 and 24 August 1937. The originals are in the Austrian National Library.

65 I say possibly because while there is nothing in the Mahabarata or Puranic stories about the mythical couple that relates to snakes, lust, or purity as and antidote to poison, later popular versions of the legend and Savitri cult accounts do talk of Satyavan dying as a result of snake bite. See Anita Ray, *Icon of Feminine Perfection: The Legend and Cult of Savitri* (forthcoming).

66 Gandhi to Nirmala Gandhi, 21 July 1936.

67 Gandhi to Nirmala Gandhi, 25 July 1936.

68 Gandhi to Francisca Standenath, April 1947.

69 Gandhi to Francisca Standenath, 16 May 1947. The original is in the Austrian National Library.

70 Gandhi to Francisca Standenath, 9 July 1947. See also Gandhi to Francisca Standenath, 22 October 1947.

71 Sudhir Kakar, *Mira and the Mahatma*, New Delhi: Penguin, 2004, pp.134-35.

72 Helene Haussding to Gandhi, 29 April 1925.

73 Helene Haussding, 'Bei Mahatma Gandhi im Ashram Sabarmati', *Westermanns Monatshefte* (1927), May, no.143, p.79.

74 Helene Haussding to Gandhi, 19 July 1925.

75 Helene Haussding to Gandhi, 12 March 1926.

76 Gandhi to Helene Haussding, 3 April 1926.

77 Gandhi to Devdas Gandhi, 3 April 1926.

78 See Gandhi to Mrs.Perin Captian, 9 and 22 June 1926.

79 Haussding, 'Bei Mahatma Gandhi im Ashram Sabarmati', p.79.

80 Gandhi to Pyarelal Nayar, 9 July 1926.

81 Gandhi to Mathuradas Trikumji, 22 August 1926.

82 See Gandhi to S.E.Stokes, 1 September 1926.

83 Gandhi to Helene Haussding, 17 September 1926.

84 Gandhi to Ashram Women, 10 January 1927.

85 'Speech at Pandharpur', *Young India*, 10 March 1927.

86 C.B. Dalal (comp.), *Gandhi: 1915-1948: A Detailed Chronology*, New Delhi: Gandhi Peace Foundation, 1971, p.65.

87 Haussding, 'Bei Mahatma Gandhi im Ashram Sabarmati', p.82.

88 Although she was the sister of the leading mill-owner, Sarabhai was the chief labour organiser in the historic mill workers' strike of early 1918 that Gandhi ended up leading.

89 Gandhi to Anasuyabehn Sarabhai, 7 February 1927.

90 Gandhi to Helene Haussding, 2 June 1927.

91 Gandhi to Helene Haussding, 23 June 1927.

92 Helene Haussding to Gandhi, 25 June 1927.

93 Gandhi to Helene Haussding, 11 August 1927.

94 Gandhi to Helene Haussding, 20 December 1927.

95 Helene Haussding to Gandhi, 27 April 1928.

96 Gandhi to Helene Haussding, 1 July 1929.

### Disciples after Gandhi: Marjorie Sykes and Catherine Mary Heilemann

1 See P.T.Thomas, 'Foreword', to Martha Dart, *Marjorie Sykes: Quaker Gandhian*, York: Sessions, 1993, p.viii.

2 For Marjorie Sykes' life, see Dart, *Marjorie Sykes*; Majorie Sykes, 'Oral History Transcript', no.441, 16 August 1985, Nehru Memorial Library, New Delhi; and Surendran Purushotham, 'Marjorie Sykes: A Disciple of

Christ and Gandhi', *Gandhi Marg* (2003), vol.25, no.1, pp.90-95. For her relationship with Gandhi, see Jehangir P. Patel and Marjorie Sykes, *Gandhi: His Gift of the Fight*, Rasulia, Hoshangabad: Friends Rural Centre, Rasulia, 1987. For a selection of her writings, see Marjorie Sykes, *Transcending Tradition: Excerpts from the Writings and Talks of Marjorie Sykes* (compiled and edited by Martha Dart), York: Sessions, 1995.

3 Pat Barr, *The Dust in the Balance: British Women in India 1905-1945*, London: Hamish Hamilton, 1989, p.131.

4 Marjorie Sykes, *The Story of Nai Talim: Fifty Years of Education at Sevagram 1937-1887*, Sevagram: Nai Talim Samiti, 1988, p.7.

5 Patel and Sykes, *Gandhi*, p.47.

6 See 'Criticism Answered', *Harijan*, 31 July 1937.

7 Sykes, *The Story of Nai Talim*, p.1.

8 For the history of the Gandhian educational experiment, see Sykes, *The Story of Nai Talim*; and for her summary of what a Gandhian educational system aims to achieve, see Marjorie Sykes, 'Setting the Clock Back?', *Journal of Educational Sociology* (1955), vol.28, no.5, pp.211-17.

9 For a history of the Shanti Sena, see Thomas Weber, *The Shanti Sena: Philosophy, History and Action,* New Delhi: Orient BlackSwan, 2009.

10 See Weber, *The Shanti Sena*, pp.113-20.

11 An explanatory note in the *Collected Works of Mahatma Gandhi* to a letter from Gandhi to Saralabehn (dated 12 January 1946) describes Heilemann as an 'English Jewess'. There does not seem to be any evidence for this. From her autobiography *Vyavaharik Vedanta*, we know that her paternal grandmother was a Lutheran and that she was brought up in the Christian faith. I thank David Hopkins for pointing this out.

12 Sarala Devi, *Revive Our Dying Planet*, Nainital: Gyanodaya Prakashan, 1982, pp.3-4.

13 For the life of Saralabehn see Sarala Devi, *Vyavaharik Vedanta*, New Delhi: Gandhi Peace Foundation, 1976 (an English translation by David Hopkins, under the title *Practical Vedanta – An Autobiography*, is in press); Vimla Bahuguna, '*Stri Shakti*: Dimensions of Women Power in India', in Kamala Ganesh and Usha Thakkar (eds), *Culture and the Making of Identity in Contemporary India*, New Delhi/London: Sage/Thousand Oaks, 2005, pp.149-53; and Sunderlal Bahuguna, 'Gandhi's Betis', reproduced from the Sunday Magazine of *The Hindusthan Times*, in the pamphlet *Save Himalaya: A Tribute to Mahatma Gandhi's Two English Daughters Sarala Behn and Mira Behn*, Silyara, Uttar Pradesh: Chipko Information Centre, n.d., pp.1-4.

14 Sarala Devi to P.N. Sanwal, 5 August 1942, in Shantilal Trivedi and Radha Behn (eds), *Sarala Behn: Smriti Granth*, New Delhi/Kausani: Himalaya Seva Sangh/Lahshmi Ashram, 1984, pp.303-5.

15 Gandhi to Sarala Devi, 29 July 1945.

16 See Thomas Weber, *Hugging the Trees: The Story of the Chipko Movement*, New Delhi: Penguin, 1989, pp.29-30.

17 In this campaign Vinoba spent many years walking the length and breadth of India asking landowners to donate some of their land to the landless. See Roderick Church, 'Vinoba and the Origins of Bhoodan', *Gandhi Marg* (1983), vol.5, no.8/9, pp.469-91; and Vishwanath Tandon 'The Bhoodan-Gramdan Movement (1951-74) – A Review', *Gandhi Marg* (1983), vol.5, no.8/9, pp.492-500.

18 Sarala Devi, 'A Blue-Print for Survival in the Hills', *Himalaya: Man and Nature* (1980), vol.4, no.6, p.5.

19 In Gramdan the whole or a large part of a village was 'donated' to the total village community who would then make collective decisions relating to the village.

20 For this remarkable episode in Gandhian social revolution, see Weber, *The Shanti Sena*, pp.120-31.

**Conclusion: Gandhi and Western Women**

1 Martin Green, *Gandhi: Voice of a New Age Revolution*, New York: Continuum, 1993, p.26.

2 See Green, *Gandhi*, *passim*; and Thomas Weber, *Gandhi as Disciple and Mentor*, New Delhi: Cambridge University Press, 2007, pp.26-30.

3 Alex Aronson, *Europe Looks at India: A Study in Cultural Relations*, Calcutta: Riddhi-India, 1979, p.124.

4 Aronson, *Europe Looks at India*, p.124.

5 See, David James Fisher, 'Romain Rolland and the Popularization of Gandhi: 1923-1925', *Gandhi Marg* (1974), vol.18, no.3, p.62; David James Fisher, *Romain Rolland and the Politics of Intellectual Engagement*, Berkeley: University of California Press, 1988, pp.112-44; and V.V. Ramana Murti, 'Romain Rolland and Gandhi', *Gandhi Marg* (1966), vol.10, no.1, p.40.

6 Rajendra Prasad, *Autobiography*, Bombay: National Book Trust, 1957, p.280.

7 See S.L. Malhotra, 'A Study of Gandhi's Biographies – Joseph J. Doke and Romain Rolland', *Gandhi Marg* (1985), vol.6, no.12, p.859.

8 Romain Rolland, *Mahatma Gandhi: The Man Who Became One With the Universal Being*, New Delhi: Publications Division, Ministry of Information and Broadcasting, Government of India, 1968, p.124. For an American perspective on the sanctification of Gandhi, see Mark Juergensmeyer, 'Saint Gandhi' in John Stratton Hawley (ed.), *Saints and Virtues*, Berkeley: University of California Press, 1987, pp.187-203.

9 Publications Division, *Romain Rolland and Gandhi Correspondence (Letters, Diary Extracts, Articles, Etc.)*, New Delhi: Publications Division, Ministry of Information and Broadcasting, Government of India, 1976, p.28.

10 Gandhi to C. Rajagopalchari, 28 March 1928.

11 Sudhir Kakar, 'Gandhi and Women', in *The Essential Writings of Sudhir Kakar*, New Delhi: Oxford University Press, 2001, p.249.

12 Green, *Gandhi*, p.329.

13 'In the role of Bapu's daughter I straightened out an uncompleted relation with Kyrios Kouk [as the Greek peasants called her father].' Nilla Cram Cook, *My Road to India*, New York: Lee Furman, 1939, p.411.

14 See Max Weber, *The Theory of Social and Economic Organisations*, New York: The Free Press, 1964, especially pp.360-61.

15 See Elisabeth Puttick, *Women in New Religions: In Search of Community, Sexuality and Spiritual Power*, London: Macmillan, 1993, especially Ch.2, 'The Making of the Master-Disciple Relationship', pp.23-31.

16 See Margaret Sanger, *An Autobiography*, New York: Dover, 1971, p.483.

17 I thank Charles di Salvo for this insightful observation.

18 Gandhi to Færing, 30 June 1918.

19 Green, *Gandhi*, p.335.

20 It is not unknown for Western women to have fulfilled such roles. Margaret Noble became Sister Nivedita, a leading figure in the Ramakrishna Mission after Vivekenanda; and the French mystic Mira Richard became 'the Mother', head of Shri Aurobindo's ashram after the master retreated into seclusion.

21 See for example the Appendices to M.K. Gandhi, *Hind Swaraj or Indian Home Rule*, Ahmedabad: Navajivan, 1939, pp.105-110.

22 'Deeds Better than Words', *Indian Opinion*, 24 November 1906.

23 Gandhi to Esther Menon, 18 July 1932. The italics are mine.

24 Millie Graham Polak, 'Gandhi and Women', in Chandrashanker Shukla (ed.), *Gandhiji as We Know Him by Seventeen Contributors*, Bombay: Vora, 1945, p.47.

25 Quoted in Amartya Sen, *The Argumentative Indian: Writings on Indian History, Culture and Identity*, London: Allen Lane, 2005, p.102.

26 For this struggle, see Girja Kumar, *Brahmacharya, Gandhi & His Women Associates*, New Delhi: Vitasta, 2006.

27 Sanger, *An Autobiography*, p.471.

28 See 'A Letter', 11 September 1932.

29 Gandhi to Nilla Cram Cook, 9 June 1933.

30 Gandhi to Bala Gandhar, 23 April 1933.

31 Stanley Wolpert, *Gandhi's Passion: The Life and Legacy of Mahatma Gandhi*, New York: Oxford University Press, 2001, pp.105-6.

32 See for example Gandhi's three letters to Mirabehn immediately following her banishment from his presence on 28 and 29 September, and 2 October 1927.

33 Rosetta Splat, 'Retracing Mira Behn's Path', in Krishna Murti Gupta, (ed.),

*Mira Behn: Gandhi's Daughter Disciple: Birth Centenary Volume*, New Delhi: Himalaya Seva Sangh, 1992, p.228.

34 Splat, 'Retracing Mira Behn's Path', p.228.

35 Kakar, *The Essential Writings of Sudhir Kakar*, p.250.

36 See Gandhi letters to Mirabehn, 21 August and 7 September 1934.

37 Jill Wallis, *Mother of World Peace: The Life of Muriel Lester*, Enfield Lock, Middlesex: Hisarlik Press, 1993, p.72.

38 Wallis, *Mother of World Peace*, pp.72-73.

39 And to the degree that this appeared to be happening, one should not look only at the voluminous correspondence exchanged between the two of them, but one should also look at the numerous letters Gandhi wrote to others about Nilla, the efforts he went to in order to find out background information on her, the talks he had with those who had fallen under her spell or were trying to help her, and the lively exchange of letters he conducted with ashram leaders about whether she should be permitted to stay and under what conditions.

40 Quoted in D.S. Ramachandra Rao, 'Foreword', to Esther Færing, *'My Dear Child': Letters from M.K. Gandhi to Esther Færing*, Ahmedabad: Navajivan, 1956, p.vii.

# Bibliography

In the notes, Gandhi's own writings are referenced only with the date and title of the relevant article, or name of addressee in the case of letters, rather than the up till now standard of the date plus the volume and page reference in the *Collected Works of Mahatma Gandhi*. This is because there are now two versions of the *CWMG* and they do not correspond. The original 100 volumes included several volumes of supplementary material that was unearthed after the publication of the volume covering the relevant dates. In the revised edition, and its CD-ROM version, most of this material (there are some inexplicable omissions) has been integrated into the body of the work. The date, title and name of addressee should make a required item relatively easy to find in whichever version is used. Where no full date is available, the pages in the hard copy original standard version of the *CWMG* are provided. The item can generally be located in the CD-ROM version through the word search facility. Unless otherwise indicated, I consulted the original letters to Gandhi, or photocopies of them, in the collection at the Sabarmati Nidhi (Trust), *Gandhi Papers*, held at the Sabarmati Harijan Ashram, Ahmedabad.

Alexander, Horace, *Gandhi Through Western Eyes*, Bombay: Asia, 1969.

Amrit Kaur, Rajkumari, 'Foreword', to *Gandhi, Women and Social Injustice*, p.iii.

Amrit Kaur, Rajkumari, 'Gandhiji and Women', in Roy (ed.), *Gandhi Memorial Peace Number*, pp.166-71.

Andrews, C.F., 'Mr. Gandhi at Phoenix', *Modern Review* (Calcutta), May 1914, pp.563-66.

Aronson, Alex, *Europe Looks at India: A Study in Cultural Relations*, Calcutta: Riddhi-India, 1979.

Ashe, Geoffrey, *Gandhi: A Study in Revolution*, London: Heinemann, 1968.

Athiyaman, P., and A.R. Venkatachalapathy, 'Debate: On Gandhi, Mayo and Emilsen', *South Asia* (1989), vol.12, no.2, pp.83-90.

Aurobindo, Sri, *Savitri: A Legend and a Symbol*, Pondicherry: Sri Aurobindo Ashram Trust, 1972.

Bahuguna, Sunderlal, *Save Himalaya: A Tribute to Mahatma Gandhi's Two English Daughters Sarala Behn and Mira Behn*, Silyara, Uttar Pradesh: Chipko Information Centre, n.d.

Bahuguna, Vimla, '*Stri Shakti*: Dimensions of Women Power in India', in Kamala Ganesh and Usha Thakkar (eds.), *Culture and the Making of Identity in Contemporary India*, New Delhi/London: Sage/Thousand Oaks, 2005, pp.149-53.

Barnes, Alice, 'Introduction', to Færing, *'My Dear Child'*, pp.xii-xix.

Barr, F. Mary, *Bapu: Conversations and Correspondence with Mahatma Gandhi* (Second Edition), Bombay: International Book House, n.d.

Barr, Margaret, 'A Gandhi Centre in the Hills', in G.Ramachandran and T.K. Mahadevan (eds.), *Gandhi: His Relevance for our Times*, New Delhi: Gandhi Peace Foundation, 1964, pp.230-37.

Barr, Pat, *The Dust in the Balance: British Women in India 1905-1945*, London: Hamish Hamilton, 1989.

Besant, Annie, *An Autobiography*, London: Unwin, 1908.

Besant, Annie, *An Autobiography*, Adyar: Theosophical Publishing House, 1939.

Besant, Annie, *The Future of Indian Politics: A Contribution to the Understanding of Present-Day Problems*, Adyar: Theosophical Publishing House, 1922.

Besant, Annie, *India, Bond or Free? A World Problem*, London: Putnam's, 1926.

Birla, Ghanshayam Das, *Bapu: A Unique Association*, Bombay: Bharatiya Vidya Bhavan, 1977, vols 1 and 3.

Blain, Virginia; Patricia Clements and Isobel Grundy (eds), *The Feminist Companion to Literature in English*, London: Batsford, 1990.

Bose, Nirmal Kumar, *My Days with Gandhi*, New Delhi: Orient Longman, 1974.

Bose, Nirmal Kumar, *Selections from Gandhi*, Ahmedabad: Navajivan, 1957.

Bourke-White, Margaret, *Halfway to Freedom*, New York: Simon and Schuster, 1949.

Bourke-White, Margaret, 'Mahatma Gandhi', in Will Yolen and Kenneth Seeman Giniger (eds), *Heroes For Our Times*, Harrisburg, P.A.: Griniger, 1968, pp.88-109.

Bourke-White, Margaret, *Portrait of Myself*, New York: Simon and Schuster, 1963.

Bourke-White, Margaret, 'The Last Days with Gandhi', in Cousins (ed.), *Profiles of Gandhi*, pp.85-92.

Britain, Vera, *The Rebel Passion: A Short History of Some Pioneer Peace-makers*, London: Allan and Unwin, 1964.

Brock, Peter, 'Gandhi's Nonviolence and His War Service', *Gandhi Marg* (1981), vol.2, no.11, pp.601-16.

Brock Peter, *The Mahatma and Mother India [Essays on Gandhi's Non-Violence and Nationalism]*, Ahmedabad: Navajivan, 1983, pp.50-74.

Brown, Heloise, *'The Truest Form of Patriotism' Pacifist Feminism in Britain, 1870-1902,* Manchester: Manchester University Press, 2003.

Buchanan-Gould, Vera, *Not Without Honour: The Life and Writings of Olive Schreiner*, London: Hutchinson, 1946.

Ceadel, Martin, *Pacifism in Britain 1914-1945:The Defining of a* Faith, Oxford: Clarendon Press, 1980.

Chandra, Jyoti, *Annie Besant: From Theosophy to Nationalism*, Delhi: K.K. Publications, 2001.

Chaudhury, P.C. Roy, *Gandhi and His Contemporaries*, New Delhi: Sterling, 1986.

Chesler, Ellen, *Woman of Valor: Margaret Sanger and the Birth Control Movement in America*, New York: Simon and Schuster, 1992.

Church, Roderick, 'Vinoba and the Origins of Bhoodan', *Gandhi Marg* (1983), vol.5, no.8/9, pp.469-91.

Churchill, Allen, *The Improper Bohemians: A Re-creation of Greenwich Village in Its Heyday*, London: Cassell, 1959.

Cook, Nilla Cram, *My Road to India*, New York: Lee Furman, 1939.

Cook, Nilla Cram, 'The Theater and Ballet Arts of Iran', *The Middle East Journal* (1949), vol.3, no.4, pp.406-20.

Cousins, Norman, (ed.), *Profiles of Gandhi: America Remembers a World Leader*, Delhi: Indian Book Company, 1970.

Cronwright-Schreiner, S.C., *The Life of Olive Schreiner*, London: T. Fisher Unwin, 1924.

Dalal, C.B., (comp.), *Gandhi: 1915-1948: A Detailed Chronology*, New Delhi: Gandhi Peace Foundation, 1971.

Dalal, Chandulal Bhagubhai, *Harilal Gandhi: A Life* (Tridip Suhrud ed. and trans.), Chennai: Orient Longman, 2007.

Dart, Martha, *Marjorie Sykes: Quaker Gandhian*, York: Sessions, 1993.

Deats Richard, (ed.), *Ambassador of Reconciliation: A Muriel Lester Reader*, Philadelphia, PA: New Society Publishers, 1991.

Dell, Floyd, *Homecoming: An Autobiography*, Port Washington, NY: Kennikat, 1969.

Desai, Mahadev, 'Brave Woman Passes Away', *Navajivan*, 11 July 1936, quoted in Desai, *Day-To-Day With Gandhi*, vol.8, pp.212-16.

Desai, Mahadev, *Mahadevbhai ni Diary*, Ahmedabad: Gandhi Smarak Sangrahalaya, 1993, vol.3.

Desai, Mahadev, *The Diary of Mahadev Desai*, Navajivan: Ahmedabad, 1953, vol.1.

Desai, Mahadev, 'Miss Madeline Slade', quoted in Desai, *Day-To-Day With Gandhi*, vol.8, pp.83-84.

Desai, Mahadev H., *Day-To-Day With Gandhi [Secretary's Diary]*, Rajghat, Varanasi: Sarva Seva Sangh, 1968, vol.2, and 1973, vol.8.

Desai, Narayan, *My Gandhi*, Ahmedabad: Navajivan, 1999.

DiSalvo, Charles R., *Gandhi: A Lawyer's Transformation* (unpublished manuscript).

Doke, Joseph J., *M.K. Gandhi: An Indian Patriot in South Africa*, London: The London Indian Chronicle, 1909.

Doke, Olive C., 'Reminiscences of M.K. Gandhi', in Shukla (ed.), *Incidents of Gandhiji's Life*, pp.42-46.

Douglas, Emily Taft, *Margaret Sanger: Pioneer of the Future*, New York: Holt, Rinehart and Winston, 1970.

Emilsen, William W., 'Gandhi and Mayo's Mother India', *South Asia* (1987), vol.10, no.1, pp.69-81.

Erikson, Erik H., *Gandhi's Truth: On the Origins of Militant Nonviolence*, New York: W.W. Norton, 1969.

Faering, Esther, *'My Dear Child': Letters from M.K. Gandhi to Esther Færing*, Ahmedabad: Navajivan, 1956.

Farson, Negley, 'Indian Hate Lyric', in Eugene Lyons (ed.), *We Cover the World: By Sixteen Foreign Correspondents*, London: Harrap, 1937, pp.127-52.

Field, Harry H., *After Mother India*, New York: Harcourt, Brace and Company, 1929.

First, Ruth, and Ann Scott, *Olive Schreiner*, New Brunswick, NJ: Rutgers University Press, 1990.

Fisher, David James, *Romain Rolland and the Politics of Intellectual Engagement*, Berkeley: University of California Press, 1988.

Fisher, David James, 'Romain Rolland and the Popularization of Gandhi: 1923-1925', *Gandhi Marg* (1974), vol.18, no.3, pp.145-80.

Fisher, John, *That Miss Hobhouse*, London: Secker and Warburg, 1971.

Fletcher, Sheila, *Maude Royden: A Life*, Oxford: Basil Blackwell, 1989.

'Gandhi and Sanger Debate Love, Lust and Birth Control', *The Margaret Sanger Papers Newsletter*, no.23, Winter 1999/2000, available online at www.nyu.edu/projects/sanger/gandhi_debate.html

Gandhi, Arun and Sunanda Gandhi, *The Forgotten Woman: The Untold Story of Kastur Gandhi, Wife of Mahatma Gandhi*, Huntsville, AR: Ozark Mountain Publishers, 1998.

Gandhi, Manu, *Last Glimpses of Bapu*, Delhi: Shiva Lal Agarwala, 1962.

Gandhi, Manubehn, *Bapu – My Mother*, Ahmedabad: Navajian, 1949.

Gandhi, Manubehn, *The Lonely Pilgrim (Gandhiji's Noakhali Pilgrimage)*, Ahmedabad: Navajivan, 1964.

Gandhi, M.K., *All Men Are Brothers: Life and Thoughts of Mahatma Gandhi as Told in His Own Words* (Krishna Kripalani comp. and ed.), Calcutta: Orient Longmans, 1958.

Gandhi, M.K., *An Autobiography or The Story of My Experiments With Truth*, Ahmedabad: Navajivan, 1940.

Gandhi, M.K., *Collected Works of Mahatma Gandhi*, vols 1-100, New Delhi: Publications Division, Government of India, 1958-1991; and revised CD-ROM version, New Delhi: Publications Division, Government of India, 1999.

Gandhi, M.K., *Conquest of Self* (R.K. Prabhu and U.R. Rao comps.), Bombay: Thacker and Co., 1943.

Gandhi, M.K., *From Yeravda Mandir: Ashram Observances*, Ahmedabad: Navajivan, 1932.

Gandhi, M.K., *Gandhi on Women* (Pushpa Joshi comp.), Ahmedabad: Navajivan, 1988.

Gandhi, M.K., *Hind Swaraj or Indian Home Rule*, Ahmedabad: Navajivan, 1939.

Gandhi, M.K., *The Law of Continence* (Anand T. Hingorani ed.), Bombay: Bharatiya Vidya Bhavan, 1964.

Gandhi, M.K., *The Mind of Mahatma Gandhi* (P.K. Prabhu and U.R. Rao comp. and eds.), Ahmedabad: Navajivan, 1967.

Gandhi, M.K., *The Role of Women* (Anand T. Hingorani ed.), Bombay: Bharatiya Vidya Bhavan, 1964.

Gandhi, M.K., *Satyagraha in South Africa*, Madras: Ganesan, 1928.

Gandhi, M.K., *Self Restraint vs. Self Indulgence*, Ahmedabad: Navajivan, 1947.

Gandhi, M.K, *To the Women* (Anand T. Hingorani ed.), Karachi: the author, 1941.

Gandhi, M.K., *Women* (Bharatan Kumarappa ed.), Ahmedabad: Navajivan, 1958.

Gandhi, M.K., *Women and Social Injustice* (Bharatan Kumarappa ed.), Ahmedabad: Navajivan, 1942.

Gandhi, M.K., *Women's Role in Society* (R.K. Prabhu comp.), Ahmedabad: Navajivan, 1959.

Gandhi, Prabhudas, *My Childhood with Gandhiji*, Ahmedabad: Navajivan, 1957.

Gangadhar, D.A., *Mahatma Gandhi's Philosophy of Brahmacharya*, Bangalore: ISPCK, 1984.

Ghosh, Sudhir, *Gandhi's Emissary*, London: Cresset, 1967.

Glaspell, Susan, *The Road to the Temple*, London: Ernst Benn, 1926.

Goldberg, Vicki, *Margaret Bourke-White: A Biography*, London: Heinemann, 1986.

Gray, Madeline, *Margaret Sanger: A Biography of the Champion of Birth Control*, New York: Richard Marek, 1979.

Green, Martin, *Gandhi: Voice of a New Age Revolution*, New York: Continuum, 1993.

Greenlees, Duncan, *Gandhi Ashram*, Phalghat, Kerala: Scholar Press, 1934.

Gupta, Krishna Murti, (ed.), *Mira Behn: Gandhi's Daughter Disciple: Birth Centenary Volume*, New Delhi: Himalaya Seva Sangh, 1992.

Hancock, W.K., *Smuts: The Sanguine Years 1870-1919*, Cambridge: Cambridge University Press, 1962.

Hancock, William, and Jean van der Poel, *Selections from the Smuts Papers*, Cambridge: Cambridge University Press, 1966, vol.3.

Handlin, Mary F., 'Mayo, Katherine', in Edward T. James, Janet Wilson James, and Paul S. Boyer (eds), *Notable American Women, 1607-1950: A Biographical Dictionary*, volume 2, Cambridge: Belknap Press, 1971, pp.515-17.

Hardiman, David, *Gandhi in His Time and Ours*, Delhi: Permanent Black, 2003.

Harrison, Agatha, 'Knightsbridge, London', in Shukla (ed.), *Gandhiji as We Know Him*, pp.82-93.

Harrison, Agatha, 'Some Impressions', in Shukla (ed.), *Incidents of Gandhiji's Life*, pp.63-71.

Harrison, Irene, *Agatha Harrison: An Impression by Her Sister*, London: Allen & Unwin, 1956.

Haussding, Helene, 'Bei Mahatma Gandhi im Ashram Sabarmati', *Westermanns Monatshefte* (1927), May, no.143, pp.79-83.

Heeney, Brian, *The Women's Movement in the Church of England 1850-1930*, Oxford: Clarendon Press, 1988.

Heller, Keith, *The Woman Who Knew Gandhi*, Boston: Mariner, 2003.

Hobhouse, Emily, *Emily Hobhouse: A Memoir compiled by A. Ruth Fry*, London: J. Cape, 1929.

Hogg, Dorothy, *Memories for Tomorrow*, London: Regency Press, 1981.

Hørup, Ellen, *Gandhis Indien*, Copenhagen: H. Hagerups, 1931.

Hunt, James D., *Gandhi in London*, New Delhi: Promilla, 1978.

Hunt, James D., *Gandhi and the Nonconformists: Encounters in South Africa*, New Delhi: Promilla, 1986.

Hunt, James D., 'Suffragettes and Satyagraha', *Indo-British Review* (1981), vol.9, no.1, pp.65-76.

Hunt, James D., and Surendra Bhana, 'Spiritual Rope-Walkers: Gandhi, Kallenbach, and the Tolstoy Farm, 1910-13', *South African Historical Journal* (2007), vol.58, pp.174-202.

Jack, Homer A., 'Henry S.L. Polak', *Gandhi Marg* (1959), vol.3, no.4, pp.289-92.

Jain, Devaki, 'Gandhian Contributions Towards a Feminist Ethic', in Diana L. Eck and Devaki Jain (eds), *Speaking of Faith: Cross-Cultural Perspectives on Women, Religion and Social Change*, New Delhi: Kali for Women, 1986, pp.255-70.

James, Edward Holton, *I Tell Everything: The Brown Man's Burden (A Book on India)*, Geneva: Imprimerie Kundig, c1931.

Jha, Manoranjan, *Civil Disobedience and After: The American Reaction to Political Developments in India During 1930-1935*, Meerut: Meenakshi, 1973.

Jha, Manoranjan, *Katherine Mayo and India*, New Delhi: People's Publishing House, 1971.

Jones, E. Stanley, *The Christ of the Indian Road*, London: Hodder and Stoughton, 1926.

Juergensmeyer, Mark, 'Saint Gandhi', in John Stratton Hawley (ed.), *Saints and Virtues*, Berkeley: University of California Press, 1987, pp.187-203.

Kakar, Sudhir, *The Essential Writings of Sudhir Kakar*, New Delhi: Oxford University Press, 2001.

Kakar, Sudhir, *Intimate Relations: Exploring Indian Sexuality*, New Delhi: Penguin, 1989.

Kakar, Sudhir, *Mira and the Mahatma*, New Delhi: Penguin, 2004.

Kendall, Patricia, *Come with Me to India!: A Quest for Truth Among Peoples and Problems*, New York: Scribner's, 1931.

Kishwar, Madhu, *Gandhi and Women*, Delhi: Manushi, 1986.

Kumar, Girja, *Brahmacharya, Gandhi & His Women Associates*, New Delhi: Vitasta, 2006.

Kumar, Raj, *Annie Besant's Rise to Power in Indian Politics 1914-1917*, New Delhi: Concept, 1981.

Lader, Lawrence, *The Margaret Sanger Story and the Fight for Birth Control*, Westport, Con.: Greenwood Press, 1955.

Lal, Vinay, 'Nakedness, Non-Violence, and the Negation of Negation: Gandhi's Experiments in *Brahmacharya* and Celibate Sexuality', *South Asia* (1999), vol.22, no.2, pp.63-94.

Larsen, Tine Elisabeth, *Anne Marie Petersen: A Danish Woman in South India: A Missionary Story 1909-1951*, Chennai: Lutheran Heritage Archives, 2000.

Lester, Muriel, *Entertaining Gandhi*, London: Nicholson and Watson, 1932.

Lester, Muriel, 'Gandhiji: 1926-39', in Shukla (ed.), *Incidents of Gandhiji's Life*, pp.143-48.

Lester, Muriel, *Gandhi: World Citizen*, Allahabad: Kitab Mahal, 1945.

Lester, Muriel, *My Host the Hindu*, London: Williams and Norgate, 1931.

Lester, Muriel, *It Occurred to Me*, New York: Harper and Brothers, 1937.

Lester, Muriel, *It So Happened*, New York: Harper and Brothers, 1947.

MacMillan, Margaret, *Women of the Raj*, n.p.: Thames and Hudson, 1988.

Mahadevan, T.K., *The Year of the Phoenix: Gandhi's Pivotal Year*, New Delhi: Arnold-Heinemann, 1982.

Malhotra, S.L., 'A Study of Gandhi's Biographies: Joseph J. Doke and Romain Rolland', *Gandhi Marg* (1985), vol.6, no.12, pp.845-61.

Mashruwala, K.G., 'Foreword', to Barr, *Bapu*, pp.v-vi.

Maxwell, David, *Muriel Lester, Gandhi and Kingsley Hall*, n.p., Gandhi Foundation, n.d.

Mayo, Katherine, *Mother India*, London: Jonathan Cape, 1927.

Meer, Fatima, 'Gandhi on Women – A Critique', in Fatima Meer (ed.), *The South African Gandhi: An Abstract of the Speeches and Writings of M.K. Gandhi, 1893 - 1914*, Durban: Madiba, 1996, pp.996-1003.

Mehta, Ved, *Mahatma Gandhi and His Apostles*, London: Andre Deutsch, 1976.

Mirabehn, 'Autobiographical Note', in Gupta (ed.), *Mira Behn*, pp.295-98.

Mirabehn (ed.), *Bapu's Letters to Mira [1924-1948]*, Ahmedabad: Navajivan, 1949.

Mirabehn, 'His Daily Life', in Shukla (ed.), *Incidents of Gandhiji's Life*, pp.186-87.

Mirabehn, 'How Bapuji Trained his Followers', reproduced in Gupta, *Mira Behn*, pp.285-87.

Mira Behn [Madeleine Slade], *The Spirit's Pilgrimage*, London: Longmans, 1960.

Morton, Eleanor, *The Women in Gandhi's Life*, New York: Dodd, Mead and Co., 1953.

Muthanna, I.M., *Mother Besant and Mahatma Gandhi*, Vellore: Thenpulam, 1986.

Murphy, Stephen, 'Constructing the Mahatma: The Evolution of Gandhi's Image in his Western Biographies, 1909-1954', unpublished Master of Arts dissertation, Department of Politics, La Trobe University, 1992.

Nandy, Ashis, *At the Edge of Psychology: Essays in Politics and Culture*, Delhi: Oxford University Press, 1980.

Nandy, Ashis, *The Intimate Enemy: Loss and Recovery of Self Under Colonialism*, Delhi: Oxford University Press, 1983.

Natesan, G.A., 'Reminiscences', in D.G. Tendulkar and others (eds), *Gandhiji: His Life and Work*, Bombay: Keshav Bhikaji Dhawale, 1944, pp.208-15.

Nayar, Sushila, *Mahatma Gandhi, volume IV: Satyagraha at Work*, Ahmedabad: Navajivan, 1989.

Nayar, Sushila, *Mahatma Gandhi, volume VII: Preparing for Swaraj*, Ahmedabad: Navajivan, 1996.

Nehru, Rameshwari, 'Gandhiji and Women', in Shukla (ed.), *Incidents of Gandhiji's Life*, pp.209-14.

Nethercot, Arthur H., *The First Five Lives of Annie Besant*, Chicago: The University of Chicago Press, 1960.

Nethercot, Arthur H., *The Last Four Lives of Annie Besant*, Chicago: The University of Chicago Press, 1963.

Parel, Anthony J., *Gandhi's Philosophy and the Quest for Harmony*, Cambridge: Cambridge University Press, 2006.

Parikh, Nilam, *Gandhiji's Lost Jewel: Harilal Gandhi*, New Delhi: National Gandhi Museum, 2001.

Parry, Albert, *Garrets and Pretenders: A History of Bohemianism in America*, New York: Dover, 1960.

Patel, Jehangir P., and Marjorie Sykes, *Gandhi: His Gift of the Fight*, Rasulia, Hoshangabad: Friends Rural Centre, Rasulia, 1987.

Patel, Sujata, 'Construction and Reconstruction of Woman in Gandhi', *Economic and Political Weekly*, 20 February 1988, vol.23, no.8, pp.377-86.

Paxton, George D., 'Sonja Schlesin, Gandhi, and South Africa', *Gandhi Marg* (1999), vol.21, no.3, pp.325-38.

Paxton, George, *Sonja Schlesin: Gandhi's South African Secretary*, Glasgow: Pax, 2006.

Pierpont, Claudia Roth, *Passionate Minds:Women Rewriting theWorld*, Melbourne: Scribe, 2000.

Polak, H.S.L., 'Some South African Reminiscences', in Shukla (ed.), *Incidents of Gandhiji's Life*, pp.230-47.

Polak, H.S.L., H.N. Brailsord and Lord Pethick-Lawrence, *Mahatma Gandhi*, London: Odhams Press, 1949.

Polak, Millie Graham, 'Gandhi and Women', in Shukla (ed.), *Gandhiji as We Know Him*, pp.47-51.

Polak, Millie Graham, *Mr Gandhi:The Man*, London: Allen and Unwin, 1931.

Prasad, Rajendra, *Autobiography*, Bombay: National Book Trust, 1957.

Publications Division, *Romain Rolland and Gandhi Correspondence (Letters, Diary Extracts, Articles, Etc.)*, New Delhi: Publications Division, Ministry of Information and Broadcasting, Government of India, 1976.

Purushotham, Surendran, 'Marjorie Sykes: A Disciple of Christ and Gandhi', *Gandhi Marg* (2003), vol.25, no.1, pp.90-95.

Puttick, Elisabeth, *Women in New Religions: In Search of Community, Sexuality and Spiritual Power*, London: Macmillan, 1993.

Pyarelal, *Mahatma Gandhi, volume I: The Early Phase*, Ahmedabad: Navajivan, 1965.

Pyarelal, *Mahatma Gandhi, volume III: The Birth of Satyagraha*, Ahmedabad: Navajivan, 1986.

Pyarelal, *Mahatma Gandhi, volume IX:The Last Phase, Part I, Book I*, Ahmedabad: Navajivan, 1956.

Pyarelal, *Mahatma Gandhi, volume X: The Last Phase, Part II*, Ahmedabad: Navajivan, 1958.

Raja Singam, S. Durai, 'The Polaks and Gandhiji', *Indian Review* (1964), vol.63, May and June, pp.173-77.

Ramana Murti, V.V., 'Romain Rolland and Gandhi', *Gandhi Marg* (1966), vol.10, no.1, pp.38-51.

Rao, D.S. Ramachandra, 'Foreword', to Faering, *'My Dear Child'*, pp.vii-xii.

Rao, P. Kodanda, 'As I Knew Him', in Shukla (ed.), *Incidents of Gandhiji's Life*, pp.110-16.

Ray, Anita. *Icon of Feminine Perfection:The Legend and Cult of Savitri* (forthcoming).

Reddy E.S., and Holger Terp (editors and publishers), 'The Danish Peace Academy: Gandhi and Nordic Countries: Notes on People in Nordic Countries who Corresponded with Gandhi', available at www.fredsakademiet.dk/library/nordic/bionotes.html

Reddy E.S, and Holger Terp (eds.), *Friends of Gandhi: Correspondence of Mahatma Gandhi with Esther Færing (Menon), Anne Marie Petersen and Ellen Horup*, New Delhi, Berlin and Copenhagen: National Gandhi Museum, Gandhi-Informations-Zentrum, and The Danish Peace Academy, 2006.

Roberts, Brian, *Those Bloody Women: Three Heroines of the Boer War*, London: John Murray, 1991.

Rolland, Romain, *Mahatma Gandhi: The Man Who Became One With the Universal Being*, New Delhi: Publications Division, Ministry of Information and Broadcasting, Government of India, 1968.

Roy, Kshitis (ed.), *Gandhi Memorial Peace Number*, Shantiniketan: Visva-Bharati Quarterly, 1949.

Royden, A. Maude, 'The Peacemaker', in William Paxton, Philip Inman, C.B. Alderton, J.W. Tuffley, A. Maude Royden, Charles G. Ammon, J.G. Beaumont, and Hugh Redwood (eds), *Dick Sheppard: An Apostle of Brotherhood*, London: Chapman and Hall, 1938, pp.73-81.

Royden, Maude, 'An Englishwoman's Faith', in S. Radhakrishnan (ed.), *Mahatma Gandhi: Essays and Reflections on His Life and Work*, Bombay: Jaico, 1956, pp.206-10.

Royden, Maude, *A Threefold Cord*, London: Gollancz, 1947.

Royden, Maude, 'The Peace Army: A Sermon by A. Maude Royden, C.H., D.D., preached at the Guildhouse, Eccleston Square, W.W.1, on Sunday evening, February 28, 1932', leaflet (n.p., n.d.).

Rudolph, Lloyd I., and Susanne Hoeber Rudolph, *The Modernity of Tradition: Political Development in India*, Chicago: University of Chicago Press, 1967.

Sanger, Margaret, *An Autobiography*, New York: Dover, 1971.

Sanger, Margaret, 'A Summit Meeting on Birth Control', in Cousins (ed.), *Profiles of Gandhi*, 1970, pp.35-41.

Sarala Devi, 'A Blue-Print for Survival in the Hills', *Himalaya: Man and Nature* (1980), vol.4, no.6, pp.1-15.

Sarala Devi, *Revive Our Dying Planet*, Nainital: Gyanodaya Prakashan, 1982.

Sarala Devi, *Vyavaharik Vedanta*, New Delhi: Gandhi Peace Foundation, 1976.

Schreiner, Olive, *Dreams*, London: T. Fisher Unwin, 1894.

Sen, Amartya, *The Argumentative Indian: Writings on Indian History, Culture and Identity*, London: Allen Lane, 2005.

Seshachari, C., *Gandhi and the American Scene, An Intellectual History and Inquiry*, Bombay: Nachiketa, 1969.

Seth, A.N., 'Mira Behn – Some Reminiscences', in Gupta, *Mira Behn*, pp.257-59.

Shaw, Maude Royden, 'Master Christian?', in Roy (ed.), *Gandhi Memorial Peace Number*, pp.130-34.

Shukla, Chandrashanker (ed.), *Gandhiji as We Know Him, by Seventeen Contributors*, Bombay: Vora, 1945.

Shukla, Chandrashanker, *Gandhi's View of Life*, Bombay: Bharatiya Vidya Bhavan, 1968.

Shukla, Chandrashanker (ed.), *Incidents of Gandhiji's Life, by Fifty-Four Contributors*, Bombay: Vora, 1949.

Sinclair, Upton, *Money Writes!*, New York: Albert and Charles Boni, 1927.

Singh, Prithvi, *Baba Prithvi Singh Azad, the Legendary Crusader: An Autobiography*, Bombay: Bharatiya Vidya Bhavan, 1987.

Sinha, Mrinalini, 'Editor's Introduction', to Katherine Mayo, *Selections from Mother India*, New Delhi: Kali for Women, 1998, pp.1-61.

'Some Remarkable European Women Who Helped Gandhiji in South Africa', available on the ANC web site: www.anc.org.za/ancdocs/history/people/gandhi/6.html

Southard, Barbara, 'The Feminism of Mahatma Gandhi', *Gandhi Marg* (1981), vol.3, no.7, pp.404-22.

Spiegel, Margarete, 'How He Taught Through Letters', in Chandrashanker Shukla (ed.), *Reminiscences of Gandhiji, by Forty-Eight Contributors*, Bombay: Vora, 1951, pp.212-16.

Spiegel, Margarete, 'My Recollections of Mahatma Gandhi', *Indo Asia: Vierteljahreshefte fur Politic, Kultur und Wirtschaft Indiens* (1968), vol.10, no.4, pp.361-67.

Splat, Rosetta, 'Retracing Mira Behn's Path', in Gupta, (ed.), *Mira Behn*, pp.225-34.

Standenath, Franziska, *Vier Monate Gast Mahatma Gandhis: Indiens Freiheitskamph 1930, Gefängnisbriefe des Mahatma*, Graz: Leuschner & Lubensky, 1931.

Steger, Manfred, *Gandhi's Dilemma: Nonviolent Principles and Nationalist Power*, New York: St Martin's Press, 2000.

Swan, Maureen, *Gandhi: The South African Experience*, Johannesburg: Ravan Press, 1985.

Sykes, Marjorie, 'Frances Mary Barr, 1895-1969: A Memoir', supplement to *The Friendly Way*, April 1969, n.87, pp.2-12.

Sykes, Marjorie, 'Oral History Transcript', no.441, 16 August 1985, Nehru Memorial Library, New Delhi.

Sykes, Marjorie, 'Setting the Clock Back?', *Journal of Educational Sociology* (1955), vol.28, no.5, pp.211-17.

Sykes, Marjorie, *The Story of Nai Talim: Fifty Years of Education at Sevagram 1937-1887*, Sevagram: Nai Talim Samiti, 1988.

Sykes, Marjorie, *Transcending Tradition: Excerpts from the Writings and Talks of Marjorie Sykes* (Martha Dart comp. and ed.), York: Sessions, 1995.

Tandon, Vishwanath, 'The Bhoodan-Gramdan Movement (1951-74) – A Review', *Gandhi Marg* (1983), vol.5, no.8/9, pp.492-500.

Taneja, Anup, *Gandhi, Women, and the National Movement, 1920-47*, New Delhi: Har-Anand, 2005.

Taylor, Anne, *Annie Besant: A Biography*, Oxford: Oxford University Press, 1992.

Terp, Holger, 'Introduction', to Reddy and Terp, 'The Danish Peace Academy: Gandhi and Nordic Countries'.

Terp, Hoger, 'Mohandas Gandhi and Ellen Hørup', available at www.fred.dk/peace/hoerup5.html

Thakur, Bharti, *Women in Gandhi's Mass Movements*, New Delhi: Deep & Deep, 2006.

Thomas, P.T., 'Foreword', to Dart, *Marjorie Sykes*, pp.viii-ix.

Thomson, Mark, *Gandhi and His Ashrams*, Bombay: Popular Prakashan, 1993.

Tinker, Hugh, *The Ordeal of Love: C.F. Andrews and India*, Delhi: Oxford University Press, 1979.

Trivedi, Shantilal, and Radha Behn (eds), *Sarala Behn: Smriti Granth*, New Delhi/Kausani: Himalaya Seva Sangh/Lakshmi Ashram, 1984.

Vine, John C., 'Interview with Mrs Millie Graham Polak', 2 May 1960, in S. Durai Raja Singam, 'They Were Ready to Talk About Gandhi', unpublished manuscript, (n.d.), pp.16-20.

Voigt, Johannes H., 'Under the Spell of the Mahatma: Dr Margarete Spiegel', in Anil Bhatti and Johannes H. Voigt (eds), *Jewish Exile in India: 1933-1945*, New Delhi: Manohar, 2005, pp.150-60.

Watson, Francis, and Hallam Tennyson, *Talking of Gandhi*, New Delhi: Sangam, 1976.

Wallis, Jill, *Mother of World Peace: The Life of Muriel Lester*, Enfield Lock, Middlesex: Hisarlik Press, 1993.

Weber, Max, *The Theory of Social and Economic Organisations*, New York: The Free Press, 1964.

Weber, Thomas, 'Claiming Credit for Gandhi', *Gandhi Marg* (2005), vol.27, no.2, pp.165-78.

Weber, Thomas, 'From Maude Royden's Peace Army to the Gulf Peace Team: An Assessment of Unarmed Interpositionary Peace Forces', *Journal of Peace Research* (1993), vol.30, no.1, pp.45-64.

Weber, Thomas, 'Gandhi and the Nobel Peace Prize', *South Asia* (1989), vol.12, no.1, pp.29-47.

Weber, Thomas, *Gandhi as Disciple and Mentor*, New Delhi: Cambridge University Press, 2007.

Weber, Thomas, 'Gandhi's "Living Wall" and Maude Royden's "Peace Army"', *Gandhi Marg* (1988), vol.10, no.4, pp.199-212.

Weber, Thomas, *Hugging the Trees: The Story of the Chipko Movement*, New Delhi: Penguin, 1989.

Weber, Thomas, *On the Salt March: The Historiography of Gandhi's March to Dandi*, New Delhi: HarperCollins, 1997.

Weber, Thomas, *The Shanti Sena: Philosophy, History and Action*, New Delhi: Orient BlackSwan, 2009

Wessinger, Catherine Lowman, *Annie Besant: And Progressive Messianism (1847-1933)*, New York: Edwin Mellen Press, 1988.

West, Albert, 'In the Early Days with Gandhi', *The Illustrated Weekly of India*, 3 October 1965, pp.30-31, 33.

Williams, Gertrude Marvin, *The Passionate Pilgrim: A Life of Annie Besant*, New York: Coward-McCann, 1931.

Williams, L.F. Rushbrook, 'Indian Unrest and American Opinion', *Asiatic Review* (1930), July, pp.479-96.

Wolpert, Stanley, *Gandhi's Passion: The Life and Legacy of Mahatma Gandhi*, New York: Oxford University Press, 2001.

# Index